Become a Unity Shaders Guru

Create advanced game visuals using code and graphs
in Unity 2022

Mina Pêcheux

BIRMINGHAM—MUMBAI

Become a Unity Shaders Guru

Copyright © 2023 Packt Publishing

Group Product Manager: Rohit Rajkumar

Publishing Product Manager: Chayan Majumdar

Senior Content Development Editor: Rashi Dubey

Technical Editor: Simran Ali

Copy Editor: Safis Editing

Project Coordinator: Arul Viveaun S

Proofreader: Safis Editing

Indexer: Subalakshmi Govindhan

Production Designer: Jyoti Chauhan

Marketing Coordinator: Nivedita Pandey and Namita Velgekar

First published: July 2023

Production reference: 1130623

Published by Packt Publishing Ltd.
Livery Place
35 Livery Street
Birmingham
B3 2PB, UK.

ISBN 978-1-83763-674-7

www.packtpub.com

Contributors

About the author

Mina Pêcheux is a freelance content creator who has been passionate about game development since an early age. She is a graduate of the French Polytech School of Engineering in applied mathematics and computer science. After a couple of years of working as a data scientist and web developer in start-ups, she turned to freelancing and online instructional content creation to reconnect with what brightens her days: learning new things every day, sharing with others, and creating multi-field projects that mix science, technology, and art.

About the reviewers

Obinna Akpen is a seasoned 2D/3D game developer and e-sports champion with a passion for creating immersive gaming experiences. With over four years of experience in the industry, he has established himself as a highly skilled and innovative professional. Holding a bachelor of science in computer science, Obinna has demonstrated exceptional expertise in Unity and C# scripting, allowing him to develop captivating games that have garnered millions of downloads and a large player base.

Obinna's talent shines through in his ability to bring creative visions to life. He has a keen eye for detail and a deep understanding of game mechanics, enabling him to design and implement gameplay features that engage players and keep them coming back for more. His contributions to the game development process, from prototyping to optimization, have been instrumental in delivering successful projects.

One of Obinna's standout skills is his knowledge of shader development, particularly **High-Level Shader Language (HLSL)**, which has been a valuable asset on projects that require advanced visual effects and graphics rendering. His proficiency in this area allows him to create stunning visuals that enhance the overall gaming experience.

In addition to his technical expertise, Obinna is a natural problem-solver and critical thinker. He thrives in fast-paced environments and excels at overcoming challenges to deliver high-quality results within tight deadlines. His ability to analyze and adapt game mechanics showcases his dedication to creating games that provide enjoyable and immersive experiences for players.

Beyond his technical accomplishments, Obinna's passion for mentoring and teaching sets him apart. Through his involvement in various game development events and initiatives, he has shared his knowledge and expertise with aspiring game developers. His commitment to fostering growth and supporting emerging talent in the gaming industry reflects his belief in the power of collaboration and knowledge sharing.

Obinna's impact and success have been recognized through multiple awards and industry recognition. His dedication to his craft and his ability to push boundaries in game development have earned him accolades such as the *Game Developer of the Year* and *Most Versatile Gamer of the Year* awards. These achievements highlight his outstanding contributions and reinforce his status as a respected professional in the gaming community.

With a combination of technical prowess, creative vision, and a passion for mentorship, Obinna Akpen continues to make a significant impact in the world of game development. His dedication to creating immersive gaming experiences and his commitment to pushing the boundaries of innovation make him a valuable asset to any game development team.

Mohan Reddy Mummareddy is an accomplished Unity3D developer with expertise in **Augmented Reality (AR)**, **Virtual Reality (VR)**, **Mixed Reality (MR)**, and game development. With seven years of experience, he has delivered numerous successful projects, demonstrating proficiency in computer vision and **Artificial Intelligence (AI)** technologies. Mohan has contributed to the development of **iPhone operating system (iOS)** applications utilizing **light detection and ranging (LIDAR)** technology for **Machine Learning (ML)** training and Unity's Barracuda for model inference. He has also worked on virtual experience products, leveraging AR/VR/MR and web technologies. Mohan holds a master of technology in AR and VR, a master of business administration in marketing, and a bachelor of technology in electrical and electronics. Passionate about extended reality, he strives to push boundaries and create strong AI-enabled **Extended Reality (XR)** platforms and solutions.

Table of Contents

3

Writing Your First URP Shader   65

4

Transforming Your Shader into a Lit PBS Shader   81

5

Discovering the Shader Graph with a Toon Shader   107

Part 3: Advanced Game Shaders

6

Simulating Geometry Efficiently   141

7

Exploring the Unity Compute Shaders and Procedural Drawing   185

10

Optimizing Your Code, or Making Your Own Pipeline?   285

Part 5: The Toolbox

11

A Little Suite of 2D Shaders   323

Appendix:

Preface

Do you really know all the ins and outs of Unity shaders? Time to step up your game and dive into the new Universal Render Pipeline (URP), the Shader Graph tool, and advanced shading techniques to bring out the beauty in your 2D/3D game projects!

Become a Unity Shaders Guru is here to help you transition from the built-in render pipeline to the SRPs and learn about the latest shading tools. It dives deeper into Unity shaders by explaining the essential concepts through practical examples. You will first get a refresher on how to create a simple shading model in the Unity built-in render pipeline, and then move on to the Unity URP render pipeline and Shader Graph, discovering a wide range of applications in the process. You will explore common game shader techniques, ranging from interior mapping to burning down a candle or simulating the wobble of a fish. You will even read about alternative rendering techniques, such as ray marching.

By the end of this book, you'll have learned how to create a wide variety of 2D and 3D shaders with Unity's URP (both in HLSL code and with the Shader Graph tool), and you'll know some optimization tricks to make your games more friendly to low-tier devices.

Who this book is for

This book is intended for technical artists who have worked with Unity and want to get a deeper understanding of Unity render pipelines and its visual node-based editing tool. Seasoned game developers who are looking for reference shaders using the recent URP render pipeline may also find this book useful. Basic-level programming experience in HLSL can help you with the code-oriented chapters, and you should already be familiar with Unity, its layout, and its common usage.

What this book covers

Chapter 1, Re-Coding a Basic Blinn-Phong Shader with Unity/CG, gives a quick reminder on how to create shaders in Unity with the built-in render pipeline and the Nvdia Cg language.

Chapter 2, The Three Unity Render Pipelines, details the differences between Unity's built-in render pipeline and the two new render pipelines: the URP and the **High-Definition Render Pipeline** (HDRP).

Chapter 3, Writing Your First URP Shader, introduces the fundamentals of writing shaders for the new URP pipeline using HLSL instead of Cg.

Chapter 4, Transforming Your Shader into a Lit PBS Shader, builds on the previous chapter and shows how to integrate physically based shading in your URP shaders.

Chapter 5, Discovering the Shader Graph with a Toon Shader, introduces Unity's new node-based visual shader editing tool, Shader Graph, and explains how to use it with a common example of custom shading – toon cel-shading.

Chapter 6, Simulating Geometry Efficiently, covers a few techniques for cleverly giving the illusion of extra geometry while maintaining correct real-time performance, such as billboarding, parallax mapping, and interior mapping.

Chapter 7, Exploring the Unity Compute Shaders and Procedural Drawing, discusses what compute shaders are and how we can use them to offload computation from the CPU to the GPU and increase the performance of our games.

Chapter 8, The Power of Ray Marching, dives into an alternative rendering method where you build your entire scene just using mathematics!

Chapter 9, Shader Compilation, Branching, and Variants, shifts the focus to shader optimization and tells you how you can use various keywords in your shaders to improve the performance of your final game after the build.

Chapter 10, Optimizing Your Code or Making Your Own Pipeline?, adds to the knowledge of the previous chapter and offers another set of tricks for optimizing your shaders, as well as a basic overview of custom render pipelines.

Chapter 11, A Little Suite of 2D Shaders, takes you through the creation of a series of shaders for your sprites ranging from simple color-swapping to outlining or dissolving effects.

Chapter 12, Vertex Displacement Shaders, explains how to use the vertex displacement technique to create procedural animations or simulate the waves on a water plane.

Chapter 13, Wireframes and Geometry Shaders, teaches you about geometry shaders and highlights the limitations of this tool, especially when targeting Mac users, before taking you through a common application of the technique to create a wireframe render.

Chapter 14, Screen Effect Shaders, wraps up this book by discussing fullscreen shaders, which make it easy to apply screen-wide effects and make a personal atmosphere for your game.

Appendix: Some Quick Refreshers on Shaders in Unity, compiles a few handy worth-remembering base concepts for creating shaders in Unity, be it with the built-in render pipeline or the new URP and HDRP pipelines.

To get the most out of this book

To really benefit from this book, you should have prior experience with Unity and be familiar with the basics of shaders. The book is written with Unity 2022 LTS (Unity 2022.3.11f1), which is the most recent Unity LTS version at the time of writing this book..

Software/hardware covered in the book	Operating system requirements
Unity 2022 LTS (Unity 2022.3.11f1)	Windows, macOS, or Linux

If you are using the digital version of this book, we advise you to type the code yourself or access the code from the book's GitHub repository (a link is available in the next section). Doing so will help you avoid any potential errors related to the copying and pasting of code.

Note that this book is not based on the latest Unity 2023 editor because it is still in preview (beta version) at the time of writing this book, and therefore is subject to too many changes in the near future and is not robust enough for learning. Instead, this book is based on the Unity 2022 editor, which is currently in the Tech Stream release, and thus provides more stability.

Download the example code files

You can download the example code files for this book from GitHub at `https://github.com/PacktPublishing/Become-a-Unity-Shaders-Guru`. If there's an update to the code, it will be updated in the GitHub repository.

We also have other code bundles from our rich catalog of books and videos available at `https://github.com/PacktPublishing/`. Check them out!

Download the color images

We also provide a PDF file that has color images of the screenshots and diagrams used in this book. You can download it here: `https://packt.link/rE7c8`

Conventions used

There are a number of text conventions used throughout this book.

`Code in text`: Indicates code words in text, database table names, folder names, filenames, file extensions, pathnames, dummy URLs, user input, and Twitter handles. Here is an example: "At that point, our URP shader is set up to use the scriptable render feature, which will automatically call the compute shader we prepared in our `FillWithRed.compute` asset and return a full red opaque color for each pixel on the screen."

A block of code is set as follows:

```
using UnityEngine;
using UnityEngine.Rendering;

[CreateAssetMenu(menuName = "Compute Assets/CH07/FillWithRed")]
public class ComputeFillWithRed : URPComputeAsset {
```

```
    public override void Render(CommandBuffer commandBuffer,
        int kernelHandle) {}
}
```

When we wish to draw your attention to a particular part of a code block, the relevant lines or items are set in bold:

```
private void _GenerateGrid() {
    _cubes = new List<GameObject>();
    _cubeRenderers = new List<MeshRenderer>();
    _data = new Cube[gridSize * gridSize];
    ...
    for (int x = 0; x < gridSize; x++) {
        for (int y = 0; y < gridSize; y++) {
            ...


            _cubes.Add(g);
            _cubeRenderers.Add(r);

            _data[x * gridSize + y] = new Cube() {
                position = g.transform.position,
                color = color
            };
        }
    }
}
```

Bold: Indicates a new term, an important word, or words that you see onscreen. For instance, words in menus or dialog boxes appear in **bold**. Here is an example: "To get this incoming vector, we use the **View Direction** node – and the offset is then computed by multiplying it with a given float value."

> **Tips or important notes**
> Appear like this.

Get in touch

Feedback from our readers is always welcome.

General feedback: If you have questions about any aspect of this book, email us at customercare@packtpub.com and mention the book title in the subject of your message.

Errata: Although we have taken every care to ensure the accuracy of our content, mistakes do happen. If you have found a mistake in this book, we would be grateful if you would report this to us. Please visit www.packtpub.com/support/errata and fill in the form.

Piracy: If you come across any illegal copies of our works in any form on the internet, we would be grateful if you would provide us with the location address or website name. Please contact us at copyright@packtpub.com with a link to the material.

If you are interested in becoming an author: If there is a topic that you have expertise in and you are interested in either writing or contributing to a book, please visit authors.packtpub.com.

Download a free PDF copy of this book

Thanks for purchasing this book!

Do you like to read on the go but are unable to carry your print books everywhere?

Is your eBook purchase not compatible with the device of your choice?

Don't worry, now with every Packt book you get a DRM-free PDF version of that book at no cost.

Read anywhere, any place, on any device. Search, copy, and paste code from your favorite technical books directly into your application.

The perks don't stop there, you can get exclusive access to discounts, newsletters, and great free content in your inbox daily

Follow these simple steps to get the benefits:

1. Scan the QR code or visit the link below

https://packt.link/free-ebook/9781837636747

2. Submit your proof of purchase

3. That's it! We'll send your free PDF and other benefits to your email directly

Part 1: Creating Shaders in Unity

Before we dive into Unity's new render pipelines and modern shader creation tools, let's first take a bit of time to re-familiarize ourselves with the process of creating shaders in Unity. In this introductory part, we'll start with a quick reminder of how to implement the well-known Blinn-Phong shading model in Unity's built-in render pipeline.

In this part, we will cover the following chapter:

- *Chapter 1, Re-Coding a Basic Blinn-Phong Shader with Unity/CG*

Re-Coding a Basic Blinn-Phong Shader with Unity/CG

The art of shaders has always been known for being fairly complex. While a few math operations can easily simulate a flat 3D surface with some lighting and shadows, creating great and optimized visuals for your games can be a hard task. As a beginner, you can always copy-paste some script in the hope that it magically transforms your visuals, but to truly design your own style, you will need quite a lot of time to learn all the ins and outs. Still – shaders are definitely worth digging into, and nowadays, with engines such as Unity, we have an opportunity to discover more about this unique field step by step.

Shaders are how our computers are able to render 3D to 2D, and they are paramount to most modern video games: be it to actually show your 3D scene or to create catchy VFX to bring your world some life, they are a key element to creating visuals. Thanks to their parallel structure, they can also take advantage of our latest GPU-based architectures, and they are blazingly fast. All of this can take some getting used to, for sure; still, the results are pretty amazing once you manage to set everything up properly.

> **Need some refreshers on the fundamentals of shaders?**
>
> If you want to review some essentials on the structure of shaders, the vertex and fragment shader functions, and specific Unity semantics to feel more comfortable when tackling more advanced shading techniques in the upcoming chapters, you can have a look at the *Appendix: Some Quick Refreshers on Shaders in Unity,* at the end of the book!

So, before we dive into Unity's newest shading tools and discover the more modern render pipelines, let's get back into the swing of things with a practical example of how to design and implement a classical shading model: Blinn-Phong.

Although this model is somewhat old and has now mostly been replaced by physically-based rendering, it will be easier to wrap our heads around and discuss in this review chapter. It will also be a good opportunity to do some quick reminders about 3D lighting and about how to perform basic operations such as diffuse, ambient, and specular lighting.

So, in this chapter, we will review the basics of shader coding in Unity with the usual built-in pipeline in a hands-on example. It will take us through all the steps required to create a vertex-fragment shader, debug it, and implement a simple 3D lighting model. We will also learn a few tips for improving the user-friendliness of our material inspectors and better controlling how shader properties are exposed.

We will cover the following topics in this chapter:

- Doing a quick study of the Blinn-Phong shading model
- Setting up our shader in Unity
- Adding the ambient and specular components
- Making a top-notch inspector!

Technical requirements

To try out the samples yourself, you will need to have Unity installed (note that the examples in this chapter do not require any specific version). You will then need to create a project with the common 3D template.

You can find the code files for this chapter on GitHub at `https://github.com/PacktPublishing/Become-a-Unity-Shaders-Guru/tree/main/Assets/Chapter%2001`.

Doing a quick study of the Blinn-Phong shading model

Working with shaders can be tricky when you don't know exactly what you are planning. Although skilled technical artists can get away with some shots in the dark and develop the logic of their shader as they implement it, it is often more reassuring to anticipate the computation and the composition of the different components your shader will use.

This process of listing the features your shader needs to have is what we call defining its **shading model**. It is crucial for beginners and often pretty useful for more advanced developers, too.

To understand what this step implies, we will define the Blinn-Phong shading model we want to implement here with an easy and well-known lighting model: the **ambient/diffuse/specular model**. We will first discuss the basic diffuse lighting, then see how to add ambient lighting, and finally dive into the specular lighting to understand how to implement all three of them in our shader.

Using diffuse lighting for a basic render

Diffuse lighting is often the first step to implementing any kind of lighting for your shader. It is the direct illumination of the object by the light, or in other words, the effect by which the surface re-emits some or all of the incoming light that hits it. The color of the object depends on which part of the light is absorbed and which part is re-emitted.

This lighting does not depend on the direction you are currently facing. It is how you can render a 3D matte surface, and it is usually what you think of when you're asked to picture a 3D object floating about like this:

Figure 1.1 – A basic diffuse lighting of a 3D sphere

In the case of the Blinn-Phong model, we can compute this base surface brightness based on the position of our light source and the normal of said surface. Let's consider a schematic visualization of this direct illumination of the surface:

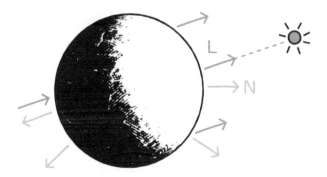

Figure 1.2 – Light vector (L) and normal vector (N), used to compute the diffuse lighting component

This diagram introduces two relevant vectors for the computation of the diffuse lighting:

- **Light vector** (L): This is the direction from the surface to the light source. Since we are assuming a single directional light source that is infinitely far away, this vector will be the same for each pixel of the object.

- **Normal vector** (N): This is the outgoing direction from the surface that is orthogonal to its tangent plane.

> **Direction versus vector?**
> Throughout this section, we will define and use various vectors that are in all directions. This basically means that we are only interested in the line along which the vector spreads and which side the arrow points; the length of the vector, however, is ignored and considered normalized to 1.

We can see in *Figure 1.2* that we want the diffuse component to be maximal when the surface is facing the light and minimal when it faces away from it. This can easily be computed by taking the dot product of the L and N vectors clamped to the [0, 1] range. This clamping can be done directly using the `saturate` function, which is common in shader languages.

Since this reflectance process is called the lambertian reflectance, this black-to-white mask is often called a **lambertian (lambert)**, and we can express it as:

```
float lambert = saturate(dot(L, N));
```

Then, to take into account the color of the light source, `lightColor`, we need to multiply this value by the `color` variable (expressed as or cast to `float3`):

```
float3 diffuseLight = saturate(dot(L, N)) * lightColor.xyz;
```

Finally, to also consider the color of the object, `color`, we simply need to re-multiply our colored diffuse lighting by this other color (again, expressed as or cast to `float3`):

```
float3 diffuseColor = diffuseLight * color;
```

As we will see in the *Setting up our shader in Unity* section, if we implement this into our fragment shader function, then we will get something similar to *Figure 1.1*.

Now that we have seen how easy it is to compute the diffuse lighting, let's see go ahead and see why ambient lighting can be a quick way to improve our lit shaders.

Better integrating the object – thanks to ambient lighting

The diffuse lighting, we just discussed is usually the first step to having your object exist in a render: it is a way to pull it out of the shadows by defining how light sources illuminate its surface. However, this first component can only go so far – in particular, the diffuse lighting is not aware of the surroundings of the object and the environment it is in.

This is why, usually, to help integrate your object into your scene, you also need to consider your environment's ambient lighting.

Ambient light is a light that does not come from any specific source – it is everywhere in the scene and illuminates slightly all the objects from all around. In a nutshell, it is light with neither an origin nor a direction. It is the light that bounces around the environment, and that allows us to see our shapes in a 3D render even if there are no specific light sources, as shown in *Figure 1.3*:

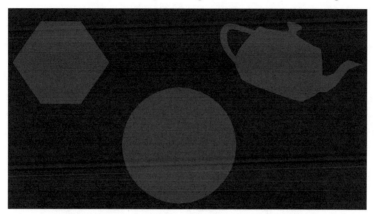

Figure 1.3 – Ambient lighting of a few random 3D shapes

It is also why, in real life, most of the time, even the side of an object that is in the shadows is not completely dark. *Figure 1.4* shows the difference between a simple diffuse material without any ambient lighting and another that integrates this second component and therefore does not have a fully black side opposite the main light:

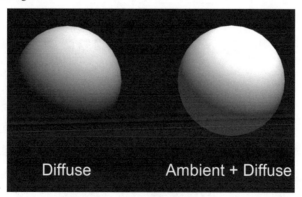

Figure 1.4 – Comparison between a shader with only a diffuse component
and a shader with both the diffuse and ambient components

Ambient light is useful in many cases, most notably whenever you want to control the overall brightness of the scene without having to adjust each light individually. For example, if you want to bring out the colors of a cartoon style, ambient light can be a nice solution.

In all generality, the ambient light component is computed as a product of intensity and color:

```
float3 ambientLight = ambientIntensity * ambientColor;
```

Note that, this time, we shouldn't multiply `ambientLight` by the color of the object because this ambient component is global to the scene and applies the same to all the shapes in the render. So, since we want this ambient lighting to be the minimum of the light that all objects in the scene get, we just need to add to our previous diffuse component to get the combination of both:

```
float3 diffuseAndAmbientColor = diffuseColor + ambientLight;
```

Of course, the tricky part can be to actually get the value of the `ambientIntensity` and `ambientColor` variables: depending on the software you use, this information can be more or less hidden inside the engine. However, we will see in the *Adding the ambient and specular components* section that in Unity, this data can be retrieved pretty easily inside of a shader code.

We are now up to speed with two light components out of three... finally, last but not least, let's recall the fundamentals of specular lighting!

Adding some light reflections with a specular

Until this point, the diffuse and ambient components we discussed were fairly easy to describe, and, in particular, they did not depend on the position of the camera at all. No matter where you render your diffuse or ambient from, the result will always be the same.

Specular lighting, on the other hand, is different. It is what causes a shiny surface (typically a plastic or a metal) to have some bright spots, glossy edges, and lighter faces, like this:

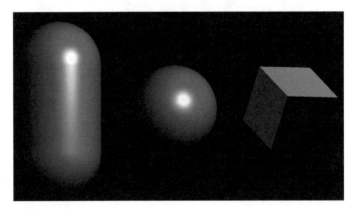

Figure 1.5 – Basic specular lighting of a capsule, a sphere, and a cube with a single directional light

Specular reflection is like a mirror reflection – if the surface is smooth enough, the incoming light rays are reflected toward the viewer's eye and create those localized highlights. The specular component, therefore, depends on three vectors:

- The (normalized) normal vector of the surface, N, as discussed for diffuse lighting

- The direction from the surface to the light source, L, as discussed for diffuse lighting

- The direction from the surface to the camera is often called the **view vector** and is denoted as V

And this is where we are finally going to talk about the "Blinn-Phong" we named our shader after! The **Blinn-Phong reflection model** is an improvement on the initial Phong model, both of which are methods for computing the speculars on a surface based on those three vectors.

The Phong model is more intuitive to understand; however, in practice, it is often less efficient and less realistic than the Blinn-Phong. This is why we are implementing the latter here. Still, to become familiar with how to compute the bright spots of a smooth surface in our render, let's first quickly go through the Phong technique.

In short, the **Phong reflection model** tries to determine how close the V vector is and the exactly reflected light vector, R. *Figure 1.6* shows this auxiliary variable, which is simply the outgoing ray of light after L has bounced off the surface:

Figure 1.6 – Light vector (L), normal vector (N), view vector (V), and reflected light vector (R), used to compute the Phong specular lighting component

Once again, the **High-Level Shader Language** (HLSL) shaders have plenty of useful built-in functions for this type of operation. Here, for example, we can use the `reflect` function and give it in the incoming vector (meaning, our outgoing light vector, L, but reversed) and the normal vector, N, to reflect around:

```
float3 R = reflect(-L, N);
```

OK, so – the Phong model checks how close we are to looking directly at the light source in a mirror, with the mirror being our object's surface. As in our diffuse computation, the "closeness" of two vectors is computed using a dot product. This leads to the following formula for Phong specular highlights:

```
float3 specularLight = saturate(dot(V, R));
```

If we implement this model and show only our specular component, we then get something resembling *Figure 1.7*:

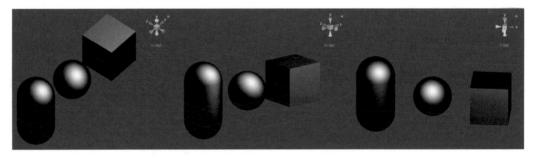

Figure 1.7 – Phong specular highlights on a capsule, a sphere, and a cube with a single directional light

As you can see in this screenshot, the specular does indeed depend on the position of the camera (you can look at the gizmo in the top-right corner to see the current view direction); however, it is not exactly the bright spot we were expecting.

This is because another important concept for specular lighting is the **glossiness** of the surface – although it is sometimes configured via its related opposite quantity, the **roughness**. The glossiness basically determines how smooth the surface is – if it is completely smooth, as a perfect mirror, then only a view vector perfectly aligned with the reflected light vector will show the specular. Conversely, if the surface has microfacets and tiny bumps, we will see specular highlights even if we are not looking at the surface in the exact direction of the reflected light vector.

> **Did you know?**
>
> The opposite of a perfect mirror surface, or in other words, a surface that makes specular highlights spread across the entire surface, is called a lambertian surface.

To apply a glossiness parameter to our specular computation, we need to use exponents. More precisely, we need to raise our `specularLight` variable to the power of our glossiness value, which here we can compute based on the normalized float value, `_Gloss`, as follows:

```
specularLight = pow(specularLight, _Gloss);
```

Because it is used as such, the gloss may also be called the specular exponent – but we will stick with the term "glossiness" here since this is way more common in game engines and 3D software.

Now, by tweaking this value, we can easily change the size of the specular highlighting to get a smooth or rough surface. *Figure 1.8* shows various examples of increasing glossiness:

Figure 1.8 – Examples of Phong specular highlights for different values of glossiness

At this point, you might be thinking that we are done and that this Phong model is all we need to create specular lighting. Why would we need to step up to another Blinn-Phong model if this one already gives us these shiny spots and edges?

To really see the issue and why Phong is not as realistic a model as Blinn-Phong, you need to increase the glossiness of your shader to get small-sized specular highlights and have a look at one of the flat faces of the cube when the light is at a steep angle, such as in *Figure 1.9*:

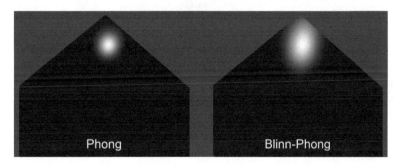

Figure 1.9 – Comparison of the specular highlight on a flat face with a
light at a steep angle using a Phong or a Blinn-Phong model

Do you notice how Phong creates a fairly round spot while Blinn-Phong stretches the light on the surface along the direction of the light source, similar to what we have in real life? Phong gives us OK results for round surfaces, but as soon as you have a flat face, it will render way too close to a perfect mirror for most use cases. On the other hand, Blinn-Phong will create anisotropic speculars that are more realistic, which is why we usually switch over to this model in 3D rendering.

In reality, it is very easy to turn Phong into Blinn-Phong. The idea is that instead of computing the following:

```
float3 specularLight = saturate(dot(V, R));
```

We will instead calculate this:

```
float3 specularLight = saturate(dot(N, H));
```

Where H is the normalized average vector between V and the L light vector called the **halfway vector** (see *Figure 1.10*):

Figure 1.10 – Diagram of the vectors required to compute the Blinn-Phong specular lighting component

The result will be approximately the same, but it gives more realistic results, handles steep angles better, and avoids cutting off the light beyond certain angle limits, contrary to Phong.

To get our halfway vector, we can simply sum L and V and normalize the result. To sum up, the Blinn-Phong specular highlights can be computed with the following formulas:

```
float3 H = normalize(L + V);

float3 specularLight = saturate(dot(N, H));

specularLight = pow(specularLight, _Gloss);
```

With this implementation, there is, however, an edge case that can cause Blinn-Phong to get slightly off track – if your camera sees the surface at an extreme angle, up to the point that the light gets behind it, then there can be some small unrealistic remnant of light on the surface. This is because we don't cull the light depending on whether it is behind the surface or not.

To fix this, we can simply use our lambertian from the diffuse lighting. Since, by definition, it is null when the surface does not face the light, we can simply multiply our specularLight variable by a check of the value of lambert, and only take into account the specular if the lambertian is not null:

```
float3 specularLight = saturate(dot(N, H)) * (lambert > 0);
```

Just like before for the diffuse component in the *Using diffuse lighting for a basic render* section, we can, of course, have these specular highlights be colored by the light source color by multiplying them together:

```
specularLight = specularLight * lightColor.xyz;
```

But the final question that needs answering is – how is this specular component composited with our two other components, the diffuse and the ambient lighting?

In short, we need to add this new component to the ones we computed before to mix together the previous shading result with these additional shiny spots:

```
float3 finalColor = diffuseAndAmbientColor + specularLight;
```

However, there is a little alternative that is interesting to point out. Let's leave the ambient light aside for now since it depends on the environment and is a global setting. Then, in the previous formula, you'll notice that the color of the light is taken into account, both in the diffuse and the specular components, but the color of the surface is only injected in the diffuse part. The specular highlights are currently not tinted by the color of the surface itself.

As a general rule, you want to leave the specular highlights as-is, as simple reflections of the light rays. But it can sometimes be interesting to also take the color of the surface into account if you want to (roughly) simulate metalness. Of course, this is a simplified model of a complex phenomenon, and if you need really realistic metal materials, you will probably have to leave Blinn-Phong behind and get into modern physically-based rendering. Still, as an approximation, this little trick of multiplying the specular highlights by the object's color can create a metal-like feeling, compared to the unaltered speculars that remind us more of plastic, as shown in *Figure 1.11*:

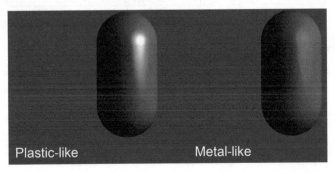

Figure 1.11 – Comparison of a specular model where highlights are not tinted
by the surface color (plastic-like) and one where they are (metal-like)

This concludes our theoretical study of the Blinn-Phong shading model. We now have reviewed everything that is relevant to implementing this shader in Unity, so let's see how to apply all of these formulas in practice!

Setting up our shader in Unity

With the Blinn-Phong model in mind, we are now ready to implement our shader with Unity's legacy render pipeline.

The overall process will be to first create our shader and a matching material so that we can assign it to a 3D object in our scene, and then gradually add more and more components to properly re-create the diffuse component of the Blinn-Phong shading model we discussed in the *Doing a quick study of the Blinn-Phong shading model* section. Before we do anything, however, let's quickly have a chat about the project requirements for this chapter so that you can test the samples yourself.

Checking your project configuration

Since we are using the built-in graphics here, you will need to create a new test project using the usual Unity 3D template. You can pick the template you want at the creation of your project, in the Unity Hub window, like this:

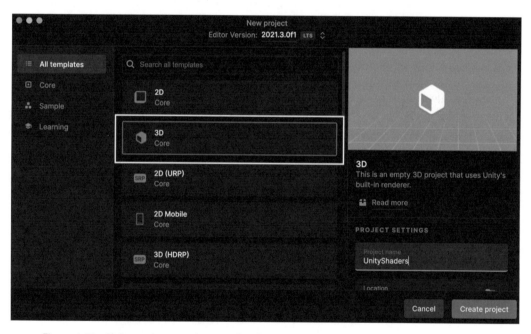

Figure 1.12 – Unity project creation panel in the Unity Hub with the 3D template highlighted

However, if you have already created a project using one of the newest render pipelines (**Universal Render Pipeline (URP)** or **High Definition Render Pipeline (HDRP)**), make sure to temporarily turn it off in your project settings if you want to use the shader we will make in this chapter. To do this, follow these steps:

1. Go to the **Edit | Project Settings...** menu.

2. Switch over to the **Graphics** section on the left.

3. At the very top of the inspector panel, in the **Scriptable Render Pipeline Settings** slot, remove the asset reference (set it to **None**).

This will re-enable the built-in renderer and allow for our legacy shader example to work properly.

Creating the shader file

Time to start writing our Blinn-Phong shader! We will follow these steps to create the shader file:

1. First, we will create a new shader asset in our project – to do this, simply right-click in the Project dock in your Unity editor and create a new shader file by navigating through the contextual menu (see *Figure 1.13*):

Figure 1.13 – Contextual menu for creating a legacy shader

You can choose whichever preset you prefer – we will remove almost all the auto-generated code to implement the shader from scratch, anyway.

2. After you've created the asset, double-click on it to open it in an IDE. Unity will have filled the file with a basic shader based on the preset you chose. But to really understand what we are doing, let's clear this and remove everything except for the top-level enclosing brackets with the name of our shader – your file should now look like this:

```
Shader "Custom/BlinnPhong"
{}
```

Defining the name and category of your shader

The first line in our shader file defines the unique reference of our shader as a path. Every forward slash in this quoted string corresponds to a level in the shader menu that unfolds in a drop-down list in the inspector panel when you pick the shader of a material. You can, of course, adjust it to your liking to organize the shaders differently in your project.

3. Then, go back to the Unity editor. You will notice that your shader is recompiled automatically. By right-clicking on your shader asset in the **Project** window, you will be able to create a material that uses this specific shader with the contextual menu:

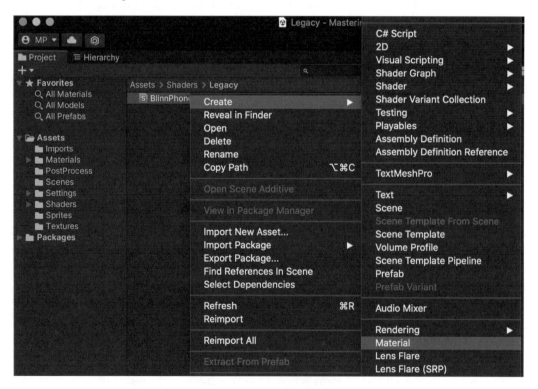

Figure 1.14 – Contextual menu for creating a material from a shader

4.   To finish setting up the test project, you need to add a 3D object (for example, a primitive sphere or a capsule) to your current Unity scene and assign it the material you created. Since this shader code is invalid, you will notice that the object appears in a magnificent flashy pink, as in *Figure 1.15*:

Figure 1.15 – Debug display of an invalid Unity shader

Even if it doesn't look right, it does verify that our shader asset is indeed used for the object's in-game render. But now, we should obviously fix our shader and turn it into a real Blinn-Phong!

The very first component we will implement will be the diffuse lighting. As we saw in the *Doing a quick study of the Blinn-Phong shading model* section, this requires that we define a color for our object and that we get the normal of our vertices to compute the diffuse contribution for the corresponding pixel.

The first step is to prepare the structure of our shader and, in particular, a property for our object color:

1.   To begin with, let's declare a new `_Color` property for our shader and give it a default value of `(1, 1, 1, 1)`, or in other words, pure white:

```
Shader "Custom/BlinnPhong" {
    Properties {
        _Color ("Color", Color) = (1, 1, 1, 1)
    }
}
```

2.   Next, we will add our `SubShader` and `Pass` blocks with a basic tag to specify that our shader is meant to be rendered as opaque:

```
Shader "Custom/BlinnPhong" {
    Properties {
        _Color ("Color", Color) = (1, 1, 1, 1)
    }
```

```
        SubShader {
            Tags { "RenderType" = "Opaque" }
            Pass
            {}
        }
    }
```

At this point, we have recomposed our famous ShaderLab nested structure, and all that is left to do is fill the `Pass` block with our low-level shader code. For now, this code will be fairly simple – we will define very basic `appdata` and `v2f` structures, have our vertex shader code pass along the data unchanged, and make the fragment shader output our color directly, such as for an unlit shader. We will follow these steps:

1. First of all, let's add the CG start and end instructions, the pragmas to identify our vertex and fragment shader functions in the script, the usual inclusion of the `UnityCG.cginc` library, and the declaration of the low-level `_Color` variable to match our exposed property:

```
Pass {
    CGPROGRAM
    #pragma vertex vert
    #pragma fragment frag

    #include "UnityCG.cginc"

    float4 _Color;
    ENDCG
}
```

2. Then, let's define our simple `appdata` and `v2f` structures. For the time being, we will simply use the position of the vertices, so each structure will have a single `float4` field with the `POSITION` or `SV_POSITION` semantic:

```
Pass {
    CGPROGRAM
    ...
    struct appdata {
        float4 vertex : POSITION;
    };

    struct v2f {
        float4 vertex : SV_POSITION;
    };
    ENDCG
}
```

3. Our data is now ready to be used as input or output by our `vert` vertex shader function. We just have to convert our incoming vertex 3D position into the equivalent 2D position in clip-space, thanks to Unity's built-in `UnityObjectToClipPos` function, like this:

```
Pass {
    CGPROGRAM
    ...
    v2f vert (appdata v) {
        v2f o;
        o.vertex = UnityObjectToClipPos(v.vertex);
        return o;
    }
    ENDCG
}
```

4. And finally, we can create a one-line fragment shader function, `frag`, that simply returns the color we defined for each pixel of our object:

```
Pass {
    CGPROGRAM
    ...
    float4 frag (v2f i) : SV_Target {
        return _Color;
    }
    ENDCG
}
```

You can now come back to the Unity editor, let the shader recompile, and admire your brand-new white shape in the **Game** view. At this point, we have made a basic unlit shader with Unity's built-in rendering pipeline that we can adjust the color of by tweaking the **Color** property exposed in the material's inspector, as shown in this screenshot:

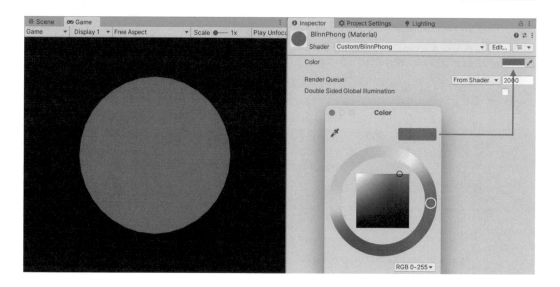

Figure 1.16 – Simple unlit shader with a color property that can be set in the inspector

The next step is to modify our unlit shader to compute some diffuse lighting.

Implementing the diffuse lighting

All right, at this point, we have a basic shader structure that allows us to render our object as unlit. But, of course, this is not what we want! It is time to draw from our previous reminders on diffuse lighting.

In the *Doing a quick study of the Blinn-Phong shading model* section, we saw that our diffuse component could be computed based on the normal of the N surface and its direction to the light, L. Let's go through each of those vectors one by one and see how we can calculate them in Unity!

First of all, the normal is easy enough to get. We can simply ask Unity to pass it in our input vertex data structure by adding a `float3` field with the `NORMAL` semantic, like this:

```
struct appdata {
    float4 vertex : POSITION;
    float3 normal : NORMAL;
};
```

Then, we have to transfer it over to the output data structure in our vertex shader function. The interpolators don't support the `NORMAL` semantic in the same way – instead, we have to store this data in our first UV set denoted by the `TEXCOORD0` semantic. Then, in our `vert` function, we need to use another Unity built-in function to convert the normal from the object space to the world space, `UnityObjectToWorldNormal`, as follows:

```
struct v2f {
    float4 vertex : SV_POSITION;
    float3 normal : TEXCOORD0;
};
v2f vert (appdata v) {
    v2f o;
    o.vertex = UnityObjectToClipPos(v.vertex);
    o.normal = UnityObjectToWorldNormal(v.normal);
    return o;
}
```

And finally, we retrieve it in the fragment shader from our interpolated data, and we apply the normalization step to get our N vector:

```
float4 frag (v2f i) : SV_Target {
    // get normalized normal for fragment
    float3 N = normalize(i.normal);
    return _Color;
}
```

A quick note on normalization

Even though the per-vertex normals Unity gives us in the `appdata` input data structure are normalized, we do need to ensure that the normal we get in our fragment shader is normalized too. This is because, since it's interpolated, there is no guarantee that this blended normal actually has a length of 1. Although it will not cause any visual issues for the diffuse lighting, you will notice a disturbing faceting with the specular highlights if you forget to re-normalize this vector before the computations.

Next up, we will get our L vector. Remember that this is the direction from the surface to the light source and that, here, we are assuming there is only one main directional light.

Luckily, this is very easy to get in Unity – the engine directly offers us a built-in `float4` variable called `_WorldSpaceLightPos0` that contains the direction of directional light or the position of a spot or point light. The fourth component is either 0 if the light is directional or 1 if the light is not directional. So, in our case, we just have to extract the first three components of this vector with the usual HLSL swizzling to get our L vector:

```
float4 frag (v2f i) : SV_Target {
    // get normalized normal for fragment
    float3 N = normalize(i.normal);
    // get (outgoing) light vector
    float3 L = _WorldSpaceLightPos0.xyz;
    return _Color;
}
```

We now have everything we need to compute our lambertian reflectance, using the formula from the *Doing a quick study of the Blinn-Phong shading model* section:

```
float4 frag (v2f i) : SV_Target {
    // get normalized normal for fragment
    float3 N = normalize(i.normal);
    // get (outgoing) light vector
    float3 L = _WorldSpaceLightPos0.xyz;
    // diffuse lighting (Lambert)
    float lambert = saturate(dot(N, L));
    return float4(lambert * _Color.xyz, 1);
}
```

At this point, if you come back to the Unity editor and wait for the shader to recompile, you'll have a shader that handles diffuse lighting and takes into account the color of the object, specified by the _Color property as we defined in *step 1* of our structure definition in the *Creating the shader file* section. For example, if you set the color to gold-yellow, you will get something similar to *Figure 1.17*:

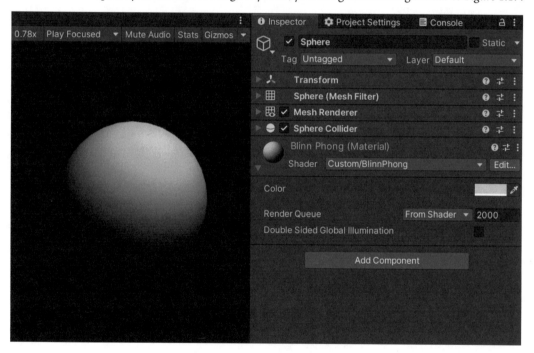

Figure 1.17 – Diffuse shader with a color property for the surface

To wrap up our implementation of the diffuse lighting, we should also make sure to get the color of the light into the mix. For now, you'll notice that if you try to change the color of the directional light in your scene, nothing happens – the object still appears yellow.

The solution here is to include the `UnityLightingCommon.cginc` library so that we can access its `_LightColor0` variable and multiply it with our `lambert` variable:

```
{
    #include "UnityLightingCommon.cginc"
    ...
    float4 frag (v2f i) : SV_Target {
        float3 N = normalize(i.normal);
        float3 L = _WorldSpaceLightPos0.xyz;

        float lambert = saturate(dot(N, L));
        float3 diffuseLight = lambert * _LightColor0.xyz;
        return float4(diffuseLight * _Color, 1);
    }
}
```

And here we are! If you try to change the color of either the object or the light, you'll see that now they both impact the final color of the pixels in the render with the same additive mix as we experience in real life. *Figure 1.18* shows how the same white sphere (meaning, with a `_Color` property equal to full white) results in different colors depending on the color of the light:

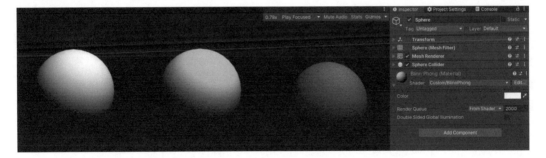

Figure 1.18 – Examples of renders with a constant white surface for the sphere but a changing light color

With that first component implemented in our Blinn-Phong shader, let's move on to the two others: the ambient and specular lighting!

Adding the ambient and specular components

Our shader now handles the diffuse lighting. However, we know that this is just part of a real Blinn-Phong model – we also need to have some specular reflections, and we should handle ambient lighting to better integrate it into the scene.

In the following sections, we will add both components one by one, starting with the ambient lighting since, as we will see, it is quick to do in Unity before taking care of the speculars.

Injecting the ambient lighting

Do you remember how, in the *Setting up our Unity shader* section, we managed to get our light direction just by calling a Unity built-in variable? Well, guess what – adding ambient lighting is just easy!

All we have to do for this step is get the UNITY_LIGHTMODEL_AMBIENT variable, and this will directly give us the ambient light to add to our previously computed diffuse component, which means we simply have to update our fragment shader function like this:

```
float4 frag (v2f i) : SV_Target {
    float3 N = normalize(i.normal);
    float3 L = _WorldSpaceLightPos0.xyz;

    float lambert = saturate(dot(N, L));
    float3 diffuseLight = lambert * _LightColor0.xyz;

    float3 ambientLight = UNITY_LIGHTMODEL_AMBIENT.xyz;
    return float4(diffuseLight * _Color + ambientLight, 1);
}
```

And with these quick modifications, we added ambient lighting to our diffuse shader. If you recompile the file, you should see that the shape is now slightly illuminated everywhere:

Figure 1.19 – Compositing of the diffuse and ambient lighting components

If you want to change the color of the ambient light, you can change this in the environment parameters of the scene. These settings are located in the **Lighting** window. To access them, follow these steps:

1. Go to the **Window | Rendering | Lighting** menu.

2. Switch over to the **Environment** tab at the top of the **Lighting** window.

3. In the inspector, you will see the ambient lighting in the **Environment Lighting** group.

Unity offers us three ways of setting the ambient color – either with a single source color, a gradient, or a skybox, which are discussed here:

- If you use the **Color** mode, then all ambient light will have the flat color you define in the color picker, as shown in *Figure 1.20*:

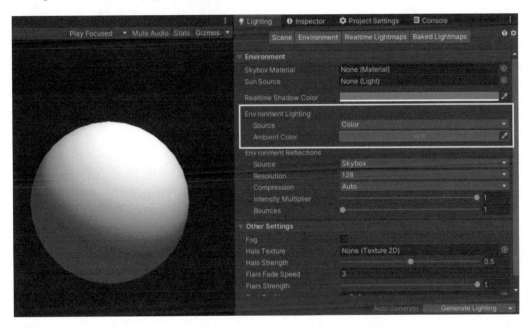

Figure 1.20 – Configuration of the ambient color for the Unity scene in the Color mode

- If you use the **Gradient** mode, you will be able to define separate colors for ambient lighting coming from the sky, the horizon, and the ground. You will have three pickers for each of those important marks, as shown in *Figure 1.21*, and the rest of the levels will blend between those references:

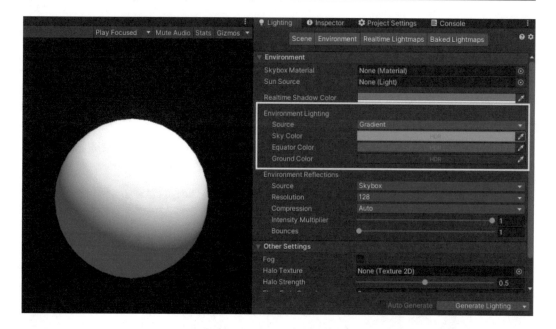

Figure 1.21 – Configuration of the ambient color for the Unity scene in the Gradient mode

Note that if you use **Gradient**, our UNITY_LIGHTMODEL_AMBIENT variable will use the sky color by default. But you can use one of the three defined color marks by replacing UNITY_LIGHTMODEL_AMBIENT with unity_AmbientSky, unity_AmbientEquator, or unity_AmbientGround.

- If you use the **Skybox** mode, then the ambient light will be computed based on the **Skybox Material** resource you pass in. This can help do more detailed lighting, but it requires a bit more setup. If you want to learn more about this, check out this documentation page from Unity at https://docs.unity3d.com/Manual/skyboxes-using.html.

We now have a shader with both the diffuse and ambient components, and we even know how to change the color of our ambient light to create a custom feel for our scene. However, this material is visually quite basic and very matte – so it is time to implement the final part of our shader: the specular.

Computing the specular lighting

As we discussed in the *Doing a quick study of the Blinn-Phong shading model* section, the only additional vector we need to prepare for computing the specular highlights with the Blinn-Phong reflection model is the view vector, V.

Remember that this is a vector that goes from the surface to the rendering eye position. To compute it, we therefore need to get the position of our main camera and the position of the fragment we are currently calculating the output value for, both in world space coordinates.

As usual, the camera position is readily available in the `UnityCG.cging` library. The `_WorldSpaceCameraPos` variable directly gives us the 3D world position of the main camera.

The world position of the vertices can be found using the vertex position in object space and the handy `unity_ObjectToWorld` matrix. Multiplying this matrix by the local vertex position converts the local coordinates to world coordinates and gives us its equivalent as a world position. We then simply need to pass it in the `v2f` data structure as our second UV set to have it interpolated and re-inputted into the fragment shader. Here are the updated parts of our shader code:

```
struct v2f {
    float4 vertex : SV_POSITION;
    float3 normal : TEXCOORD0;
    float3 worldPos : TEXCOORD1;
};
v2f vert (appdata v) {
    v2f o;
    o.vertex = UnityObjectToClipPos(v.vertex);
    o.normal = v.normal;
    o.worldPos = mul(unity_ObjectToWorld, v.vertex);
    return o;
}
float4 frag (v2f i) : SV_Target {
    float3 V = normalize(_WorldSpaceCameraPos -
        i.worldPos);
    ...
}
```

Here, we use the `normalize` function to transform our position offset into a direction.

Then, we will define our `_Gloss` property for the surface smoothness:

```
Shader "Custom/BlinnPhong" {
    Properties {
        ...
        _Gloss ("Gloss", Float) = 1
    }
    SubShader {
        Tags { "RenderType" = "Opaque" }
        Pass {
            ...
            float _Gloss;
        }
    }
}
```

Finally, we simply need to copy back the formulas we prepared during the theoretical analysis to first get the halfway vector, H, get the specular, apply glossiness, and use the light source color. We eventually composite all three components in the final return with a simple sum. Our following fragment shader function, therefore, looks as follows:

```
float4 frag (v2f i) : SV_Target {
    float3 N = normalize(i.normal);
    float3 L = _WorldSpaceLightPos0.xyz;
    float3 V = normalize(_WorldSpaceCameraPos -
        i.worldPos);

    // diffuse lighting (lambertian)
    float lambert = saturate(dot(N, L));
    float3 diffuseLight = lambert * _LightColor0.xyz;
    float3 diffuseColor = diffuseLight * _Color;

    // ambient lighting (direct from Unity settings)
    float3 ambientLight = UNITY_LIGHTMODEL_AMBIENT.xyz;

    // specular lighting (Blinn-Phong)
    float3 H = normalize(L + V);
    float3 specularLight = saturate(dot(N, H)) *
        (lambert > 0);
    specularLight = pow(specularLight, _Gloss) *
        _LightColor0.xyz;

    return float4(diffuseColor + ambientLight +
        specularLight, 1);
}
```

At the very top, we get the three vectors we require for the diffuse and specular lighting, then we compute each component, and finally, we composite them. The following diagram shows how different primitive objects look with our associated material applied to them:

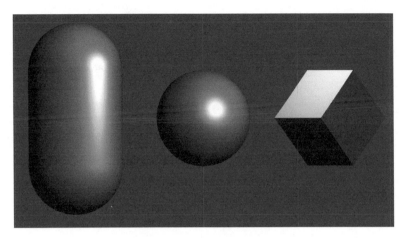

Figure 1.22 – Some applications of our final shader with the diffuse,
ambient, and specular lighting components

We have successfully implemented the model we wanted with the following components:

- The diffuse component uses the color of the surface and the light to create a base lighting that is the same no matter where the camera is

- The ambient component slightly impacts all the shapes in the render and brings out the shadows

- The specular component varies depending on the position of the rendering camera, and it simply reflects the color of the light to make this shiny plastic-like effect

There are, of course, an infinite number of ways to tweak and modify all of our settings and simulate other types of materials. Even if Blinn-Phong is a crude lighting model, we know that changing the size of the specular highlights or tinting them with the surface color can already give quite a different feel, and we also said that ambient lighting is optional.

So, to further improve this shader, let's take a bit of time to review Unity's tool for creating easy-to-use and well-controlled material inspectors.

Making a top-notch inspector!

Now that we have an example shader to test things on, we have an opportunity to quickly discuss why creating an adapted inspector is important and how to do it. The following sections will explore both of these questions.

Why should I waste time refining an editor inspector?

This is probably a question that popped into your mind if you are not yet used to customizing or creating your own tooling in Unity, and it is a valid inquiry. Given that we're talking about in-editor displays, who cares if it is a little messy? It won't impact the quality of the final game!

Well, yes... and no.

It is true that, from a very objective standpoint, the look and feel of your editor interfaces doesn't directly translate to the ones in your game. Your desk may be untidy, and still, you create amazing drawings.

However, generally speaking, it does hinder your productivity. If your interfaces are not properly designed, finding the right tool at the right time can quickly turn into a treasure hunt – it would be just like a messy in-game UI where players don't know where to read their health points or where is the information on their current target.

This is even more true with these editor tools actually since the people who use them, your artist teammates or clients, expect them to be work tools. They are not here to have fun and be lenient about a few errors here and there. They want to get to their goal swiftly and without any headaches, so it is crucial that your tools guide them. In particular, your tools should relieve your users of thinking about how to use the interface... they probably already have enough thinking about what they want to make with it!

Your editor tools should thus be clear and, when applicable, aware of the context. In other words, they should possess the following attributes:

- **Clarity**: A Unity editor tool should not require you to read hundreds of pages in a manual to understand how it works. You should be able to quickly understand what variables you are changing and how they impact the final result just by looking at the interface and trying it out a few times.

  Note that this also means tools should usually be quite focused – don't try to create ultimate swiss-knives that can do everything because those will most probably confuse your users. Instead, narrow down the specific task you want to help them with, or at the very least break down the interfaces into multiple parts for each important subtask, which brings us to our next point.

- **Context-awareness**: When building a Unity editor tool, you have an amazing advantage compared to someone who makes real-world drills or screwdrivers – your interface can adapt dynamically! This can be via the use of tabs or sections or even with an auto-generation of a different layout based on what is currently selected, the preferences of the users, and so on. This is key in presenting all the information you want to the user in a readable manner.

  If your tool is supposed to cover a variety of use cases, always try your best not to flood your users with too much data and take advantage of these context-adapted layout mechanics. Otherwise, the users will end up throwing away your tool before they understand all of its power.

This may seem like it is a bit of overkill in our case – after all, we just want to show some variables in an inspector to better configure our shader, right?

However, there are numerous ways of displaying those variables, and some will instinctively feel more in sync with the way they actually behave behind the scenes. So, time to dive in and see some easy examples of how to guide users who are discovering our shader via the interface!

Faking Booleans?

To begin with, we can look at a simple option in our shader – whether or not we should use ambient lighting. We've said that there are many cases where this is useful, but there are still other examples where you could want your shadows to be really dark and mysterious.

Ideally, this option should be available as a toggle with an on/off value, like a Boolean variable. However, we know that shaders cannot use Boolean variables – this is why, rather, we need to use Unity's additional ShaderLab attributes to adapt our interface and fake these discrete values.

First of all, we will implement the logic. We just need to add an _UseAmbient float property and then check its value to use or ignore the ambientLight value, as we did in the *Doing a quick study of the Blinn-Phong shading model* section, with the lambertian to cut off the unwanted specular highlights:

```
Shader "Custom/BlinnPhong" {
    Properties {
        ...
        _UseAmbient ("Use Ambient", Float) = 1
    }
    SubShader {
        Tags { "RenderType" = "Opaque" }
        Pass {
            ...
            float _UseAmbient;
            float4 frag (v2f i) : SV_Target {
                ...
                // ambient lighting (direct from Unity
                    settings)
                float3 ambientLight =
                    UNITY_LIGHTMODEL_AMBIENT.xyz;
                ambientLight = ambientLight *
                    (_UseAmbient > 0);
                ...
            }
        }
    }
}
```

In this code snippet, I used a `float` variable for `_UseAmbient` and then checked whether it is strictly positive to use it as a Boolean in my computation. From a logical point of view, this trick solves our issue and hides the fact that this was initially a float. However, in the UI... we get a number input that accepts any values! *Figure 1.24* shows how, for a random negative value, we do have the toggling of the ambient light, but we also have a very unintuitive interface:

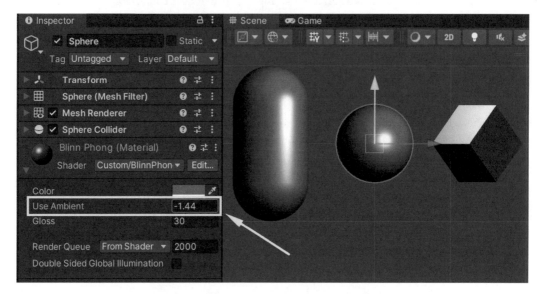

Figure 1.23 – Default display of a float input as a free value

To turn it into a checkbox and make it more straightforward to use, we'll just go back to our shader code and, at the very top, add a `[Toggle]` attribute to our `_UseAmbient` property:

```
[Toggle] _UseAmbient ("Use Ambient", Float) = 1
```

This means that this float variable, although it could technically still take an infinite number of values, will only be editable via an on/off toggle in the inspector (and thus take the values 0 or 1), like this:

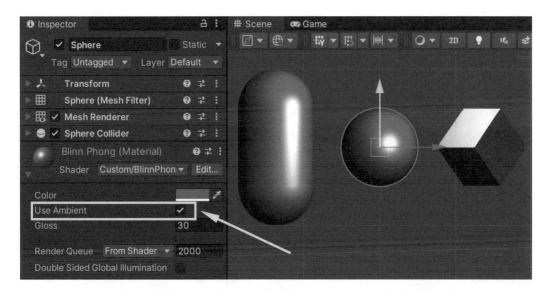

Figure 1.24 – Customized display of our float as an on/off toggle

This is already a nice improvement on our previous interface, but we can do more!

Improving our glossiness display

Another annoying part of our interface is that the _Gloss variable is currently a number that can range from one to the hundreds. Even worse, this large value range is non-linear – as the glossiness increases, you need to crank it higher and higher to actually see a difference. In many reference Unity materials, however, this setting is displayed as a linear slider that goes from 0 to 1, so how come our value doesn't work this way?

The trick to getting this more intuitive display is to remap our _Gloss value to an exponential curve – this way, we can keep it in the [0, 1] range and keep the exponential behavior under wraps. For the user, glossiness will just be a normalized float that goes from a fixed low value of 0 (a very rough surface) to a fixed high value of 1 (a very mirror-like surface).

There are various ways of remapping the value, but often multiplying our input by a small coefficient and putting it in an exp2 function (meaning we compute 2 to the power of our input) gives a good result. We can also avoid the low values of glossiness that cause strange visual artifacts by artificially increasing our specular exponent value with a base minimum.

The exact formula, suggested by Freya Holmér in one of her videos (see https://www.youtube.com/watch?v=mL8U8tIiRRg&t=11892s) and wildly adopted since then, contains a few magic numbers that are not completely intuitive, but it works really well:

```
float specExponent = exp2(_Gloss * 8) + 2;

specularLight = pow(specularLight, specExponent) * _LightColor0.xyz;
```

With these modifications, our shader now works fine with a _Gloss value between 0 and 1. For the cherry on top, let's actually convert our float to a slider with this range so that users directly know the minimum and maximum value they can use.

To do this, we simply have to change the type of our _Gloss property from Float to Range(0, 1):

```
_Gloss ("Gloss", Range(0, 1)) = 1
```

Unity will know that this property is a float that can only take its values in the [0, 1] range, and that should be displayed as a slider in the inspector. *Figure 1.25* shows us the final result:

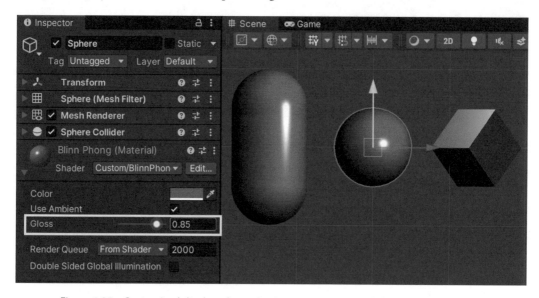

Figure 1.25 – Customized display of our glossiness property as a slider in the [0, 1] range

Note that we could also use the same toggle or slider trick if we wanted to switch between the "plastic-like" and "metal-like" speculars. You could define another _Metalness float value in the [0,1] range, use it to tint the specular component and show it with one or the other type of display, depending on whether you want a continuous or discrete value.

These various modifications to our UI make it way more intuitive and quicker to use than our previous insanely diverse float values. We are now gently guiding the users to pick the proper settings and tweak our shader in a viable way.

A few additional tricks

To wrap up this focus on the customization of our property displays, here are some other interesting attributes that can help you improve your material inspectors:

- [HideInInspector]: This attribute will hide the property that follows it in the inspector. This can be interesting if you are still in the development phase and want to keep some alternative property in your code for posterity without it polluting your inspector.

- [NoScaleOffset]: This attribute will remove the **Tiling** and **Offset** fields that appear by default next to texture slots in the inspector. This can be useful if your texture should be used as-is, and users should be prevented from changing its scale or its offset.

- [MainColor] and [MainTexture]: By default, Unity will consider that the property called _Color is the main color, and the property called _MainTex is the main texture. Those are the values you will access in your C# scripts if you get Material.color or Material.mainTexture. The [MainColor] and [MainTexture] attributes let you define the properties that follow as the main color and the main texture in your material, even when they are not named _Color and _MainTex.

- [Normal]: This attribute tells Unity that only normal maps are accepted for this texture property. If you try to use a texture asset that has not been marked as a normal map in its import settings into the slot matching this texture property, you will get a warning in the inspector, which can help with debugging.

With all these examples, we now have various techniques and tools for improving our material inspectors and making them clear to use for our users. We also know why it is important to devote time to these improvements and how even a simple UI such as our shader options here can be improved with some additional steps.

Summary

Over the course of this chapter, we have reviewed a famous shading model for 3D rendering: Blinn-Phong. We recalled the fundamentals of 3D lighting, and we saw how to compute and composite the components of a basic lighting model, the ambient/diffuse/specular model.

We then applied our theoretical study of the Blinn-Phong model in Unity to create our own Blinn-Phong shader with the built-in legacy pipeline.

Finally, we covered a few tricks and tools for improving our material inspectors so that users can easily tweak the settings of our shader.

You should now feel at ease with all the base concepts of writing shaders with Unity's built-in render pipeline, applying them on objects, thanks to materials, and setting their properties in the inspector, which means that you are ready to dive into Unity's new shading tools!

The next chapter will introduce us to this new world by exploring the other rendering pipelines Unity offers and explaining when they are useful and how to use them in your game projects.

Going further

If you're curious about the basics of Unity shader coding (in particular, using the legacy pipeline and the Cg language) or about the Blinn-Phong model, here are a few interesting resources to check out or continue your journey from:

- Unity legacy shaders:

  - *Unity 5.x Shaders and Effects Cookbook*, A. Zucconi (2016): `https://www.packtpub.com/product/unity-5x-shaders-and-effects-cookbook/9781785285240`

  - *Unity 2021 Shaders and Effects Cookbook - Fourth Edition*, J. P. Doran (2021): `https://www.packtpub.com/product/unity-2021-shaders-and-effects-cookbook-fourth-edition/9781839218620`

  - *Writing shaders* (official documentation), Unity: `https://docs.unity3d.com/Manual/shader-writing.html`

  - *Unofficial repository with Unity's built-in shaders (per Unity version)*, TwoTailsGames (2017-2020): `https://github.com/TwoTailsGames/Unity-Built-in-Shaders`

- The Blinn-Phong model:

  - *Basic Lighting*, J. de Vries (2014 –): `https://learnopengl.com/Lighting/Basic-Lighting`

  - *Advanced Lighting*, J. de Vries (2014 –): `https://learnopengl.com/Advanced-Lighting/Advanced-Lighting`

Part 2:
Stepping Up to URP
and the Shader Graph

Now that we've brushed up on our knowledge of creating shaders with the Unity built-in render pipeline, it's time to level up our shader skills and learn about Unity's new shader tools. In this second part, we'll begin by talking about Unity's new Scriptable Render Pipelines (such as the URP and HDRP pipelines). Then, we'll focus on the URP pipeline and see how to write shaders for this render pipeline, both in HLSL code and using the new node-based visual editing tool – the Shader Graph.

In this part, we will cover the following chapters:

- *Chapter 2, The Three Unity Render Pipelines*
- *Chapter 3, Writing Your First URP Shader*
- *Chapter 4, Transforming Your Shader into a Lit PBS Shader*
- *Chapter 5, Discovering the Shader Graph with a Toon Shader*

2

The Three Unity Render Pipelines

Now that we have seen a basic example of how to create a shader using Unity's built-in render pipeline in *Chapter 1*, we are ready to dive into the newest shading tools and discover the modern render pipelines!

Indeed, while the built-in render pipeline is a good way to start and get familiar with making your own shaders, it is slowly becoming a legacy tool. Nowadays, Unity game makers are encouraged to explore the new **Scriptable Render Pipelines** (**SRPs**), which are embodied by the **Universal Render Pipeline** (**URP**) and **High-Definition Render Pipeline** (**HDRP**). With their optimized graphics, easy-to-use no-code shading tools, great postprocessing effects, and cross-platform support possibilities, those new render pipelines are now in the spotlight, and the built-in render pipeline pales in comparison. To become a modern Unity technical artist, you should definitely know and utilize these new resources to further widen your knowledge, participate in this new community of shader enthusiasts, and improve your game renders!

So, in this chapter, we will provide a brief overview of the main differences between the legacy render pipeline and the new SRP ones to better understand their various limitations and advantages. We will be covering the following topics:

- Using the built-in render pipeline
- Stepping up with the URP render pipeline
- Going realistic with the HDRP render pipeline
- Diving deeper into the SRPs

Technical requirements

To try out the samples yourself, you will need to have Unity installed, with a version from 2019 or later. You will then need to create either of the following:

- A project with the common 3D template, which you will then upgrade to use the URP or HDRP render pipelines (see the *Stepping up with the URP render pipeline* section)

- A project with the new 3D URP or 3D HDRP template, which you can temporarily force to use the built-in render pipeline, as shown in the *Setting up our shader in Unity* section of *Chapter 1*

You can find the code files for this chapter on GitHub at `https://github.com/PacktPublishing/Become-a-Unity-Shaders-Guru/tree/main/Assets/Chapter%2002`.

Using the built-in render pipeline

Up until now, we have looked at Unity's **built-in or legacy render pipeline**. This was a good way to learn how to make shaders in this game engine. However, this pipeline also has its share of limitations.

So, in this first section, let's discuss the advantages and drawbacks of this pipeline, as well as how we can extend it, thanks to `CommandBuffers`.

A handy but limited pipeline

The built-in pipeline has several advantages:

- The most obvious plus is that it is readily available as soon as you create a new Unity project with a basic template. It lets you get familiar with the whole toolchain of shaders, materials, and mesh renderers.

- Since it's been around for a long time, the built-in render pipeline is also compatible with a large number of pre-existing shaders, VFX, third-party tools, and learning resources.

- Of course, because it is a general-purpose render pipeline, it handles most of the common use cases you might work on as a beginner Unity developer, and it is among the most widely supported pipelines. Be it for a 2D or a 3D game, with baked or real-time lighting, with reflection probes or global illumination, with particle systems or custom shaders, with or without postprocessing, the built-in renderer covers it all.

With the proper time and knowledge, it can even create pretty good renders, such as this great one from Unity's demo project "The Courtyard" (the following image is by Unity and available at `https://assetstore.unity.com/packages/essentials/tutorial-projects/the-courtyard-49377`):

Figure 2.1 – Render of "The Courtyard," a Unity demo project made with the built-in render pipeline

The key issue, however, is that most of these features are subject to severe limitations:

- The particle systems, for example, are handled by the **Shuriken** tool, which runs on the CPU. Although it allows us to create basic systems, it is quickly limited in terms of performance and cannot exceed thousands of particles.

- Postprocessing modules have to be installed via the **Post-Processing V2** package.

- Of course, as we've seen before, writing custom shaders requires you to know the HLSL language, and to be ready to dive into scripting.

The built-in pipeline does compensate for these problems by allowing quite extensive customization and easy-to-configure cherry-picked optimizations.

But the real interesting feature of this pipeline for advanced shader developers is the ability to intervene in the rendering process, thanks to hooks and `CommandBuffers`.

The power of CommandBuffers

In short, the idea behind `CommandBuffers` is to give Unity developers a say on how the scene is rendered by letting them stack one or multiple rendering commands in a buffer and then execute this list of commands at a given point. These commands can be fairly diverse, such as drawing a given mesh, setting a global shader property, or picking the active render target. These buffers are, therefore, an interesting way to extend the built-in render pipeline, or even mimic rendering tools from other pipelines.

A very common example of built-in `CommandBuffers` is the implementation of decals, which are not available by default (although **Projectors** can be a valid workaround), or the creation of a blurry glass effect, such as the one shown in *Figure 2.2*:

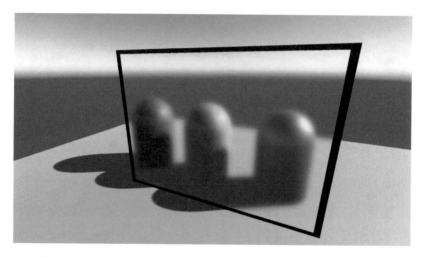

Figure 2.2 – A blurry refraction effect in the Unity built-in render pipeline

Let's have a look at this last example to better understand how to use `CommandBuffers`.

This effect works by first rendering the skybox and the opaque objects behind the glass, then capturing this intermediary render as an image, blurring it, and re-sampling it for the glass panel in front. To do this, we will need a shader for the glass object, another shader for the blur effect, and a C# script to implement our `CommandBuffers` in, and to use the blur shader.

So, first things first, let's prepare our shaders. The glass is quite simple – all we have to do is define a texture field for the blurred image (it doesn't even need to be exposed in the **Inspector**) and then sample it according to the right UV coordinates.

Now, the trick is to get those UV coordinates because here, we are not simply pasting a texture onto an object. What we want here is to apply an effect on the pixels behind our glass object to distort the UVs of the background content and create our blur filter, similar to what a grab pass does. Luckily, Unity has a built-in function for that, `ComputeGrabScreenPos`, so we can easily write our shader by following these steps:

1. First, we will set up our `Queue` and `RenderType` tags, and we will prepare our overall shader structure:

    ```
    Shader "FX/Glass/Blurry" {
        SubShader {
            Tags { "Queue"="Transparent"
                "RenderType"="Opaque" }
    ```

```
                Pass {
                    CGPROGRAM
                    #pragma vertex vert
                    #pragma fragment frag
                    #include "UnityCG.cginc"

                    sampler2D _GrabBlurTexture;

                    struct appdata {
                        float4 vertex : POSITION;
                    };
                    struct v2f {
                        float4 vertex : POSITION;
                        float4 uvgrab : TEXCOORD0;
                    };
                    ENDCG
                }
            }
        }
```

Take note that the uvgrab field will be computed in the vertex shader part, so we don't need to declare any UV coordinate semantic in the incoming appdata structure, and that these grab-pass UVs are float4, because they represent special UVs with extra data.

2. Then, inside the vertex shader function, we will get our vertex position in clip space and our grab-pass UVs, thanks to the built-in functions:

```
v2f vert (appdata v) {
    v2f o;
    o.vertex = UnityObjectToClipPos(v.vertex);
    o.uvgrab = ComputeGrabScreenPos(o.vertex);
    return o;
}
```

3. Finally, in the fragment shader function, we will sample our blurred texture with those grab-pass UVs by doing some projections. These are necessary because the UV coordinates of a grab pass are not float2 as usual but float4, and they cannot be directly passed to a usual tex2D sampling function:

```
half4 frag (v2f i) : SV_Target {
    return tex2Dproj (_GrabBlurTexture,
        UNITY_PROJ_COORD(i.uvgrab));
}
```

The second shader we need to create is not a material shader like the ones we saw up to that point, but a compute shader that computes our blur effect faster on the intermediary render. We will discuss this concept of compute shaders in more detail in *Chapter 8*, so we will not dive into too many details for now. However, if you want to check out the shader for yourself, you can find it in the GitHub repository of the book at `https://github.com/PacktPublishing/Become-a-Unity-Shaders-Guru`.

Alright, so at that stage, we are going to assume that we have our glass shader and associated material that we can put on our glass object to apply the blurred render as a grab-pass texture, plus we have another compute shader to actually compute this blur on the intermediary render. The last step is therefore to bring everything together in a C# script thanks to `CommandBuffers`.

> **Important note**
>
> In this section, we will show the basic usage of `CommandBuffers`. This example is not optimized and production-ready, but rather detailed and readability-oriented!

This script will need to set up various buffers for the cameras in our scene that take a picture of the current render, apply the blur, and feed it to the glass material shader. We will put it on our glass object in the scene so it can trigger this specific behavior when it is rendered.

4. To begin with, to keep a quick-access reference to the cameras in the scene and the `CommandBuffer` variable associated with each of them, we can define a dictionary mapping and do our setup and cleanup whenever the glass object is enabled or disabled:

```
using UnityEngine;
using UnityEngine.Rendering;
using System.Collections.Generic;

public class CommandBufferBlur : MonoBehaviour {
    private Dictionary<Camera,CommandBuffer> _cameras
        = new Dictionary<Camera,CommandBuffer>();

    private void Cleanup() {
        foreach (var cam in _cameras)
            if (cam.Key)
                cam.Key.RemoveCommandBuffer(
                    CameraEvent.AfterSkybox,
                        cam.Value);
        _cameras.Clear();
    }
    public void OnEnable() {
        Cleanup();
    }
    public void OnDisable() {
        Cleanup();
```

```
        }
    }
```

You'll notice that our `Cleanup` function uses one of the rendering hooks we mentioned at the beginning of this section. Here, the `CameraEvent.AfterSkybox` value allows us to target this specific stage of the rendering process and remove our custom buffer of commands from it.

5. Then, let's use the `OnWillRenderObject` built-in hook to run our logic whenever the glass object is rendered by any camera in the scene. We will start by checking whether the object is indeed active, and by getting a reference to our current camera to try and fill its buffer. If it's already registered in our dictionary, it means we've already prepared everything, and we can just exit early. Here's the corresponding C# code:

```csharp
public void OnWillRenderObject() {
    var act = gameObject.activeInHierarchy && enabled;
    if (!act) {
        Cleanup();
        return;
    }
    var cam = Camera.current;
    if (!cam) return;
    CommandBuffer buf = null;
    if (_cameras.ContainsKey(cam)) return;
}
```

6. The next step is to prepare a material to apply our blur shader on. Contrary to most Unity materials, we won't actually apply it to any mesh in our scene, but rather make it a runtime asset for our blur filter computation, because it is just used in our intermediary calculations. To do this, we simply have to create a new `Material` object based on our blur shader the first time we use it, set its `HideFlags` bitmask property to prevent it from being saved in the assets, and then cache it in our script for further reuse, like this:

```csharp
public class CommandBufferBlur : MonoBehaviour {
    public Shader _blurShader;
    private Material _material;
    ...

    public void OnWillRenderObject() {
        ...
        if (!_material) {
            _material = new Material(_blurShader);
            _material.hideFlags =
                HideFlags.HideAndDontSave;
        }
    }
}
```

7. Finally, we have to take care of really filling in our `CommandBuffer` instance for the current camera. This process can be decomposed into five parts:

I. Initializing the buffer: Before we do anything, we have to create our `CommandBuffer` variable and add it to our dictionary as follows:

```
public void OnWillRenderObject() {
    ...
    buf = new CommandBuffer();
    _cameras[cam] = buf;
}
```

II. Capturing the current render in a **RenderTexture (RT)**: Then, we need to take the current camera render as an image and store it in an RT – this will allow us to work on those pixels and apply our blur. To do this, we can use the `Blit` buffer command, which copies a set of pixels from a source to a destination texture, like here:

```
public void OnWillRenderObject() {
    ...
    int screenCopyID = Shader.PropertyToID("_Screen
        CopyTexture");
    buf.GetTemporaryRT (screenCopyID, -1, -1, 0,
        FilterMode.Bilinear);
    buf.Blit (BuiltinRenderTextureType.CurrentActive,
        screenCopyID);
}
```

III. Prepare 1-pixel-smaller RTs to blur this image: The idea at this stage is to copy the contents of our screen RT to slightly smaller RTs and mix them to perform a Gaussian blur. We will use the separable property of this algorithm, which allows us to first compute the blur on one 1D axis and store the results, and then feed these unfinished results to another blur on the other 1D axis to get our final convolution. This is why we need two smaller RTs, and a 1-pixel margin to be able to get the neighbors for each pixel, as shown here:

```
public void OnWillRenderObject() {
    ...
    int blurredID = Shader.PropertyToID("_Temp1");
    int blurredID2 = Shader.PropertyToID("_Temp2");
    buf.GetTemporaryRT (blurredID, -2, -2, 0,
        FilterMode.Bilinear);
    buf.GetTemporaryRT (blurredID2, -2, -2, 0,
        FilterMode.Bilinear);

    // copy screen RT into tmp RT, release screen RT
    buf.Blit (screenCopyID, blurredID);
```

```
        buf.ReleaseTemporaryRT (screenCopyID);
    }
```

IV. Feed the temporary RTs to our compute shader: Now, it is finally time to perform our blur! By setting some global variables with the use of the SetGlobalVector buffer command, we can actually parametrize our blur shader so that it computes the Gaussian convolution on a given 1D axis. Then, we just have to input the data to perform this computation on, thanks to the Blit command, as in *step III*:

```
public void OnWillRenderObject() {
    ...
    // horizontal blur 1
    buf.SetGlobalVector("offsets", new Vector4(
        2.0f/Screen.width,0,0,0));
    buf.Blit (blurredID, blurredID2, _material);
    // vertical blur 1
    buf.SetGlobalVector("offsets", new Vector4(
        0,2.0f/Screen.height,0,0));
    buf.Blit (blurredID2, blurredID, _material);
    // horizontal blur 2
    buf.SetGlobalVector("offsets", new Vector4(
        4.0f/Screen.width,0,0,0));
    buf.Blit (blurredID, blurredID2, _material);
    // vertical blur 2
    buf.SetGlobalVector("offsets", new Vector4(
        0,4.0f/Screen.height,0,0));
    buf.Blit (blurredID2, blurredID, _material);
}
```

V. Using the resulting texture and hooking up the CommandBuffer variable: Last but not least, we have to tell our glass object's shader to use the blurred texture (thanks to another global variable, this time for a texture), and tell the render pipeline to use this whole chain of commands by hooking it up to the CameraEvent.AfterSkybox step:

```
public void OnWillRenderObject() {
    ...
    buf.SetGlobalTexture("_GrabBlurTexture",
        blurredID);
    cam.AddCommandBuffer (CameraEvent.AfterSkybox,
        buf);
}
```

For the cherry on top, you can add the [ExecuteInEditMode] attribute above the entire script to have it automatically refresh in the editor, even when the game is not currently running:

```
[ExecuteInEditMode]
public class CommandBufferBlur : MonoBehaviour { ... }
```

If you add this script to the glass object in the scene and put the blur shader in its **Inspector** slot, you should see that now, no matter how many cameras there are in your scene, each one gets a blurred effect on the objects behind the glass panel, like in *Figure 2.3*:

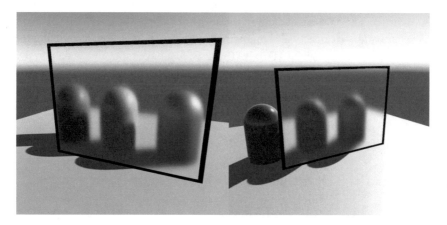

Figure 2.3 – The blurry refraction effect rendered by multiple cameras at once

This concludes our overview of the built-in render pipeline. In this section, we've examined how the built-in render pipeline can be a good introduction to the system of materials and shaders in Unity, how it offers a wide gallery of features, and how it can be extended, thanks to CommandBuffers.

However, since 2019, Unity has promoted the use of its new SRPs and is pushing forward the URP render pipeline as the new all-in-one solution. So, let's see how this other tool differs from the one already at our disposal!

Stepping up with the URP render pipeline

The URP is one of the two new SRP templates. It is meant to be highly customizable via a gallery of tools, scalable to ensure your projects are cross-platform between mobiles and desktops, and all-around a more optimized rendering solution than the built-in render pipeline. However, it is not installed by default in all your Unity projects, and we need a few preliminary steps to get a project URP-ready.

So, in the following sections, we will discuss how URP helps foster creativity and support multiple platforms. Then, we will examine the new node-based visual editors it offers, and finally, we will have a look at how to get and set up the URP in a project (both a new and an existing one).

A powerful pipeline for all creators

The URP is gradually becoming the standard for most Unity projects because of its wide variety of applications, its ease of use, and its scalability. Initially called the **Light-Weight Render Pipeline** (**LWRP**), it has always been about finding a good trade-off between quality and performance.

One of the important philosophies behind URP is to give Unity creators a way to transition from the built-in render pipeline to the new SRP tools. This is why, among other things, URP handles 2D and 3D rendering, has camera stacking to continue the multi-camera support, has the same various light types, and also has light cookies and reflection probes. There is a one-to-one mapping for the built-in shader types to matching URP shaders, too, so that you can easily upgrade your materials for this new rendering environment. Since the Unity 2020 LTS version, URP has even deferred rendering and screen space ambient occlusion, as requested by many users.

All of this makes URP a great solution for many use cases, and today, unless you really want to start from a blank project, going for URP instead of the built-in renderer for your games is often the better choice.

For example, just like the built-in render pipeline, URP offers a range of lighting techniques, with both direct and indirect lighting tools. But it also has a CPU-to-GPU lightmapper to improve the performance of the rendering on low-tier devices, such as mobiles, and three rendering paths to optimize your rendering depending on the type of game you're making (forward rendering, deferred rendering, or 2D rendering).

> **How to choose the right rendering path**
>
> To put it simply, forward rendering is the most common rendering path. It is nice for optimizing materials and lighting computations, and it scales well for various platforms. Deferred rendering is interesting whenever you have a large number of lights and want to avoid the heavy toll of those multiple sources that would occur with forward rendering. Finally, 2D rendering is optimized for global 2D lights and shadows.

URP has always been about keeping as high performance as possible to help you create games and apps for low-tier platforms such as mobiles, tablets, or even XR (meaning AR or VR). It gives you a lot of control over your performance resources to optimize your project and create smooth games everywhere.

Then, if you want to apply some cinematic effects to your scene, URP will offer you ready-made postprocessing effects, such as Depth of Field, Bloom, Motion Blur, Vignette, or even Lens Flares.

Just as an example, here is a screenshot from the famous Viking Village sample project by Unity Technologies, which was ported to the URP while still preserving the ambience and nice postprocessing (the following image is by Unity and available at `https://assetstore.unity.com/packages/essentials/tutorial-projects/viking-village-urp-29140`):

Figure 2.4 – Render of the Viking Village, a Unity sample project ported to URP

URP can also be customized or studied via its open source code, and you can tune some of its passes and features out to learn how it is built step by step.

> **Exploring the URP source code**
>
> If you want to discover the inner mechanics of the URP, you can see its source code here: `https://github.com/Unity-Technologies/Graphics`.

In short, URP is a way to get both realistic and artistic rendering styles with high performance, and to ensure platform compatibility from high-end desktops and consoles to low-tier mobiles. It works both for 2D and 3D rendering and provides tools for developers and artists alike, especially its new graph-based editing tools.

Making shaders and VFX with graphs

URP was designed to widen the circle of shader makers and include non-developers as well, so as to better integrate artists in the rendering process. Typically, if you're somewhat connected to the internet, you might have noticed that in the last few years, there have been more and more tutorials, videos, and tweets featuring shaders as a graph of nodes. That's thanks to the new SRP node-based visual editors!

For many years, Unity shaders have been all about coding. Even if the built-in shader code relies on the common CG/HLSL shading languages (see *Chapter 1*) and is therefore fairly straightforward for a specialized technical artist, shaders used to be quite daunting for everyone else. There were some side projects and store assets made by the community to visualize your graphs and work in a no-code fashion, such as the well-known **Amplify Shader Editor**, but no official tool. And, up to this day, if you stick with the built-in render pipeline, Unity will provide you with lots of neat libraries to include, but no visual editing whatsoever.

> **Need visual editing for your built-in render pipeline?**
> For reference, here is the page of the Amplify Shader Editor: `https://assetstore.unity.com/packages/tools/visual-scripting/amplify-shader-editor-68570`.

But with the arrival of the SRPs, Unity also introduced a node-based visual editor called **Shader Graph**. This completely transformed the Unity shader community by opening the field to more casual developers and enthusiasts, and brought back the fun to shaders!

Here is an example of a shader made in the node-based visual Shader Graph editor:

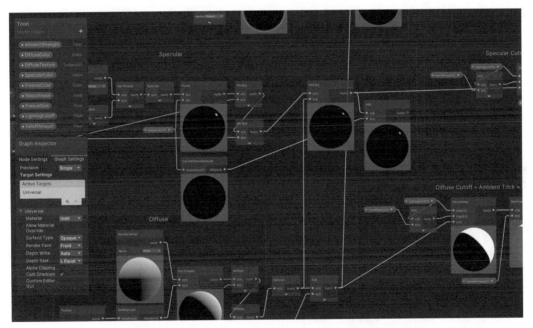

Figure 2.5 – A shader made in the node-based visual Shader Graph editor (the text within this image is not important, and the image intends only to show an overall graph example)

Like many no-code tools, it primarily aims at giving artists direct control over the visuals of the games. This can be very beneficial in small teams because it lightens the schedule of developers and lets the creative team experiment with more original ideas.

In truth, even as a coder, Shader Graph can be a great way to speed up your process and avoid unnecessary complexity. Although programming a shader in code with the new render pipelines is possible, it can quickly become tedious. At the same time, Shader Graph gives you instant feedback at every node (which means every step) of your process and offers you numerous readily available functions to quickly create advanced effects.

> **Another graph for VFX?**
>
> Parallel to this Shader Graph, Unity also developed another node-based tool for VFX, aptly named the VFX Graph, to create particle systems with a similar visual tool. This VFX Graph is available for all SRPs and, since it leverages the power of GPUs, handles more complex and demanding systems than the previous Shuriken tool. However, this also means it will not work on mobiles, so be sure to choose the right tool depending on your project's needs.
>
> Using the VFX Graph makes it possible to create complex and impressive visual effects very quickly and with immediate feedback on the result, which is extremely handy during the development phase.

With this quick review of the URP basics in mind, it's now time to see how to install it in a Unity project to actually test it out in practice!

Installing the URP

Alright, now, before discussing the various advanced shading techniques you may use with the URP, let's make sure you can set up all the tools you need to test out the URP yourself.

> **About the Unity version**
>
> Don't forget that the URP is only available with Unity 2019 and later, so you should have at least the 2019 version installed if you want to try this out. Also, the menus and field names I give here are for the Unity 2021 version, so they might be slightly different in other versions.

There are basically two situations to consider:

- First, if you haven't created your Unity project yet, you should download and use the 2D URP or 3D URP template (see *Figure 2.6*):

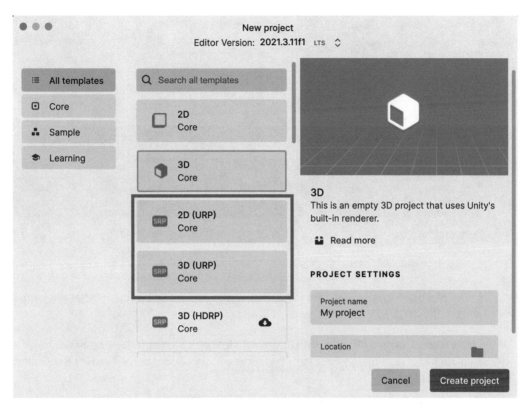

Figure 2.6 – List of startup templates for a new Unity project

This will automatically import all the necessary packages, and it will configure everything so that your project is ready for use upon launch.

- Second, if you already have a project and you want to have it use the URP, you can switch render pipelines by adding a few packages and updating your project settings.

The first step is to install the **Universal RP** package using the **Package Manager**. To do this, simply open the **Package Manager** and look through the Unity Registry packages:

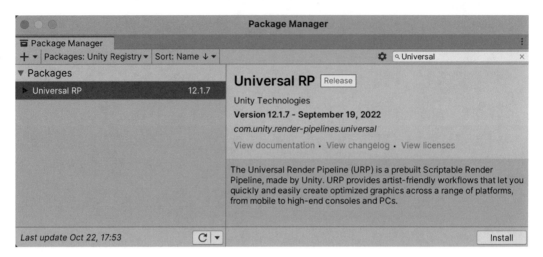

Figure 2.7 – Universal RP package in the Package Manager window

Now that the pipeline is ready, you need to configure your project to use it instead of the built-in render pipeline. To do this, you need to do the following:

1. Create a new **Universal Render Pipeline Asset** anywhere in your project – you can find it as usual, by right-clicking in your **Project** window and navigating to the **Create | Rendering | URP Asset** menu.

2. Then, open your **Project Settings** window by going to **Edit | Project Settings…**.

3. Switch to the **Graphics** section.

4. In the **Scriptable Render Pipeline Settings** field, add the URP asset from before (see *Figure 2.8*):

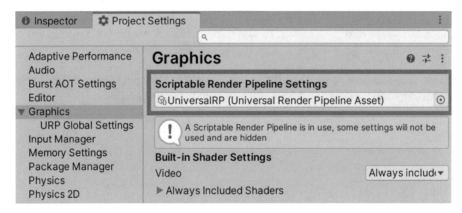

Figure 2.8 – Screenshot of the Graphics section in the Project Settings panel with the URP asset assigned

You can always go back to the built-in render pipeline by removing this asset from the **Scriptable Render Pipeline Settings** field, selecting **None** instead.

The tricky part, however, is usually converting your current shader and materials for the new render pipeline. Since the shaders for the built-in pipeline are not compatible with URP shaders, you have to do the conversion manually. Luckily, there is a tool to help speed up this conversion. You can access it as follows:

1. Go to **Edit | Rendering | Materials**.
2. Click **Convert Selected Built-in Materials to URP** to auto-transform all the materials currently selected in your **Project** window.

> **Important: Backing up the project!**
>
> Keep in mind that those changes cannot be undone, so if your project contains important data, you should do a backup first.

The postprocessing tools are different between the built-in and URPs, too. So, if you already had the **Post Processing Version 2** package installed, you will need to remove it and instead use URP's integrated postprocessing solution to re-create your effects.

The downside to this switch is that the URP postprocessing does not support custom effects yet. Still, there are some workarounds to this limitation, and, at the time of writing this book, the URP roadmap is featuring this as "in-progress." Also, though there is currently no official workflow to create custom postprocessing with URP, all Unity packages are open source, thus allowing us to go and dig into the available effects (**Bloom**, **Vignette**, etc.) to create our own postprocessing effects with a similar method.

Now that we've explored the URP and seen its diverse applications and advantages, let's discuss the other SRP: the high-definition pipeline.

Going realistic with the HDRP render pipeline

Contrary to the URP, which is meant to handle diverse use cases and platforms, the HDRP focuses on a more specific application – the creation of 3D (hyper)photorealistic renders for high-end platforms, such as desktops or consoles.

The need for such a rendering tool has emerged for different reasons – most notably, because, as Unity has reached more and more diverse communities, it eventually spread to the film industry. CGI movie teams are now starting to see game engines as a way to get real-time high-level graphics, so Unity had to offer tools to create photorealistic renders inside the engine. Hence, the HDRP!

You might have already seen what the HDRP is capable of if you've watched Unity's famous Unity short films, or if you've tried out the HDRP sample scene template – here is a screenshot from this hyper-realistic scene:

Figure 2.9 – Screenshot from the HDRP sample scene template

In a nutshell, the HDRP is aimed specifically at creating stunning realistic visuals and, as such, it does not really concern itself with low-tier device performance or cross-platform support. The goal of this pipeline is to typically produce high-fidelity graphics, thanks to cutting-edge techniques and tools from the movie industry. And there are no compatibility checks to validate, to hinder these results. With HDRP, you target the most efficient high-end platforms, and you put everything in place to produce the most amazing and life-like visuals possible. This does, however, mean that HDRP cannot support mobiles or 2D, so you should keep this in mind when you design your project and pick your render pipeline.

Just like the URP, HDRP shaders can be created either via HLSL or using the new Shader Graph, so non-technical artists can participate in making your project's visuals. Other than that, in terms of features, HDRP's quest for realism is supported by various options and specificities of the pipeline, such as the following:

- Physical cameras: By providing real-life camera settings for the lens and the aperture of the device, the HDRP ensures that photography specialists have all they need to re-create a realistic camera.

- Physically based lighting: The pipeline also accommodates lighting configuration using real-world units such as lumen or lux, and physical quantities such as color temperature instead of an abstract light color.

    Moreover, in HDRP, lighting can use rasterization, light baking, raytracing, or path tracing to produce gorgeous images compatible with different environments, and the pipeline contains several tools to create impressive atmospheres, thanks to HDRI and volumetrics.

- Multiple anti-aliasing options: To avoid jagged edges and unrealistic aliasing, HDRP provides us with anti-aliasing tools, at both the hardware and software levels. On the one hand, we can enable **Multi-Sampling Anti-Aliasing** (**MSAA**) to drastically improve the visuals, but at a very high cost. On the other hand, we can use other types of anti-aliasing that are applied as postprocessing effects and reduce the aliasing for less computing power, such as **Fast Approximate Anti-Aliasing** (**FXAA**) or **Temporal Anti-Aliasing** (**TAA**).

Anti-aliasing in Unity (MSAA, FXAA, and TAA)

The anti-aliasing used by your Unity project can be configured either by going to the **Project Settings | Frame Settings | HDRP Default Settings** menu and setting the default value for the anti-aliasing (along with some additional options) or in the project's HDRP asset (for MSAA).

To make a better-informed choice, here's a quick summary of the three possible anti-aliasing for HDRP:

- **MSAA**: This algorithm is the most powerful but also the most demanding in terms of computing resources, since it happens at the hardware level. Here, we tell Unity to increase or decrease the number of samples to use to render the image, which directly translates to more or less accurate images but also longer or shorter rendering times. Setting the samples count to its maximum (as we'll see later in this section) boosts the visual's quality but requires the built game to run on a high-end platform such as a computer or a console.

- **FXAA**: At the other end of the spectrum, FXAA is a fast-approximation algorithm applied as a postprocessing effect on the rendered image. So, this time, Unity doesn't let us play with the render samples – the algorithm just tries to remove as many jagged lines as possible on the already rendered image. This anti-aliasing scheme is interesting for mobiles and platforms that don't support motion vectors.

- **TAA**: TAA is sort of an in-between. It is still a postprocessing effect, but it uses motion vectors and gives better results than FXAA. It is usually a good choice for computers or desktops to lighten the load, compared to MSAA.

When using MSAA, **MSAA Sample Count** determines how many samples per pixel the effect uses, and therefore how smooth the edges will be, as well as how demanding the anti-aliasing is. *Figure 2.10* shows the difference between a scaled-up HDRP render with no aliasing and one with **MSAA Sample Count** set to its maximum of **8X** (the following images are by Unity and available at `https://docs.unity3d.com/Packages/com.unity.render-pipelines.high-definition@9.0/manual/`):

Figure 2.10 – Comparison between two MSAA Sample Count values: None and 8X

- **A wide range of material properties for realism**: With subsurface scattering, translucency, iridescence, anisotropy, and more, the HDRP has all the tweaks you might want for your life-like scenes.

To balance out these high requirements and still allow HDRP projects to run on some slightly older or less performant machines, the pipeline has a few additional tricks up its sleeve. Most notably, the HDRP can use a dynamic resolution to maintain a stable frame rate and extend the range of supported platforms a little. This option is a way to rescale the viewport, so it adapts to the varying resolutions on different devices. You can also define various quality levels for your target platforms, and various settings in those quality levels – or even overrides on a per-camera or per-light basis to direct all the computing power to the elements that really require it.

Finally, the HDRP also has a built-in **Graphics Compositor** to easily merge the renders of your Unity scenes with external sources, such as videos or images. There are various techniques for compositing your Unity renders, but the most common one is using the graph-based composition tool, as shown in *Figure 2.11*:

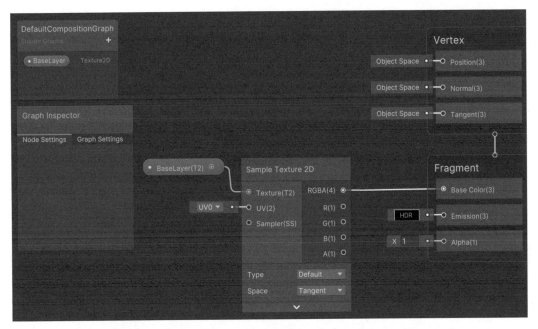

Figure 2.11 – Screenshot of the default HDRP node-based composition graph

Having a multi-camera setup in HDRP

By default, HDRP does not support a multi-camera setup, like the built-in or URP renderers. Rather, you should use a custom pass to draw your game objects at custom points and create a full-screen mix of your passes, or the **Graphics Compositor** to blend together multiple camera viewss to the same render target.

The interesting thing is that installing HDRP in your Unity project works just the same as for the URP setup we saw in the *Stepping up with the URP* section. You can either choose a template or install the **High Definition RP** package, and then add an HDRP asset to your project's graphics settings. There are a few additional configuration steps, but the HDRP plugin comes with a helper to properly re-update your project, so the transition should go fairly smoothly. This means that you can very easily switch between the two to better understand the differences.

To sum up, although it is not as cross-platform as URP, the HDRP's ability to create realistic and detailed scenes makes it an interesting tool for showcases or even full CGI movies, and it offers a range of tools for creating high-fidelity renders with realistic cameras, compositing internal and external sources, or applying powerful postprocessing effects that illuminate your renders.

Still, the URP and HDRPs share some interesting features since they are both based on the SRP object. So, to finish our review of Unity's render pipelines, let's have a more in-depth look at the SRPs themselves.

Diving deeper into the SRPs

One of the core ideas with the new SRPs is to allow developers even more granularity in the customization of their rendering process by letting them code their entire rendering pipeline. It is a continuation of the `CommandBuffers` we saw in the *Using the built-in render pipeline* section, but with more choice and more control.

This can be particularly valuable if you want to optimize your graphics or your rendering resources in a certain way, typically to better fit low-tier platforms. For the more devoted graphics programmer, it is a great feature because creating your own custom render pipeline from start to finish is the ultimate way to merge aesthetics and performance.

Note that while there is no extensive documentation on that topic yet and it does involve more work than just using one of the templates, we will go through the basics of this in *Chapter 10*. Another approach to tackling this steep learning curve can also be to use the framework's customization capabilities to add or remove some features and deconstruct the existing templates for analysis.

But of course, while having a customizable pipeline is great, most people will be just fine sticking to the available templates. So, the Unity team had to make sure that those URP and HDRP frameworks already offered a high-enough performance. This was made possible thanks to a rewrite of low-level engine parts, and in particular a native integration of some CPU-to-GPU data transfers.

In short, up until now, the flexibility of Unity's rendering engine, for example, the ability to change any property of a material at any time during a frame, was accompanied by some hard work for the CPU to properly communicate all this data to the GPU memory. As you can see in *Figure 2.12* (image by Unity, available at `https://blog.unity.com/technology/srp-batcher-speed-up-your-rendering`), the system had to continuously check and feed the contents of the GPU buffers so that the shader code would have the right input data:

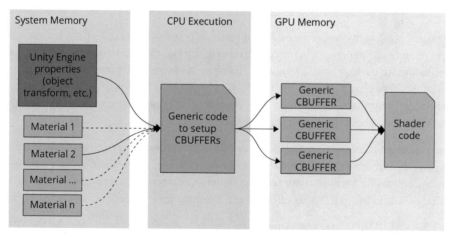

Figure 2.12 – Standard Unity rendering workflow

But with the SRPs, Unity introduced a new tool, the SRP Batcher, to improve this process. This optimization speeds up the CPU by storing the material content in GPU memory with data persistence, and using a specific code path for the update of per-object built-in engine properties, as shown in *Figure 2.13* (image by Unity, available at `https://blog.unity.com/technology/srp-batcher-speed-up-your-rendering`):

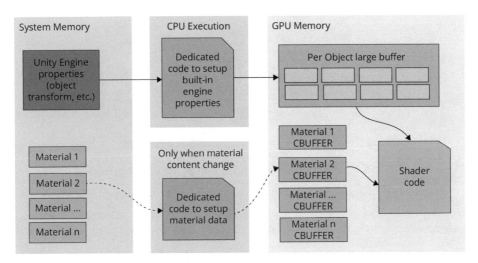

Figure 2.13 – SRP Batcher rendering workflow

This SRP Batcher should be enabled by default in URP, but you can always check whether it is enabled or not in the properties of the current SRP. For example, you can check whether SRP Batcher is enabled in the URP asset by first switching the **Inspector** to **Debug** mode by right-clicking on the tab and then clicking on the second option:

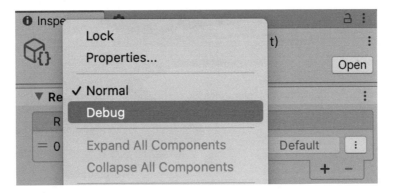

Figure 2.14 – Screenshot of how to switch the Inspector panel from Normal to Debug mode

Then, scroll down to the **Use SRP Batcher** option:

Figure 2.15 – Screenshot of a URP asset with the Use SRP Batcher option enabled

There are, however, two requirements to the SRP Batcher being used for the rendering of an object:

- The object has to be a mesh (it cannot be a particle or a skinned mesh)
- The shader must be compatible with the SRP Batcher

If you work with built-in lit and unlit shaders from the HDRP and URP templates, those requirements will be filled automatically. But if you're working on some cutting-edge visuals and want to check whether your shader is compatible, you can always select your shader and check for compatibility in the **Inspector**:

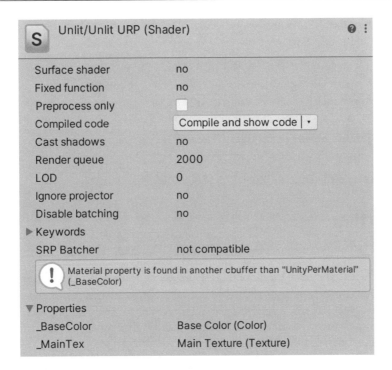

Figure 2.16 – Screenshot of a shader Inspector not compatible with the SRP Batcher

We will see how to write a custom SRP shader in HLSL that is compatible with the SRP Batcher in *Chapter 10*. For now, let's just remember this optimization trick is possible, and that we will have to take some extra steps in the future to ensure that our custom shader scripts use the SRP to its full potential.

What's also really neat is that a single scene can mix SRP Batcher-compatible and non-SRP Batcher-compatible objects – the rendering process will just use the SRP Batcher code path for the former, and the standard (slightly slower) code path for the latter.

However, just like with the optimization feature, you should always profile your game with and without the SRP Batcher to ensure that, in your current use case, it does lead to significant improvements.

Summary

In this chapter, we discussed the three pipelines Unity offers us – the built-in render pipeline, the URP, and the HDRP. We saw how these templates differ from one another, what their strengths and limitations are, and how we can customize their features to better understand the rendering process in Unity.

We also took this opportunity to introduce some tools and techniques that we will discuss in more detail in upcoming chapters, such as compute shaders and `CommandBuffers`.

Finally, we saw how the SRPs themselves are designed for performance, and how we can optimize our shaders, thanks to the SRP Batcher.

A key point of this analysis is that today, the URP is slowly becoming the de facto solution for Unity rendering. With its diverse applications, its out-of-the-box optimizations, and its beginner-friendly shader creation tools, such as Shader Graph, it is slowly taking over the built-in pipeline. This is why, in the rest of this book, we will focus on the URP and its shaders, via both code and the node-based editor, to implement modern and optimized visual effects.

To begin with, in the next chapter, we will see how to write a simple URP shader in HLSL code to get familiar with the little adjustments it requires in our ShaderLab scripts!

Going further

If you're curious about the differences between the three Unity render pipelines or `CommandBuffers`, here are a few interesting resources to check out or continue your journey with:

- The Unity render pipelines:

    - *Render pipelines* (official documentation), Unity: `https://docs.unity3d.com/Manual/render-pipelines.html`

    - *What are the Unity render pipelines and which to use? | HDRP vs URP 2022*, B. Dickinson (2022): `https://www.youtube.com/watch?v=xS6g15XL8jQ`

    - *Scriptable Render Pipeline: What You Need To Know*, Unity (2018): `https://www.youtube.com/watch?v=2wUPgl7upnU`

    - *SRP Batcher: Speed up your rendering*, A. Carré: `https://blog.unity.com/engine-platform/srp-batcher-speed-up-your-rendering`

- `CommandBuffers`:

    - *Extending Unity 5 rendering pipeline: Command Buffers*, A. Pranckevičius (2015): `https://blog.unity.com/technology/extending-unity-5-rendering-pipeline-command-buffers`

    - *Using Command Buffers in Unity: Selective Bloom*, L. Reid (2018): `https://lindenreidblog.com/2018/09/13/using-command-buffers-in-unity-selective-bloom/`

    - Official API reference of the `CommandBuffer` object, Unity: `https://docs.unity3d.com/ScriptReference/Rendering.CommandBuffer.html`

3

Writing Your First URP Shader

Thanks to the first two chapters, we are now familiar with both the old way of writing shaders using the built-in render pipeline and the idea that we could improve our workflow by switching to the new **Universal Render Pipeline** (**URP**). However, we still don't know exactly what this implies for our shader scripts, and how to actually create our effects with this new setup.

Although Unity now puts the node-based shader editing in the foreground with its Shader Graph, it is still interesting to know what goes on behind the scenes and to have an idea of how to write shader code for this new render pipeline via code. This will give you more knowledge of the overall shading pipeline and help you decipher some obscure documentation or a discreet thread on a great but rare shader effect, and be useful if your shaders require some custom functions – for which you will need to write your own scripts.

So, throughout this chapter, we will learn how to write a simple unlit shader for the URP using HLSL code to get familiar with the differences between the legacy built-in render pipeline shader scripts and the URP-compatible ones.

To do this, we will cover the following topics:

- Structuring a Unity HLSL shader
- Having a peek at shader includes and tags
- Writing our unlit URP shader

Technical requirements

To try out the samples yourself, you will need to have Unity installed, with a version from 2019 or later. You will then need to create either of the following:

- A project with the common 3D template, which you will then upgrade to use the URP or HDRP render pipelines (see the *Stepping up with the URP render pipeline* section of *Chapter 2*)
- A project with the new 3D URP or 3D HDRP template (see the *Stepping up with the URP render pipeline* section of *Chapter 2* for guidance on how to download and pick this template)

You can find the code files for this chapter on GitHub at `https://github.com/PacktPublishing/Become-a-Unity-Shaders-Guru/tree/main/Assets/Chapter%2003`.

Structuring a Unity HLSL shader

When we worked on our simple Blinn-Phong shader in *Chapter 1*, we discussed the syntax of Unity shaders. We saw that all these files are composed of an overarching wrapper using the ShaderLab syntax and that inside it, we find blocks such as `Properties`, `SubShader`, and `Pass`. The real "meat" of the code, so to speak, is the low-level shader logic written in between the `CGPROGRAM` and `ENDCG` lines. This is the hardware shader code that performs the actual computation.

All of this can be summarized as follows:

```
Shader "Custom/MyLegacyShader" {
    Properties { ... }
    SubShader {
        // subshader tags
        Pass {
            // pass tags
            // (optional: blend mode setup)
            // (optional: z-testing setup)
            // (optional: culling setup)
            CGPROGRAM
            // low-level hardware logic
            ENDCG
        }
    }
}
```

This representation is fairly crude, but the good news is that it is still mostly valid for the new **Scriptable Render Pipelines (SRPs)**!

Whether you are using the built-in render pipeline or the new URP, you will still have this ShaderLab wrapper with its nested hierarchy. This is nice because it means we can devise a recipe for translating our old shaders into new ones, compatible with the URP. The only thing to keep an eye out for at the ShaderLab level will be the shader tags, so we will specially focus on that in the *Having a peek at shader includes and tags* section.

In truth, the real difference will be for the low-level hardware logic part definition. Indeed, whereas the built-in pipeline relies on **Cg** (which is a shading language by Nvidia that is now deprecated), the URP uses another, way more common shading language called the **High-Level Shading Language** (**HLSL**). This is why, nowadays, HLSL is considered the best tool for writing shaders in Unity, and you should focus your study on this language rather than Cg. The two languages are very similar to one another, so the logic implementation in itself will be almost identical. However, the integration of this HLSL chunk inside the ShaderLab container will require some changes compared to our previous legacy shaders.

So, what difference does it make for our shader scripts exactly?

The main thing to keep in mind when switching over to this new HLSL-based shader scripting in Unity is that, now, rather than having everything under the CGPROGRAM/ENDCG block, you will need to separate the includes from the real implementation. This is done by using the HLSLINCLUDE/ENDHLSL and HLSLPROGRAM/ENDHLSL blocks. The includes will also be exported out of the Pass block, inside of its parent SubShader, so that they can be shared more easily between each Pass instance.

This means that a typical URP shader script will be slightly different, and more along the lines of the following:

```
SubShader {
    // subshader tags
    HLSLINCLUDE
    // include HLSL-compatible libraries
    // define properties
    // define data structure (appdata, v2f)
    ENDHLSL
    Pass {
        // pass tags
        // (optional: blend mode setup)
        // (optional: z-testing setup)
        // (optional: culling setup)
        HLSLPROGRAM
        // use pragmas to link vertex/fragment shader
            functions
        // define vertex/fragment shader functions
        ENDHLSL
    }
}
```

Here, we can spot the new blocks that replace our old CGPROGRAM/ENDCG, plus an important note about libraries – they have to be HLSL-compatible.

This will probably be the biggest friction point in going from the built-in render pipeline shader scripting to the new URP/HLSL-based version: includes, libraries, and built-in functions have changed. If you've been coding Unity shaders for a long time, all the neat tools you might be used to, such as UnityCG.cginc or UnityObjectToClipPos, are now gone. There are, of course, equivalents, and sometimes even more apt and flexible built-in variables and methods, but the fact is that you will need to re-adapt to this new world.

To avoid some pitfalls and common traps, let's have a closer look at these shader includes, and check out how some common tools have been replaced in the new URP shader scripting ecosystem.

Having a peek at shader includes and tags

After this quick overview of the new shader script structure for URP, we now know that there has been an important change with the includes.

Thus, to better understand why and how it has changed, let's briefly discuss how to import the new core shader tools for URP/HLSL shader scripts and how to update some of our most common built-in variables and function calls provided via macros. We will then talk about the two important shader tags you need to be aware of when writing shaders for URP.

Including the URP core module

As we discussed in the *Structuring a Unity HLSL shader* section, the new HLSL-based shader scripts cannot use the classic `.cginc` shader includes, as their predecessors did. Because they are based on the HLSL language, they have to include libraries written in that language, and more precisely in our case, modules from the new URP shader library.

The most common is the following:

```
#include "Packages/com.unity.render-pipelines.universal/ShaderLibrary/
Core.hlsl"
```

This line, albeit long, is pretty much an equivalent of the usual one for legacy shader code:

```
#include "UnityCG.cginc"
```

However, you'll notice that this time, it is an HLSL file and it is prefixed with a long folder path-like string. This is because, up to this day, the SRPs haven't been integrated inside of the Unity editor yet – we saw in the *Stepping up with the URP render pipeline* section of *Chapter 2* that preparing a project to use the URP requires some installation and configuration steps. To use the URP, you have to install a specific package, the **Universal RP** package, from the **Package Manager**.

And guess what? If you take a look at the list of packages in your project, select the **Universal RP** package, and look at its information, you'll notice this reference code:

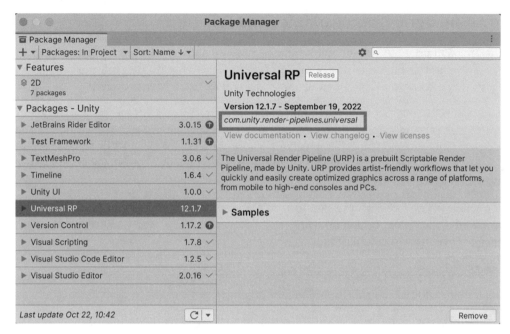

Figure 3.1 – Unique reference code of Universal RP shown in the Package Manager

The reference code we have in *Figure 3.1* is the unique ID of this package, and you can see how it is part of the path to the Core.hlsl library we just mentioned earlier in this section. By using this packaging system, Unity ensures that nobody is obligated to use the URP, but that anyone who wants to can do so easily and in a very clear manner.

The downside of having a full address like this is obviously how long the line is, but once you get used to it and you've understood what it means, I believe it is actually more informative than the plain old UnityCG.cginc.

> **What about a lit shader?**
>
> If you want your shader to take into account lights and shadows, then using just the Core. hlsl module will not be enough. You will need to include another module from the same library, Lighting.hlsl. We will see this in detail in the upcoming chapter, *Chapter 4*, but for your information, here is the include:
>
> ```
> #include "Packages/com.unity.render-pipelines.universal/
> ShaderLibrary/Lighting.hlsl"
> ```

If you want to dive in deeper, you can have a look at the source code of these library files in Unity's GitHub repository, at the following URL: https://github.com/Unity-Technologies/ Graphics/tree/master/Packages/com.unity.render-pipelines.universal/ ShaderLibrary.

Updating our built-in variables and functions

Something important to keep in mind is that because we don't use the same language or includes anymore, we also have to switch up some parts of our toolbox. While the data structures stay identical, and the semantics are the same, many of our shader writing habits have to evolve.

There is an `HLSLSupport.cginc` library that is automatically included in your legacy code (meaning when compiling code with a `CGPROGRAM` block) to help smooth the transition and allow for cross-platform compilation, but it will not be used for a shader using `HLSLPROGRAM` blocks. Thus, you will still need to remember a few transformations if you plan on writing up-to-date shader scripts for the URP.

For example, a very frequent operation you can perform in your vertex shader function code is the conversion of the vertex position from object to clip space. With the legacy built-in render pipeline, remember that this was done like this:

```
float4 clipPosition = UnityObjectToClipPos(v.vertex);
```

With the new URP, however, it changed to this:

```
float4 clipPosition = TransformObjectToHClip(v.vertex.xyz);
```

So, to help you translate your shaders, here is a summary of common Cg-to-HLSL Unity built-in macro or snippet equivalents:

Cg version (built-in render pipeline) or action	HLSL version (Universal Render Pipeline)
Library includes	
`UnityCG.cginc`	`Packages/com.unity.render-pipelines.universal/ShaderLibrary/Core.hlsl`
`AutoLight.cginc`	`Packages/com.unity.render-pipelines.universal/ShaderLibrary/Lighting.hlsl` `Packages/com.unity.render-pipelines.universal/ShaderLibrary/Shadows.hlsl`
Space transforms	
Get pre-translated object-to-world matrix	`GetObjectToWorldMatrix`
Get world-to-object matrix	`GetWorldToObjectMatrix`
Transform world to homogeneous clip space	`GetWorldToHClipMatrix`
Transform view to homogeneous clip space	`GetViewToHClipMatrix`
`UnityObjectToClipPos`	`TransformObjectToHClip`
`UnityWorldToClipPos`	`TransformWorldToHClip`
`UnityViewToClipPos`	`TransformViewToHClip`

UnityObjectToViewPos	TransformWorldToView
Transforms a `float3` position in object space to another `float3` position in world space	TransformObjectToWorld
Transforms a `float3` position in world space to another `float3` position in object space	TransformWorldToObject
Transforms a `float3` position in world space to another `float3` position in view space	TransformWorldToView
Other preprocessor macros	
`UNITY_PROJ_COORD(a)`	`a.xy / a.w`
`UNITY_DECLARE_SHADOWMAP(tex)`	`TEXTURE2D_SHADOW_PARAM(textureName, samplerName)`
`UNITY_SAMPLE_SHADOW(tex, uv)`	`SAMPLE_TEXTURE2D_SHADOW(textureName, samplerName, coord3)`
`UNITY_SAMPLE_SHADOW_PROJ(tex, uv)`	`SAMPLE_TEXTURE2D_SHADOW(textureName, samplerName, coord4.xyz/coord4.w)`
Texture sampling	
`sampler2D _BaseMap;` `float4 _BaseMap_ST;` or `UNITY_DECLARE_TEX2D(_BaseMap)`	`TEXTURE2D(_BaseMap);` `SAMPLER(sampler_BaseMap);`
`UNITY_DECLARE_TEX2D_NOSAMPLER(_BaseMap)`	`TEXTURE2D(_BaseMap);`
`tex2D(_BaseMap, i.uv);` or `UNITY_SAMPLE_TEX2D_SAMPLER(_BaseMap, _BaseMap_ST, I.uv)`	`SAMPLE_TEXTURE2D(_BaseMap, sample_BaseMap, I.uv)`

Figure 3.2 – Conversion table for some frequently used Unity shader built-in variables and functions

The table in *Figure 3.2* can help you spot which pipeline shader code you're reading is intended for, and convert a shader script of your own from a legacy to a modern version.

Picking the right tags for our shader

If you are working on a basic shader with just a single SubShader block, or even a single Pass block, then most of the time you will get away with using the same tags as for a legacy shader (if you need a refresher on what those tags are, don't hesitate to look up the *Exploring SubShader and Pass tags* section of *Appendix, Some Quick Refreshers on Shaders in Unity*).

But if your code contains multiple SubShader blocks, or multiple Pass blocks, you might have to help Unity understand what is intended for the URP and which pass should be used when. More precisely, we can specify our SubShader and Pass tags like this:

- To specify which SubShader Unity should use, you can take advantage of the RenderPipeline tag, and typically in our case, set its value to UniversalPipeline, like this:

```
SubShader {
    Tags = { /* other tags */
        "RenderPipeline"="UniversalPipeline" }
    ...
}
```

This is an interesting tool for defining several implementations of your shader for the different Unity render pipelines and still making sure that the engine chooses the right one for the current context. Note that Unity will pick the first SubShader that can be run on the GPU, so this tag is mostly here to enforce the use of a specific SRP.

For example, a shader with the following SubShader blocks would be compatible with the URP (using the first block), the HDRP (using the second block), and the built-in render pipeline (using the third block as a fallback):

```
Shader "Custom/MultiCompatibleShader" {
    SubShader {
        Tags = { "RenderPipeline"="UniversalPipeline"
            }
        ...
    }
    SubShader {
        Tags = { "RenderPipeline"="HDRenderPipeline" }
        ...
    }
    SubShader {
        Tags = {}
        ...
    }
}
```

You can also define an actual fallback shader after all your `SubShader` blocks, to ensure that the engine is never left hanging, with the `Fallback` keyword:

```
Shader "Custom/ShaderWithFallback" {
    SubShader { ... }
    Fallback "Path/To/Shader/And/Name"
}
```

- A complex shader can also have multiple passes that are used at different stages of the render. Most of the time, you'll want to define several `Pass` blocks to have parts of your shader with different `LightMode` tags.

  The most common `LightMode` tag for URP is `UniversalForward`:

  ```
  Pass {
      Tags { "LightMode"="UniversalForward" }
  }
  ```

  This is the tag you should use for any pass that computes the rendering of geometry with lighting, thanks to the forward rendering path.

  Other frequently used values are `Universal2D` for when you're using the 2D renderer, `DepthOnly` or `DepthNormalsOnly` for when you're computing a depth texture, and `ShadowCaster` for when you're computing the casting of shadows.

For a full list of the available `Pass` tags in URP and their exact usage, see `https://docs.unity3d.com/Packages/com.unity.render-pipelines.universal@14.0/manual/urp-shaders/urp-shaderlab-pass-tags.html`.

> **Important note**
>
> If you browse the net for shader examples, you might find some people using the `PassName` and `UsePass` combo. The idea is that Unity allows us to name our `Pass` blocks with the `Name` keyword to then reuse them elsewhere, thanks to the `UsePass` keyword. However, this is not recommended in terms of performance because it hinders the SRP Batcher. We will discuss this in more detail in *Chapter 10*.

Alright – now that we are clear on what an HLSL-based shader script looks like, let's wrap up this introductory chapter on URP shaders with a hands-on example to cement all of these understandings.

Writing our unlit URP shader

With all this theory out of the way, it's time to write our first URP shader! For this first example, we will go for something simple – we will design a basic unlit shader that accepts a base color and a main texture.

Figure 3.3 shows what the shader will look like on a few primitive shapes with a simple checker texture and a red color:

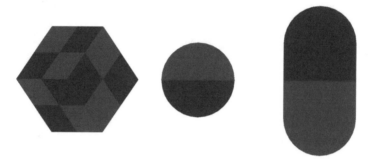

Figure 3.3 – Example of primitive shapes with our unlit URP shader applied

> **Important note**
>
> The shader we will design in this chapter will not be production-ready. It was simplified to facilitate the exploration of HLSL-based programming but does not use some of the basic optimization tricks URP offers (in particular, it is not compatible with the SRP Batcher).

To get ready to write our unlit URP shader, let's follow these steps:

1. Create a new shader script file by right-clicking on our **Project** panel and going to the **Create | Shader | Unlit Shader** menu (note that you can choose whichever preset you want since we will replace all of its content anyway!).

2. Open this file in your favorite IDE and remove everything inside.

3. Fill it with the following script skeleton:

```
Shader "Unlit/UnlitURP" {
    Properties {}
    SubShader {
        Pass {}
    }
}
```

We are now ready to implement our first URP shader in HLSL code. We will do so as follows:

1. First, we will prepare our shader properties. For this shader, we will have a `Base Color` property (of the `Color` type) and a `Main Texture` property (of the 2D type):

```
Properties {
    _BaseColor ("Base Color", Color) = (1, 1, 1, 1)
    _BaseMap ("Main Texture", 2D) = "white" {}
}
```

2. Then, we're going to take care of our includes and variables definition. As we said before, this is done in an `HLSLINCLUDE`/`ENDHLSL` block, like this:

```
HLSLINCLUDE
#include "Packages/com.unity.render-pipelines.universal/
ShaderLibrary/Core.hlsl"

float4 _BaseColor;

TEXTURE2D(_BaseMap);
SAMPLER(sampler_BaseMap);

struct appdata {};
struct v2f {};
ENDHLSL
```

3. Our `appdata` and `v2f` structures are written the same as in a legacy shader – here, we just need the position of our vertex and the main UV coordinates, so that we can use our texture property:

```
struct appdata {
    float4 vertex : POSITION;
    float2 uv : TEXCOORD0;
};

struct v2f {
    float4 vertex : SV_POSITION;
    float2 uv : TEXCOORD0;
};
```

Naming conventions

Here, I have kept the `appdata` and `v2f` names for our vertex and fragment input data structures to ease out the transition from legacy shader scripting. The URP convention is, however, to rather use `Attributes` (instead of `appdata`) and `Varyings` (instead of `v2f`). But remember that, ultimately, these are just arbitrary names – as long as you are consistent throughout your entire script, the shader will work just fine!

4. Now, the next step is to handle the HLSL low-level shader logic implementation in an HLSLPROGRAM block. This is done in Pass by defining our vertex and fragment shader functions:

```
Pass {
    HLSLPROGRAM
    #pragma vertex vert
    #pragma fragment frag

    v2f vert(appdata v) {
        v2f o;
        o.vertex = TransformObjectToHClip(
            v.vertex.xyz);
        o.uv = v.uv;
        return o;
    }

    float4 frag(v2f i) : SV_Target {
        float4 baseTex = SAMPLE_TEXTURE2D(_BaseMap,
            sampler_BaseMap, i.uv);
        return baseTex * _BaseColor;
    }
    ENDHLSL
}
```

And here we are! With just these few lines, we've written up an unlit URP shader that can receive an optional texture and a base color through its exposed properties. You can notice that, all in all, and apart from the modified built-in macros as mentioned in the *Having a peek at shader includes and tags* section, the core of the implementation is roughly identical to a legacy shader script.

If we assign it to some objects, we can then configure it in the inspector panel:

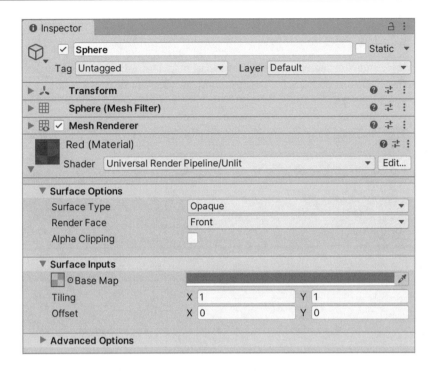

Figure 3.4 – Material inspector for our unlit URP shader

It is also worth noting that the inspector for materials that use an SRP shader is not exactly the same as the one for materials using built-in shaders. *Figure 3.5* provides a side-by-side comparison of the inspector we had for the legacy Blinn-Phong shader from *Chapter 1* and our new unlit URP shader:

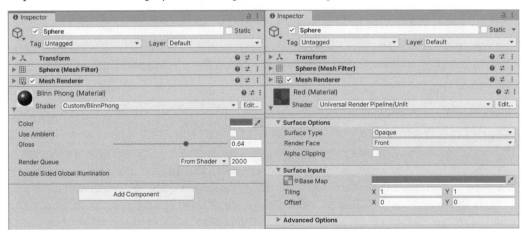

Figure 3.5 – Comparison of the material inspector for legacy
shading (on the left) and URP shading (on the right)

This means that, from a user point of view, it is clear whether a material (and more precisely the shader it uses) can be used in a URP project as is or not.

But the really nice and cool feature of this new material inspector is that, in URP, we now have access to a set of **Surface Options** that make it easy to set the blending mode or the z-testing parameter for our material (see *Figure 3.6*):

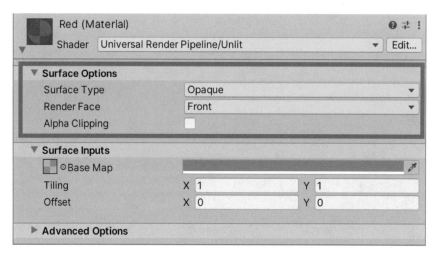

Figure 3.6 – Easy-to-use Surface Options section to further customize the material

This **Surface Options** section offers us three or four parameters:

- **Surface Type**: To choose between **Opaque** and **Transparent** renders

- **Blending Mode** (only available when **Surface Type** is set to **Transparent**): To choose whether the object should be blended in **Alpha**, **Premultiply**, **Additive**, or **Multiply** mode

- **Render Face**: To set what type of culling to use (the default **Front** value corresponds to back-face culling, while **Back** is for front-face culling, and **Both** is to disable culling entirely)

- **Alpha Clipping**: To quickly discard any pixel with an alpha value below a certain threshold and get transparency even for materials with **Surface Type** set to **Opaque** (although the alpha will be an on/off Boolean value that does not allow for semi-transparency)

The reason this **Surface Options** section is extremely useful is that it can be configured per material, even when they share the same base shader. In other words, even non-developer team members can play around with those **Surface Options** to help design the visual effects! For example, we could take our unlit shader and create two materials from it, one with the red opaque color and another with a semi-transparent blue and front-face culling (which you can observe most notably on the cubes in these screenshots):

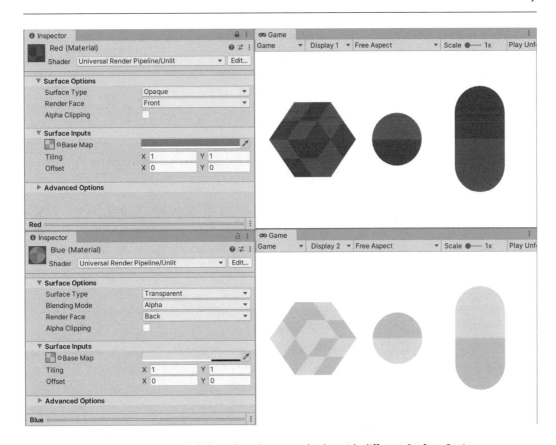

Figure 3.7 – Two materials based on the same shader with different Surface Options

This simple example of an unlit shader showed us how to build a URL/HLSL shader step by step, and it allowed us to highlight the important novelties compared to writing legacy shaders, from both a developer viewpoint and a user viewpoint.

Summary

In this chapter, we discussed the fundamentals of programming shaders with Unity's new URP.

We studied the evolutions of ShaderLab and low-level hardware shader logic syntax between the built-in render pipeline and our new setup, and in particular, we zoomed into some common macro translations that are worth mentioning. We also got an overview of the frequently used tags to help the Unity engine handle cross-platform shaders that contain multiple `SubShader` and/or `Pass` tags.

Finally, we applied the theory to a simple example and implemented an unlit URP shader with two properties: a base color and a main texture. We also took this opportunity to look at the material inspector and how, with the new SRPs, it now provides us with some interesting extra options that are material-specific.

This concludes our first look at how to program HLSL-based shaders for the Unity URP – we now have a good idea of how these scripts are structured and how this structure differs from the one of legacy shaders. We are now ready to jump into the next chapter, where we will tackle a more complex example: the creation of a lit physically based shaded URP shader script!

Going further

If you're curious about the fundamentals of writing URP shaders, here are a few interesting resources to check out or continue your journey with:

- URP official documentation: `https://docs.unity3d.com/Packages/com.unity.render-pipelines.universal@10.10/manual/index.html`

- Official GitHub repository of the URP library: `https://github.com/Unity-Technologies/Graphics/blob/master/Packages/com.unity.render-pipelines.universal`

- *Universal Render Pipeline in Unity 2019 – Overview & Tutorial*, Unity (2019): `https://www.youtube.com/watch?v=m6YqTrwjpP0`

- *Evolving game graphics with the Universal Render Pipeline | Unite Now 2020*, Unity (2020): `https://www.youtube.com/watch?v=Bvl9rCVbMas`

- *Unity Basics - Shader Code in URP*, D. Ilett (2021): `https://danielilett.com/2021-04-02-basics-3-shaders-in-urp/`

- *Writing Shader Code in Universal RP (v2)*, Cyanilux (2021): `https://www.cyanilux.com/tutorials/urp-shader-code/`

4

Transforming Your Shader into a Lit PBS Shader

In *Chapter 3*, we discovered the basics of programming a shader for the new **Universal Render Pipeline** (**URP**) using HLSL code. We saw how it differs from legacy shader scripting, focused on a few commonly used built-in variables and functions that must be changed when switching over to this new ecosystem, and eventually applied all of this theory to a hands-on example. As a result, by the end of that chapter, we had a simple unlit URP shader with a base color and a main texture property.

This was a nice introduction to the topic, but of course, modern video games only rarely ship with this rough a shading level – while having all of your objects unlit could be a conscious artistic choice, it would be interesting to also be able to create lit shaders, right?

This is why, in this chapter, we will build upon the unlit URP shader we wrote previously and implement all that is required to take into account the main and additional lights. The goal will be to recreate a shader capable of computing **physically based shading** (**PBS**).

> **Important note**
> The shader we will create in this chapter will be more advanced and present most of the features Unity's official URP lit PBS shader does, but it will be a slightly simplified version. In particular, we won't discuss additional passes and emission. Also, it won't be optimized, so it shouldn't be used as is in production. As usual, I'll explain things so that they are easy to understand and won't overwhelm you with details.

We will be covering the following topics in this chapter:

- Discovering Unity PBR-related tooling
- Coding our lit PBS shader logic

Technical requirements

To try out the samples yourself, you will need to have Unity installed, with a version from 2019 or later. You will then need to create either of the following:

- A project with the common 3D template, which you will then upgrade to use the URP or HDRP render pipelines (see the *Stepping up with the URP render pipeline* section of *Chapter 2*)

- A project with the new 3D URP or 3D HDRP template (see the same section for guidance on how to download and pick this template)

You can also find all the code files for this chapter, including a more advanced version of the shader we will create here, on GitHub at `https://github.com/PacktPublishing/Become-a-Unity-Shaders-Guru/tree/main/Assets/Chapter%2004`.

Discovering Unity PBR-related tooling

Nowadays, many video games aim for renders that are as realistic as possible, and the PBR, or PBS, has become a new standard. It is, therefore, an important technique to master for modern technical artists, so let's see how to apply it in Unity when using the URP pipeline.

In the following sections, we will have a quick glance at the shader keywords and variants that are required to make our shader lit. Then, we will have a quick look at the important tooling the URP provides us with for PBR, set up our shader keywords, and finally, introduce the four data structures our shader will use.

A quick overview of shader keywords and variants

So, before we actually dive into adding lighting to a URP shader and turning it into a lit PBS shader, we need to have a quick look at the notion of **shader keywords** and **shader variants**. We will not go into a fully detailed explanation here because we will have another in-depth run at those concepts in *Chapter 10*, but we will provide a rough take on the key ideas.

Shader keywords and variants are tools to easily turn some parts of your shader code on or off, depending on the environment it is run in. To be more precise, the idea is to define some specific keywords that can be enabled or disabled per material to use different variants of your shader. These variants can be computed and chosen at runtime if you use the `#pragma multi_compile` directive, or at compile time if you use the `#pragma shader_feature` directive. This way, you can easily centralize the different versions you want in the same shader script file to support different platforms, graphics quality, or performance limitations.

For example, to use the `#pragma multi_compile` directive, you would do something like this:

```
#pragma multi_compile _A _B _C ...
#ifdef _A
  // Compile this code if A is enabled
#endif
#ifndef _B
  // Compile this code if B is disabled
#else
  // Compile this code if B is enabled
#endif
#if defined(_A) || defined(_C)
  // Compile this code if A or C is enabled.
#endif
```

This snippet shows how to check for the keywords that are currently defined, thanks to the `#ifdef`, `#ifndef` (which stands for "if not defined"), `#else`, and `#endif` directives. The third check also exemplifies how to merge multiple conditions using C-like operators (`||` is the "or" operator, `&&` is the "and" operator, and `!` is the "not" operator).

If you only have two variants and want to quickly generate a scenario where both are disabled, you can use an underscore for the first keyword:

`#pragma multi_compile _ _A _B`

The `#pragma shader_feature` directive works in a similar way, except that the variants are computed at the time of the build. Any unused variant will just be stripped out completely. This can reduce build times and make for a lighter export, but it's not recommended if you plan on enabling and disabling keywords at runtime, since the corresponding variant of the shader might not be included in the build.

If you only have two variants in your `#pragma shader_feature` directive, then it will automatically generate the third one for the case where both are disabled – you don't need to add any underscore.

> **Note**
> The number of shader variants grows exponentially, so it can increase fairly quickly if you add several keywords. Moreover, you are limited to a maximum of 256 global keywords per project; thus, you should always try to normalize and reuse your keywords between shaders.

Finally, it is important to point out that we can also use the local versions of our two directives, `#pragma multi_compile_local` and `#pragma shader_feature_local`. We are still limited to a maximum of 64 keywords per shader, but it helps to better encapsulate our data.

Alright, with this short digression complete, we are now ready to discuss the tools that URP has for us to help with lighting, especially PBS!

Taking advantage of the built-in PBR lighting helpers

If you are an old-time Unity shader user, you are probably used to the idea that physically based rendering in Unity requires surface shaders. These were the legacy method to create realistic visuals with lighting, and starting with Unity 5, they could be used to create PBR materials that followed the two main PBS principles:

- **Energy conservation**: The surface can never reflect more light than the total incoming light (except for special cases, such as emissive materials that create additional light)

- **Microgeometry**: The surface can have some geometry at the microscopic level to better simulate its smoothness

However, in URP, these surface shaders have disappeared! Instead, the new pipeline now offers us various shading models, both lit and unlit – and PBS is one of those lit models.

This might seem scary because it implies that you'll have to rethink your lighting workflow. However, the good news is that URP does provide really interesting helpers and built-in functions to handle lighting computations, in its `Lighting.hlsl` file.

> **Diving into the source code**
>
> Don't forget that you can find all the source files for URP (such as the `Lighting.hlsl` library) on Unity's GitHub: `https://github.com/Unity-Technologies/Graphics`.

Most of the common operations are, therefore, fairly easy to add to our custom shaders. We will see in *Chapter 5* how to create our own basic toon-styled lighting using those helpers. But, in this instance, since we want to recreate a very common lighting scheme (namely, PBR lighting), we have an even easier way to add this lighting computation – the pipeline actually has a fragment function we can include to directly take care of it, `UniversalFragmentPBR`.

However, if you look at the code of the `UniversalFragmentPBR` function in Unity's official GitHub repository, you will soon understand that it relies on two things that are new to us:

- This method assumes that you have a few keywords defined in your shader to properly compute some of its values

- It expects two input parameters of type `InputData` and `SurfaceData`, which are two custom data structures we need to define and fill in beforehand

So, let's go through each preparation step in more detail.

Adding the right include statements and keywords to our shader

The first step is to ensure that our shader has all the necessary environment settings, which is why we have to add a few keywords at the top of the code, and to include some HLSL library files. Here, more specifically, we will need Core.hlsl and Lighting.hlsl.

In regards to the Core.hlsl library, we can keep it at the beginning of our HLSLINCLUDE block, as usual:

```
Shader "Custom/URP Lit PBS" {
  Properties { ... }
  SubShader {
    Tags { ... }
    HLSLINCLUDE
    #include "Packages/com.unity.render-pipelines
        .universal/ShaderLibrary/Core.hlsl"
    // define properties
    ENDHLSL
    Pass {
      HLSLPROGRAM
      ...
      ENDHLSL
    }
  }
}
```

However, for the Lighting.hlsl include, it's a bit different – since some functions inside it require specific keywords to work properly, we need to define them first inside our HLSLPROGRAM block, and then add the include afterward.

So, let's think about what we need. What we want is to design a lit shader that supports the most usual PBS options, which are as follows:

- **Albedo (with color and texture)**: The base color of our objects will be given by a color variable and a main texture slot.

- **Alpha clipping**: If turned on, our shader will use a threshold to discard any pixels with an alpha below a certain value, and create transparent areas in our surface. The shader, however, will use an opaque render, so we will not allow for semi-transparency.

- **Specular or metallic reflections**: To get shiny reflections on our surface, we will support either a metallic-based workflow or a specular gloss workflow (such as the one we saw in *Chapter 1*), with an option to toggle between the two.

- **Occlusion**: To better integrate our objects into a scene, we will let users add an occlusion map if they want to specify in more detail how indirect lighting should impact a model (typically, this is used to avoid having the same amount of indirect lighting in cracks and concave parts of the mesh, since, in real life, those zones would receive less light).

- **Normals**: We will accept a normal map to simulate surface imperfections and bumps.

Other than that, the shader should obviously work with one or more light sources. We'll also make sure that it works with baked lighting and global illumination by allowing for the use of lightmaps.

> **Do you want even more features?**
>
> Here, we won't integrate support for an emissive surface or fog to keep things slightly more concise, but you can have a look at the GitHub repo for this book for a more advanced version of the shader that supports both those options: `https://github.com/PacktPublishing/Become-a-Unity-Shaders-Guru`.

All of this means that to properly take advantage of the helpers in the `Lighting.hlsl` file and have all these options, we have to set up several keywords, which can be roughly classified into three categories:

- **The material keywords**: These keywords are related to the properties of the material itself – for example, whether or not it should use alpha clipping, and whether or not we should have an occlusion map. We will define them as follows:

```
// Material Keywords
#pragma shader_feature_local _NORMALMAP
#pragma shader_feature_local_fragment _ALPHATEST_ON
#pragma shader_feature_local_fragment _ALPHAPREMULTIPLY_ON
#pragma shader_feature_local_fragment _METALLICSPECGLOSSMAP
#pragma shader_feature_local_fragment _OCCLUSIONMAP
#pragma shader_feature_local_fragment _SPECULAR_SETUP
#pragma shader_feature_local _RECEIVE_SHADOWS_OFF
```

- **The URP keywords**: These keywords are related to the render pipeline options we want to enable for the rendering of our shader. We will define them as follows:

```
// URP Keywords
#pragma multi_compile _ _MAIN_LIGHT_SHADOWS _MAIN_LIGHT_SHADOWS_
CASCADE _MAIN_LIGHT_SHADOWS_SCREEN
#pragma multi_compile _ _ADDITIONAL_LIGHTS_VERTEX _ADDITIONAL_
LIGHTS
#pragma multi_compile_fragment _ _ADDITIONAL_LIGHT_SHADOWS
#pragma multi_compile_fragment _ _SHADOWS_SOFT
#pragma multi_compile_fragment _ _SCREEN_SPACE_OCCLUSION
#pragma multi_compile _ LIGHTMAP_SHADOW_MIXING
#pragma multi_compile _ SHADOWS_SHADOWMASK
```

- **The Unity keywords**: These keywords are related to the base Unity render options (which are common to all pipelines) that we want to enable for our shader. We will define them as follows:

```
// Unity Keywords
#pragma multi_compile _ LIGHTMAP_ON
#pragma multi_compile _ DIRLIGHTMAP_COMBINED
```

All these keywords are fairly self-explanatory, and we will look at them in more detail in the upcoming *Coding our lit PBS shader logic* section. When combined, they will allow us to set up a really cool PBR lighting in our shader! Also, remember that they are used by the helpers we want to include from the Lighting.hlsl library, so we have to name them exactly as shown in the previous code snippet. We will need to add them at the beginning of our HLSLPROGRAM block, like this:

```
HLSLPROGRAM
// KEYWORDS --------------------------------------
// Material Keywords ...
// URP Keywords ...
// Unity Keywords ...
ENDHLSL
```

With these last four snippets, we have a good idea of what our keywords section will look like. Following that, we'll finally be able to include the Lighting.hlsl library to indeed get all the nice built-in macros and functions we are interested in, using the package base URL and the exact path of the file, as follows:

```
HLSLPROGRAM
// KEYWORDS --------------------------------------
// Material Keywords …
// URP Keywords ...
// Unity Keywords ...
#include "Packages/com.unity.render-pipelines
.universal/ShaderLibrary/Lighting.h"sl"
ENDHLSL
```

This is already a big step forward – with these keywords and include statements, we have set up a large chunk of the required structure for our shader. Before we dive into the actual coding, however, there are still a couple of concepts that we have to discuss, and they are the new data structures, InputData and SurfaceData.

Understanding the PBR data structures

In the previous chapters, the shader scripting examples we discussed had two data structures to define – the data input to the vertex shader function (which we called appdata), and the data input to the fragment shader function (which we called v2f, standing for "vertex-to-fragment"). The URP physically based shading relies on those two data structures, plus two new ones, SurfaceData and InputData.

Firstly, when we do PBR, it is better to use other names for our appdata and v2f structures. In Lighting.hlsl and related library files, these structures are instead named Attributes and Varyings, respectively. Although these are just names and don't make a profound difference, we want to include and use built-in tools in this case; therefore, we have to obey their conventions. That's why, in this lit PBS shader, we will use the Attributes and Varyings names for our well-known data structures, rather than appdata and v2f, respectively.

These data structures should contain enough information for our vertex and fragment shaders to set up all the data for PBR lighting, so we will define them as follows.

- The Attributes block has to contain the position, normal, and optionally the tangent (if we are using a normal map) in object space, plus the UVs and the lightmap UVs to sample the shadows properly. This results in the following definition:

```
struct Attributes {
    float4 positionOS : POSITION;
    #ifdef _NORMALMAP
    float4 tangentOS : TANGENT;
    #endif
    float4 normalOS : NORMAL;
    float2 uv : TEXCOORD0;
    float2 lightmapUV : TEXCOORD1;
};
```

You'll see in this snippet that we use an if-check directive (#ifdef) to add the tangentOS field to our structure only when necessary – this helps improve the performance of our shader and strip it down to the bare minimum, excluding any unused option.

- The Varyings block is a bit more complex. We have to transfer some of the data converted from object space to other spaces, but we also have to handle the lightmap and shadow-related information. Let's start with the "easy" part, the converted data, which should look like this:

```
struct Varyings {
    float4 positionCS : SV_POSITION; // CS: clip space
    float3 positionWS : TEXCOORD0;   // WS: world space
    float2 uv : TEXCOORD1;

    #ifdef _NORMALMAP
        half4 normalWS : TEXCOORD2;
```

```
        half4 tangentWS : TEXCOORD3;
        half4 bitangentWS : TEXCOORD4;
    #else
        half3 normalWS : TEXCOORD2;
    #endif
};
```

Here, we use the different UV channels as usual with the various TEXCOORD# semantics, and we store some conversions of our initial vertex data in clip and world space.

For the lightmap and shadow-related data, we will take advantage of a nice set of macros that is available for us in the Lighting.hlsl file:

```
#if defined(LIGHTMAP_ON)
    #define DECLARE_LIGHTMAP_OR_SH(lmName, shName,
        index) float2 lmName : TEXCOORD##index
    #define OUTPUT_LIGHTMAP_UV(lightmapUV,
        lightmapScaleOffset, OUT) OUT.xy = lightmapUV.xy *
            lightmapScaleOffset.xy + lightmapScaleOffset.zw;
    #define OUTPUT_SH(normalWS, OUT)
#else
    #define DECLARE_LIGHTMAP_OR_SH(lmName, shName,
        index) half3 shName : TEXCOORD##index
    #define OUTPUT_LIGHTMAP_UV(lightmapUV,
        lightmapScaleOffset, OUT)
    #define OUTPUT_SH(normalWS, OUT) OUT.xyz =
        SampleSHVertex(normalWS)
#endif
```

In our case, we can use the first macro in our Varyings structure to define either a lightmapUV or vertexSH field. We will also have a check for another keyword defined in Unity's URP library code, REQUIRES_VERTEX_SHADOW_COORD_INTERPOLATOR – if this value is true, then we should compute an extra field for our structure with the shadow coordinates for a given vertex position.

We just have to be careful not to have any overlap in the UV channels, especially with the dynamic number of attributed channels, depending on the value of the _NORMALMAP keyword – this is why the next UV channel we will use is TEXCOORD5 (and not TEXCOORD3), in order to ensure it never conflicts with previously written data:

```
struct Varyings {
    ...
    DECLARE_LIGHTMAP_OR_SH(lightmapUV, vertexSH, 5);
    #if defined(
        REQUIRES_VERTEX_SHADOW_COORD_INTERPOLATOR)
        float4 shadowCoord : TEXCOORD6;
    #endif
}
```

Now, let's focus briefly on the new data structures PBR requires, the `SurfaceData` and `InputData` structures.

The `SurfaceData` structure contains all the input we will find on the standard URP lit shader, and it also samples the required textures – in the current v15 version of URP, it is defined like so:

```
struct SurfaceData {
    half3 albedo;
    half3 specular;
    half  metallic;
    half  smoothness;
    half3 normalTS;
    half3 emission;
    half  occlusion;
    half  alpha;
    half  clearCoatMask;
    half  clearCoatSmoothness;
};
```

Actually, we don't need to write it in our own shader, since we can get it just by including the `SurfaceInput.hlsl` file in our `HLSLPROGRAM` block! Similarly, by including the `Core.hlsl` library, we also indirectly include the `Input.hlsl` file and the `InputData` structure inside it, which provides some extra information about lighting computations (again, based on URP v15):

```
struct InputData {
    float3   positionWS;
    float4   positionCS;
    float3   normalWS;
    half3    viewDirectionWS;
    float4   shadowCoord;
    half     fogCoord;
    half3    vertexLighting;
    half3    bakedGI;
    float2   normalizedScreenSpaceUV;
    half4    shadowMask;
    half3x3  tangentToWorld;
};
```

We will see in the next section, *Coding our lit PBS shader logic*, how to initialize these structures to prepare them for the PBR lighting fragment function. However, for now, let's just recap what the general organization of our shader is at this point.

At the very top of the code, we have a `Properties` block that, currently, is completely empty. We will shortly add various fields here to really control what our shader looks like. Then, we have our `SubShader` with the usual URP tags, and the `HLSLINCLUDE` block with the include of the `Core.hlsl` file. Finally, we have `Pass` with an `HLSLPROGRAM` block and, inside, a list of keywords (in three categories), the include of `Lighting.hlsl` and `SurfaceInput.hlsl`, and the definition of our `Attributes` and `Varyings` data structures. Here is the overview of this setup:

```
Shader "Custom/URP Lit PBS" {
  Properties {}
  SubShader {
    Tags { "RenderPipeline"="UniversalPipeline"
      "RenderType"="Opaque" "Queue"="Geometry" }
    HLSLINCLUDE
    #include "Packages/com.unity.render-pipelines
        .universal/ShaderLibrary/Core.hlsl"
    ENDHLSL
    Pass {
      HLSLPROGRAM
      // KEYWORDS --------------------------------------
      // Material Keywords ...
      // URP Keywords ...
      // Unity Keywords ...
      #include "Packages/com.unity.render-pipelines
          .universal/ShaderLibrary/Lighting.hlsl"
      #include "Packages/com.unity.render-pipelines
          .universal/ShaderLibrary/SurfaceInput.hlsl"

      struct Attributes { ... };
      struct Varyings { ... };
      ENDHLSL
    }
  }
}
```

With this preparation done, it is time to implement the actual functions that use all this data to create PBR lighting in our shader!

Coding our lit PBS shader logic

Alright, we now have a nice structure for our PBS lit shader with the proper keywords and include statements. We also know what our data structures look like, so the next step is to discuss how to compute all these fields and fill in the logic to use all of this.

In the upcoming sections, we will prepare the various properties that our shader will offer to users to better control the shading result, then see how to initialize our `SurfaceData` and `InputData` structures, and finally, design the vertex and fragment shader functions.

Preparing our shader properties

We saw in the *Discovering Unity PBR-related tooling* section that we wanted our shader to support the most frequent PBS options – albedo, metallic or specular reflections, occlusion, normals, and so on.

Of course, we want our users to be able to tweak all of these parameters, so we want to expose various properties in the inspector panel for them. Let's have a look at each option and see what input we need to offer for it:

- **Albedo**: Since we want to have a main texture and a base color, the properties associated with this option will be identical to what we had in our unlit URP shader:

```
Properties {
  [MainTexture] _BaseMap("Base Map", 2D) = "white" {}
  [MainColor]   _BaseColor("Base Color", Color) = (1,
    1, 1, 1)
}
```

- **Alpha clipping**: With this parameter, we need to control two things – whether we want to clip the alpha or just leave our object fully opaque and, if we are clipping, which alpha threshold should be used for the discard process. The first setting is easy to change – because we included `SurfaceInput.hlsl` and `Core.hlsl`, our shader is actually already configured to clip the alpha if the `_ALPHATEST_ON` keyword is enabled or keep it as is otherwise. For the second setting, we just have to add a float value for the alpha cutoff value, between 0 and 1.

  We saw in *Chapter 1* that we can use the `[Toggle]` attribute in a shader `Property` block to transform a float value into a Boolean with the discrete values of 0 and 1. What is even nicer is that we can optionally pass a keyword to this `[Toggle]` attribute to have the checkbox directly update the value of the keyword. However, since we still need to apply this attribute to a property, we have to use a dummy reference to hold this toggle, like this:

```
Properties {
  ...
  [Toggle(_ALPHATEST_ON)] _AlphaClipToggle ("Alpha
    Clipping", Float) = 0
}
```

This property now appears as a checkbox in the material's inspector panel with the **Alpha Clipping** label (see *Figure 4.1*). For the cutoff threshold, we can simply use a Range property type to constrain our float to the right values:

```
Properties {
  ...
  _Cutoff ("Alpha Cutoff", Range(0, 1)) = 0.5
}
```

The [Toggle] attribute on the _ALPHATEST_ON keyword results in the following inspector for our material:

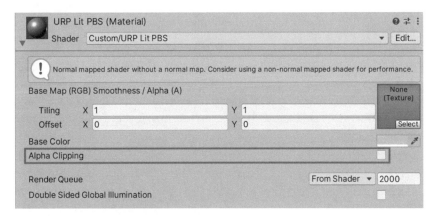

Figure 4.1 – The custom toggle property directly linked to our _ALPHATEST_ON keyword

- **Specular or metallic reflections**: Again, here, we have to consider several options because users should be able to first choose between a specular and a metallic workflow, and then configure each with more parameters. A simple solution is to have a toggle for the workflow and then simply show all the options, only taking into account the ones that match.

The choice of the workflow (specular or metallic) is controlled by our _SPECULAR_SETUP keyword – when this value is on, we use specular reflections, and when it's off, we use metallic reflections. So, let's add another dummy property with a [Toggle] attribute on this keyword:

```
Properties {
  ...
  [Toggle(_SPECULAR_SETUP)] _MetallicSpecToggle
    ("Workflow: Specular (if on) or Metallic (
      if off)", Float) = 0
}
```

In specular mode, we can consider two options – the specular gloss and the specular color:

```
Properties {
  ...
  _SpecGloss("Specular Gloss", Range(0, 1)) = 0.5
  _SpecColor("Specular Color", Color) = (0.5, 0.5,
    0.5, 0.5)
}
```

In metallic mode, we only have the `_Metalness` property (from 0 to 1) that tells us how reflective the surface should be:

```
Properties {
  ...
  _Metallic("Metallic", Range(0, 1)) = 0
}
```

One last improvement we can make is allowing users to pass in specular or metalness maps – this is a nice and easy way to specify exactly where reflections should happen on the surface. Here, we will keep things simple and define just one map that is used either as a specular map or a metalness map:

```
Properties {
  ...
  _MetallicSpecMap("Metallic/Specular Map", 2D) =
    "black" {}
}
```

However, this map should not collide with the global specular reflections we would compute otherwise if there is no given map. Thus, we also need to include a toggle for whether we use a specular/metallic map or not, which again is actually decided by one of our keywords – _ METALLICSPECGLOSSMAP. To do this, let's add another dummy property with `[Toggle]` before our texture property declaration attribute, like this:

```
Properties {
  ...
  [Toggle(_METALLICSPECGLOSSMAP)]
    _MetallicSpecMapToggle ("Use Metallic/Specular
      Map", Float) = 0
  _MetallicSpecMap("Metallic/Specular Map", 2D) =
    "black" {}
}
```

- **Normals**: This option will also rely on a texture (a normal map) and a float parameter to configure the bump scale, or in other words, how high our simulated surface perturbations should go. Overall, it's fairly similar to what we did previously for the specular – we will use a toggle to turn the usage of normal maps on or off, which is linked to our _NORMALMAP keyword, add a texture property, and then add a `Float`-typed property for the scale:

```
Properties {
  ...
  [Toggle(_NORMALMAP)] _NormalMapToggle ("Use Normal
    Map", Float) = 0
  [NoScaleOffset] _BumpMap("Normal Map", 2D) = "bump"
    {}
  _BumpScale("Bump Scale", Float) = 1
}
```

You can see I have added the [NoScaleOffset] attribute to my _BumpMap property because, for this type of texture, we don't need to have tiling and offset inputs (they are applied as is on the surface).

- **Occlusion**: This last set of properties is quite similar to the normals – the occlusion will also use a map, and a strength parameter (except, this time, it is constrained to the 0–1 range). Therefore, we can create our toggle (on the _OCCLUSIONMAP keyword) and define the texture property and the strength slider:

```
Properties {
  ...
  [Toggle(_OCCLUSIONMAP)] _OcclusionToggle (
    "Use Occlusion Map", Float) = 0
  [NoScaleOffset] _OcclusionMap("Occlusion Map", 2D) =
    "white" {}
  _OcclusionStrength("Occlusion Strength",
    Range(0, 1)) = 1
}
```

Remember that _BumpMap should be a normal map texture, but an occlusion map should be a grayscale image.

With all these properties in place, we now have an inspector for our shader that looks like *Figure 4.2*:

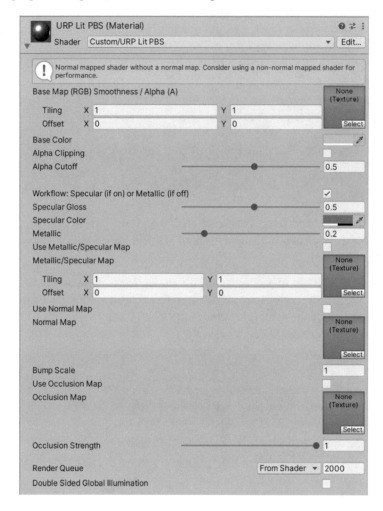

Figure 4.2 – The inspector panel for our URP lit PBS shader

We could, of course, improve it in various ways, typically with a custom editor GUI, but I won't go into too much detail on that here and, instead, keep the focus on the shader itself.

> **Do you want to see a custom shader inspector GUI example?**
>
> The GitHub for the book contains a basic custom GUI inspector for our shader that slightly improves all the displayed properties, making it easier to switch between specular/metallic workflows or configure the various maps. Don't forget that you can find it here: `https://github.com/PacktPublishing/Become-a-Unity-Shaders-Guru`.

The last step is to actually define all these properties in our HLSLINCLUDE block with the matching HLSL variable types.

Overall, it is the same process as for the unlit URP shader we made in *Chapter 3*, but there are a couple of handy built-in assignments that have already been taken care of for us. Most notably, because we include the SurfaceInput.hlsl file, our _BaseMap and _BumpMap texture properties will automatically be given the appropriate samplers. So, we just have to handle our _MetallicSpecMap, our _OcclusionMap, and all the other Float and Color-typed properties we just declared, like this:

```
HLSLINCLUDE
#include "Packages/com.unity.render-pipelines
  .universal/ShaderLibrary/Core.hlsl"

TEXTURE2D(_MetallicSpecMap); SAMPLER(
  sampler_MetallicSpecMap);
TEXTURE2D(_OcclusionMap);    SAMPLER(sampler_OcclusionMap);

float4 _BaseColor;
float4 _BaseMap_ST;
float  _Cutoff;
float  _SpecGloss;
float4 _SpecColor;
float  _Metallic;
float  _BumpScale;
float  _OcclusionStrength;
ENDHLSL
```

Our shader is now parametrized and set up properly – let's move on to the real computation part, starting by discussing how to initialize all of our data structures.

Initializing our data structures

As we saw in the *Discovering Unity PBR-related tooling* section, our shader will use four data structures – the usual Attributes and Varyings (equivalent to appdata and v2f, respectively), and the new InputData and SurfaceData structures.

Attributes will be auto-filled by Unity itself, based on the semantics we asked for; Varyings will be created and prepared in the vertex shader function, as usual.

But the question remains for InputData and SurfaceData – when are they used, and when should we initialize their various fields?

In fact, those two data structures are only used in the fragment shader function – we need to set them up so that we can pass them to the built-in `UniversalFragmentPBR` helper function, which computes the PBR lighting for us. However, because our lighting computation is a bit more complex than what we did for our previous shaders, we should avoid cramming everything in the fragment shader this time.

Rather, we are going to create specific functions for the initialization of our `InputData` and `SurfaceData` structures so that this process is easy to call in our fragment shader. In this instance, we will follow the organization of the official URP lit PBS shader that uses `void` initialization functions with an `out` parameter (meaning that instead of returning our updated structure, we pass it in and modify it in place).

So, let's start with the initialization of the `SurfaceData` structure, which contains the core fields required for PBR lighting. The URP library once again offers us various helpers to get our different values, but there are still a few sampling methods we will need to write ourselves. The following snippet shows a summary of how our `SurfaceData` initialization process will go:

```
// additional custom sampling functions (not built-in)
half SampleOcclusion(float2 uv) {}
half4 SampleMetallicSpecGloss(float2 uv, half albedoAlpha) {}

void InitializeSurfaceData(Varyings i,
out SurfaceData surfaceData) {
  surfaceData = (SurfaceData)0; // fill all fields with
                                 defaults
  // sample albedo + normals (built-in)
  // sample occlusion + metallic/spec gloss (use custom
     methods)
  // finish preparing metallic/specular fields depending
  // on the current workflow
}
```

This overview snippet should be quite straightforward – first, we initialize all the fields in our `SurfaceData` structure with their default values so that we don't have any incomplete initialization errors. Then, we sample our various textures and use our properties to compute all the relevant fields in our data structure. The important point is that, while some sampling processes such as the albedo or normal map extraction are already included, taken from the URP library, we have to write the occlusion and gloss sampling functions on our own.

Let's start with the easy-to-use built-in functions for the albedo and normal maps sampling. The beginning of our `InitializeSurfaceData` will look like this:

```
void InitializeSurfaceData(Varyings i,
out SurfaceData surfaceData) {
  surfaceData = (SurfaceData)0; // fill all fields with
```

```
                        defaults

  half4 albedoAlpha = SampleAlbedoAlpha(i.uv,
    TEXTURE2D_ARGS(_BaseMap, sampler_BaseMap));
  surfaceData.alpha = Alpha(albedoAlpha.a, _BaseColor,
    _Cutoff);
  surfaceData.albedo = albedoAlpha.rgb * _BaseColor.rgb;
  // ...
}
```

In this snippet, we use the `SampleAlbedoAlpha` helper to get our main texture along with its alpha channel, and then we pass this alpha value to the `Alpha` method with the `_BaseColor` and the `_Cutoff` values. This is where, behind the scenes, URP will check whether the `_ALPHATEST_ON` keyword is enabled, and either apply alpha clipping or leave the object fully opaque. Finally, we mix the main texture color with the base color to get our final albedo color, and we assign it to the `albedo` field of the `SurfaceData` structure.

Sampling the normal map works exactly the same – we can use the built-in `SampleNormal` function and give it our `_BumpMap` texture property to get the normals in tangent space, and set the `normalTS` field of our data structure:

```
void InitializeSurfaceData(Varyings i,
out SurfaceData surfaceData){
  ...
  surfaceData.normalTS = SampleNormal(i.uv,
    TEXTURE2D_ARGS(_BumpMap, sampler_BumpMap), _BumpScale);
  // ...
}
```

Now, we need to write our custom sampling methods for the occlusion and the metallic/specular gloss. It might sound like a big endeavor, but guess what? The URP library source code can actually help us yet again!

There is one file that defines some `SampleOcclusion` and `SampleMetallicSpecGloss` functions, which is called `LitInput.hlsl`. We did not include it because it also automatically adds quite a lot of complexity to a shader by adding more properties, such as parallax or detail maps (as well as all the matching functions). So, it would have suddenly charged our shader with numerous features that are not essential to this HLSL scripting introduction (and that you can explore and discover in your own time anyway, now that you are familiar with the URP online repository).

However, `LitInput.hlsl` is still very useful to us here because we can go ahead and extract the `SampleOcclusion` and `SampleMetallicSpecGloss` functions from it.

So, here is our `SampleOcclusion` function:

```
half SampleOcclusion(float2 uv) {
#ifdef _OCCLUSIONMAP
  half occ = SAMPLE_TEXTURE2D(_OcclusionMap,
    sampler_OcclusionMap, uv).g;
  return LerpWhiteTo(occ, _OcclusionStrength);
#else
  return 1.0;
#endif
}
```

This function checks for the `_OCCLUSIONMAP` keyword to check whether we're currently using an occlusion map or not. If we are, then we sample it, and we remix the result with white depending on our `_OcclusionStrength` parameter; otherwise, we simply output pure white (which is equivalent to global ambient lighting with no occlusion whatsoever). Thanks to the built-in `LerpWhiteTo`, if the `_OcclusionStrength` parameter is set at zero, then we have just pure white as well, and then, as it increases, we get more and more of the grayscale areas stored in the occlusion texture.

Similarly, let's take the `SampleMetallicSpecGloss` function from the `LitInput.hlsl` file (I've adapted it slightly because we named our smoothness gloss property `_SpecGloss`, not `_Smoothness`):

```
half4 SampleMetallicSpecGloss(float2 uv, half albedoAlpha) {
  half4 specGloss;
#ifdef _METALLICSPECGLOSSMAP
  specGloss = half4(SAMPLE_METALLICSPECULAR(uv));
  specGloss.a *= _SpecGloss;
#else
  #if _SPECULAR_SETUP
    specGloss.rgb = _SpecColor.rgb;
  #else
    specGloss.rgb = _Metallic.rrr;
  #endif
  specGloss.a = _SpecGloss;
#endif
  return specGloss;
}
```

Check out the advanced version

If you look through the actual URP source code, you'll see I've simplified this function. Here, this version doesn't take into account the `_SMOOTHNESS_TEXTURE_ALBEDO_CHANNEL_A` keyword (which basically offers another way to input your specular smoothness as a channel in your main texture). However, remember that the GitHub repo for this book contains a more advanced version of the shader where, for example, this keyword is supported!

In this snippet, we first check our _METALLICSPECGLOSSMAP keyword to check whether we need to sample a texture or compute the reflections completely from scratch:

- If we have a map, then we just read its contents and remultiply the alpha channel with our gloss parameter to dim it properly.

- If we don't have a map, then depending on our workflow (metallic or specular), we need to either consider the specular color (our _SpecColor property), or the value of the _Metallic property – since this _Metallic is a single float, we have to swizzle it into a three-component vector with the rrr suffix.

- In both cases, note that we store the glossiness in the alpha channel. This is not to be interpreted as any sort of transparency – here, we simply consider our half4 return value as a combination of four half values, so we just decide to keep the glossiness in the last slot.

With these new functions in our shader, we are now ready to finish up our InitializeSurfaceData method with the occlusion and metallic/specular computation, like this:

```
void InitializeSurfaceData(Varyings i,
out SurfaceData surfaceData){
  surfaceData = (SurfaceData)0;

  half4 albedoAlpha = SampleAlbedoAlpha(i.uv,
    TEXTURE2D_ARGS(_BaseMap, sampler_BaseMap));
  surfaceData.alpha = Alpha(albedoAlpha.a, _BaseColor,
    _Cutoff);
  surfaceData.albedo = albedoAlpha.rgb * _BaseColor.rgb;

  surfaceData.normalTS = SampleNormal(i.uv,
    TEXTURE2D_ARGS(_BumpMap, sampler_BumpMap), _BumpScale);

  surfaceData.occlusion = SampleOcclusion(i.uv);

  half4 specGloss = SampleMetallicSpecGloss(i.uv,
    albedoAlpha.a);
#if _SPECULAR_SETUP
  surfaceData.metallic = 1.0h;
  surfaceData.specular = specGloss.rgb;
#else
  surfaceData.metallic = specGloss.r;
  surfaceData.specular = half3(0.0h, 0.0h, 0.0h);
#endif
  surfaceData.smoothness = specGloss.a;
}
```

You can see that, after sampling our occlusion and metallic/specular gloss values, we have to recheck our current workflow to assign the result to the right field in our `SurfaceData` structure, also resetting the other one. Then, we re-extract the glossiness value from the alpha channel where we stored it earlier and assign it to the `smoothness` field of our data structure.

Alright, we are now done with our first initialization function, `InitializeSurfaceData`! Let's wrap up this setup step with the other data structure, `InitializeInputData`, which is as follows:

```
void InitializeInputData(Varyings input, half3 normalTS, out InputData
inputData) {
  inputData = (InputData)0;
  inputData.positionWS = input.positionWS;

#ifdef _NORMALMAP
  half3 viewDirWS = half3(input.normalWS.w,
    input.tangentWS.w, input.bitangentWS.w);
  inputData.normalWS = TransformTangentToWorld(normalTS,
    half3x3(input.tangentWS.xyz, input.bitangentWS.xyz,
      input.normalWS.xyz));
#else
  half3 viewDirWS = GetWorldSpaceNormalizeViewDir(
    inputData.positionWS);
  inputData.normalWS = input.normalWS;
#endif

  inputData.normalWS = NormalizeNormalPerPixel(
    inputData.normalWS);
  viewDirWS = SafeNormalize(viewDirWS);
  inputData.viewDirectionWS = viewDirWS;

#if defined(REQUIRES_VERTEX_SHADOW_COORD_INTERPOLATOR)
  inputData.shadowCoord = input.shadowCoord;
#elif defined(MAIN_LIGHT_CALCULATE_SHADOWS)
  inputData.shadowCoord = TransformWorldToShadowCoord(
    inputData.positionWS);
#else
  inputData.shadowCoord = float4(0, 0, 0, 0);
#endif

  inputData.bakedGI = SAMPLE_GI(input.lightmapUV,
    input.vertexSH, inputData.normalWS);
  inputData.normalizedScreenSpaceUV =
    GetNormalizedScreenSpaceUV(input.positionCS);
  inputData.shadowMask =
    SAMPLE_SHADOWMASK(input.lightmapUV);
}
```

Overall, this function is quite self-explanatory. We just create a new `InputData` structure with default values and then use the various built-in helpers of Unity's URP to fill in our fields.

With this second method added to our shader, we have made another big step forward!

Setting up the vertex and fragment shader functions

OK, now that we have all the logic to initialize our `InputData` and `SurfaceData` structures, it is time to bring everything together and create our vertex and fragment shader functions.

I will stick with the conventions we have used up till this point and name those two functions `vert` and `frag`. We will start by adding the pragma directives to declare those functions and preparing some empty methods, so here is a schematic overview of our current `HLSLPROGRAM` block structure:

```
HLSLPROGRAM
#pragma vertex vert
#pragma fragment frag
... (keywords, structures, initialization logic)

Varyings vert(Attributes i) { }
half4 frag(Varyings i) : SV_Target { }
ENDHLSL
```

We know that the fragment shader function will mostly involve calling our previous functions, so let's do this first – the idea is to get our `Varyings` interpolated data, use our initialization functions on it to fill our `SurfaceData` and `InputData` structures, and finally, call the `UniversalFragmentPBR` helper function to get our PBR-lit color – hence, the following code:

```
half4 frag(Varyings i) : SV_Target {
  SurfaceData surfaceData;
  InitializeSurfaceData(i, surfaceData);

  InputData inputData;
  InitializeInputData(i, surfaceData.normalTS, inputData);

  half4 color = UniversalFragmentPBR(inputData,
    surfaceData);
  return color;
}
```

The vertex shader function is slightly more complex because we have to properly handle the different cases given by our numerous keywords. Luckily, though, we have a good set of built-in macros and functions to help us set it all up. Our `vert` function will, therefore, look like this:

```
Varyings LitPassVertex(Attributes i) {
  Varyings v;

  VertexPositionInputs positionInputs =
    GetVertexPositionInputs(i.positionOS.xyz);
#ifdef _NORMALMAP
  VertexNormalInputs normalInputs =
    GetVertexNormalInputs(i.normalOS.xyz, i.tangentOS);
#else
  VertexNormalInputs normalInputs =
    GetVertexNormalInputs(i.normalOS.xyz);
#endif

  v.positionCS = positionInputs.positionCS;
  v.positionWS = positionInputs.positionWS;

  half3 viewDirWS =
    GetWorldSpaceViewDir(positionInputs.positionWS);
  half3 vertexLight =
    VertexLighting(positionInputs.positionWS,
      normalInputs.normalWS);

#ifdef _NORMALMAP
  v.normalWS = half4(normalInputs.normalWS, viewDirWS.x);
  v.tangentWS = half4(normalInputs.tangentWS, viewDirWS.y);
  v.bitangentWS = half4(normalInputs.bitangentWS,
    viewDirWS.z);
#else
  v.normalWS =
    NormalizeNormalPerVertex(normalInputs.normalWS);
#endif

  OUTPUT_LIGHTMAP_UV(i.lightmapUV, unity_LightmapST,
    v.lightmapUV);
  OUTPUT_SH(v.normalWS.xyz, v.vertexSH);

#if defined(REQUIRES_VERTEX_SHADOW_COORD_INTERPOLATOR)
  v.shadowCoord = GetShadowCoord(positionInputs);
#endif

  v.uv = TRANSFORM_TEX(i.uv, _BaseMap);
```

```
    return v;
}
```

Once again, that logic is quite easy to read, and we can see that URP has a well-furnished toolbox right at our disposal! Now, we finally have a shader that can compile and provide us with a visual – the following figure shows the result on some basic shapes, with a basic albedo texture, a normal map, some metallic reflections, and even alpha clipping:

Figure 4.3 – Our final URP lit PBS shader applied to various primitives

So, finally, we have successfully implemented our physically based shading in URP step by step, and we have discussed various useful tools that Unity provides for HLSL shader scripting.

Summary

In this chapter, we worked on the fundamentals of writing HLSL shaders for the new URP pipeline by studying a very common shader for modern video games – a PBS lit shader.

We talked about all the built-in helpers and functions the URP offers to help us design lighting, especially for such a common type of shading. We also focused on shader keywords and the additional data structures that physically based shading requires, compared to our previous unlit shader.

We then coded the logic of our shaders to display various properties and properly initialize the data structures. Finally, we saw how to pass all the required data in our vertex and fragment shader functions.

Now, we are fairly familiar with the basics of HLSL-based shaders for the Unity URP pipeline, and we even know where to look for built-in macros and handy ready-made functions. This is important for an advanced Unity technical artist because it means that you will be able to explore the ecosystem of the URP shaders in the future and draw ideas or tricks from this base material.

However, as we saw earlier in this book, there is another side to creating shaders in URP – making your own amazing visuals, thanks to Shader Graph! Therefore, it is now time to shift gears and discover this new tool. In the next chapter, we will see how to use the node-based editor by creating our own toon shader.

Going further

If you're curious about setting up lighting in URP and writing more complex HLSL shaders, here are a few interesting resources to check out to continue your journey:

- *Unity 5.x Shaders and Effects Cookbook*, A. Zucconi (2016): `https://www.packtpub.com/product/unity-5x-shaders-and-effects-cookbook/9781785285240`

- *Unity 2021 Shaders and Effects Cookbook - Fourth Edition*, J. P. Doran (2021): `https://www.packtpub.com/product/unity-2021-shaders-and-effects-cookbook-fourth-edition/9781839218620`

- *Physically based rendering*, Wikipedia (2023): `https://en.wikipedia.org/wiki/Physically_based_rendering`

- *(PBR) Theory*, J. de Vries (2014 –): `https://learnopengl.com/PBR/Theory`

- *URP official Lit Shader*: `https://github.com/Unity-Technologies/Graphics/blob/v8.3.1/com.unity.render-pipelines.universal/Shaders/Lit.shader`

- *Official GitHub repository of the URP library*: `https://github.com/Unity-Technologies/Graphics/blob/master/Packages/com.unity.render-pipelines.universal`

Discovering the Shader Graph with a Toon Shader

Up until now, in this book, we have focused on shaders written with code. We first saw the legacy way of using Cg for the built-in render pipeline, and we then explored the more recent HLSL-based shader scripting for the new URP.

This knowledge of what goes on under the hood is fundamental if you wish to really make advanced and optimized shaders. However, with the introduction of the Shader Graph tool in the SRP pipelines, non-developers have now started to take a look at shader creation too, and many have joined the community of technical artists to share their own amazing visuals.

So, in this chapter, we are going to explore this second route and discuss the basics of using the Shader Graph by working on a frequent indie aesthetic: toon-shading!

We will do so by covering the following topics:

- What is the Shader Graph?
- Learning the essentials of Shader Graph
- Improving our toon shader

Technical requirements

To try out the samples yourself, you will need to have Unity installed, with a version from 2019 or later. You will then need to create either of the following:

- A project with the common 3D template, which you will then upgrade to use the URP or HDRP render pipelines (see the *Stepping up with the URP render pipeline* section of *Chapter 2*)
- A project with the new 3D URP or 3D HDRP template (see the same section for guidance on how to download and pick this template)

You can also find all the code files for this chapter on GitHub, at `https://github.com/PacktPublishing/Become-a-Unity-Shaders-Guru/tree/main/Assets/Chapter%2005`.

What is the Shader Graph?

To begin with, let's do a quick review of what the Shader Graph is exactly.

In the next sections, we will see what this tool is useful for and who it can benefit, how we can add it to a Unity project, and how to navigate its interface.

A tool for everyone...or not

As we have mentioned previously in *Chapter 2*, the **Shader Graph** is a new node-based shader creation tool Unity added to the engine in 2017, when they added the SRP pipelines. This visual tool was made with multiple goals in mind:

- Ease-of-use: First and foremost, the Shader Graph is meant to be beginner-friendly – in particular, it simplifies the process to allow artists and non-coders from the team to actively participate in the development of the graphics. But it can even be useful for shader developers too because it usually makes prototyping more straightforward and more pleasant.

- Instant feedback: Another key characteristic of the Shader Graph is that it provides immediate results for each step of your process – or in this case, each node in your graph. This is extremely powerful because it can help you deconstruct a shader someone shares with you to understand it better, and to create your own shaders in an iterative manner.

- Faster development: All this boils down to an enjoyable and quick workflow where changes are reflected almost instantly on your model, and many commonly used operations in shaders are readily available to you via the built-in nodes.

Though these features are great and significantly lowered the barrier to entry into the world of shaders for many people, remember that the Shader Graph is still just a tool...meaning that to create really great results, you must have really great knowledge!

It is also crucial to keep in mind that the Shader Graph is primarily designed to work with the SRP pipelines, namely the HDRP and URP. Starting from Unity 2021.2, it is now compatible with the legacy built-in render pipeline, but most of the resources on the internet focus on using the Shader Graph for URP or HDRP, so you would probably be better off creating a project with one of these modern render pipelines (or upgrading an existing project) if you want to use this tool to its fullest potential.

This is not to rain on the parade: I personally love the Shader Graph, and I think it is a superb addition to the game engine's toolbox. I would recommend it to any newcomer to shader creation, and to any enthusiast who has just dived into Unity and wants to get familiar with this domain. But don't forget that, in the end, those nodes still run code in the background, and that all of this is mostly a packaging for the kind of HLSL code we saw in the two previous chapters.

Anyway, with all these warnings and unasked-for safety notes out of the way, let's get to it and see how to integrate the Shader Graph into our Unity project!

Installing the Shader Graph

This step will be short and easy. In a nutshell, the Shader Graph, available through an official Unity package, is so linked to the SRP pipelines that whenever you install either the HDRP or URP to your project, the Shader Graph is automatically installed alongside it.

Typically, if you create a new project with the URP template (as shown in the *Stepping up with the URP render pipeline* section of *Chapter 2*), the Shader Graph will be available as soon as you enter the editor.

Because the Shader Graph is packaged apart from the URP and HDRP, you could technically update them independently via your **Package Manager** window. However, it is recommended to keep them in sync. Therefore, usually, the best course of action is to start from a SRP template or install the render pipeline from the Package Manager, and leave it to Unity to handle the dependencies such as the Shader Graph.

If you are curious as to which version of Shader Graph your project is using (for example, because you want to look up the documentation online and wish to read the correct one that matches your exact version), you can change your project settings to show these dependencies explicitly. The process is as follows:

1. Open the **Edit | Project Settings** panel.
2. Go to the **Package Manager** section.
3. Toggle on the **Show Dependencies** option, as illustrated in *Figure 5.1*:

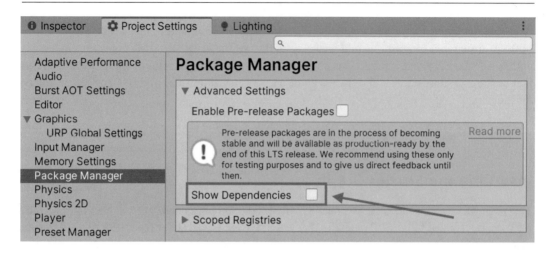

Figure 5.1 – Package Manager-related project settings to show the package dependencies

Now, if you open your Package Manager, you will notice that whenever you click on a package, you see all the dependencies it has and all the other packages it is a dependency for:

Figure 5.2 – Details of a package with its upstream and downstream dependencies

With all that said, it is time to finally explore this new tool and discover the interface of the Shader Graph.

Discovering the Shader Graph tool

If you are new to using the Shader Graph, the very first things you will have to wrap your head around are the new types of assets this workflow relies on.

While legacy and HLSL shaders were scripts written in text files, graph-based shaders are created using Shader Graph assets. If you're curious and you try to open one in a text editor, you'll actually see that these are JSON-like text files that reference nodes, mark positions, store links in between the components, and more. But these assets are mostly meant to be examined and edited via the Shader Graph window itself.

When you create your Shader Graph asset, you have several choices:

- URP/HDRP presets (depending on the pipelines installed in your project): Unity has multiple presets to quickly create shaders for URP/HDRP that are either lit or unlit, for sprites or meshes, or even for decals.

- Built-in presets (in Unity 2021.2+): Similarly, Unity provides us with a lit and an unlit preset compatible with the built-in render pipeline.

- Blank Shader Graph: This creates a completely empty shader with no node inside. It cannot be used as-is, but it ensures you are not dragging along some unused features auto-injected by a preset.

- Sub Graph: Finally, thanks to Sub Graphs, you can create small pieces of shader logic that you then assemble in other Sub Graphs or in Shader Graph assets to build the full process.

This last point brings us to a great advantage of Shader Graph-based workflows: they are inherently modular. Because you can very easily chop down your shader logic into groups, or Sub Graphs, or **Custom Function** nodes, it is possible to test just one of the features and then bring it together with another, or to recombine it in some other way to create a completely different effect. We will see how to use Sub Graphs in the upcoming section, *Learning the essentials of Shader Graph*.

For now, however, let's take one of the basic URP presets, create a new Shader Graph asset, and open it in the Shader Graph editor window to see what sort of tools we have at our disposal. We will do the following:

1. First, we will right-click in our **Project** dock and go to the **Create | Shader Graph | URP | Lit Shader Graph** menu.

2. This will create a new Shader Graph asset in our project, which we can name as we want – for example, here, I'll name it `Toon` to anticipate the example for this chapter.

3. Then, we can double-click on the asset to open it in the Shader Graph editor.

This will open a window in our Unity layout that we can dock where we want, which looks like this:

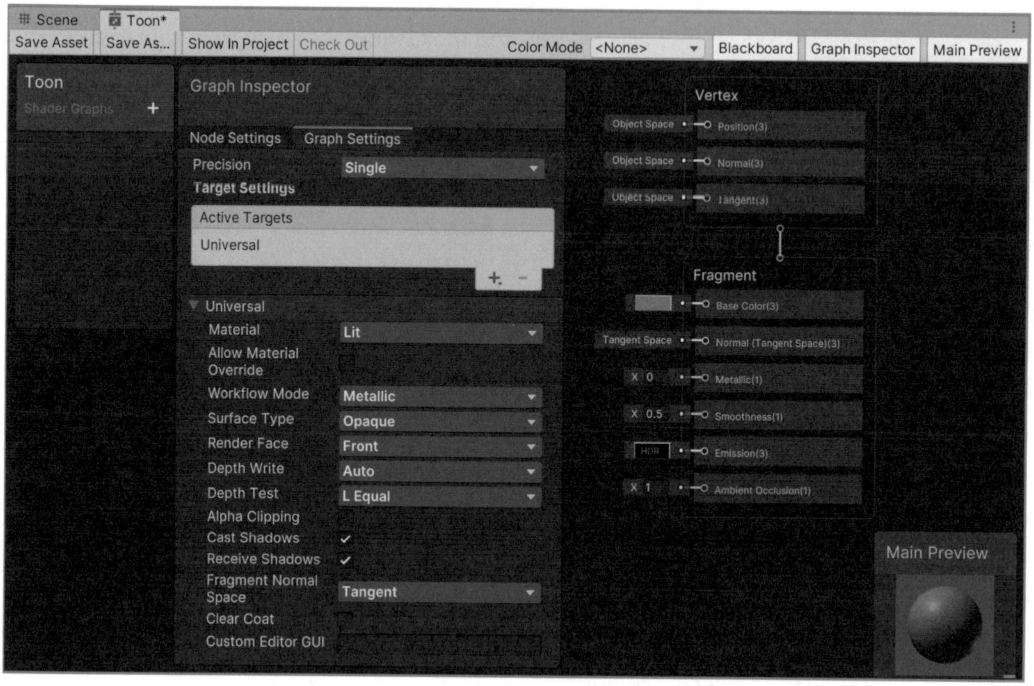

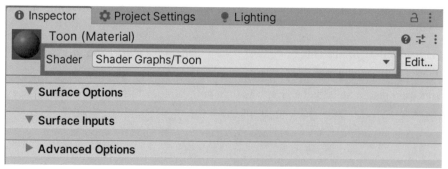

Figure 5.3 – Shader Graph editor window for a simple lit URP graph-based shader asset

Figure 5.3 shows us the important parts of the Shader Graph's interface:

- At the very top, the name of the tab is the name of our shader. This is defined by the name of the asset in the project, and it will directly determine the path of this shader when we assign it to a material. For example, in our case, we can create a new material asset based on our **Toon** shader, as shown in *Figure 5.4*.

Figure 5.4 – Inspector of a material using our "Toon" shader

- In the top-left corner of the Shader Graph editor, we have the **Blackboard** and **Graph Inspector** panels. These floating panels can be toggled on and off with the corresponding **Blackboard** and **Graph Inspector** buttons in the top-right, and they can be moved where you want inside the **Shader Graph** window.

  The **Blackboard** panel is where we define our exposed parameters, the ones that show up in the inspector of a material using this shader. Here, we can add, remove, or re-order the properties to create a neat inspector for our teammates who will use the shader.

  The **Graph Inspector** panel allows us to tweak the parameters of our graph, of the currently selected node, or of the currently selected variable if there is one. For now, it shows the settings of our graph, such as the target render pipeline (URP), whether our material is lit or not, what type of reflections workflow we use, how z-testing and culling are configured, and more. We see that most of the shader options we discussed in the previous chapters are available here with clear names and easy-to-use pickers.

- In the bottom-right corner, we have the **Main Preview** panel, which shows us the current result of our shader on various primitives. Again, this can be enabled or disabled with the **Main Preview** button in the menu bar at the top. Depending on the type of mesh you plan to apply your shader on, you can switch the shape in the preview to another by right-clicking on it and selecting a better-suited primitive.

- Last but not least, you'll notice that our graph is not empty. Because we chose a URP preset and not a blank graph, Unity auto-created a set of very special nodes, which are the outputs of the shader and define the final surface appearance of the shader.

  This group of nodes, here on the right side of **Graph Inspector**, is the end point of the Shader Graph asset, called the **Master Stack**. There can be only one per shader, and it contains the two common stages of a shader: the vertex and the functions. Here, the **Vertex** and **Fragment** groups are called "contexts" – and they can contain different blocks, depending on the type of shader we are creating.

  You can link nodes to the **Vertex** context to have the logic execute in the vertex function, to the **Fragment** context for the fragment function, or to both for both stages.

Alright, we are now familiar with the components of the Shader Graph editor interface. Let's see how to use all of these tools to actually create a node-based shader gradually – it's time to make our own toon shader!

Learning the essentials of Shader Graph

This quick introduction to the Shader Graph workflow was nice, but to truly understand how to use all of these new tools, we are going to go through a real example – the creation of a cel-shaded outlined shader.

Although it is not actively developed anymore, the main inspiration for our toon shader will be Unity's open source project *Chop-Chop* (available at `https://github.com/UnityTechnologies/open-project-1`). *Figure 5.5* shows a screenshot of what we are aiming for:

Figure 5.5 – Screenshot of Chop-Chop, Unity's first open source project

In this section, we will first discuss the features we want our shader to have, then implement each in turn: the albedo, the alpha clipping, the emission, and the specular.

An overview of the toon shader

Before diving into the implementation of our shader, let's quickly list the different features we want it to have. To recreate something similar to Unity's cel-shaded look, we will need to handle the following:

- Albedo: Just like our lit PBS shader from *Chapter 4*, our toon shader will have to support a base color and a base texture.

- Alpha clipping: The shader will be rendered opaque, but we will make sure to handle alpha clipping to still have some basic cutout transparency.

- Emission: Because we are creating a more cartoony look here, it can be interesting to integrate an emissive property into our material, based on a black-and-white map and a specific intensity. This can be a good way to highlight some details or set up better ambiances.

- Toon lighting: Of course, we'll want our shader to have the famous cel-shading type of shading, where the delimitation between lit and dark areas is not a smooth gradient, but rather hard color bends (see *Figure 5.5* for an example).

There will, however, be some differences with the reference shader from *Chop-Chop*. Indeed, if you look at Unity's open source project repository, you'll see that its toon shader also supports the following:

- Mix lighting and shadow attenuation: It can take into account the baked lighting from the scene, the light probes, and the **global illumination (GI)**

- Specular: The materials can have some reflections based on specular computations

Our version will not handle these features because I wanted to keep it short and focus on the main cel-shaded lighting computation. Our version will be diffuse, and use real-time lighting computation. But, of course, feel free to look through the original resource to add this extra layer of complexity!

The rest of the features are, luckily, not that hard to implement in Shader Graph. To keep a modular approach and segment our work, we will use Sub Graphs to handle the various steps, and then have the Toon shader be just the final combination process.

So, first things first, let's discuss how to set up the albedo of our shader.

Implementing the albedo feature

We know that our albedo will consist of a texture with an additional color tint. The first step is therefore to define those properties in our shader.

To do this, we'll go to our **Blackboard** panel, click on the plus sign in the top-right corner, and select the **Color** type (see *Figure 5.6*, on the left). Then, we will set the display name of our new property (here I chose `Base Color`) and select it to edit its properties in the **Graph Inspector** panel (see *Figure 5.6*, on the right). In particular, I like to have my property references have underscores only at the beginning, and I'd prefer the default color to be white instead of black.

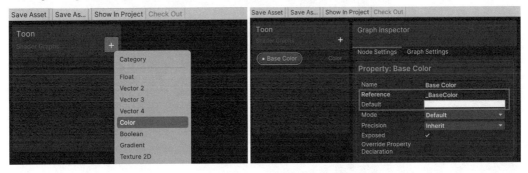

Figure 5.6 – Creation of a new property of the Color type, with the editing of some of its properties

We can then do the same for our main texture by creating another property of the `Texture2D` type, and renaming its reference to `_MainTexture` (by giving it this exact name, it will automatically be considered the main texture of this shader by the URP pipeline).

Now, to instantiate these properties as nodes in our graph, we can simply drag them to the area in the middle of the graph:

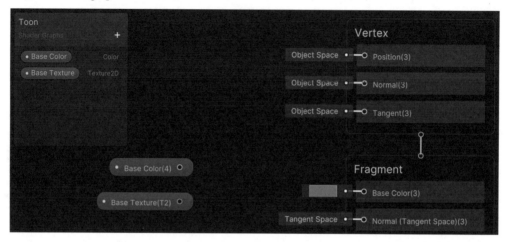

Figure 5.7 – Node instances of our Base Color and Base Texture properties in the graph

The idea is then to sample our texture to extract the color from it and multiply this color with our base color to tint it properly. Here is a screenshot of the resulting graph:

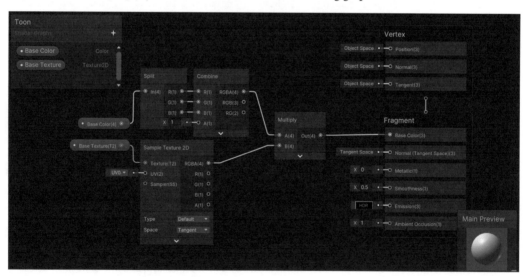

Figure 5.8 – Sampling and tinting of the main texture to compute the albedo

The process is as follows:

1. Sampling the texture: This can be done using an aptly named **Sample Texture 2D** node, to which we pass our main texture by connecting the **Base Texture** node to its **Texture** input slot (like at the bottom of *Figure 5.8*).

2. Tinting the color with our base color: Then, we simply need to add a **Multiply** node to multiply the **RGBA** output of the sampling node with the **Base Color** node...except that we don't want the alpha of the base color to impact our visual (remember we only want alpha clipping)! Thus, we need to separate the four channels of our **Base Color** node with a **Split** node and recombine just the **R**, **G**, and **B** channels with a **Combine** node, to eventually get our tint without the alpha data (see the top of *Figure 5.8*).

3. When you recombine the channels, be very careful to initialize the alpha channel to 1, or else the alpha clipping we will set up later will simply discard everything!

4. Outputting the result: Finally, we can connect the output of our **Multiply** node to the **Base Color** socket of the **Fragment** context to apply our final tinted texture as the albedo for our shader (see the right side of *Figure 5.8*).

At this point, our shader creates a simple lit render with a main texture and a base color. You can save the modifications by clicking on the **Save Asset** button in the top-left corner of the **Shader Graph** window (see *Figure 5.3*) and then apply it on some meshes to try it out, like in *Figure 5.9*:

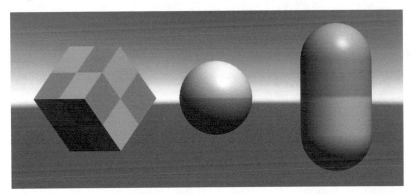

Figure 5.9 – Examples of our shader with the albedo feature on three primitives

You see that, thanks to the Shader Graph and Unity's presets for the graph, it is really easy to set up a basic lit shader with common albedo properties. However, you can probably guess that, as we add more features to our shader, the graph will quickly get quite big, and fairly unreadable.

To avoid this issue, a good practice is to use Sub Graphs – in our case, we want to extract the nodes we created and linked so far to an asset of the Sub Graph type called Albedo. This is easy to do – we just need to select all of our nodes before the Master Stack, right-click on one of them, and go to the **Convert To | Sub-graph** menu, as shown in *Figure 5.10*:

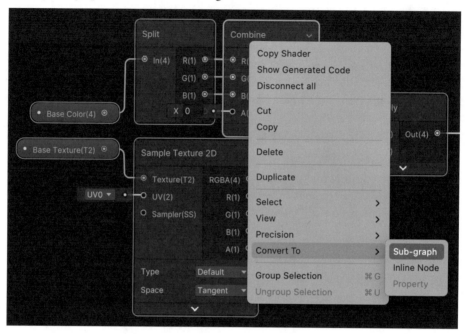

Figure 5.10 – Conversion menu to extract the select nodes as a new Sub Graph asset

This conversion process will have two consequences:

- A new Sub Graph asset named Albedo will be added to your project. It will contain all the nodes we had selected along with their connections, a copy of all the properties these nodes use at one point or another in their own **Blackboard** panel, and an output matching the type of the last node in the chain (here, our **Multiply** node returns a Vector4 value, because we are multiplying colors with four channels). You can re-open and re-edit it at any time by double-clicking on it in the **Project** window to display it in a new tab using the Shader Graph editor.

- Inside our original Shader Graph (the Toon asset we are currently working on), the nodes that have been extracted will be replaced by an instance of the new Albedo Sub Graph asset with its inputs and output already connected as they were before.

To sum up – we have simplified the visual structure of the graph by extracting a logical and self-contained chunk of it to its own Sub Graph, but the behavior is still exactly the same!

With this base visual in place, let's keep going and add the support for alpha clipping.

Adding alpha clipping

Luckily, enabling alpha clipping for a Shader Graph asset is very straightforward. If we open our **Graph Inspector** panel and switch over to the **Graph Settings** tab, then we see that we have an **Alpha Clipping** option we can turn on. And, as soon as it is enabled, you will notice that in the **Fragment** context, two new blocks automatically get added – **Alpha** and **Alpha Clip Threshold** (see *Figure 5.11*):

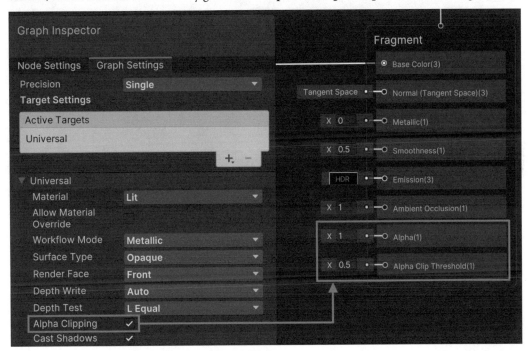

Figure 5.11 – Graph settings with the Alpha Clipping property
enabled, and corresponding blocks in the Master Stack

All we have to do is connect the alpha output from our albedo in the **Alpha** input, and create another property for the clip threshold to make it easy to control for the users. Here is the detailed walk-through:

1. First, we will connect the output of our **Albedo** node to a new **Split** node, and extract only the alpha component from it to link this value to the **Alpha** input of the Master Stack.

2. Then, we will add a new property to our shader of the `Float` type, drag it to the shader editing zone, and connect it to the **Alpha Clip Threshold** block.

Figure 5.12 shows the resulting graph, with the specific properties of our new clip threshold property:

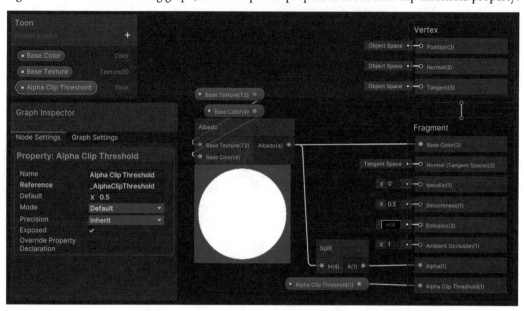

Figure 5.12 – Alpha clipping logic for our shader

And with that, our shader now handles alpha clipping with a customizable threshold, and we're ready to tackle its next feature: emission.

Handling emission

As we said in our first subsection, *An overview of the toon shader*, our emission will rely on a map and an intensity. The overall logic will therefore be very similar to our albedo setup – we will sample the emission texture, multiply it with the intensity to dim it accordingly, and output the final result as the emission color.

There are, however, two important things to note:

- The final color will have only the **R**, **G**, and **B** channels because it doesn't make sense to have alpha on the emission, so our emission chunk should output a `Vector3` value.

- We will need to mix this emission with the albedo component we computed previously in the *Implementing the albedo feature* section. Fortunately, this combination is very simple since, by definition, emission is additive, and should therefore just be added to the albedo to get our final shader color.

With all this in mind, let's implement our emission. At this point, you should be pretty familiar with the process:

1. First, we will define two new properties in our shader of the `Texture2D` type (for **Emission Map**) and `Float` (for **Emission Intensity**), like this:

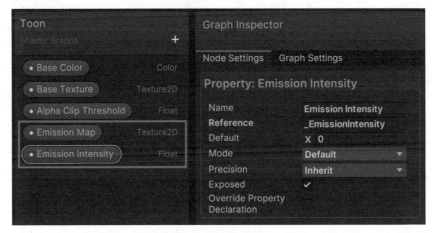

Figure 5.13 – New emission-related properties in our shader

2. Then, we will sample the texture and multiply it with the intensity, with the same chain of nodes as in the *Implementing the albedo feature* section:

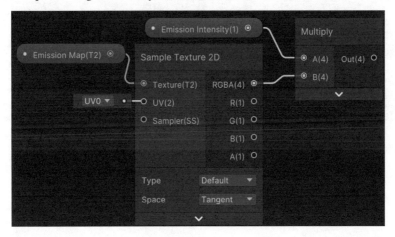

Figure 5.14 – Emission sampling and intensifying logic chunk

3.   We will extract these nodes to a Sub Graph to simplify our main graph and ensure that its output is a `Vector3` and not a `Vector4` value (see *Figure 5.15*):

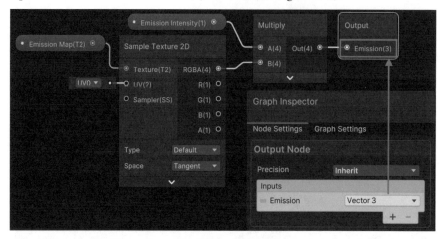

Figure 5.15 – Emission Sub Graph asset with a Vector3 output

4.   And finally, we will add the result of this new **Emission** node to the output of our **Albedo** node (see *Figure 5.16*). The result will be our new value for the base color of the shader.

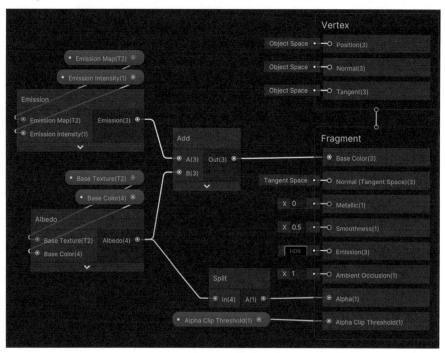

Figure 5.16 – Final mix of the albedo and the emission in our shader graph

Now, if you pay attention to this image, you will notice something strange – we are not using our emission value in the **Emission** slot of the **Fragment** context. Why is that?

The reason we are sticking to the **Base Color** block is that the **Emission** output won't stay in our Master Stack for long. Indeed, for now, our graph settings contain a major flaw – we have set up our shader to be lit. However, this auto-lighting, despite being very useful for many cases, is absolutely not what we want here – as now, we have a PBS shading with smooth shadows and color gradients and not a toon shading! To produce a toon shading like in *Chop-Chop*, we need to compute the lighting ourselves.

So, first, we need to turn our graph to the **Unlit** mode, as shown in *Figure 5.17* (you'll notice that most blocks of the **Fragment** context have disappeared):

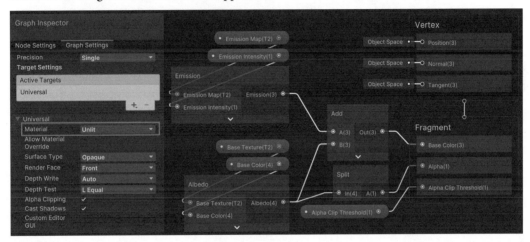

Figure 5.17 – Overview of our shader after switching to Unlit material mode

And then, with that fix done, we can finally dive into the core of our toon shader – the definition of a custom lighting scheme.

Setting up the lighting

After setting up our albedo, emission, and alpha clipping, and after making our shader unlit, we are down to a very basic result with a flat render (see *Figure 5.18*):

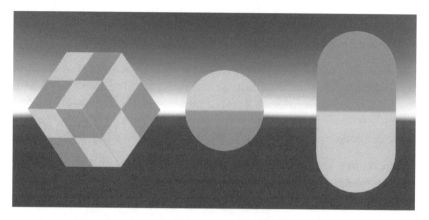

Figure 5.18 – Visual result of our shader after switching to Unlit material mode

So, what we need to do now is re-inject lighting computation, but with our own shading model, so that it creates a cel-shaded render and not the default physically based shading. Also, remember that our system will take into account the main light and the additional lights in the scene, but not the baked lighting, GI, or lighting probes.

Our toon shading scheme will rely on a few important elements:

- `CustomLighting.hlsl`: An HLSL script containing two helper functions:

  - `MainLight_float`, which returns the main light contribution at a given world position

  - `AdditionalLights_float`, which returns the contribution of all additional lights in the scene at a given world position

  You can see with these two function name examples that, when defining custom functions for a graph-based shader, you specify what type of variable it returns as a suffix in the name. Here, we always return a `float` value, so all function names end in `_float`.

  I will not copy the content of this HLSL script here, as it is directly available in the GitHub repository of this book (`https://github.com/PacktPublishing/Become-a-Unity-Shaders-Guru`). It is a simplified version of the one provided in the GitHub repository of *Chop-Chop* without the specular and shadow attenuation-related code. The important thing is to save this text file as an `.hlsl` file in your project assets, as we will need to reference it later on in our graph.

- `MainLight`: A Sub Graph asset that uses the **Custom Function** node (hooked to the `MainLight_float` method inside `CustomLighting.hlsl`). It will handle the self-shadowing process, apply cel-shading and tinting to the main light, and output its final contribution to the object's shading.

- `AdditionalLights`: Another Sub Graph asset that does the same but with the `AdditionalLights_float` method to calculate the contribution of all additional lights in the scene.

- `ToonShading`: The Sub Graph for the final aggregation of main and additional lights, and the combination of everything with the albedo.

Let's go through each Sub Graph in order to build our lighting model.

Coding our custom lighting computation

For the `MainLight` Sub Graph asset, the starting point is to add a **Custom Function** node. We'll edit its properties to link it to the `CustomLighting.hlsl` script, set up the name of the function to use to `MainLight_float`, and finally, add the proper input and output variables to match the method prototype (*Figure 5.19* shows the final setup). Note that the input position is given in absolute world space.

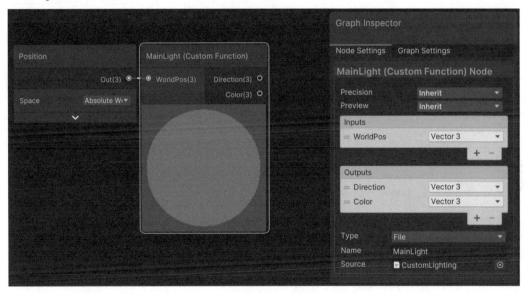

Figure 5.19 – Computation of the base main light contribution with a Custom Function node

The self-shadowing can be computed as the dot product between the normal of the surface and the light direction in the same way that we made our Lambert shadows in *Chapter 1*. So, our `MainLight` graph now looks like this:

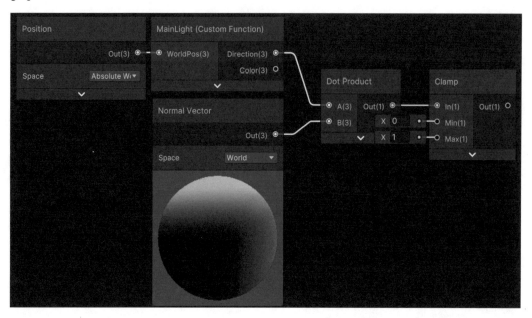

Figure 5.20 – Additional computation of self-shadowing based on the main light contribution

The problem is that this computes a basic light contribution with smooth color transitions. We need to introduce specific transformations to create our cel-shaded look.

Basically, the idea will be to apply the technique of **ramp shading** – we will convert the smooth color transitions on our model to sharp color changes by sampling manually-defined gradients. These gradients will convert the basic (smooth) light contribution to new (discrete) colors defined by custom color ramps. This will allow us to remap the initial light contribution to harder transitions, and also to avoid having completely black or white areas, which is often a nice way to get an overall brighter look.

Our core tool for this will be the **Sample Gradient** node, which allows us to create a unique gradient or use a preset, and then sample it at a given (normalized) input value to get the corresponding color. *Figure 5.21* shows an example of the remapping of an initial grayscale range to another set of colors, thanks to this node:

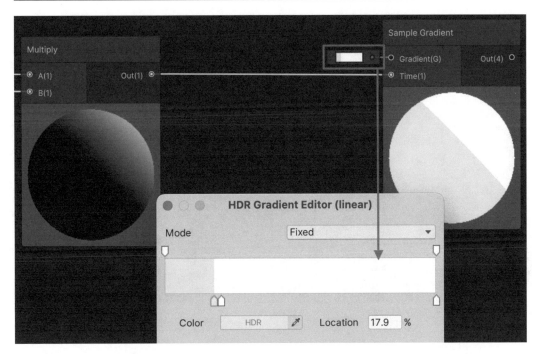

Figure 5.21 – Remapping from smooth color transitions to hard color bends using ramp shading

In this screenshot, the floating panel at the bottom shows what the sampled color ramp looks like exactly: we use a **Fixed** mode to get hard transitions and remap the different shadow levels to specific values to better integrate the contribution of these lights in our shading model. This gradient can obviously be tweaked to better fit your style, so feel free to test various changes and see how they affect the final render of the mesh.

An important point, however, is that we want our cel-shading to impact the way we transition from the lit to the dark areas, but not the final color of the lighting, as this should depend on the color of the light itself. So, we need to apply this ramp shading on the amount of light that is given by the shadow computation *before* it is tinted with the light color, like in *Figure 5.22*:

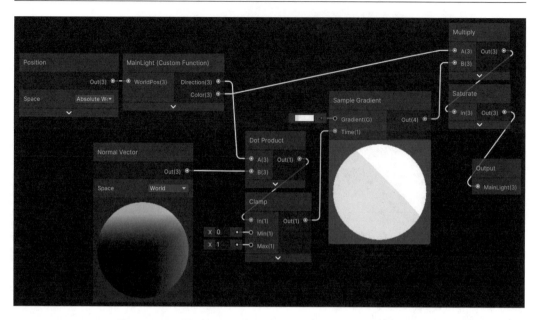

Figure 5.22 – Final MainLight Sub Graph logic with cel-shading

In this screenshot, we see that we get the basic lighting from the self-shadowing logic, then use ramp shading to transform our color transitions, tint the result with the light color, saturate it to avoid any invalid value and stay in the 0-1 range, and finally, set this as the output value of our Sub Graph.

We now have our main light contribution with cel-shading applied!

Setting up our other lights

The `AdditionalLights` Sub Graph follows the same logic. We will use the **Custom Function** node (but with the `AdditionalLights_float` function assigned) to get the initial lighting computation, and then use a **Sample Gradient** node to make it cel-shaded.

The only difference is that, here, the color is not separated from the base intensity, as we had for the main light, because we are computing the contribution of all the other lights in the scene (which could potentially have various colors, and therefore result in a mixed color).

So, here, to only impact the lightness of the lit areas and not their colors, it is best to extract the total amount of light by converting the value to the **HSV** color space, and then doing the ramp shading only on the value channel. This can be done easily, thanks to the **Colorspace Conversion** node, and gives us the process illustrated in *Figure 5.23*:

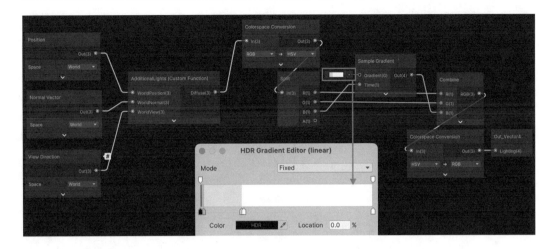

Figure 5.23 – AdditionalLights Sub Graph logic with cel-shading

This graph contains the different steps we just discussed – on the left, we use our custom HLSL function to get the total contribution from all additional lights; then, we have a conversion to the **HSV** color space, the application of ramp shading, and a conversion back to **RGB** color space.

Bringing everything together

Finally, the `ToonShading` Sub Graph is the easiest of them all – it is just here to pack all lighting computation steps together and add them easily to our final `Toon` shader graph.

It simply takes the albedo as an input (so that it can apply the lighting on it directly), and computes the total light contribution by summing the main light result from our `MainLight` Sub Graph and the additional lights output from the `AdditionalLights` Sub Graph, as shown in *Figure 5.24*:

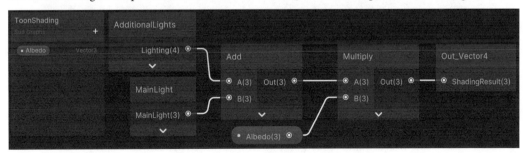

Figure 5.24 – Final ToonShading Sub Graph logic

At this point, our lighting computation is done, and the only step that remains is integrating it into the final shader. We will inject it just after our albedo computation and before the emission addition, like this:

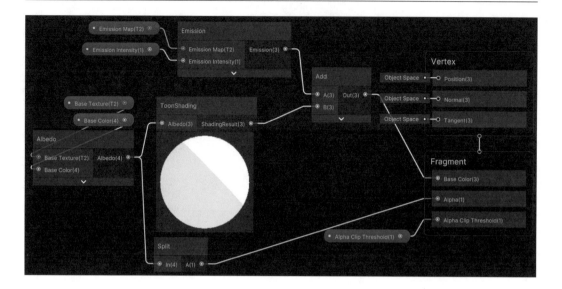

Figure 5.25 – Final Toon shader graph

And there we are! If we enable the shadows on our lights in the scene and in the URP pipeline settings, we can see in the scene that we now have a nice cel-shaded look for our objects:

Figure 5.26 – Small scene with various applications of our toon shader

In this section, we have created a cel-shaded based on the one from Unity's *Chop-Chop* open source project and took this opportunity to explore the ins and outs of the Shader Graph tool. But there are still a few improvements we could make to boost our shader even more.

Improving our toon shader

Up to this point, we have set up the basis of a toon shader to have a custom cel-shading system. To bring it further, we can explore another common feature for cartoon renders, and discuss how to use the Shader Graph tools to organize our graph better.

So, in the following sections, we will add an outline to our shader, and see some interesting techniques to make our shader easier to read and use.

Adding an outline to our shader

Many toon shaders combine the cel-shading with a contour to remind of the aesthetics of comics. This can give your render a nice look, and it is also a good way to highlight the characters, or the important elements in your scene and separate them from the background.

To give you an idea of how it impacts the visual, *Figure 5.27* shows what our scene will look like with the new outline feature applied:

Figure 5.27 – Small scene using our toon shader with its new outline feature

To create this contour, the idea is to compute some additional data about our object, namely the depth and normals, to then derive a per-object outline from them. To do this, we will need to import another HLSL script with a helper function, add a few nodes to our `Toon` shader, and most importantly, create a custom **scriptable render feature** for our URP settings. In a nutshell, this render feature will be a customization and an improvement of the URP pipeline, so that it actually computes some extra information on the render for us.

Let's do this step by step:

1. To begin with, you will need to import the C# script that implements the custom renderer feature: `DepthNormalsFeature.cs`. The goal of this script is to generate a commonly used texture that URP doesn't provide out of the box – the map of the color and depth discontinuities in the render, called `_CameraDepthNormalsTexture`. Basically, this is a useful complement

to the two textures that URP *does* output by default, which are `_CameraColorTexture` and `_CameraDepthTexture`, and it will let us compute the "border" of our objects, and therefore the position of our outlines.

You should get this file in the GitHub repository of this book, and add it to your assets. Then, don't forget to actually assign it as a custom renderer feature in your URP pipeline for this project! This can be done in the **Inspector** panel of the URP renderer data asset, at the bottom, by clicking the **Add Renderer Feature** button and selecting the **Depth Normals Feature** option (see *Figure 5.28*):

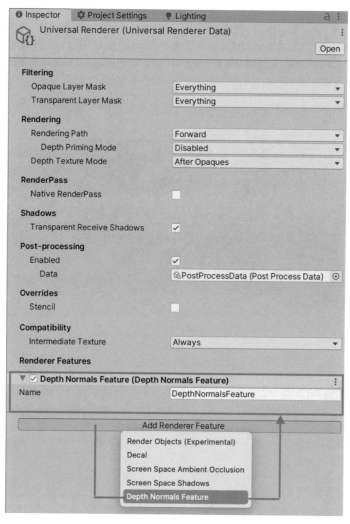

Figure 5.28 – Setup of our new custom scriptable render feature in the URP settings

2. The next step is to take advantage of this new renderer feature in our shader logic. For this, you will also have to import the `Outline.hlsl` file from the GitHub repository of this book and add it to your assets, so that it is accessible from a **Custom Function** node. If you open it, you will see that it contains two functions:

- `DecodeNormal`: An internal function that can extract the normal value back from the `_CameraDepthNormalsTexture` resource we generated previously

- `OutlineObject_float`: A function we can use in our **Custom Function** node to actually process our `_CameraDepthTexture` and `_CameraDepthNormalsTexture` resources to compute the proper edge result

3. Once you've added the `DepthNormalsFeature.cs` and `Outline.hlsl` files to your project, you will be able to implement the outline effect in the `Toon` shader by referencing the HLSL function in a **Custom Function** node, and multiplying the output with the surface color we had up to this point. Be careful, though, because `OutlineObject_float` returns the edge as a positive mask, so we have to reverse it with a **One Minus** node (as shown in *Figure 5.29*).

The outline feature also requires three new inputs – the desired thickness, the normals sensitivity, and the depth sensitivity (to control how the discontinuities in these values should impact the contouring), as shown here:

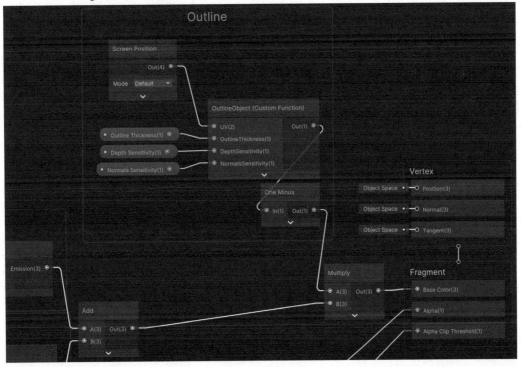

Figure 5.29 – Improvement of our Toon shader with the new outline feature and its related properties

With these quick modifications, we now have a nice edge detection setup to make our render look even more like the style of comic books, and we got a first glance at a new interesting feature of the URP, the scriptable render features.

Organizing the graph better

To end this chapter, we are going to quickly go through a few other good practices, which you should keep in the back of your head whenever you work with the Shader Graph tool.

We have already seen in the *An overview of the toon shader* section how splitting the logic into Sub Graphs helps simplify the different stages, and increases modularity. However, some of our graphs could be improved a bit more by adding notes or groups with well-chosen titles. This is usually a great technique to clearly identify the purpose of a set of nodes, and better communicate the overall logic to your teammates or your future self.

For example, *Figure 5.30* shows how we could group some of our nodes and add notes to our Toon shader to increase the readability of the graph:

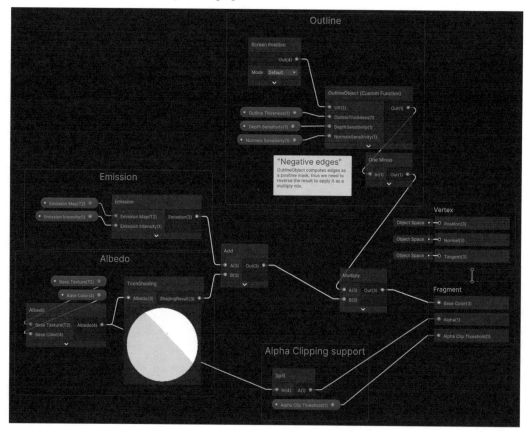

Figure 5.30 – Toon shader with groups and notes

To group nodes, you can either select the nodes, do a right-click, and go down to the **Group Selection** command, or press *Ctrl + G* (*Cmd + G* on a Mac). To add notes, you should right-click on the background and choose the **Add Sticky Note** command.

Another cool feature for future users of your shader is to have the properties in the material inspector be categorized. This ensures you create intuitive editing tools where properties are clearly identified.

We can add categories for our properties in the **Blackboard** panel by clicking the + button and choosing the **Category** type, and then dragging our properties into the different groups (see *Figure 5.31*).

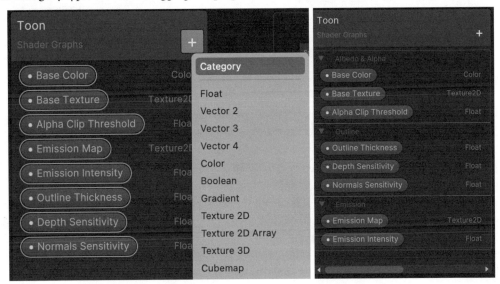

Figure 5.31 – Creation of categories for the properties of our Toon shader

This will transform our material's inspector by sorting and organizing the various inputs – the following figure compares the inspector before and after this improvement:

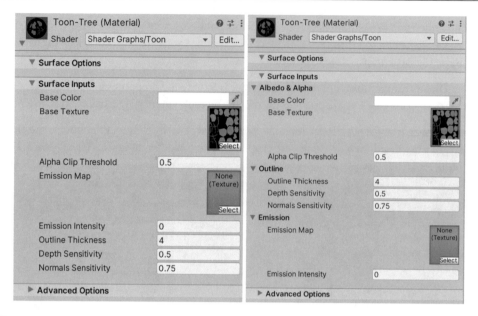

Figure 5.32 – Comparison of the inspector of our shader before and after adding property categories

Finally, as we discussed in *Chapter 1*, it is always useful to properly set the mode of our inputs and typically use sliders when a value should be limited to a range. We can do this easily for graph-based shaders by editing the settings of a property in the **Blackboard** panel and changing its mode. Typically, *Figure 5.33* shows the new settings we could apply to our **Alpha Clip Threshold** value to enforce it is always in the 0-1 range, and how the use of sliders would change the inspector:

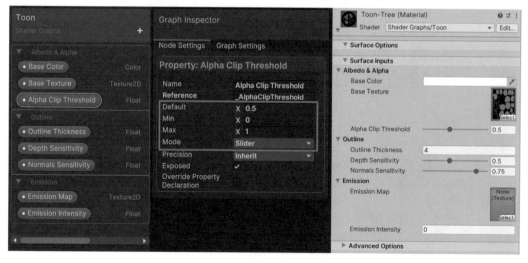

Figure 5.33 – Improvement of the inspector display using the Slider mode for some float properties

There are, of course, many other conventions you could put in place in your team to facilitate collaborative work, and to make clear assets that everyone can use easily and quickly. But, for now, we will stick to these three improvements in the organization of our graph, and enjoy our new toon shader with cel-shading and outlines!

Summary

In this chapter, we discovered how to work with the Shader Graph to create our shaders using a node-based visual editor.

We first explored the main benefits of this alternate workflow compared to the creation of shaders via code and then detailed the Shader Graph editor interface.

Then, we worked on a practical example and created a toon shader inspired by the one in Unity's first open source project, *Chop-Chop*. This allowed us to learn how to use Sub Graphs to make our logic modular and easy to read, how to do basic texture sampling and color tinting, and how to compute more advanced values, such as lighting contribution, thanks to custom HLSL functions. We also took advantage of the technique of ramp shading to turn our smooth color gradients into sharp color transitions to produce a cel-shaded look in our renders.

In the last section, we introduced the notion of a scriptable render feature to provide our URP with more features and used this tool to add an outline to our objects. Finally, we discussed a few useful tips to better organize our graphs, such as node groups and property categorization.

Now that we are familiar with the fundamentals of Shader Graph, we are ready to build upon this knowledge and take on more difficult challenges! In the next chapter, we will focus on various shading techniques we can use to simulate geometry and details at a low cost – billboarding, interior mapping, and parallax mapping.

Going further

If you're curious about Shader Graph or implementing custom lighting in URP (especially toon shading), here are a few interesting resources to check out or continue your journey from:

- Shader Graph:

  - *Intro to Shader Graph*, Cyanilux (2021): `https://www.cyanilux.com/tutorials/intro-to-shader-graph/`

  - *How To Use All 200+ Nodes in Unity Shader Graph*, D. Ilett (2021): `https://www.youtube.com/watch?v=84A1FcQt9v4`

- *Unity Shader Graph Introduction - Basic Shader Graph Tutorial*, Game Dev Bill (2020): `https://www.youtube.com/watch?v=FLVNfBQgeQc`

- *Shader Graph fundamentals in Unity*, PabloMakes (2021): `https://www.youtube.com/watch?v=nDsTBk6eano`

- Custom (toon) shading:

  - *Custom Lighting in Unity URP Shader Graph! Ready for Toony Lights! 2021.1 | Game Dev Tutorial*, Ned Makes Games (2021): `https://www.youtube.com/watch?v=GQyCPaThQnA`

  - *Making a Zelda-style Cel Shading Effect in Unity Shader Graph*, D. Ilett (2021): `https://www.youtube.com/watch?v=lUmRJRrZfGc`

  - *Unlocking The Power Of Unity's Scriptable Render Pipeline*, Game Dev Guide (2023): `https://www.youtube.com/watch?v=9fa4uFm1eCE`

  - *AMAZING Free OUTLINE for URP (Screen Space Outline Unity)*, SpeedTutor (2022): `https://www.youtube.com/watch?v=VpIIFdwTKyQ`

  - *Outline Post Process in Unity Shader Graph (URP)*, D. Ilett (2023): `https://www.youtube.com/watch?v=VGEz8oKyMpY`

  - *Hull Outline Shader in Unity URP Using Renderer Features and Culling! 2020.3 | Game Dev Tutorial*, Ned Makes Games (2020): `https://www.youtube.com/watch?v=1QPA3s0S3Oo`

Part 3: Advanced Game Shaders

To continue our journey into the world of shaders, we'll discuss some advanced techniques to create more realistic renders efficiently and take advantage of the power of our GPUs to make some computations faster. In this third part, we'll study a variety of must-know tools for advanced technical artists, such as parallax mapping, interior mapping, compute shaders, and even the famous ray marching rendering method.

In this part, we will cover the following chapters:

6

Simulating Geometry Efficiently

As you probably know, video games, just like movies, are very much about devices and tricks to make the viewers believe what the creator wants. However, with games, because you have to actually display a completely made-up world from scratch, your illusion has to also hold up to some standards in terms of performance – otherwise, the whole thing will crumble instantly.

This issue of finding the right trade-off between visuals and efficiency appears very frequently with shader creation, obviously. A good technical artist should be able to create stunning effects with a minimal computational cost. This search for efficient visual artifice has led to the invention of many techniques, in particular to try and fake geometry. This is because, ultimately, rendering many polygons is always hard on machines.

So, in this chapter, we will discuss three common shader tricks for adding geometry, details, or transformations to our objects in an optimized way, by covering the following topics:

- Using billboarding for in-game UI displays
- Faking depths and heights with parallax mapping
- Creating hundreds of rooms with one cube... and interior mapping

Technical requirements

To try out the samples yourself, you will need to have Unity installed, with a version from 2019 or later. You will then need to create either of the following:

- A project with the common 3D template, which you will then upgrade to use the URP or HDRP render pipeline (see the *Stepping up with the URP render pipeline* section of *Chapter 2*)
- A project with the new 3D URP or 3D HDRP template (see the *Stepping up with the URP render pipeline* section of *Chapter 2* for guidance on how to download and pick this template)

You can also find all the code files for this chapter on GitHub, at `https://github.com/PacktPublishing/Become-a-Unity-Shaders-Guru/tree/main/Assets/Chapter%2006`.

All the textures used for the parallax mapping and interior mapping shaders are also available in the repository, in the `Chapter 06` folder – the PBR texture packs were downloaded from the full CC0 content `ambientcg.com` website.

Using billboarding for in-game UI displays

It is quite common in games to have outdoor scenes with a lot of vegetation, be it trees, bushes, ferns, or a bit of everything. At first sight, these might look like complex assets to optimize and render, since you have all these leaves to show everywhere, requiring a high enough density for the player to really feel the foliage volume... but that's where the trickery comes in!

To fake this effect of leaves all around you without having to model millions of polygons of foliage, game creators have developed a nice technique over the years: **billboarding**.

In short, this shading ruse allows us to have some objects face the camera at all times – for example, the leaves in our trees – and thus, use just an image instead of a heavy 3D model. In a completely different context, billboarding can also be applied to extra-diegetic elements such as pickups and UI so that they are more readable in the scene.

In the next sections, we will see what billboarding is exactly, and how we can implement it using Shader Graph to create a simple in-game health bar.

Understanding the concept of billboarding

Suppose we are working on a 3D action-adventure game where the player's avatar always stays at the center of the screen, and the camera follows it from above (see *Figure 6.1*).

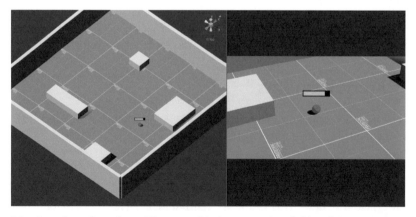

Figure 6.1 – Overview of our demo 3D game with the scene view (left) and the game view (right)

Because our hero will encounter monsters of all sorts, we have a basic health bar in our game – and you see it is fixed above the head of our player, since it is a core element of gameplay. This health bar should follow the avatar when it moves, but also look like a flat 2D UI element (this is particularly important for avoiding deformations due to perspective, which could lead to wrong readings from the player and the disastrous death of the hero!).

As we want the health bar to move along with the player, it seems logical to implement it as a 3D object in the scene, parented to this object. This will directly hook the health bar's position to the player's, and ensure the whole system moves together. However, it also means that the health bar will rotate when the avatar turns, instead of staying flat, as shown in *Figure 6.2*:

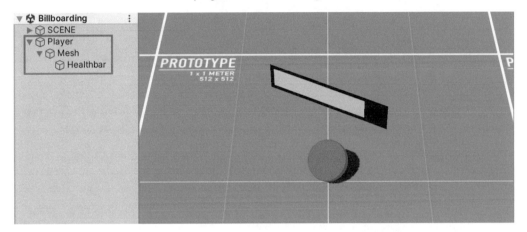

Figure 6.2 – Basic parenting of the health bar under the player object, which causes unwanted rotation

There are various solutions to solve this rotation issue.

The most straightforward approach would be to re-update the transform of the object so that it constantly looks at the camera... but this is very unoptimized! The required computations and space conversions from local to world coordinates will surely take quite a toll on the performance of your game.

A way more efficient technique to have your object track the camera and face it continuously is billboarding. In a nutshell, the idea of a billboarding shader is to compute the direction from the camera to the object and adjust the rendering angle so that the object always looks toward the camera.

Computing the direction via shaders is better than doing it by hand with an actual update of the transform for the following reasons:

- The computation is off-loaded from the CPU to the GPU, which implies faster calculations
- The engine will take care of rendering the object properly, and your game code will not be polluted with these low-level concerns

Figure 6.3 shows an example of our in-game health bar object without any billboarding (on the left) and with billboarding (on the right):

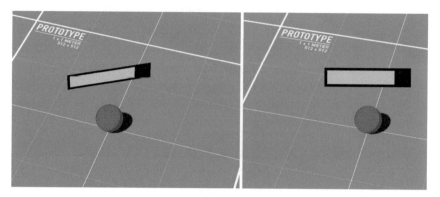

Figure 6.3 – Comparison between the health bar 3D object without and with billboarding

In *Figure 6.3*, thanks to billboarding, we see that our 3D health bar object appears flat, like a 2D HUD, although it is actually included in the world. This setup checks the two conditions we asked for:

- The health bar will follow the player perfectly (because it is a child of its transform)
- However, it won't take its rotation; rather, it will always face the camera

Now that we know why billboarding can be interesting and powerful for this specific example, let's see how to actually implement it in Unity.

Implementing billboarding in Shader Graph

Alright – with all this in mind, it is time to make our own billboarding shader and create a unique health bar auto-adjusting material.

As we said in *Chapter 5*, a Shader Graph asset always ends with its Master Stack. This output contains two contexts, **Vertex** and **Fragment**, which match the usual vertex and fragment functions in a shader script.

When we created our toon shader, we only had to compute values for blocks in the **Fragment** context, because we wanted to leave the geometry unchanged. This time, however, our billboarding effect is all about vertex displacement and clever re-positioning of the geometry to simulate a continuously 2D flat object.

Note that the shader will also contain some logic for the fragment output, obviously. We want to have a health bar with a (normalized) `Health` property that controls the length and color of the fill, and also set up some optional parameters to create a border around the rectangle to better separate it from the background. But this is not the focus of our current discussion, so if you're curious as to how you can use **Step** and **Rectangle** nodes to make your own dynamic health bar shader, just have a look at the full shader in the GitHub repository of this book (available at `https://github.com/PacktPublishing/Become-a-Unity-Shaders-Guru`).

The billboarding shader is set up like this:

1. First, we take the position of our vertex in object space, which is given by the **Position** node. This node is set to **Object** mode. Except that we are going to think of it as the coordinates of the billboard in view space – this is indeed equivalent if we consider the billboard is centered at the origin of the world.

> **Re-adjusting the coordinates' scale**
>
> Note that, in this step, we also have to re-adjust the scale of the original coordinates because the output of a **Position** node in **Object** mode is local and doesn't take into account this overall deformation.

This logic corresponds to the following group of nodes in the graph:

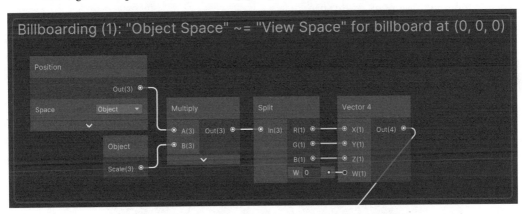

Figure 6.4 – Graph of the nodes group for the first step of the billboarding computation

2. Then, we will convert this assumed "view space" back to world space, thanks to the **Transformation Matrix** node using the **Inverse View** matrix option. This will effectively bring back our billboard to the camera position.

This logic corresponds to the following group of nodes in the graph:

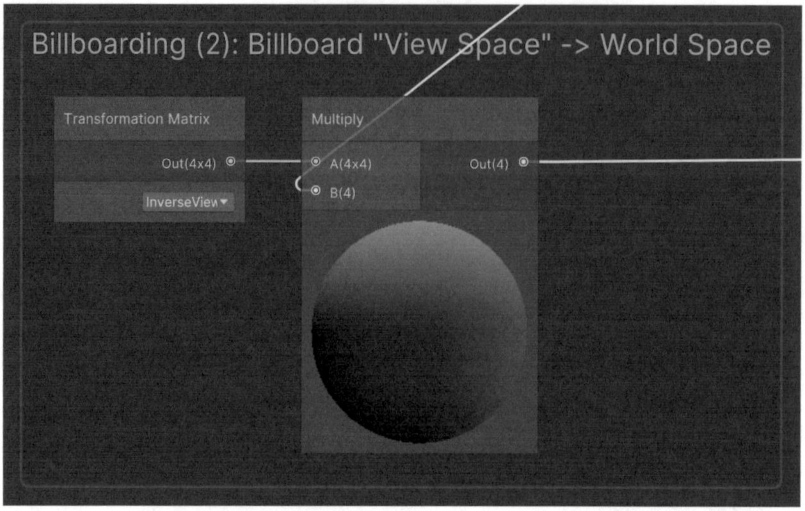

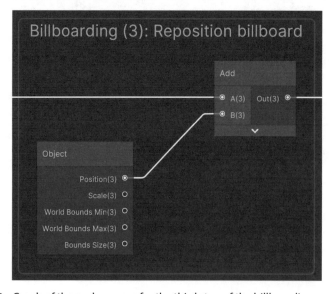

Figure 6.5 – Graph of the nodes group for the second step of the billboarding computation

3. The next step is to place the billboard in the real position of our health bar object. To do this, we just have to add our result from *step 2* to the **Position** output of an **Object** node to offset our output position in world space.

    This logic corresponds to the following group of nodes in the graph:

Figure 6.6 – Graph of the nodes group for the third step of the billboarding computation

4. Finally, because the **Position** slot in the **Vertex** context expects the position to be given in object space, we will convert it one last time from world to object space. This is easy to do, thanks to the **Transform** node, which offers various input and output spaces.

This logic corresponds to the last group of nodes in the graph:

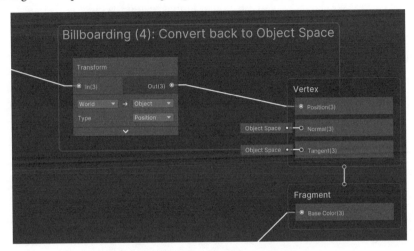

Figure 6.7 – Graph of the nodes group for the second step of the billboarding computation

Figure 6.8 shows the overall graph for this billboarding shader, and how each of the four node groups we just described is interconnected:

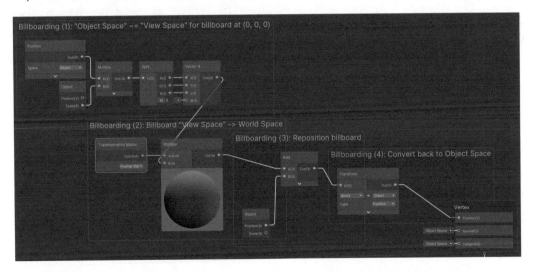

Figure 6.8 – Final billboarding logic for our health bar shader (the text within this figure is not important, and the figure intends only to show the complete graph logic)

With just these few nodes, our shader now always renders the object so it faces the camera, and we are sure that the players won't be disturbed by perspective when they look at our in-game HUD. The nice part is that because we're doing these adjustments via a shader, it will be very efficient and easy to apply to other objects by giving them the right material!

So, with this first health bar shader, we've seen that billboardsing is a great technique for mixing 3D and 2D elements in your game scenes. It allows you to avoid annoying perspective deformations and get your HUD to follow your 3D objects, or create dense vegetation without needing to model and render an insane amount of leaves.

But what if, now, we tried to do the opposite, and go from 2D to 3D? What if, with just minimal geometry and a texture, we could re-create bumps and cracks to simulate a chunk of land or a pool of lava?

Faking depths and heights with parallax mapping

We've seen that billboarding makes it easy to highlight elements in a 3D scene by tweaking their transform and that it can also be used to render vegetation efficiently.

The problem is that this technique can only go so far in simulating geometry. If you walk toward a tree using billboarding and examine its leaves, you might eventually see that there is no real geometry there.

A better way to create this illusion of depth without needing any additional geometry or textures is to have our shader displace the UVs just in the right way for our brains to think there is more volume to see than what is really in the scene. This technique is called parallax mapping, and it was first introduced by Tomomichi Kaneko et al. in a 2011 article (available for free over here: `https://www.researchgate.net/publication/228583097_Detailed_shape_representation_with_parallax_mapping`).

So, in the next sections, we will examine this second trick, discuss a common issue we can have with naive implementations, and finally, see a couple of examples by creating several shaders based on this technique.

Reviewing the basics of parallax mapping

As its name implies, **parallax mapping** is a shading technique that relies primarily on an optical effect called parallax, the process by which objects in the distance seem to move slower than objects in the foreground. In physics, and in particular astronomy, parallax can be used to determine distances; but in video games, we often use it "in reverse," so to speak, to simulate distance.

Typically, if you put a sprite behind another and have it move slower when the camera translates, it will look like it's further away, and you will get the feeling it is a background image at the horizon. If you've ever browsed through the website of the amazing Firewatch game (`https://www.firewatchgame.com/`), then you'll have seen this effect on the landing page:

Figure 6.9 – Screenshot of Firewatch's website where parallax is used to fake distances with 2D sprites

In *Figure 6.9*, we see that when we scroll down the page, the various 2D elements move to follow the movement, but they have different speeds depending on the depth layer they are supposed to be on: elements in the foreground move quicker, and elements in the background stay mostly in place.

In practice, parallax mapping plays around with the location of the UV coordinates depending on the incoming viewing angle to displace the visuals and simulate depth. This way, we can use simple textures but project them as if there were actual 3D depth and details.

To get a first feel for this 3D faking via displacement effect, we could draw inspiration from Oliver Loftus's great tutorial series on parallax mapping from 2020 (`https://www.artstation.com/blogs/loftus/9B67/parallax-mapping-in-blender-part-1`), which describes the first steps in implementing this technique in Blender. If we convert his setup to the Unity Shader Graph, we can make a very basic parallax mapping shader such as this one (*Figure 6.10* just shows the overall graph; each part of the graph is then chopped into zoomed-in views in the following figures):

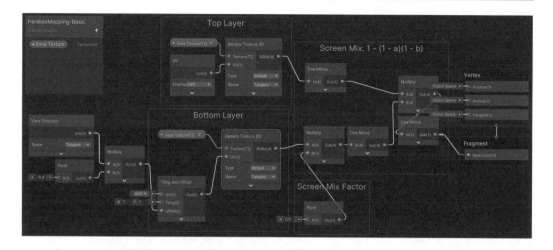

Figure 6.10 – Basic parallax mapping shader with a fixed offset (the text within this figure is not important, and the figure intends only to show the complete graph logic)

This graph presents the overall architecture, and it can be decomposed as follows:

- In the **Top Layer** group (see *Figure 6.11*), we first get our default UVs and use them to sample our texture as we would normally for albedo computation. This will be the base map for our plane.

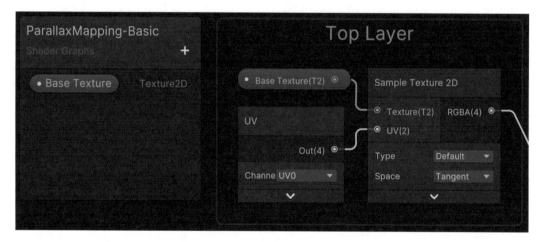

Figure 6.11 – Top Layer block of the basic parallax mapping shader

- Then, in the **Bottom Layer** group (see *Figure 6.12*), we sample the texture again, but this time with UV coordinates that are offsetted by a small amount based on the current view angle. To get this incoming vector, we use the **View Direction** node – and the offset is then computed by multiplying it by a given float value.

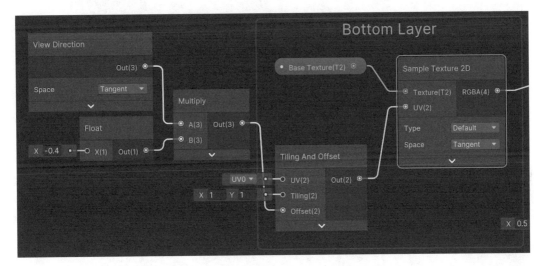

Figure 6.12 – Bottom Layer block of the parallax mapping shader

If this offset factor is positive, then the second layer will appear above the base one, and if it is negative, it will appear below it. Usually, it is best to keep the second layer below the base; otherwise, we risk having the render be cropped by the border of the real geometry and the effect break down for the viewer. We could of course turn this value into a property if we wanted to let the users tweak it to control the strength of the displacement.

- The final mix of the two layers is done in screen blend mode to have lighter areas take over without any need for additional masking (see *Figure 6.13*). But we could change the mix blend type to create other depth effects – for example, having a grid on top of some flowing water or lava.

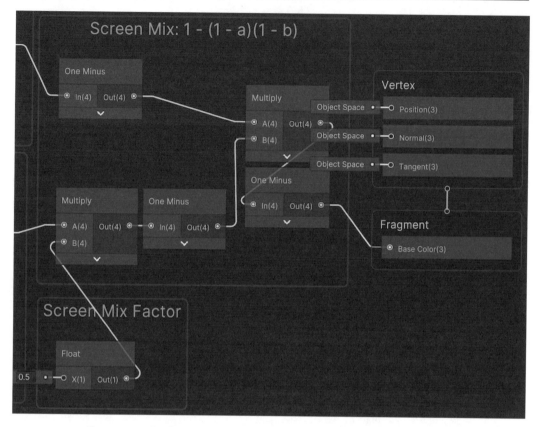

Figure 6.13 – Final mixing of the layers in the basic parallax mapping shader

If you create a material from this shader and apply it on a simple primitive plane, you will get a result similar to what is shown in *Figure 6.14* (the gizmo in the top-right corner shows the current camera angle, and we see the render adapts depending on this view direction). So, this shader simulates a sort of 3D drop shadow, using only 2D textures and four vertices.

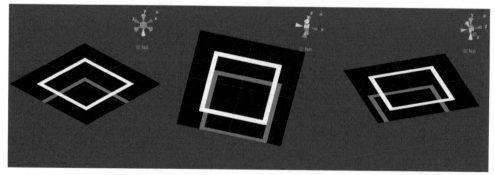

Figure 6.14 – Example of a plane with a basic parallax mapping shader from three points of view

A key thing to note in the graph from *Figure 6.12* is that **View Direction** uses the **Tangent** mode. Indeed, throughout this section, we will work extensively with the tangent space… so let's get a quick refresher before going further!

The **tangent space**, sometimes called the texture space, is the space in which the UV texture coordinates are specified. It is set up like this:

- Its right vector corresponds to the U axis

- Its up vector corresponds to the V axis (or -V, depending on the software)

- Its forward vector corresponds to the (outgoing) normal of the face

Typically, that's the space that normal maps frequently use – hence the blueish tints we usually see in these textures (for example, the one shown in *Figure A.9* of *Appendix, Some Quick Refreshers on Shaders in Unity*).

A fundamental property of the tangent space is therefore that it is relative to the surface of the object. This will be crucial in our case, because it will ensure that our visual is properly adjusted on the plane no matter where it is or what direction it is facing.

The other important idea is that by blending in more offsetted samplers, we could effectively simulate a 3D geometry just by cleverly displacing our texture and mimicking a vertical stack of multiple thin layers:

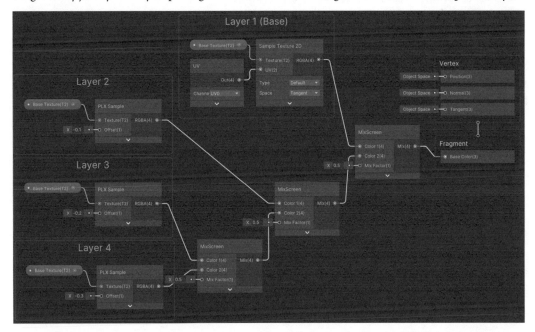

Figure 6.15 – Improved parallax mapping shader with multiple parallax samples (the text within this figure is not important, and the figure intends only to show the complete graph logic)

Figure 6.15 shows a basic example with just four layers, where each `Layer N` node group uses a **PLX Sample** Sub Graph asset, which is built from the logic of the **Bottom Layer** group from *Figure 6.12*.

Because there are only four layers, the 3D resolution is quite low and we thus see the crude trick:

Figure 6.16 – Example of a plane with the multi-layer parallax mapping shader from three points of view

But if we had more detailed textures with varying tints of gray to fake more layers, we wouldn't be able to distinguish between them anymore and it would feel like a real 3D shape. For example, we could use gradients or thresholds to better control which parts of the textures should be taken into account, and potentially exclude some data from one or more of these imaginary layers.

The only problem is that, right now, if you look closely at *Figure 6.14* and *Figure 6.16*, you will notice that our basic shader logic has an issue: the fake 3D volume we are simulating shrinks and stretches along the vertical axis depending on the camera angle! When we are looking at the plane from above, our layers look further away than when we look at the object from the side.

So, first of all, let's quickly see how to fix this problem. And then, we will see a few neat effects we can create thanks to this technique!

Fixing our squash-and-stretch issue

The logic we set up in the introduction of this section lays the foundation for working with parallax mapping, but it shows an annoying squash-and-stretch effect of the volume. This is because the view direction is `Vector3`, while the UV coordinates are `Vector2`, and thus we basically lose the third dimension during our computation. So, to fix this, we need to update our shader logic to re-adjust our UV offset along the vertical axis.

The new logic will look as follows (again, this is just an overview of the new graph – *Figure 6.18* then shows a more detailed view of the new node group on the left):

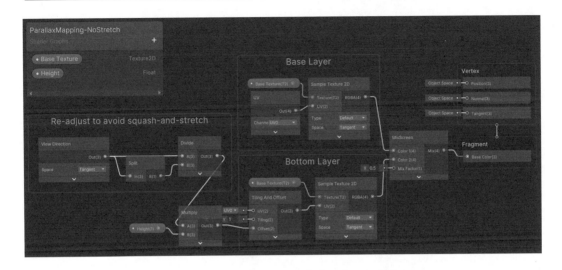

Figure 6.17 – Adjusted parallax mapping shader to avoid the squash-and-stretch issue (the text within this figure is not important, and the figure intends only to show the complete graph logic)

The only difference in this graph is the leftmost block where we re-adjust our coordinates, and that zoomed-in looks like this:

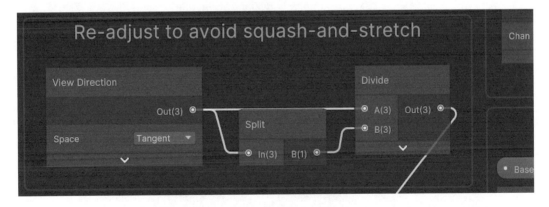

Figure 6.18 – UV re-adjustment logic to avoid the squash-and-stretch issue

You see that we solve our issue by dividing the view direction by its own Z component, which essentially scales the 2D components of this vector by the third one. It is just like placing an image on a plane somewhere in the scene and then scaling the image by the distance to the camera to have it maintain a consistent size.

If we test this improved version of our parallax mapping shader on our plane, we see that the volume stays even no matter the view angle, so we have gotten rid of the stretching problem:

Figure 6.19 – Example of a plane with the adjusted parallax mapping shader from three points of view

We now have a good idea of how parallax mapping works and how we can simulate a basic 3D volume with it. Time to level up and use this trick to create more interesting effects – the first of which will be some cracked ice!

Creating cracked ice with dithering

We saw, in the *Reviewing the basics of parallax mapping* section, that by sampling our textures with different offsets, we can create a vertical stack of layers and simulate depth (as shown, for example, in *Figure 6.12*). This could be used to create a cracked ice shader with some fake depth by having the cracks point downward.

As an example, consider *Figure 6.20*. In this figure, the left part shows a plane with a simple PBR cracked ice material – the textures are nice, so we get some bumps and speculars depending on the incoming angle of light, but it still feels quite flat. The right part shows the same plane with an improved shader where we use parallax mapping to deepen the cracks and add depth to the ground. This instantly gives more realism to the scene, although our geometry is still just four vertices and we haven't added any more textures.

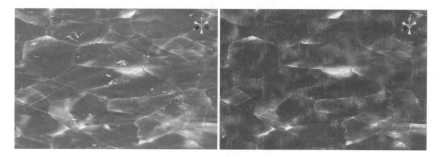

Figure 6.20 – Example of a cracked ice shader without and with a parallax mapping effect

This kind of effect can be implemented in two ways: using multi-layering or vertical stretch.

Multi-layering

We could continue with our idea of re-sampling the color texture with different displacements (as in *Figure 6.20*), and then mix all the outputs to create a column of ice cracks that appear deeper and deeper. With a simpler texture (to better see the effect), we could get results like the ones in *Figure 6.21*, where we have a first example with a large step in between each layer and a second example with a smaller step.

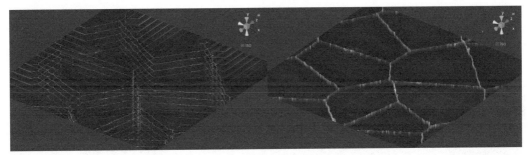

Figure 6.21 – Example of a multi-layer cracked ice shader with two different step values in between layers

We see that, with enough iterations and a tiny step value from one layer to another, we get a basic effect of volume in our ice layer.

To implement this sort of shader, we could obviously have multiple sample chunks and merge them by hand… but a better idea would be to create a custom HLSL function that automatically iterates a given amount of time between 0 and our total parallax offset, and samples our ice crack texture multiple times to fill each level. This is quite straightforward – if you're interested in the detailed implementation of this shader, take a look at the GitHub repository of this book (`https://github.com/PacktPublishing/Become-a-Unity-Shaders-Guru`), which contains this version of the cracked ice shader.

Vertical stretch

Another way to really convey the impression of depth and bridge together our top and bottom layers would be to have some blur in between the two in order to fake all the volume in the middle. To do this, we could stretch our bottom layer vertically to extend the cracks from the surface all the way to the offsetted plane at the bottom.

Let's go through this step by step:

1. First of all, we will prepare a little Sub Graph asset called **Tex Samplers** to easily pack together the sampling of our color, roughness, and normal maps. This will make our end graph simpler to read, and it is very simple to do – we just have to use some **Sample Texture 2D** nodes (for the normal map, we can also take advantage of the **Normal From Texture** node to pass in the normal strength).

    Here is the graph of the **Tex Samplers** Sub Graph:

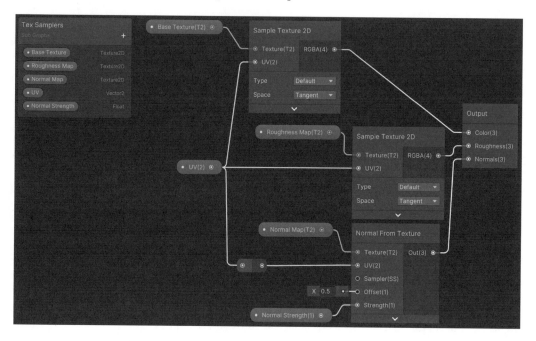

Figure 6.22 – Tex Samplers Sub Graph asset to group the sampling of color, roughness, and normal maps

2. Now, we can use this tool in a shader to get our color, roughness, and normals for the base top and bottom layers. This piece of shader logic looks like this:

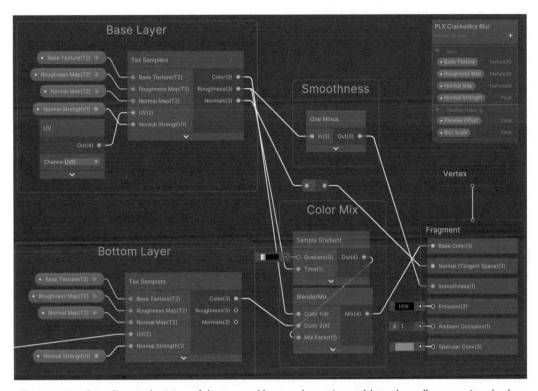

Figure 6.23 – Sampling and mixing of the top and bottom layers in our blurred parallax mapping shader

Here, I've voluntarily hidden the computation of the offsetted UVs for the bottom layer, because we will focus on this in more detail in the next step. For now, let's take a look at the right part of *Figure 6.23*. You can notice two things: one, we need to invert the roughness map sampling because Unity uses smoothness, not roughness; two, we mix the colors of the top and bottom layers based on the roughness map.

The **Blender Mix** node is a Sub Graph I created to reproduce the **Mix RGB** node available in Blender. If we examine the Blender open source code (https://gitlab.com/ideasman42/blender/-/blob/dyntopo_knife/source/blender/blenkernel/intern/material.c#L1429), we see that this mix uses a very simple formula: color = (1 - factor) * color1 + factor * color2. So, here is the matching code from my **Blender Mix** Sub Graph:

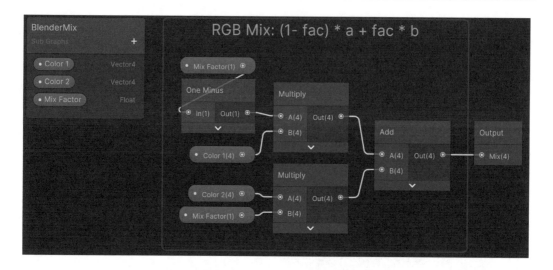

Figure 6.24 – Blender Mix Sub Graph re-implementing the Mix RGB node from Blender

You also see in *Figure 6.23* that by using our roughness map as the mix factor, we ensure that our top layer color is predominant on the rough parts, and the bottom layer color shows more on the rest of the surface. However, we need to remap it slightly to ensure the right mix. We can do this by sampling a gradient (just like we did for our ramp shading in *Chapter 5*).

3. The last part of this graph is the actual computation of the bottom layer UV... with the blur effect (see *Figure 6.25*)! So – how does it work?

The idea here is to use a white noise that spreads across the surface and, for each point of this noise, to get a different height between 0 and 1. This way, we will have random values across our surface that we can remap to our height range, which goes from 0 (at the surface) to our total parallax offset (at the bottom). This randomness will avoid the very visible downward repetitive pattern that we get with our first shader, the one shown in *Figure 6.21*, and it is inspired by the dithering trick (used in VFX and sound design) where you intentionally add noise to your data to stylize it or hide some repeating patterns.

In our case, the process is implemented using a **Simple Noise** node with a tweakable scale (the effect usually looks best when it is in the thousands), a **Sample Gradient** node to have the low end of the cracks fade out rather than stopping abruptly, and finally, a **Remap** node to transform our random values in the [0, 1] range to values in the [0, total parallax offset] range:

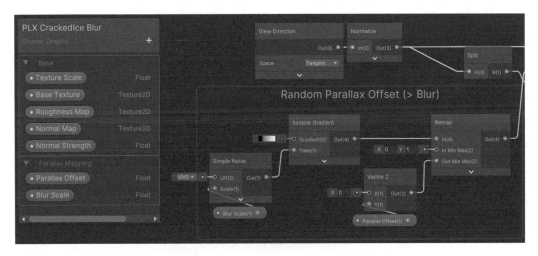

Figure 6.25 – Computation of the stretched and offsetted UVs in our blurred parallax mapping shader

All of this combined (plus some slight re-adjustments of the bottom layer color not detailed here) gives us the really cool effect we demoed in *Figure 6.20* (on the right). Thanks to parallax mapping, we've added a lot of depth to this basic plane without requiring any additional geometry or textures.

In truth, because this effect is so valuable and powerful, Unity has prepared two built-in nodes for it: the **Parallax Mapping** and **Parallax Occlusion Mapping** nodes! So, let's have a peek at those tools and see how to set up some PBR materials with parallax mapping in a matter of seconds.

Taking advantage of the built-in nodes

So far, we've created graphs where parallax mapping was re-implemented from scratch. This allowed us to get familiar with the inner workings of this technique, but this is not the most optimized way to include this feature in our materials.

To help us set up parallax mapping quickly and efficiently, Unity has two built-in nodes: the **Parallax Mapping** and **Parallax Occlusion Mapping** nodes, which differ in terms of complexity:

- **Parallax Mapping**: This node uses a single-step process to compute the UV displacement and does not take occlusion into account. It is fast and good as a first approximation, but it may lack control and finesse.

- **Parallax Occlusion Mapping**: This node is a more evolved version of the **Parallax Mapping** node that runs a multi-step process, and therefore usually provides a better result overall.

Figure 6.26 presents three examples of physically based rendered materials with an additional parallax mapping feature created, thanks to the **Parallax Occlusion Mapping** node.

Figure 6.26 – Examples of PBR materials with parallax mapping

The difference between the two nodes will be particularly visible if you crank up the parallax offset to a fairly high value. This is because you can tell **Parallax Occlusion Mapping** to use more iterations in its computation, so it creates a better 3D geometry simulation with fewer artifacts... apart from the edges! *Figure 6.27* shows a side-by-side comparison of the same parallax mapping setup with a **Parallax Mapping** node and a **Parallax Occlusion Mapping** node:

Figure 6.27 – Comparison of the Parallax Mapping and Parallax Occlusion Mapping nodes

You see that, on the right, we get a better volume effect in the middle, but the edges are very distorted. Note that this could be hidden by having some additional meshes on the borders (as in *Figure 6.26*), and the distortion only happens when the parallax offset value is set really high.

These nodes are extremely easy to use in a Shader Graph asset. We just need to pass in our heightmap texture for the displacement, and we directly get the displaced UVs to sample all of our other PBR textures, as shown in *Figure 6.28* (see the following figures after this one for more detailed views):

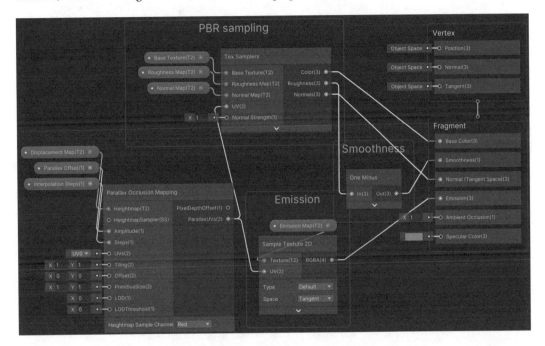

Figure 6.28 – Graph using the built-in Parallax Occlusion Mapping node (the text within this figure is not important, and the figure intends only to show the complete graph logic)

We see in *Figure 6.28* that the graph is composed of three main parts:

- The **PBR sampling** nodes group at the top, which extracts all the relevant data from the color, roughness, and normal maps and creates a physically based shading for the geometry:

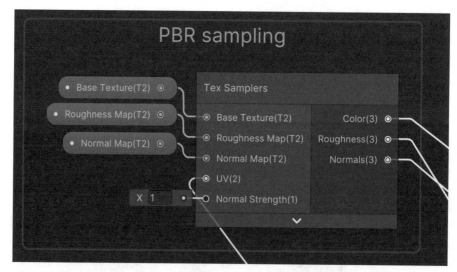

Figure 6.29 – Graph of the PBR sampling group in the parallax mapping shader

- The **Parallax Occlusion Mapping** node on the left, which uses the displacement map to create the parallax effect:

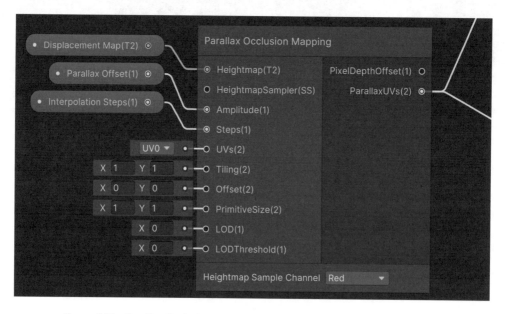

Figure 6.30 – Parallax Occlusion Mapping node in the parallax mapping shader

- The final `Emission` and `Smoothness` node groups, which recombine everything on the right:

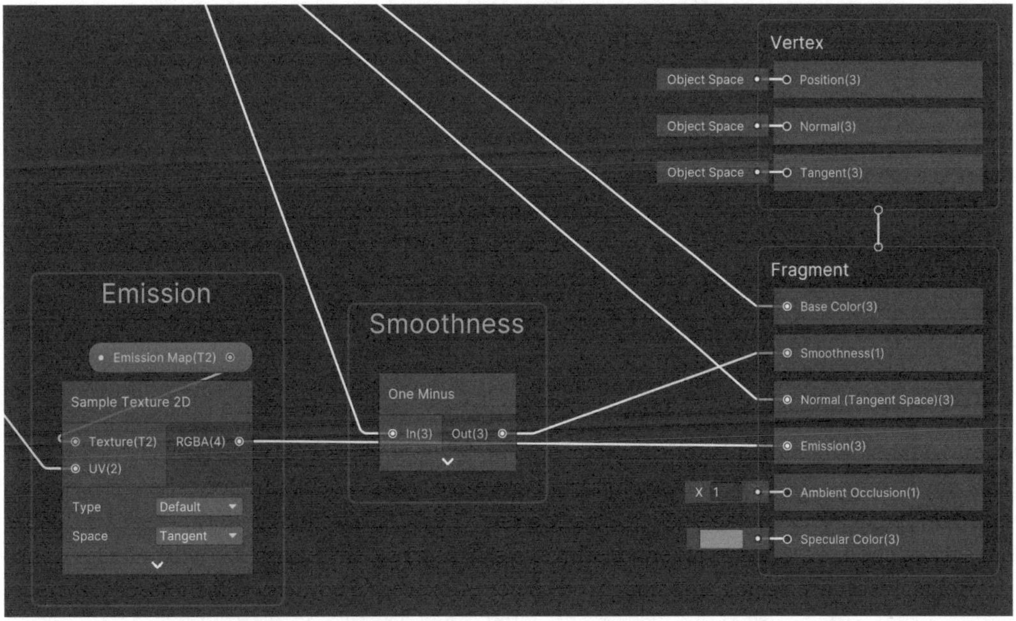

Figure 6.31 – Emission and Smoothness groups for the final combination in the parallax mapping shader

In this graph, the `Emission Map` property should be optional and initialized to a black texture so that if your material doesn't have a reason to use emission and you don't assign a texture to this slot, the default value won't disturb the visual. The `Interpolation Steps` property should also be set as an integer. Finally, you can set the `Normal Map` texture to the `Normal Map` mode to have the property's inspector auto-warn you if the texture you try to input in this slot is not in the right format.

With this very simple graph, we can easily create a chunk of stone ground with depth, thanks to parallax mapping, just by picking out a few PBR textures:

Figure 6.32 – Example of a plane with PBR textures and a parallax
mapping shader from three points of view

Of course, the **Parallax Mapping** and **Parallax Occlusion Mapping** nodes don't cover all the possible use cases – if you need your parallax mapping effect to behave in a very specific way, or if you don't have a heightmap available, you probably won't be able to use them. Still, in most cases, it can be a great first step to set up everything and introduce the effect in your scene.

> **Working without a heightmap**
>
> If you don't have a heightmap texture for your shader, then you can also rely on procedural generation, and use mathematics to create it. Although it can sometimes be difficult to find the right formula if your surface imperfections are complex, this allows you to quickly change the map and even incorporate some randomness into it!

All these examples showed us that parallax mapping is a great technique for faking geometry on a flat surface to give it more details and make it appear more realistic. But could we go even further? Could we simulate deeper volumes to get actual rooms, using just one texture and this idea of UV re-location?

Creating hundreds of rooms with one cube… and interior mapping

Throughout the *Faking depths and heights with parallax mapping* section, we examined a fairly old and common technique for faking depth with a minimal amount of base geometry: parallax mapping. But in the last few years, there is another trick that shader artists have started to work on more and more, which specifically aims at creating great interior rooms in buildings very efficiently.

For example, if you have ever played the amazing 2019 *Marvel's Spider-Man* PS4 video game, you might have noticed that they managed to populate the interior of their buildings in a pretty convincing way (see *Figure 6.33*; image from `https://polycount.com/discussion/204601/interior-mapping-in-spider-man-ps4`).

Figure 6.33 – The PS4 Marvel's Spider-Man video game from 2019 (by Sony Interactive Entertainment) used interior mapping to give depth to the buildings in the city

However, as you've probably guessed, they didn't actually model each and every room in each and every building of the city: this would require so much computing power that the game couldn't run! Rather, they took advantage of this new shading technique that also plays around with UVs to create false geometry: interior mapping.

In the following sections, we will explore this shading trick by first introducing the theory behind it, and then implementing a simple interior mapping shader with Shader Graph.

What is interior mapping?

The **interior mapping** technique was originally published by Joost van Dongen in the Ogre forums in 2007, and then in a whitepaper a year later (available for free at https://www.proun-game.com/Oogst3D/CODING/InteriorMapping/InteriorMapping.pdf). Since then, it has been used in many games, including the *SimCity* series, the *BioShock* games, and *Forza Horizon 4*.

Compared to older methods, such as having a simple image of the room interior behind your window (see *Figure 6.34*; image from https://www.gtagaming.com/ by the author of the module, *devilgtaIV*), interior mapping creates a far better illusion of depth and helps avoid the uncanny valley issue (which often arose with the basic image, because our eyes are very used to seeing interiors in real life, and could detect the unrealistic render).

Figure 6.34 – Example of an image-based shop facade from a community mod for GTA IV (by devilgtalV)

The key idea with interior mapping is that rather than modeling entire rooms behind the windows and making the poly-count of the scene skyrocket with every single building, we are going to use a shader that uses images to fake this inset geometry. Similar to parallax mapping, this shader will adjust the UVs of the interior of our rooms to show us what we would actually see of the interior, given our current camera angle, if this room contained real props. This means that in the end, our entire room will be a simple plane with four vertices onto which an image is projected just in the right way to mimic the depth of a volume, as illustrated in *Figure 6.33*.

Now, how do we do this? The process goes something like this:

1. First, since the whole point of our shader is to adjust the render relative to the current camera angle, we will obviously need to know exactly what this direction is. So, the logic of our interior mapping process will heavily rely on doing a raycast, or in other words, computing the ray from the camera to the current pixel on the object's surface.

    We already saw, in the *Faking depths and heights with parallax mapping* section, that this ray can be obtained directly using the **View Direction** node and the tangent space.

    Also, because we are looking from the exterior of the building, the part of this ray that we will really be interested in is the segment that goes from the pixel on the surface to the intersection point on the theoretical room side behind it (see *Figure 6.35*).

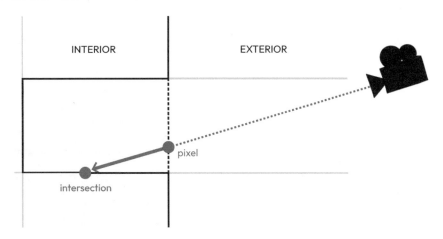

Figure 6.35 – Our shader will work on the segment of the camera-to-pixel ray inside the building

As the ceilings and walls are infinite geometric planes that we assume to be at certain coordinates based on the uniform room size, we will ultimately need to calculate intersections between a ray and a plane, which is a very low-cost operation and allows for great performances.

2. Then, we have to notice something important: though a room technically has six sides (the ceiling, the floor, and the four walls), when we look at a room through a window, we can only see up to three sides out of these six (see *Figure 6.36*). The question is therefore: which side out of these three does our pixel belong to?

Figure 6.36 – When looking into a building through a window, we
can only see up to three sides of the room interior

To determine this, the trick will be to compute the intersection points of our ray with the three planes, and then take the one that is closest. We can get an idea of this by looking at *Figure 6.35* and thinking through the various cases we could have.

If the ray is going straight down, like in the illustration, then it will intersect with the floor first, and it should indeed be the side that is rendered. If it slightly tilted to the side, then it might collide with a wall first, in which case the render will show this wall instead of the floor. And of course, if the ray goes in a horizontal line with nothing else on the way, we will see the back wall of the room. The same goes for camera rays oriented upward that will show either the ceiling, the side walls, or the back wall.

Once we have identified which wall we need to display, we will have to find what the starting pixel position maps to on this imaginary plane, and then sample the image of this side at this transformed point.

Once again, this shading trick relies on the tangent space to ensure that the renders create consistent rooms and don't distort the texture on the fake walls.

This quick description also tells us that interior mapping is fairly cheap in terms of computation, and is therefore an immense resource-saver. Thanks to this technique, we will be able to add great backdrops to our windows without burdening the scene with geometry. We will just use an image for the entire room, and we won't even need transparent materials for the windows, which also boosts the performance. We will see, in the upcoming *Setting up a node-based interior mapping shader* section, that we can even tile multiple images to instantly transform this basic plane into a multi-store building. This will allow for efficient yet very lively environments, so it's definitely a nice trick to have in your technical artist toolbox!

But, to implement it properly, we need to take some time to explain the different steps well. And, to begin with, we need to talk a bit about these images we want to map as room interiors. Because, unlike our previous shaders, this one is not going to use textures.

A quick note on cubemaps

All the shaders we've worked on up until now used fairly common asset types: we had colors, sliders, textures, and so on. But for interior mapping, we are going to rely on something else: a **cubemap**.

In its most frequent usage, a cubemap is a collection of six square textures that form the six faces of an imaginary cube that surrounds the object and therefore represents the reflections in the environment on the surface of this object. This is why cubemaps are often used for skyboxes or environment reflections.

In our case, we will basically reverse the cube so that the cubemaps contain the inside of the cube and not the environment around it. But from a technical point of view, it will be the same type of asset: we will have six images for each side of our room packed together in a cubemap image asset.

Unity actually provides us with three ways of adding cubemaps to our project:

- If we have prepared the cubemap beforehand in some other software as six square images (one for each face), we can import it into the project using a legacy cubemap asset. To do this, we need to go to the **Assets | Create | Legacy | Cubemap** menu and then fill in the textures for each of the six sides, like on the left of *Figure 6.37*.

- A cubemap can also be prepared as a single image. To import this image as a cubemap, you can include it as a texture in **Default** mode and set its shape to **Cube** in the import **Inspector** panel, like on the right of *Figure 6.37*.

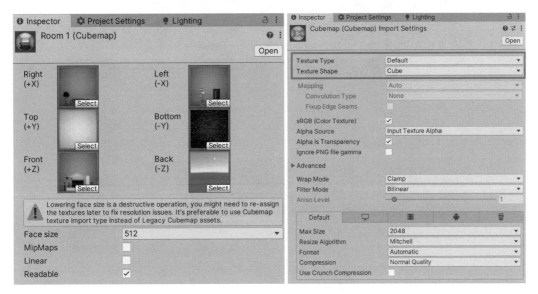

Figure 6.37 – Comparison of the two methods for importing
cubemaps from external sources (legacy or new)

Note that the technique shown on the right of *Figure 6.37* is now the recommended way for importing cubemap assets from external sources. Unity supports the common ways to organize a cubemap (and it will auto-detect the one your texture uses). *Figure 6.38* shows some of the frequently used setups you can choose for your cubemap if you want to import your image with this technique (image by Unity; available at `https://docs.unity3d.com/Manual/class-Cubemap.html`).

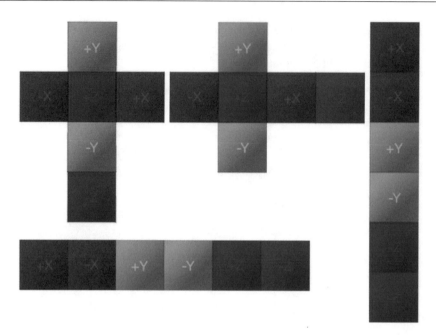

Figure 6.38 – Some common cubemap setups that Unity will auto-detect and cut down properly on import

- If we want to have a full Unity workflow, we can even create a cubemap from a 3D scene. By placing a camera in the center and executing a basic script, you can turn your geometry into a cubemap asset. However, if you do this, remember that it's usually better to squish your assets on the walls to avoid stretching the final image.

  You can find an example of a cubemap generation script in the GitHub repository of this book (`https://github.com/PacktPublishing/Become-a-Unity-Shaders-Guru`).

The GitHub repository of the book also contains several cubemap assets, in both legacy and non-legacy modes, so that you can test the shader easily.

Setting up a node-based interior mapping shader

Now that we have a basic understanding of the interior mapping logic and we have gone through these reminders about cubemaps, it's time to see how to implement this technique in Unity using Shader Graph.

Our process will consist of these five steps:

1. **UV recentering**: Usually, UVs are centered around the edge of a face – their origin is at the bottom-left corner of the face, and they then go up to 1 on each U/V axis along the face. However, here, to combine these values with the view direction, we need to re-center them around the middle of the face, because the view direction is centered around this middle point and not the edge. This is quite easy to do – we just have to chain together a **Frac** node (to avoid any invalid values and basically clamp the vector to the 0-1 range), a **Multiply** node with a factor of 2, and a **Subtract** node with a factor of 1. *Figure 6.39* shows the graph chunk that implements this, and we see that the process will indeed offset and resize the UV coordinates of our face to be around the middle of the face, since the values are remapped from the [0, 1] range to the [-1, 1] range.

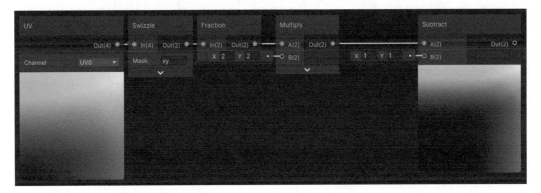

Figure 6.39 – Remapping of our UVs from the [0,1] to the [-1, 1] range

2. **Depth append**: The next step is to append a third dimension to our `Vector2` UVs, because remember that we plan on sampling a cubemap and not a texture, which requires `Vector3`. But the question is: what Z value can we "invent" here? Actually, if we come back to our notion of tangent space from before, we see that, in that space, the Z axis is the normal of our face. If we go in the negative, then our Z value could correspond to the fake depth our room should have – the Z coordinate could thus be the theoretical inset offset of the back wall of our room, the distance we would have from the back of the room to the building facade if we really had geometry.

Since we don't really have 3D volume, in our case, this parameter will be decided on by the users themselves. So, let's create a new parameter, `Depth`, in our graph, which is of the `Float` type, and add it to our graph. We will negate it in the logic. This way, users will enter a positive value for the depth, which is more intuitive, but we will get an inset in the right direction. To append this new coordinate to our `Vector2` UVs, we can use a **Split** node to separate the X value from the Y value, and then recombine everything in a **Combine** node, as shown in *Figure 6.40*:

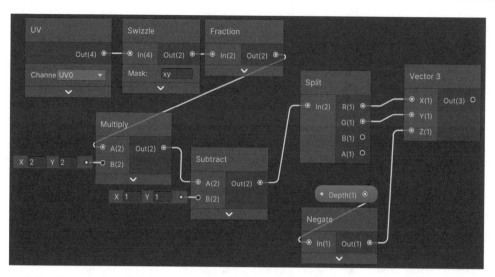

Figure 6.40 – Computation of the transformed UVs with the Depth property appended as the Z coordinate

3. **Depth sampling**: Now, suppose that, as a first experiment, we try to mix the view direction in tangent space with our UVs by adding them together. Then, we'll use the **Sample Reflected Cubemap** node to extract the data from our `Cubemap` property and pass it the result of the sum as the **ViewDir** value. Finally, we'll plug the result into the **Base Color** output of our shader (see *Figure 6.41*).

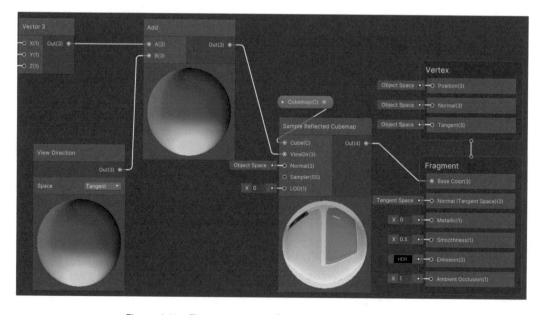

Figure 6.41 – First experiment of a cubemap sampling graph

If we apply this on a quad in our scene, we see that we are starting to get some appearance of a room inside, but it is clearly not perfect. We do feel like we are looking inside the building, but the image is flipped upside-down, and it is stretched in a strange way; the map is not at all like the nice hard wall edges we expected:

Figure 6.42 – First result of cubemap sampling at different camera angles

4. **Fixing the flip issues**: The upside-down issue comes from the fact that we need to convert our data from the OpenGL convention to the DirectX convention (where the Y axis is reversed). We can fix it quite easily simply by negating our UVs – this will basically ensure that the mapping feels like the texture is going away from the camera, rather than toward it, and in particular, it will fix the vertical mirroring (see *Figure 6.43*).

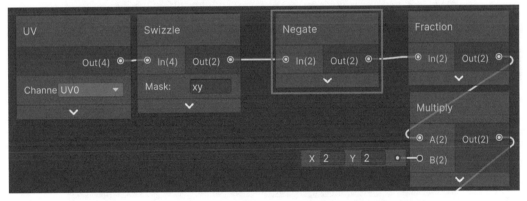

Figure 6.43 – Negation of the UVs to flip them back in the right direction

5. **Computing the projection**: But now comes the real meat of our shader – we need to fix our projection so that it actually resembles a room! Our goal here is to apply some transformations to the view direction, so it performs the raycast we discussed in the *What is interior mapping?* section and finds which wall to display and sample the pixel from.

We could technically do this raycasting by using the in-going view direction of the pixel in tangent space and doing some dot products for the three possible sides. Then, we would simply need to check which one is closer and extract the data from this side texture. This is typically the method that Erik Nordeus used in his tutorial (available here: `https://www.habrador.com/tutorials/shaders/2-interior-mapping/`) as a direct application of Joost van Dongen's whitepaper.

However, over the years, people have improved on this basic approach, and the common way to do interior mapping in modern workflows is a bit different, as we will discuss in the next subsection.

Optimizing the projection computation

Here, to compute our raycasting and do the projection, we are going to use a new-and-improved technique that is now commonly used by game developers, which consists of the following steps:

1. The first transformation we will compute is the per-component reciprocal of our view direction in tangent space, using the **Reciprocal** node (see *Figure 6.44*).

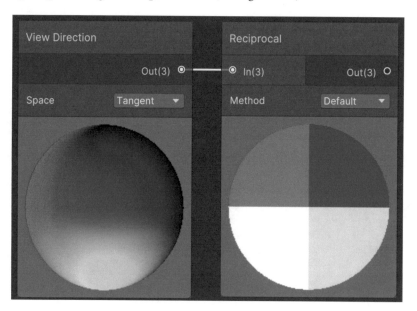

Figure 6.44 – Computation of the per-component reciprocal of the view direction

This essentially performs the raycasting from our camera position to the window plane, but the result is not really understandable on its own, so let's just keep going and see how this transformed vector can be used to calculate interesting values.

2. To begin with, let's consider our UV recentering logic and the additional `Depth` parameter that we append to create a 3D vector:

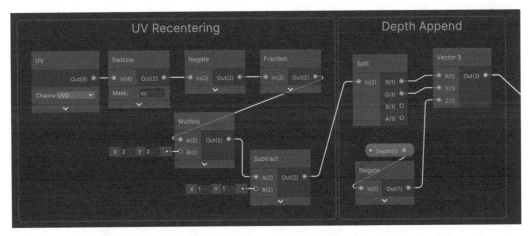

Figure 6.45 – Re-organization of our UV transformation in two node groups

Well, we can multiply our reciprocal by the result of the Depth Append node group like this:

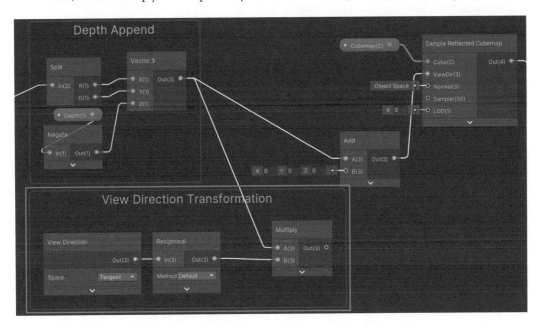

Figure 6.46 – Update of our shader graph with the new view direction transformation part

This will give us an interesting rework of our UVs where the positive X and Y values change depending on the current camera angle (see *Figure 6.47*). This is the visualization of our ray intersection with the three possible theoretical sides of the room, considering the current view.

Figure 6.47 – Visualization of the ray planes intersections on three possible sides of the room

3. In parallel, we will do something else – we will take the absolute value of the reciprocal (using an **Absolute** node) and subtract our previous product from this new result. This will basically compute the distance from the window to the intersection with each imaginary side of the room in one go:

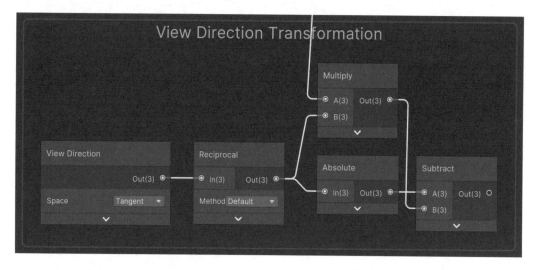

Figure 6.48 – Update of our shader graph with additional transformations on the view direction

4. And finally, all that's left to do is take the minimum of these values, meaning the minimum distance from the window to the intersection point, like this:

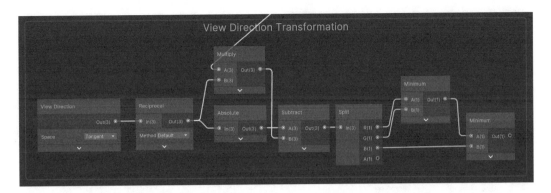

Figure 6.49 – Final transformation of our view direction to get the
minimum distance from the window to the intersection point

Figure 6.50 shows the display of this minimum distance, which is a float. We see that we do have a very small value near the window (because the distance is almost null) and a very high value in the back of the room (because the distance is greater).

Figure 6.50 – Visualization of the minimum distance from the window to the intersection point

We can now re-multiply this distance by the view direction to get an actual `Vector3` value that corresponds to the little chunk of raycast inside the room (illustrated as the solid red arrow in *Figure 6.35*), between the window and the side we hit. This final result is what we will use in our **Add** node from before, to properly reconstruct the whole ray and get the exact UV coordinates to sample our cubemap at, as shown in *Figure 6.51*.

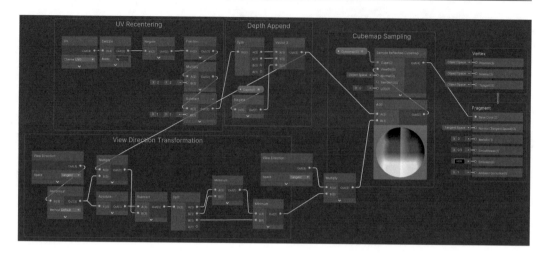

Figure 6.51 – Final graph of our interior mapping shader (the text within this figure is not important, and the figure intends only to show the complete graph logic)

If you create a material from this shader, load up a cubemap, and apply it on a quad, then you will get similar results to the ones in *Figure 6.36*.

Adding an extra tiling property

As a little bonus, a final improvement we can make to our shader is to add a `Tiling` property to be able to create one or more rooms in our facade. This will be `Vector2` that just determines the number of repetitions on the horizontal and vertical axes. This way, we will go even further and create multiple interiors on a single face!

To include this property in our UV computation, we simply need to use the **Tiling And Offset** node (which directly outputs a `Vector2` by default) and pass in our property in its **Tiling** input slot:

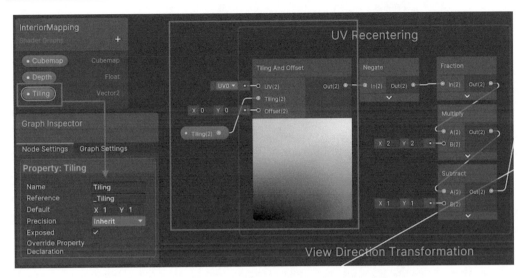

Figure 6.52 – Extra tiling feature in our interior mapping shader graph

If we set the tiling to 2 on each axis, we will then instantly get four rooms in our building facade that all behave like a real interior would (see *Figure 6.53*)!

Figure 6.53 – Example of a tiling of 2 on a quad with and without extra
objects for the facade, and the matching material Inspector

Of course, we could have some logic on top of all that to show different cubemaps from one room to another, and introduce more visual diversity to better dupe players – this would simply require extracting our current logic to a Sub Graph and then calling one of multiple instances that each use various cubemaps based on some given pattern.

> **Want to see the advanced version?**
>
> If you are interested in how this randomization could work, have a look at the GitHub repository of this book (`https://github.com/PacktPublishing/Become-a-Unity-Shaders-Guru`). It contains an improved version of the shader with this additional logic for interior variations based on multiple cubemaps.

Anyway, there you go! You are now able to create an interior mapping in your Unity games, and you will be able to show hundreds of rooms in your buildings, thanks to a couple of cubemaps.

Summary

In this chapter, we discovered various tricks to efficiently simulate geometry and details on our objects.

In the first section, we discussed the technique of billboarding, an easy-to-implement and yet very powerful tool for displaying "3D as 2D" in a Unity scene, and render vegetation or in-game HUD elements.

Then, we talked about parallax mapping and studied how this technique can create a fake depth effect, with no additional geometry or textures required – we saw we just need to displace the UVs on our surface in a clever way, based on the current view angle. We implemented a few Unity shaders with this feature, both from scratch and with the help of the URP built-in nodes.

Finally, we explored one last trick to simulate volume that derives from parallax mapping, called interior mapping. We learned that using just a cubemap asset, this tool allows us to create great-looking rooms inside of buildings with minimal computational cost, and that it is a significant improvement on older techniques such as simply placing an image of the building interior behind the window.

So, we now know several techniques to simulate geometry on our surfaces easily – this is a great example of the power of shaders and how they can help optimize our renders, thanks to their highly parallel execution and their low-level intrinsics. But did you know that all this performance can also be used for pure computations and not just visuals? This is what we will study in the next chapters as we dive into Unity's compute shaders and ray marching.

Going further

If you're curious about billboarding, parallax mapping, or interior mapping, and you want to learn more on these topics, here are a few interesting resources to check out or continue your journey with.

Billboarding

- *Implementing a Billboard Shader in Unity Shadergraph*, William from Noveltech (2021): `https://www.noveltech.dev/unity-billboard-shader-shadergraph/`

- *Cg Programming/Unity/Billboards*, Wikibooks (2022): `https://en.wikibooks.org/wiki/Cg_Programming/Unity/Billboards`

- Forum thread: *Unity Matrix P and matrix MV equlivant* (2018-present): `https://forum.unity.com/threads/unity-matrix-p-and-matrix-mv-equlivant.692932/`

Parallax mapping

- *Advanced shaders in Unity: Parallax mapping*, E. Nordeus: `https://www.habrador.com/tutorials/shaders/3-parallax-mapping/`

- *Parallax Mapping in Unity Shader Graph*, AE Tuts (2019): `https://www.youtube.com/watch?v=LKhGqKYOmbo`

Interior mapping

- *Building SimCity: Art in the Service of Simulation*, O. Quigley (2013, at GDC conference): `https://www.gdcvault.com/play/1017823/Building-SimCity-Art-in-the`

- *Creating an Interior Mapping Shader using Unity's Shader Graph - Game Dev Sandbox*, Game Dev Guide (2020): `https://www.youtube.com/watch?v=dUjNoIxQXAA`

- *Advanced shaders in Unity: Interior mapping*, E. Nordeus: `https://www.habrador.com/tutorials/shaders/2-interior-mapping/`

7

Exploring the Unity Compute Shaders and Procedural Drawing

Up until now, we have focused mainly on the most common application of shaders in video games: the rendering of objects in 3D scenes. We have seen various tools and techniques and studied complex shading tricks, but they all aimed at visualizing some geometry on our 2D screen.

However, shader scripting is a very interesting type of development that can be used to solve other problems, too. For example, because, at its core, it is about writing low-level code to run in parallel for many data points, the art of shader creation can be transposed to another fascinating topic: the efficient processing of expensive computational tasks.

In Unity, it is possible to greatly increase the speed of some large calculations by taking advantage of the power of shaders and offloading the work from the CPU to the GPU, using compute shaders. This, in turn, can lead to delightful advanced techniques in the field of procedural drawing.

So, in this chapter, we will study how shader scripting can be used to perform complex computations quickly. In order to introduce the basics in detail, we won't go into complex applications and will stick with fairly simple experiments. But hopefully, this will give you all the keys you need to then look around the internet and study more advanced examples of compute shaders for real game features!

In this chapter, we will cover the following topics:

- Discovering compute shaders and compute buffers
- Generating a grid of randomized cubes
- Applying a compute shader-based screen effect in URP

Technical requirements

To try out the samples yourself, you will need to have Unity installed.

The *Generating a grid of randomized cubes* section is compatible with both the legacy and URPs, but the *Applying a compute shader-based screen effect in URP* section will require that you use Unity 2019 or later and set up a URP project. To do this, you can do either of the following:

- Start with the common 3D template, and then upgrade it to use the URP render pipeline (see the *Stepping up with the URP render pipeline* section of *Chapter 2*)

- Start with the new 3D URP template (see the *Stepping up with the URP render pipeline* section of *Chapter 2* for guidance on how to download and pick this template)

You can also find all the code files for this chapter on GitHub, at `https://github.com/PacktPublishing/Become-a-Unity-Shaders-Guru/tree/main/Assets/Chapter%2007`.

Discovering compute shaders and compute buffers

Compute shaders are quite a unique tool that has many applications, such as the rendering of procedurally generated shapes (see *Figure 7.1*, a screenshot taken from `https://www.youtube.com/watch?v=WWI07UQbJ9E`) or the large calculations in a complex system.

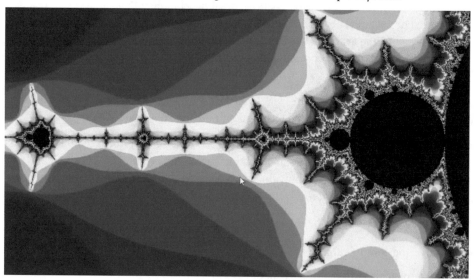

Figure 7.1 – Render of the Mandelbrot Set using compute shaders

In the following sections, we will see what compute shaders are exactly, why they can be useful, how they work hand in hand with compute buffers to properly share data between the CPU and the GPU, and how they are structured.

What are compute shaders?

In a nutshell, **compute shaders** are a specific type of shader script that are meant to offload processing from the CPU to the GPU.

The main idea is that because the GPU runs code in parallel, it can achieve better performance for computationally intensive tasks and large amounts of data – typically, heavy rendering algorithms or simulations that need to be run on many instances. By comparison, classic C# execution on the CPU is often much slower for complex, demanding tasks, because the architecture of the CPU works sequentially, and is therefore not designed to handle such heavy computation.

It can thus be interesting to leverage the power of your hardware to lighten the load on your CPU and leave it free to perform other more "common" tasks.

> **Important note about GPU execution**
>
> Of course, as is always the case with parallel execution on the GPU, we have to ensure that we can abstract our process as a set of instructions that is identical for all executors (although the input data can obviously help separate between very different cases). While we are used to this for material shaders, it can sometimes require a bit of rework of the initial algorithm in the case of simulations or purely computational tasks, in order to fit the GPU architecture.

Also, compute shaders are written in pure HLSL – contrary to Unity material shaders, there is no ShaderLab wrapping around the code, but just a few specific pragma directives. So, writing compute shaders is usually pretty straightforward for technical artists, and it should be a natural extension of your toolbox if you ever want to get into game optimization.

Once you have written a compute shader, you will need to call it from your C# logic (which is run on the CPU) to tell Unity to invoke this specific piece of code on the GPU and link it into your process at this precise time. This is quite easy to do, thanks to the ComputeShader C# class, and we will see various examples of how to dispatch our calculations to a compute shader program in the *Generating a grid of randomized cubes* and *Applying a compute shader-based screen effect in URP* sections.

In terms of applications, compute shaders can be used in many situations, from postprocessing and heavy rendering tasks to fluid simulation, mesh skinning, physics computation, pathfinding, large-scale animation, or even geometry building. Basically, whenever you have a scenario where many similar instances have to execute the same task, be it actual agents stuck in a maze or virtual points in space, compute shaders can be a nice trick to make your program more efficient.

The specific case of geometry shaders

A very focused usage of compute shaders that is growing in the community is as a tool to replace geometry shaders (which we will briefly discuss in *Chapter 13*). Indeed, because the newest Apple platforms don't support these geometry shaders anymore, people are searching for a fully cross-platform replacement – and compute shaders are now slowly coming in as the better solution.

If you're curious about concrete applications of compute shaders in games, you can have a look at Ned Makes Games's YouTube channel, where he has covered, among other things, a few usages of this tool: how to model and animate grass blades (see *Figure 7.2*, a screenshot taken from `https://www.youtube.com/watch?v=DeATXF4Szqo`), how to generate and save a mesh asset, how to replace geometry shaders with compute shaders, and more.

Figure 7.2 – An endless field of grass animated using compute shaders

OK, now – all of this sounds great, and the idea of offloading heavy processes to the GPU is very attractive, but there is still one major topic we need to discuss, and that's the data sharing between the CPU and the GPU. Because, if you are a bit familiar with computer architecture, you might be aware that, by default, the data that a program uses resides on the CPU (so on the C# side) and not on the GPU.

So, the question is: how can we transfer the data to the GPU for our calculations, and then retrieve the results to use them in our C# logic on the CPU?

Using compute buffers to pass data between the CPU and the GPU

As we said in the *What are compute shaders?* section, compute shaders can sometimes be used to speed up pure abstract computation – such as a complex physics simulation, or some fluid mechanics. In that case, we obviously want to pass in some data to our process so that it knows the context of the problem, and then retrieve the results at the end to actually use the calculations in the rest of our program.

This means that our compute shaders, which are run on the GPU, need to be able to read and write data that is also used by our main routine... which is executed on the CPU!

To do this data transfer, the solution is to use **compute buffers**, which are little chunks of memory on the GPU that both shaders and C# scripts can read from and write to. These buffers are therefore the backbone of our data exchange routine: our CPU C# logic will upload the initial data to set the context for the computation, then pass it on to the GPU for the computation phase, during which the data will be updated, and finally read the new data from the compute buffer to get back the results.

These buffers are like arrays: they hold elements of a specific data type in contiguous cells, and we can get or set the values by accessing the cells with integer indices.

The data type can be either a built-in data type (such as integer or float) or a custom data structure composed of several fields. If you define a matching data structure on the HLSL side in your compute shader, then you will be able to pass it between the CPU and the GPU in a compute buffer. But because Unity has some "augmented" C# types that don't exist in HLSL, you will need to be careful to properly convert your structure field data types to the right HLSL native type in your compute shader code. Typically, Vector3 will become float3, or Color will become float4.

Also, an important thing to keep in mind is that when working with compute buffers, you are responsible for computing the size of each element in the buffer in bytes (also called the **stride** of the buffer), because you will need to tell the program exactly the amount of memory to allocate for your buffer when you first set it up.

Don't worry, though – this is not that hard! C# has a really nice tool to help us with that: the sizeof function, which basically returns the size of a given type in bytes. And for composite types such as Vector2 or Vector3, we simply need to add up the individual sizes. For example, the following lines of code give us the size of an integer, a float or Vector3:

```
int intSize = sizeof(int);
int floatSize = sizeof(float);
int vector3Size = sizeof(float) * 3;
```

If we want to transfer a custom structure, then its size is the sum of the sizes of all of its fields. The following snippet shows how it would work for a basic data structure with a position, a normal, and a UV field:

```
struct VertexData {
    public Vector3 position;
    public Vector3 normal;
    public Vector2 uv;
}
int vector2Size = sizeof(float) * 2;
int vector3Size = sizeof(float) * 3;
int vertexDataSize = vector3Size * 2 + vector2Size;
```

Then, inside the compute shader HLSL code, the equivalents of the C# ComputeBuffer class are the StructuredBuffer<T> and RWStructuredBuffer<T> types.

The RW prefix at the start of RWStructuredBuffer<T> stands for "read/write" – this is a type of variable that can be read from and written to the GPU memory by the compute shader. StructuredBuffer<T>, on the other hand, is a read-only data buffer.

As you can see, they are generic types, meaning that you can specialize them with the exact type of data your buffer elements have. So, a compute buffer of floats will be received on the GPU side as a StructuredBuffer<float> variable or a RWStructuredBuffer<float> variable.

Similarly, the HLSL language also supports other types, such as Texture1D, Texture2D, and Texture3D (plus all the matching read/write types) to exchange data stored in a specific number of dimensions.

But enough with the theory – let's jump back into Unity and create a compute shader to really see how these assets are structured!

Creating and studying the structure of a compute shader

To better understand how to write a compute shader, it is time to dive back into our game engine and look at this new asset type up close. We won't tackle the C# calls and dispatch phase yet (we will see that in the upcoming *Generating a grid of randomized cubes* section), and will instead focus on the shader code itself.

You can create a new compute shader script in Unity very easily, simply by going to the creation contextual menu and choosing this type of asset in the **Shader** submenu:

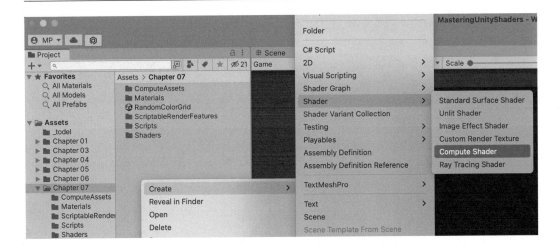

Figure 7.3 – Contextual menu for the creation of a compute shader asset

This will create a new script file in your project with the `.compute` extension, which contains the following boilerplate code:

```
#pragma kernel CSMain

RWTexture2D<float4> Result;

[numthreads(8,8,1)]
void CSMain (uint3 id : SV_DispatchThreadID) {
    Result[id.xy] = float4(id.x & id.y, (id.x & 15)/15.0,
        (id.y & 15)/15.0, 0.0);
}
```

We can decompose this snippet into four parts:

- The first line is a pragma directive that specifies the name of a function in this shader. This function will be compiled as a compute shader kernel, which we will be able to call from the C# logic. There must be at least one `#pragma kernel` directive in any compute shader, but we can actually have as many as we want.

- If there is only one kernel function, then your C# logic will be able to invoke it by using the `ComputeShader.Dispatch` method and passing it in index 0, which corresponds to the first (and only) kernel function in the compute shader. If you have multiple kernel functions, then you can use the `ComputeShader.FindKernel` method to first get back the index of a function by name, and then give it to the `ComputeShader.Dispatch` call.

- Then, we declare a read/write 2D texture to store our results in, using the `RWTexture2D` generic type. We pass it a specific `float4` subtype, which means that each point in this 2D grid will have four components (typically, four color channels if we want to use the result as an RGBA image).

- The last part defines our kernel compute function, `CSMain`. There are a few important things to note about the way this function is written:

  - Above our function definition, we use the `[numthreads]` attribute to tell the GPU how we expect the computation to be spread on our GPU among the available thread groups.

  - The three numbers in braces are the number of groups required in the X, Y, and Z dimensions.

  - The function automatically receives an input parameter from Unity: the unique identifier of the thread running the computation on the GPU, here called `id`. This reference is an integer vector with three components that correspond to its position in each thread group along the X, Y, and Z dimensions of the GPU (so it is directly determined and bounded by the maximum of the thread groups along that dimension, specified by the `[numthreads]` attribute). We can get its x, y, and z values to get the "position" of the thread. The `id` variable is also often used to fill the right cell in our result grid since it is unique for each execution and perfectly identifies each GPU task instance.

  - The function doesn't return any data directly – instead, it updates the shared data resource with the results of the computation, so that they can then be retrieved by the C# logic on the CPU.

The default compute shader code is a basic computation that creates a nice full-screen geometric pattern:

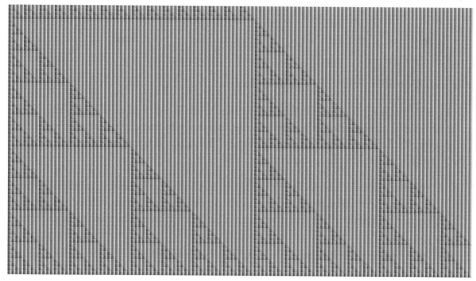

Figure 7.4 – Visualization of the default compute shader screen effect

With this theory and sample demo out of the way, let's get to an actual application of compute shaders for computation optimization and study how the randomization of a large grid of cubes compares on the CPU and the GPU.

Generating a grid of randomized cubes

Alright – we now know what compute shaders and compute buffers are. To truly understand how they can be used in a real-life scenario, however, let's discuss a basic example where compute shaders can greatly improve performance: the generation of a grid of randomly positioned and colored cubes.

We will first see how this simple process can be performed with a naive approach that runs on the CPU to get familiar with the problem, and then explore the limitations of this implementation. Finally, we will transfer our logic over to the GPU by using a compute shader and see how it boosts our performance.

Writing a naive C# implementation

Before diving into GPU offloading and performance enhancement, it stands to reason that we must first establish a baseline – or, in other words, a reference to compare our "improved" version against. So, first, let's create a simple implementation of our random color grid system with the usual C# scripting. The process will therefore run on the CPU, and it will allow us to test the advantages and limitations of this execution as opposed to running the logic on the GPU.

> **Important disclaimer**
>
> The random color grid example shown in this subsection and the upcoming ones is a re-arrangement of the amazing getting started tutorial by Matt on his Game Dev Guide channel, available here: `https://www.youtube.com/watch?v=BrZ4pWwkpto`. I simply integrated the initial grid generation logic, renamed some variables, and added comments. Kudos and many thanks to him for producing such a superb introduction to the topic!

Our scene will be very simple: we will simply have a camera, a main light, and an empty game object with a C# script called `RandomColorGrid.cs`.

In this script, we will first generate a grid of cubes when the game starts, and then show a basic GUI button to randomize these cubes – the randomization will modify two attributes on each cube: its Z position and its color.

Figure 7.5 shows a screenshot of the scene at startup:

Figure 7.5 – Screenshot of our color grid randomization test scene

We see in *Figure 7.5* that we have the grid of cubes and the **Randomize (CPU)** button in the top-left corner. We will eventually add a second button to randomize using the GPU, but for now, let's focus on the CPU version.

The size of our grid and the difficulty of the randomization process will be controlled by two parameters in our C# class:

- `gridSize`: The number of cubes along one edge of the grid (the grid contains `gridSize * gridSize` cubes in total)

- `nRandomizations`: The number of times to repeat the randomization process when the GUI button is clicked – this is an easy way to simulate a compute-intensive process without having to generate a huge number of cubes to begin with

By default, we will have `gridSize = 50`, and `nRandomizations = 1`, but these properties will be public and so they will be exposed and quick to change in the **Inspector** panel when we select our empty object with the C# script component (see *Figure 7.6*).

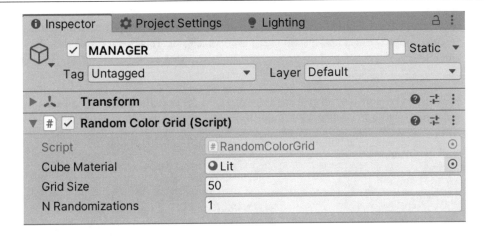

Figure 7.6 – Inspector of our RandomColorGrid C# script component

You can see in *Figure 7.6* that the script also requires a reference to a material, which will be applied to the cubes during the generation phase. Here, I'm using Unity's built-in URP lit material.

With all that in mind, let's implement our RandomColorGrid class to perform the process on the CPU. We can build it gradually as follows:

1. **Script initialization**: First, we have the base contents of the script that declare the various properties we talked about, and call our grid generation logic in the Start function, like this:

```
using System.Collections.Generic;
using UnityEngine;

public class RandomColorGrid : MonoBehaviour {
    public Material cubeMaterial;
    public int gridSize = 50;
    public int nRandomizations = 1;

    private List<GameObject> _cubes;
    private List<MeshRenderer> _cubeRenderers;

    private void Start() {
        _GenerateGrid();
    }

    private void _GenerateGrid() {}
}
```

2. **Grid setup**: Then, we will fill the `_GenerateGrid` function with two nested loops that iterate through the grid and instantiate a cube in each slot. This method will also need to store references to the cubes and their renderers in lists so that we can reuse them later on, when we randomize the grid.

The code will ensure the full grid has a size of 10 on the horizontal and vertical axes, and it will scale and position the cubes accordingly to fit everything – here is the snippet:

```
private void _GenerateGrid() {
    _cubes = new List<GameObject>();
    _cubeRenderers = new List<MeshRenderer>();

    GameObject g; MeshRenderer r;
    float cubeSize = 10 / (float)gridSize;
    for (int x = 0; x < gridSize; x++) {
        for (int y = 0; y < gridSize; y++) {
            g = GameObject.CreatePrimitive(
                PrimitiveType.Cube);
            g.transform.SetParent(transform);
            g.transform.localScale = Vector3.one *
                cubeSize;
            g.transform.position = new Vector3(
                x * cubeSize, y * cubeSize,
                    Random.Range(-0.1f, 0.1f));

            Color color = Random.ColorHSV();
            r = g.GetComponent<MeshRenderer>();
            r.material = new Material(cubeMaterial);
            r.material.SetColor("_BaseColor", color);

            _cubes.Add(g);
            _cubeRenderers.Add(r);
        }
    }
}
```

You will notice that, for the material, we can't just use the reference asset as is. Instead, we need to create a new instance from this asset, using the `Material` constructor. This is important because during the randomization phase, we want to change properties independently on each cube, so their materials have to all be different instances.

3. **CPU randomization**: Then, we will get to the meat of our script and work on the randomization process.

As we said before, we will want to iterate through our entire grid (containing `gridSize * gridSize` cubes) multiple times, as determined by the `nRandomizations` integer value. This will help us simulate a "heavy" process by artificially increasing the workload. For each cube, we will set its Z position to a random number between -0.1 and +0.1, and we will set its color to a new random value.

Thanks to our previously filled-in references in the _cubes and _cubeRenderers lists, this is quite straightforward to do:

```
public class RandomColorGrid : MonoBehaviour {
    ...

    private void _RandomizeCPU() {
        GameObject g;
        for (int r = 0; r < nRandomizations; r++) {
            for (int c = 0; c < _cubes.Count; c++) {
                g = _cubes[c];
                g.transform.position = new Vector3(
                    g.transform.position.x,
                        g.transform.position.y,
                            Random.Range(-0.1f, 0.1f));
                _cubeRenderers[c].material.SetColor(
                    "_BaseColor", Random.ColorHSV());
            }
        }
    }
}
```

4. **Basic GUI**: Finally, we will have to set up a very basic UI so that we can actually call our randomization logic. To do this, let's take advantage of Unity's IMGUI system (the legacy and easy-to-use but basic UI API), which allows us to create buttons in just a few lines of code, simply by hooking into the OnGUI function:

```
public class RandomColorGrid : MonoBehaviour {
    ...

    private void OnGUI() {
        Rect r = new Rect(10, 10, 200, 40);
        if (GUI.Button(r, "Randomize (CPU)")) {
            _RandomizeCPU();
        }
    }
}
```

5. **Bonus – measuring execution time**: To help us compare the results of our randomization computations as we change the `gridSize` and `nRandomizations` parameters, we can also add a simple execution time log that tells us how long the whole randomization process took, by wrapping the `_RandomizeCPU` function code with the following lines:

```
public class RandomColorGrid : MonoBehaviour {
    ...

    private void _RandomizeCPU() {
        float timeStart = Time.realtimeSinceStartup;

        // (... previous code)

        float timeEnd = Time.realtimeSinceStartup;
        float t =  timeEnd - timeStart;
        Debug.Log($"Execution time: {t.ToString("f6")}
            sec");
    }
}
```

If we add this script to our empty game object and run the scene, we will see that we get the expected screen shown in *Figure 7.5*, and that we can call the randomization process to change the Z position and color of all the cubes in the grid.

Of course, we have to restart the scene if we want to modify the `gridSize` parameter. This is because the grid is generated at the start and, therefore, cannot react to later changes in the `gridSize` value. But the `nRandomizations` parameter can be switched out for lower or higher values on the fly to test out the efficiency of our setup.

So, does our CPU-based logic stand a chance, or is it too limited?

Examining the limitations of our CPU implementation

Now that we have a basic script to establish a baseline, let's run it in several configurations to see how `gridSize` and `nRandomizations` impact the execution time, and whether this CPU process can be used as is in a real game or whether it is too slow.

Figure 7.7 lists various configurations with the final execution time in seconds averaged over multiple trials:

Grid size	Number of cubes	Number of randomizations	Average execution time over three tests (in seconds)
10	100	1	~0.0003
50	250	1	~0.007
100	10,000	1	~0.03

Grid size	Number of cubes	Number of randomizations	Average execution time over three tests (in seconds)
50	250	2	~0.015
50	250	10	~0.07
50	250	100	~0.7
50	250	1,000	~7
50	250	5,000	~37.4
50	250	10,000	~78.1

Figure 7.7 – Results of the CPU-based randomization process for various configurations

These results show us that as `gridSize` and `nRandomizations` get higher, the execution time grows too (and `gridSize` causes a larger increase).

This is absolutely consistent with our code: because we have `gridSize * gridSize` cubes in our grid, the complexity of our algorithm evolves as the square of this parameter; and because we have `nRandomizations` loops, it evolves linearly with regard to this parameter.

But, of course, this means that even with a limited amount of cubes, if the calculations are too intensive, the CPU will start to really struggle. The bottom half of the table in particular is proof that in a real-case scenario, using basic C# logic will soon be very limiting.

So, let's test how using compute shaders can help us optimize these calculations and greatly reduce our execution time.

Optimizing the process with compute shaders

OK – our previous tests in the *Writing a naive C# implementation* section have shown that although our CPU randomization process was easy to implement, it also comes with quite the limitations. As soon as the computations start to get too intensive, the required time skyrockets and makes it hard to consider for an actual game. We need to find a way to make these calculations faster; luckily, our GPU is here to help!

We saw, in the *Discovering compute shader and compute buffers* section, that invoking HLSL logic from C# is actually quite straightforward: once we have written a compute shader in a `.compute` asset, we can interact with it by filling the data in compute buffers and dispatching calls. Basically, Unity provides us with a few easy-to-use functions to send data to the GPU and load results back from it and take advantage of the highly efficient GPU parallel execution.

Let's convert our CPU logic to the GPU equivalent by setting up a compute shader and extending our RandomColorGrid C# script to offer this other alternative. We will do so by taking the following steps:

1. **Compute shader setup**: To start things off, we need to create our compute shader – we will make a new RandomColorGrid.compute asset, and fill it with the following basic content:

   ```
   #pragma kernel CSMain

   [numthreads(10,1,1)]
   void CSMain (uint3 id : SV_DispatchThreadID) {}
   ```

   To keep things simple, we will keep all the threads in the X dimension – hence the unitary values for the two other dimensions in the [numthreads] attribute. This is obviously not optimal, since we are not using our GPU to its full potential, but it will make computing the "position" of the current thread easier.

2. **HLSL structure and utilities**: Then, we will implement the structure to represent the data we want to compute for our cubes during the randomization process – the position and the color fields. Remember that we need to use basic HLSL types, so our structure will look like this:

   ```
   struct Cube {
       float3 position;
       float4 color;
   };
   ```

   To get our C# script configuration parameters, we will also define two float values for the total number of cubes and the number of randomization iterations; and of course, we will need to pass in our cube data from and to the C# side with a read/write structured buffer:

   ```
   RWStructuredBuffer<Cube> cubes;
   float nCubes;
   float nRandomizations;
   ```

   Next up, we have to prepare a function to generate some random numbers easily. Even though there is no built-in tool for this in HLSL, there are many places on the internet where we can find nice one-liners to create pseudo-randomness, such as this one:

   ```
   float rand(float2 co) {
       return (frac(sin(dot(co.xy, float2(12.9898,
           78.233))) * 43758.5453)) * 1;
   }
   ```

   Our compute shader is now ready for computation – we have all the information we need to perform the randomization.

3. **GPU randomization**: To finish our compute shader, we need to fill in the CSMain function to actually run the randomization process using all of the parameters and tools we prepared in step 2.

Because we are only using the X dimension for the threading, we know that the unique identifier of the current cube we are working on only depends on the x component of the id input parameter. This identifier will allow us to get and re-apply the data for our cube by accessing this index in the cubes structured buffer:

```
void CSMain (uint3 id : SV_DispatchThreadID) {
    Cube cube = cubes[id.x];
    // apply randomization
    cubes[id.x] = cube;
}
```

Now, we need to create a loop that iterates nRandomizations times, and in each iteration, use our rand function to get a random Z position and a random color. Since it takes in two parameters, we will need to find a way to prepare various arguments that are as unique to this cube as possible.

For the position, we can actually compute a "relative position" from the cube's ID, pass it in the rand tool, and assign the result back as the Z position for the cube:

```
void CSMain (uint3 id : SV_DispatchThreadID) {
    Cube cube = cubes[id.x];

    float p = id.x / nCubes;
    for (int i = 0; i < nRandomizations; i++) {
        float zPos = rand(float2(p, cube.position.z));
        cube.position.z = zPos;
    }

    cubes[id.x] = cube;
}
```

For the color, we can just play around with the components of the cube's current color to basically remix them into some other color:

```
void CSMain (uint3 id : SV_DispatchThreadID) {
    // ...
    for (int i = 0; i < nRandomizations; i++) {
        // ...
        float r = rand(float2(cube.color.r,
            cube.color.g));
        float g = rand(float2(cube.color.g,
            cube.color.b));
        float b = rand(float2(cube.color.b,
            cube.color.r));
        cube.color = float4(r, g, b, 1);
    }
```

```
    cubes[id.x] = cube;
}
```

Our compute shader is now complete and ready to be invoked from the C# script.

4. **Referencing and invoking the compute shader**: Now that we are done with the HLSL part, we just need to reference our shader asset in the C# RandomColorGrid class and set up the alternative UI and workflow to execute our GPU-based process.

First, we will create a C# structure that matches the one in our compute shader and contains the per-cube data (this time, with handy Unity types). We will also declare an array of that struct type in the class to store our cubes' data:

```
public class RandomColorGrid : MonoBehaviour {
    public struct Cube {
        public Vector3 position;
        public Color color;
    }

    private Cube[] _data;
    ...
}
```

Then, when we generate the grid, we will also fill in this new _data array with instances of our Cube structure containing the initial parameters for each of our cubes:

```
private void _GenerateGrid() {
    _cubes = new List<GameObject>();
    _cubeRenderers = new List<MeshRenderer>();
    _data = new Cube[gridSize * gridSize];
    ...
    for (int x = 0; x < gridSize; x++) {
        for (int y = 0; y < gridSize; y++) {
            ...

            _cubes.Add(g);
            _cubeRenderers.Add(r);

            _data[x * gridSize + y] = new Cube() {
                position = g.transform.position,
                color = color
            };
        }
    }
}
```

The next step is to create a variable to reference our compute shader and write up a
_RandomizeGPU function that sets up its parameters and invokes it. This method will need
to first prepare the buffer of cube data, then set the parameters of the compute shader based
on the C# configuration variables, then dispatch the call to the shader, and finally retrieve the
data back from the GPU to the CPU and apply the results to the cubes. All in all, here are the
updates to our script:

```csharp
public class RandomColorGrid : MonoBehaviour {
  public ComputeShader computeShader;

  ...

  private void _RandomizeGPU() {
    // compute size of our Cube struct
    int vector3Size = sizeof(float) * 3;
    int colorSize = sizeof(float) * 4;
    int totalStructSize = vector3Size + colorSize;

    // prepare buffer with the right size + set data
      values
    ComputeBuffer cubesBuffer = new ComputeBuffer(
      _data.Length, totalStructSize);
    cubesBuffer.SetData(_data);

    // setup compute shader fields
    computeShader.SetBuffer(0, "cubes", cubesBuffer);
    computeShader.SetFloat("nCubes", _data.Length);
    computeShader.SetFloat("nRandomizations",
      nRandomizations);

    // invoke compute shader
    computeShader.Dispatch(0, _data.Length / 10, 1,
      1);

    // read data back into buffer to get results on
      the C# side
    cubesBuffer.GetData(_data);

    for (int i = 0; i < _cubes.Count; i++) {
      Cube c = _data[i];
      _cubes[i].transform.position = c.position;
      _cubeRenderers[i].material.SetColor(
        "_BaseColor", c.color);
    }
```

```
        // clean up buffer
        cubesBuffer.Dispose();
    }
}
```

Finally, we can add a new button in our GUI to call our GPU-based randomization function:

```
private void OnGUI() {
    if (GUI.Button(new Rect(10, 10, 200, 40),
        "Randomize (CPU)"))
    {

        _RandomizeCPU();
    }
    if (GUI.Button(new Rect(220, 10, 200, 40),
        "Randomize (GPU)"))
    {

        _RandomizeGPU();
    }
}
```

If we assign our RandomColorGrid.compute asset to the new **Compute Shader** slot of the RandomColorGrid C# script component (see *Figure 7.8*), we will then be able to re-run our game and try out the GPU-based randomization process.

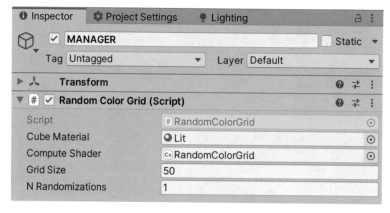

Figure 7.8 – Inspector of our improved RandomColorGrid C# script component

Our new UI offers us two possibilities: the previous CPU-based calculations or the new GPU-based version.

Again, we can of course wrap the _RandomizeGPU function with some time checks to easily get the execution time of this new workflow. Then, by re-creating the same conditions as in the *Examining the limitations of our CPU implementation* section, we can compare how this compute time evolves as the task becomes more intensive.

Figure 7.9 shows the results for the GPU version, presented in the same way as the previous evaluation of the CPU-based process (see *Figure 7.7*):

Grid size	Number of cubes	Number of randomizations	Average execution time over three tests (in seconds)
10	100	1	~0.0016
50	250	1	~0.025
100	10,000	1	~0.06
50	250	2	~0.026
50	250	10	~0.028
50	250	100	~0.028
50	250	1,000	~0.03
50	250	5,000	~0.04
50	250	10,000	~0.047

Figure 7.9 – Results of the GPU-based randomization process for various configurations

In *Figure 7.9*, the new averaged execution times are extremely valuable, because they highlight the two main features of GPU computing:

- For a low amount of calculations, using the GPU is often worse than using the CPU. That's because, ultimately, the data has to be stored on the CPU, so to do the computation on the GPU, we need to transfer the data to and back from the GPU as a preprocessing and postprocessing step. This means that there is some incompressible time that has to be taken into consideration, and that is not absorbed by the actual gain in compute time if the data is too small.

- On the other hand, the GPU clearly shines whenever we are dealing with intensive computational tasks, such as our artificially large multi-randomizations with a high value for the nRandomizations parameter. The bottom half of the table in *Figure 7.9* actually shows a crucial result: once the data transfer time is passed, we can greatly increase the number of calculations without seeing a significant change in the execution time (the last three rows, for nRandomizations = {1000, 5000, 10000}, display fairly similar compute times, although the workload has been multiplied by 10!).

This example of a cube grid randomization is, of course, more of an experiment than an actual game mechanic, but it demonstrates the power of compute shaders. We could easily see how to take advantage of these optimizations for pathfinding, procedural data generation, large physics and fluid simulations, particles, and VFX.

But to continue our exploration of compute shaders, let's see another common use case for them: the creation of efficient postprocessing effects and full-screen renders.

Applying a compute shader-based screen effect in URP

So far, we have seen how to use compute shaders to optimize calculations on pure data. We eventually used the information to modify cube visual properties, but it was a sort of "side-effect" to make it easier to see the results: in theory, we could have simply stuck to the compute part and measured the execution time to compare our CPU and GPU process performances.

Still, screen effects and postprocessing are big applications of compute shaders, so we definitely need to have a look at how we can use these shaders to directly render something on our screen.

To test things out, we are going to create a very simple compute shader that fills the screen with red pixels. The goal is thus to effectively end up with a fully red screen. I know, it is not a very exciting idea, but it will be a good way to understand the basics of using compute shaders in a URP project without too much distraction!

In the following sections, we will first see why, in URP, this requires us to set up a new custom feature for our renderer and then use it to run a compute shader-based screen effect.

Preparing custom URP render assets

OK, so – we want to have a shader script that efficiently loops through all the pixels on screen and returns some value for them, here a full red opaque color.

With the legacy built-in pipeline, it used to be that you could simply add a script on the camera in your scene and override the `OnRenderImage` hook with a bit of logic that invokes your compute shader. In just a dozen lines, you would be done, and the C# code was able to call the HLSL logic inside your compute shader asset.

But, with the new SRPs, such as URP, the setup process is slightly more complex. Most importantly, we don't have the `OnRenderImage` function to override anymore and, instead, we need to create a custom scriptable render feature, just as we did in *Chapter 5*. In order to use a compute shader to calculate screen effects, we need to prepare the following objects in our Unity URP project:

- `URPComputeAsset.cs`: An abstract C# class that will serve as a model to declare ScriptableObjects to hold all of the relevant data for a compute shader, as well as the reference to the compute shader asset itself. By having this abstract class at the top of the inheritance tree, we will be able to easily create assets for each of the compute shaders we want to use as screen effects, while ensuring these child classes contain all the necessary functions for the custom scriptable render feature to use them.

- `URPComputePass.cs`: A C# class that uses the data defined in the `URPComputeAsset` instance. This data is used to invoke the compute shader during the rendering process. This class inherits from the `ScriptableRenderPass` built-in Unity class and uses `CommandBuffers` to intervene in the render workflow (just like the legacy pipeline extensions we saw in *Chapter 2*).

- `URPComputeFeature.cs`: A third C# class that brings everything together and creates a scriptable render feature for the URP that uses the `URPComputePass` logic – this is the script that will allow us to actually include the whole process in our URP settings, similar to what we did for the outline feature in *Chapter 5*.

- `FillWithRed.compute`: The actual compute shader asset with the low-level HLSL code that performs the per-pixel computation. In our case, it will be very basic, since we want to always return a red color – you can recognize the structure we saw in the previous sections:

```
#pragma kernel CSMain
RWTexture2D<float4> Result;


[numthreads(8,8,1)]
void CSMain (uint3 id : SV_DispatchThreadID) {
    Result[id.xy] = float4(1,0,0,1);
}
```

- `ComputeFillWithRed.cs`: The wrapper ScriptableObject for our compute shader that inherits from our previous `URPComputeAsset` class and contains a reference to our `FillWithRed.compute` asset. This object is just a binder between the low-level side and the URP rendering process. Fortunately, this class will be very short and easy to write, because we don't need to do anything for this basic compute shader (we don't have any data to pass in or initialize, and so we don't need any extra parameters):

```
using UnityEngine;
using UnityEngine.Rendering;


[CreateAssetMenu(menuName = "Compute Assets/CH07/FillWithRed")]
public class ComputeFillWithRed : URPComputeAsset {
    public override void Render(
        CommandBuffer commandBuffer,
            int kernelHandle) {}
}
```

As you can see in this snippet, the `ComputeFillWithRed` class doesn't actually declare additional logic compared to its parent class, `URPComputeAsset`. The only difference between the `URPComputeAsset` and `ComputeFillWithRed` classes is that the latter is a derived class that can be instantiated – and here, we make it quick to do so by adding the `[CreateAssetMenu]` attribute on our class so that it shows up in our creation contextual menus (as we will see later in *Figure 7.12*).

I won't go into the exact contents of the three C# scripts, which we just discussed, for the scriptable render feature because they are quite long and not that fascinating. In a nutshell, these three C# scripts use the various hooks Unity provides us with for classes that derive from the `ScriptableRenderFeature` and `ScriptableRenderPass` classes to integrate the additional calculations of the compute shader in the rendering process.

You can find the C# scripts along with all the code for this chapter in the GitHub repository of the book, and the scripts are directly adapted from Ryan J. Boyer's superb "URP Compute" GitHub project (available here: `https://github.com/ryanslikesocool/URP-Compute`). The only important difference apart from the script names and namespaces is that, in the `URPComputePass.cs` file, we don't use the `Hidden/AddShader` resource but the `Unlit/Texture` shader reference for the auto-generated render material, because `Hidden/AddShader` is not available anymore.

This means that, in your **Project Settings** panel, you have to make sure that you add this extra shader reference to the list of the shaders that are always included. To do this, do the following:

1. Open the **Edit | Project Settings...** window and go to the **Graphics** section.

2. In the section labeled **Always Included Shaders**, increase the size to 8 and use the picker to browse the built-in assets; select the `Unlit/Texture` one:

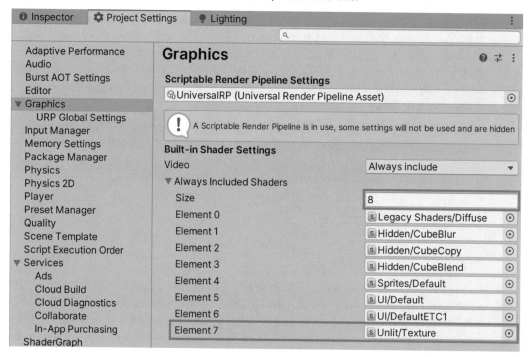

Figure 7.10 – Project configuration with the additional pre-included shader

This will allow the scriptable render feature to create a material based on this shader if it doesn't have a reference to one yet, and use it for the rendering process.

Integrating our compute shader in the URP

Now that we've added all these assets to our project, we will need to configure the URP to actually use them. We already saw the basics of how to do that in *Chapter 5*, but here there a few other steps we need to take to use our custom compute feature:

1. First, we need to tell our URP renderer to use our custom feature. Remember that, to do this, we need to select our URP data asset and, in its **Inspector** panel, at the bottom, click **Add Renderer Feature** and pick our **URP Compute Feature**. *Figure 7.11* shows what the URP data looks like for the sample project in the GitHub repository of this book, with both the outline feature from *Chapter 5* and the new compute feature we just integrated:

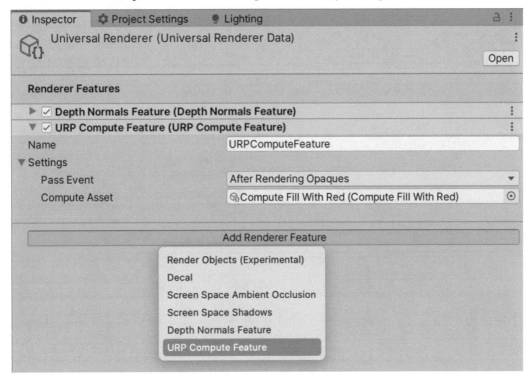

Figure 7.11 – Addition of our new URP Compute Feature to the URP settings

2. However, you'll notice in *Figure 7.11* that in my **URP Compute Feature** section, I need to assign a URPComputeAsset instance. To create this **Compute Fill With Red** compute asset, which links to the FillWithRed.compute logic, I used my ScriptableObject to create a menu like the one shown in *Figure 7.12*:

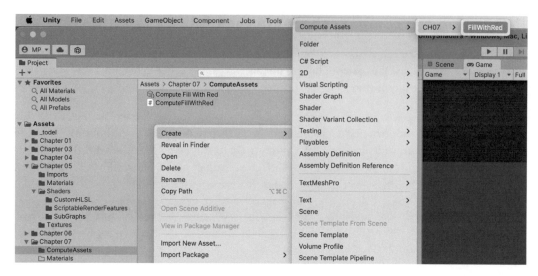

Figure 7.12 – Contextual menu for the creation of a new URPComputeAsset ScriptableObject instance

3. And then, with this new asset selected, I picked our compute shader and assigned it in the **Inspector** panel (see *Figure 7.13*) to tell the renderer what shader to use exactly.

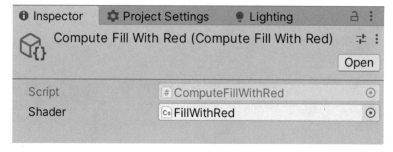

Figure 7.13 – Setup of our URPComputeAsset ScriptableObject to use the FillWithRed compute shader

At that point, our URP is set up to use the scriptable render feature, which will automatically call the compute shader we prepared in our `FillWithRed.compute` asset and return a full red opaque color for each pixel on the screen. So, you should see that the scene and the game view turn to completely red renders, as shown in *Figure 7.14*:

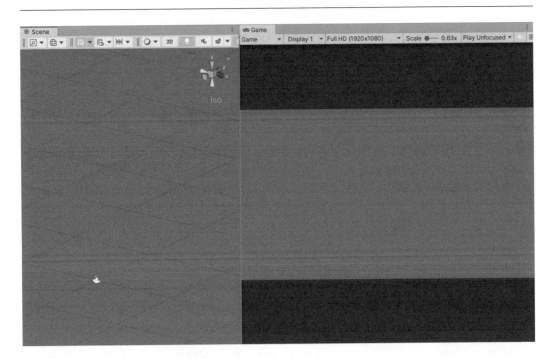

Figure 7.14 – Scene and game views with our compute shader-based screen effect enabled

Again, it's not that attractive, but it shows that our entire process works well and that we can indeed perform an intensive task (filling the entire screen every time it needs to redraw) in a very efficient way, thanks to our compute shader.

The same technique could be used to create some simulations, such as Conway's famous Game of Life, a maze generation algorithm, or a postprocessing filter (like in this tutorial by Bronson Zgeb about a URP pixelate effect: `https://bronsonzgeb.com/index.php/2021/07/25/pixelate-filter-in-urp-using-compute-shaders/`).

But anyway – here we are. We now have a basic understanding of how to use custom shaders for full-screen effects in URP!

Summary

In this chapter, we dived into the compute shaders and the compute buffers, and we explored how these tools can be used in a variety of situations to render demanding visuals or optimize heavy computations.

We first zoomed in on the base concepts and introduced how compute shaders allow us to offload processing from the CPU to the GPU by defining HLSL kernel functions for parallel execution and transferring data via compute buffers.

We then implemented a basic grid randomization process on the CPU and studied how refactoring our code to use the GPU improved the performance significantly by reducing the execution time, in particular, for large amounts of data.

Finally, we talked about another common application of compute shaders, namely the postprocessing and screen effects, and we saw how to set up a URP project to handle this special type of rendering, thanks to a new custom render feature.

Of course, compute shaders are a vast topic, and they have hundreds of applications – some quite esoteric, and others very practical – so we only scratched the surface here! But there is a well-known and beautiful application of compute shaders that deserves its own chapter: ray marching. Basically, this technique goes one step further than the parallax mapping and interior mapping tools we discussed in *Chapter 6*, and uses the power of compute shaders to render geometry from pure maths. Because who says we need to have geometry at all to begin with?!

So, in the next chapter, we will dive into this other amazing shader trick and see how we can create fully procedural 3D scenes.

Going further

If you're curious about procedural drawing and compute shaders, here are a few interesting resources to check out or continue your journey with:

- *Getting Started with Compute Shaders in Unity*, Game Dev Guide (2020): https://www.youtube.com/watch?v=BrZ4pWwkpto

- *Intro to Compute Shaders in Unity URP! Replace Geometry Shaders 2020.3 | Game Dev Tutorial*, Ned Makes Games (2020): https://www.youtube.com/watch?v=EB5HiqDl7VE&list=PLAUha41PUKAY7PHFqblsla9uPi0cCcJEy

- *Unity Compute Shader Tutorial - The Mandelbrot Set*, Coderious (2020): https://www.youtube.com/watch?v=WWI07UQbJ9E

8

The Power of Ray Marching

In *Chapter 6*, we saw a few techniques to boost basic geometry and add details to cubes or planes using textures and clever shading tricks. We explored how parallax mapping and interior mapping are nice and easy-to-understand techniques because they make you manipulate common asset types, namely meshes and images.

The issue with these methods, however, is that they require your team to produce the aforementioned assets. If the members of your game development team don't have the time or skills to create the right textures or the right base geometries, you won't be able to apply your shader to anything!

To counteract this issue, a growing trend is procedural generation, which basically is about using controlled randomness to auto-create viable parts of your game based on a set of rules. This idea of scripted generation is particularly interesting if you are more into development than art, you want to produce assets quickly and in a modular way, or you need infinite re-creation capability (be it to increase replay value or to generate endless levels), for example.

And, of course, procedural generation can also be applied to... environments and scenes! Thanks to the Unity compute shaders we discussed in *Chapter 7*, and an amazing technique called ray marching, it is possible to create entire 3D spaces based just on code that simulates the perception a camera would have of the equivalent 3D scene. We can even use this tool to create other advanced visuals, such as clouds.

So, in this chapter, we will study the basic principles of ray marching. Then, we will see how to implement it in Unity step by step to create various shapes in a fully procedural way. Finally, we will see how to apply it to the rendering of clouds. We will therefore cover the following topics:

- Understanding the fundamentals of ray marching

- Entering a world of primitives...

- Studying a common use case – the rendering of volumetric clouds

Technical requirements

To try out the samples yourself, you will need to have Unity installed, with a version from 2019 or later. You will then need to create either of the following:

- A project with the common 3D template, which you will then upgrade to use the URP or HDRP render pipeline (see the *Stepping up with the URP render pipeline* section of *Chapter 2*)

- A project with the new 3D URP or 3D HDRP template (see the *Stepping up with the URP render pipeline* section of *Chapter 2* for guidance on how to download and pick this template)

We will also rely on the custom scriptable render feature we coded in *Chapter 7*, so make sure you either implement or download the `URPComputeAsset.cs`, `URPComputePass.cs`, and `URPComputeFeature.cs` files from the GitHub repository of this book, at `https://github.com/PacktPublishing/Become-a-Unity-Shaders-Guru/tree/main/Assets/Chapter%2008`.

Understanding the fundamentals of ray marching

Before diving into the practical applications and implementation tricks of ray marching, let's first have a quick run through the concepts it relies on.

In the upcoming sections, we will first introduce the concept of **signed distance functions** (SDFs) for representing arbitrarily complex shapes, then understand how this notion can be used to actually compute 3D renders, and finally, have a look at how to add shading to ray marching visualizations.

Describing a shape with SDFs

At the core of the ray marching process is a concept called the **signed distance function**, or **SDF**. To put it simply, SDFs are mathematical functions that take a point in space (represented by its X, Y, and Z coordinates) and return how far it is from a surface.

It may seem like a strange idea to compute surfaces at first, but the power of SDFs is that they can describe quite complex shapes in just a few lines, and they allow us to render surprising geometries. *Figure 8.1* shows an example of ray marching with a two-lines-of-code-signed distance function:

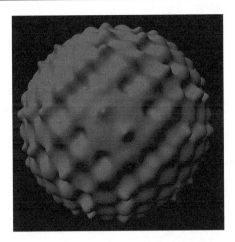

Figure 8.1 – Sphere with displacement rendered using ray marching

A basic example of SDF is that of a sphere: suppose you have an (imaginary) 3D sphere centered at C and with a radius of r, as in *Figure 8.2*, and you consider a 3D point, P, next to it.

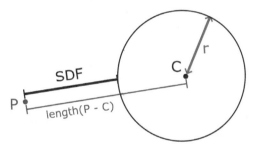

Figure 8.2 – Schematic representation of the imaginary 3D sphere and SDF for a given point P

Then, you can easily compute the distance from P to the closest point on the sphere's surface with the following formula: `float sdf = length(P - C) - r`.

So, if we consider evaluation points P around the sphere, we can approximately map out the shape of the sphere in the chunk of space we are looking at, although we didn't import a mesh!

Now, you might have noticed that we are not talking about "distance functions" but "*signed* distance functions." Indeed, a key characteristic of SDFs is that they give a signed distance to the surface (meaning that it can be positive or negative), which allows us to also specify whether our point P is inside or outside the surface. Since the only information we have about our imaginary geometry is this SDF, this additional property is obviously essential to determining the direction of our faces and where the inner volume of our 3D surface lies.

Let's extend *Figure 8.2* to show the three possible cases for our point P – inside the sphere, at the surface of the sphere, or outside the sphere:

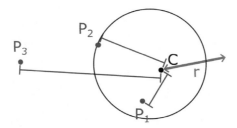

Figure 8.3 – Overview of three possible cases for P (inside, on, or outside the sphere)

We see in *Figure 8.3* that our SDF for this sphere can return negative, null, or positive numbers depending on the case:

- If P is inside the sphere (see P_1 in *Figure 8.3*), then `length(P - C) < r`, so `length(P - C) - r < 0`

- If P is on the sphere (see P_2 in *Figure 8.3*), then `length(P - C) = r`, so `length(P - C) - r = 0`

- If P is outside the sphere (see P_3 in *Figure 8.3*), then `length(P - C) > r`, so `length(P - C) - r > 0`

Alright – this looks like a concise and yet powerful way to represent a 3D surface... but how can we actually use those SDFs to render something?

Turning SDFs into renders with the ray marching loop

So far, we have discussed a purely mathematical concept, the SDF. We got a glimpse of how it can relate to the description of a 3D surface, but we don't yet have a clear link between defining an SDF and rendering a procedurally generated 3D scene.

This is where our main technique of **ray marching** comes in.

As the name implies, ray marching works by generating many rays from the camera (one for each pixel on screen) and taking steps along them. Each of those steps on each of those rays will give evaluation points to compute the value of the SDF. And so, by aggregating all those results in a fragment shader, we will eventually get a rendered image of this procedural scene, derived just from the mathematics of our SDF.

To better understand the process and discuss some of its details, let's take a little example. We will consider this map of a 3D scene we want to render using ray marching (the area shaded in gray is the inside of the shape):

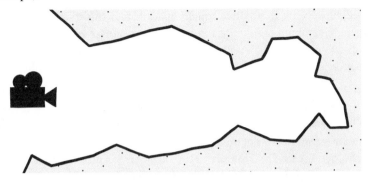

Figure 8.4 – Example of a scene to render with ray marching

To apply ray marching here, the idea would be to do the following:

1. **Define the SDF**: First, we would need to code up an SDF to represent this surface. It would obviously be a bit harder than for the sphere we worked on previously, but thanks to the great adaptability of SDFs, we could technically find an algorithm that always returns the distance to this surface for a given point in the 3D space.

2. **Generate the rays**: Then, we would need to generate our rays to know along which lines to evaluate our points. It seems logical to consider rays that originate at the position of the camera and move forward in order to render the part of the space that faces our camera. But, since we need results for each pixel in the image to get a complete render, we will have to generate one ray per pixel and basically use the position of this pixel on the screen to get the small offset for our ray (see *Figure 8.5*).

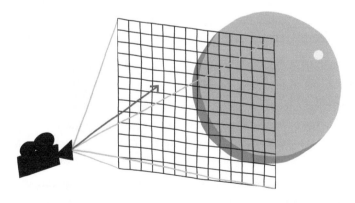

Figure 8.5 – Origin points for the camera rays

3. **March along the rays**: The next step is to perform the steps along each ray. To do this, we will first decide on a maximum number of steps. Then, we will start at our camera position and move along the ray until we reach this count.

The trick, however, is to not take equally spaced steps. Although this could work, it would require a high amount of iterations to get accurate enough results. And most importantly, it would distribute the search evenly along the ray even though there might be some areas that require more granularity, and others that can be traversed more quickly.

To avoid this issue, a better solution is to use **distance-aided ray marching** (sometimes called sphere tracing) to move forward in a more clever and optimized way. In short, the idea is to build a little bubble around our evaluation point and see when it hits our 3D surface – we can compute this easily, thanks to our SDF. Since this minimal distance before hitting the surface is by definition the smallest distance to the surface (remember that this is how we defined the SDF), it means that we can safely take a step along our ray with a length equal to this distance without running the risk of missing the surface.

So, our marching steps will look like the ones shown in *Figure 8.6* – we will compute evaluation points at irregular intervals, based on the distance to the surface we computed previously, and thus create an efficient and yet perfectly accurate chain of "check bubbles":

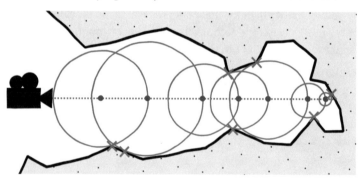

Figure 8.6 – Marching process along one ray with the distance-aided ray marching trick

The position of the n-th point is therefore computed by combining the ray origin (the camera's position) and the ray direction (the slightly offsetted forward vector) with the distance we've already traveled, which is the sum of the SDF evaluation for the n - 1 previous step points.

Note that, as is often the case in computer science, this is where you will need to do a trade-off between the accuracy of the result and the required computing power. The more steps you take, the better the results... but the longer and more demanding the calculations!

4. **Stopping the rays**: There are two important improvements we should make to this algorithm, though, to avoid useless computations and optimize the calculations.

At the moment, we see that if we hit a wall (meaning if our surface is in front of the camera and our ray therefore gets right into it), the loop will keep going until it has finished all its steps, even though the distance will be almost null and all the evaluation points will be crammed together in the same spot. To avoid this, we could check for the distance to the surface we got from our SDF and, if it is below a small, predefined threshold, consider that this means we are blocked and should stop the computation for this ray here.

Conversely, if the 3D object we are rendering is not placed on the route of the ray at all, our SDF results might quickly get out of hand and give us evaluation points at an insanely high distance from the camera. To tackle this issue, the best idea is to limit our computation to a reasonable volume of the 3D scene and consider a far-clipping plane for the camera: if the traveled distance gets above this second threshold, then we just break the loop and consider that this pixel has the background color because the ray couldn't "see" any object to render.

We now have a bird's-eye view of the ray marching process, and we could already implement a valid script to put all of that into action. There is, however, one important thing we need to discuss to finalize this theoretical study of the concept: how to re-integrate shading when rendering with this method.

Upping the ante with basic shading

Indeed, as we saw in the previous chapters of this book, shading is at the heart of 3D renders. This is partly why shaders are called that, actually: they are programs that compute the right color for the pixel on screen based on the object's inherent properties *and* its interactions with the lights in the scene.

But since, with ray marching, we have neither a 3D mesh nor a light, how can we apply these principles? How can we get shadows and volumes to really give the viewer the feeling that we are rendering a scene in three dimensions (as in *Figure 8.1*), and not just an arrangement of flat 2D geometric figures?

The trick, as always, is to play around with the mathematics to simulate the proper visuals – in our case, we are going to extend our ray marching algorithm so that it also computes the normals of the surface. As we saw in *Chapter 1*, this will provide us with all the data we need to set up a diffuse/specular lighting model.

Of course, the difficulty here is that we are not dealing with well-known shapes such as a sphere or a cube, for which we have explicit formulas to compute the normals. Because the SDFs can be arbitrarily complex, we have to find a method that can work with any shape.

The solution is to approximate these normals by computing, at each evaluation point, what we call the **gradient** of the distance field. Basically, the gradient is the extension of the notion of derivative to higher dimensions, so here it is a quantity that represents how the distance value evolves when we move just a tiny bit around our evaluation point. We can get it by considering little offsets around the point along the X, Y, and Z axes in the negative and positive directions, and evaluating our SDF at those nudged positions.

Once normalized, this gradient will be a great approximation of the surface's normal at that evaluation point, and it will make it easy to compute the shading for our surface. We will see the detailed calculations in the upcoming *Entering a world of primitives...* section, but it will rely on the same basic ideas we discussed for our Blinn-Phong lighting in *Chapter 1*.

Also, because the normal is computed dynamically, the shading will remain consistent no matter the deformations we add to our surface, or the imaginary objects we add to our procedural scene.

Alright – after this simple overview of SDFs, ray marching, and dynamic shading, let's see how to actually apply all of this in practice by creating our own procedural scenes in Unity!

Entering a world of primitives...

We saw in *Chapter 7* that compute shaders are an excellent way to process large data quickly – which is typically what we need for ray marching, since in every frame, we have to step through many rays (one per pixel) to render the scene!

Our ray marching logic will therefore be written in a compute shader file, and then called from a C# script at the time of the render as a full-screen effect. So, the process will reuse the custom scriptable render feature (URPComputeFeature) we prepared in *Chapter 7*, and we will go through the same steps as in the *Applying a compute shader-based screen effect in URP* section of *Chapter 7*.

In the upcoming sections, we will therefore start by preparing a basic compute shader to render a single sphere using ray marching, and then improve it to handle multiple shapes of different types.

Rendering a sphere with ray marching

To begin with, let's set up a first basic ray marching compute shader to get the gist. For now, we will just render a single sphere in the middle of the screen, so this shader will be called RaymarchingSphere.compute. The shader will also allow us to tweak the color of the sphere's surface, plus the direction and the intensity of the (virtual) directional light to use for shading in our ray marching process.

Figure 8.7 demonstrates the final result for a basic light coming from the top-left corner and a blue surface color:

Figure 8.7 – Render of a single blue sphere with basic Lambert-like shading using ray marching

First things first, we can draw inspiration from our `FillWithRed.compute` asset from *Chapter 7*, and initialize our `RaymarchingSphere.compute` shader with the following content:

```
#pragma kernel CSMain

RWTexture2D<float4> Result;

[numthreads(8,8,1)]
void CSMain (uint3 id : SV_DispatchThreadID) {
    Result[id.xy] = float4(0, 0, 0, 1);
}
```

Then, we should also create an associated `URPComputeAsset`-derived C# class to use in our `URPComputeFeature` section of the URP settings (as shown in *Figure 8.10*) that corresponds to this compute shader – `ComputeRaymarchingSphere.cs`. We will set up this script with this snippet of code:

```
using UnityEngine;
using UnityEngine.Rendering;

[CreateAssetMenu(menuName = "Compute Assets/CH08/Raymarching Sphere")]
public class ComputeRaymarchingSphere : URPComputeAsset {

    public override void Render(
        CommandBuffer commandBuffer,
            int kernelHandle) {}

}
```

Now, let's create a ScriptableObject from this `ComputeRaymarchingSphere` C# class and set it as the reference for our `URPComputeFeature`:

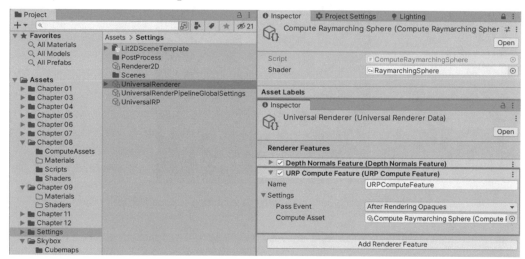

Figure 8.8 – Configuration of the URP project settings to use the ComputeRaymarchingSphere shader

At this point, you should see that your scene and game views just turned completely black, like this:

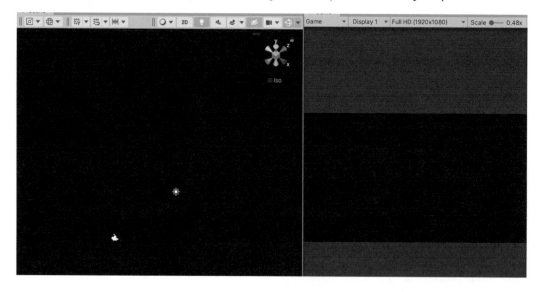

Figure 8.9 – Initial black render from the ComputeRaymarchingSphere in the scene and the game views

Of course, the point is to actually render something – so time to upgrade our compute shader!

We will do these improvements gradually in our compute shader and our `ComputeRaymarchingSphere` C# class, by going through the same stages as in the *Understanding the fundamentals of ray marching* section.

Defining the SDF

For starters, we need to set up our SDF to represent the shape's surface. We saw, in the *Understanding the fundamentals of ray marching* section, that in the case of a sphere, we can use the following formula:

```
float sdf = length(P - C) - r
```

This means that in our compute shader, we can define a new utility to easily sample our SDF for any given 3D point, p, like this:

```
float sdfSphere (float3 p, float3 c, float r) {
    return length(p - c) - r;
}
```

We can then use this function in another higher-level method, called `mapSceneSdf`. Although, here, our example assumes there is only one shape in the scene, it can be useful to have this second level of abstraction to differentiate between the shape and the scene, and optionally combine multiple shapes.

Anyway, in our case, this `mapSceneSdf` function will be extremely simple and just call the `sdfSphere` function with some arbitrary pre-determined position and radius values:

```
float mapSceneSdf (float3 p) {
    float sphere = sdfSphere(p, float3(0, 0, 1), 5);
    return sphere;
}
```

Now that we have "modeled" our virtual scene by inputting its exact SDF, we need to have our camera cast rays onto it to truly get a render.

Generating the rays

We know that the first part of the process of generating our rays for the render is to get all the ray origins and directions, for each of the pixels on screen.

Contrary to a usual material shader, compute shaders don't have UV coordinates. Instead, we saw in *Chapter 7* that we need to use the thread dispatch ID, which is a handy unique reference to compute some thread-specific data, such as the "position" of the compute cell. So, how can we use it to determine our pixels?

The trick is to get the size of our render image (which we can deduct from the size of our `Result` output buffer) to renormalize the thread ID along the X and Y coordinates, which will give us an equivalent of UV coordinates (with $(0, 0)$ in the bottom-left corner and $(1, 1)$ in the top-right corner).

To make our lives easier, we can then remap these values to the [-1, 1] range to reposition the (0, 0) point at the center of the screen – this is more akin to what a normal camera does, and it will help us when we get to actually specifying shape locations by hand in the next subsection, *Upgrading our procedural generation logic to handle a multi-shape render*.

We will do all of this in our `CSMain` function:

```
[numthreads(8,8,1)]
void CSMain (uint3 id : SV_DispatchThreadID) {
    // transform pixel to [-1,1] range
    uint width, height;
    Result.GetDimensions(width, height);
    float2 uv = float2(id.xy / float2(width, height) *
        2 - 1);

    Result[id.xy] = float4(0, 0, 0, 1);
}
```

The next step is to get our ray origin – we know that this should be our camera position in world space coordinates, so we can compute it like this:

```
float4x4 CameraToWorld;

[numthreads(8,8,1)]
void CSMain (uint3 id : SV_DispatchThreadID) {
    // transform pixel to [-1,1] range...

    // create ray origin from camera pos in world space
    float3 rayOrigin = mul(CameraToWorld, float4(0, 0, 0,
        1)).xyz;

    Result[id.xy] = float4(0, 0, 0, 1);
}
```

Here, I am using the `CameraToWorld` matrix to convert my vector from camera space to world space. This matrix will be stored as a `float4x4` GPU data buffer and passed to the shader from our CPU logic, where we will be able to retrieve it using the C# `Camera` API.

Finally, we have to get the ray direction. The process is slightly more complex than for the origin because, for now, we only have our UV equivalent in screen space. So, we need to first compute this direction in screen space and then convert it to world space, via the camera space.

Again, we can do this using Unity conversion matrices, namely the `CameraInverseProjection` matrix (to get from screen to camera space) and, as before, the `CameraToWorld` matrix (to get from camera to world space).

And, of course, don't forget that a direction should be normalized! So, in the end, this all boils down to the following calculations:

```
float4x4 CameraToWorld;
float4x4 CameraInverseProjection;

[numthreads(8,8,1)]
void CSMain (uint3 id : SV_DispatchThreadID) {
    // transform pixel to [-1,1] range...
    // create ray origin from camera pos in world space...

    // create ray direction from UVs
    //   (converted to: screen -> camera -> world space)
    float3 rayDirection = mul(
        CameraInverseProjection, float4(uv, 0, 1)).xyz;
    rayDirection = mul(CameraToWorld, float4(rayDirection,
        0)).xyz;
    rayDirection = normalize(rayDirection);

    Result[id.xy] = float4(0, 0, 0, 1);
}
```

OK, we now have our ray origins and directions for each pixel in the render. The next step is to actually march along those to compute the right color for our pixel.

Marching along the rays

For the marching process, we will make another dedicated function in our compute shader, `raymarch`, to call from our `CSMain` to fill in the `Result` buffer:

```
float3 raymarch(float3 rayOrigin, float3 rayDirection) {
    return float3(0, 0, 0);
}

[numthreads(8,8,1)]
void CSMain (uint3 id : SV_DispatchThreadID) {

    Result[id.xy] = float4(raymarch(rayOrigin,
        rayDirection), 1);
}
```

This `raymarch` function will be the heart of our render logic, where we evaluate each sample point and call our SDF to gradually determine the right color for this pixel, as described in *Figure 8.6*. By default, the function will just return a black color: this determines the background color for our render, for the pixels where the surface wasn't hit.

To actually march through the ray, let's implement a `while` loop that runs until we reach the maximum trace distance and accumulates the traveled distance at each iteration:

```
static const float MINIMUM_HIT_DISTANCE = 0.001f;
static const float MAXIMUM_TRACE_DISTANCE = 1000.0f;

float3 raymarch(float3 rayOrigin, float3 rayDirection) {
    float totalDistanceTraveled = 0;
    while (totalDistanceTraveled < MAXIMUM_TRACE_DISTANCE)
    {

        totalDistanceTraveled += dist;
    }
    return float3(0, 0, 0);
}
```

In this snippet, I've used `static const` variables to store some global arbitrary constants: `MINIMUM_HIT_DISTANCE` and `MAXIMUM_TRACE_DISTANCE`.

`MINIMUM_HIT_DISTANCE` will be the threshold for a hit – if our SDF is below this value, then we will consider that we have found the surface and we should stop there. So, we will simply compute the color for our pixel based on our current position, and exit the raymarch process for this ray.

`MAXIMUM_TRACE_DISTANCE` will be our stop limit for the raymarching: if we get to this value, then we will consider the scene surface is not in front of the camera at this pixel, and we should therefore return the background color.

Our sampling position is easy to calculate from the ray origin and the current traveled distance, therefore we can get the SDF value at each iteration like this:

```
float3 raymarch(float3 rayOrigin, float3 rayDirection) {
    float totalDistanceTraveled = 0;
    while (totalDistanceTraveled < MAXIMUM_TRACE_DISTANCE)
    {
        float3 currentPosition = rayOrigin +
            totalDistanceTraveled * rayDirection;
        float dist = mapSceneSdf(currentPosition);
        totalDistanceTraveled += dist;
    }
    return float3(0, 0, 0);
}
```

Now, we can check our `dist` against `MINIMUM_HIT_DISTANCE` to know whether we hit the surface – and in that case, we will just return the surface color as is:

```
float3 SurfaceColor;
float3 raymarch(float3 rayOrigin, float3 rayDirection) {
```

```
    float totalDistanceTraveled = 0;
    while (totalDistanceTraveled < MAXIMUM_TRACE_DISTANCE)
    {
        float3 currentPosition = rayOrigin +
            totalDistanceTraveled * rayDirection;
        float dist = mapSceneSdf(currentPosition);

        if (dist <= MINIMUM_HIT_DISTANCE) {
            return SurfaceColor;
        }

        totalDistanceTraveled += dist;
    }
    return float3(0, 0, 0);
}
```

Again, we can use a data buffer to input the surface color via our C# class and expose this information to the users in the editor – this is why I am using a `SurfaceColor` property here: we will fill the value for this color option in the `ComputeRaymarchingSphere` script, thanks to an input in the **Inspector**.

Because, indeed, to really render our scene using ray marching, we also have to work on our C# script.

Updating our C# class

At this point, our `RaymarchingSphere.compute` shader is already able to give us some pixel colors and compute an image. However, we have to call this `RaymarchingSphere.compute` shader properly from the CPU side, and in particular, we need to pass it all the required variables and buffers in our `ComputeRaymarchingSphere` C# class.

In a nutshell, the point will be to use the `Render` method in this C# script to extend the logic from the parent `URPComputeAsset` abstract class and compute some additional information. We will then store all this data in the `CommandBuffer` instance we are given so that `URPComputeFeature` can retrieve it later on and use it as the current context during the compute shader dispatch.

Here is the updated version of our `ComputeRaymarchingSphere` class:

```
public class ComputeRaymarchingSphere : URPComputeAsset {
    public Color surfaceColor = Color.white;

    public override void Render(
    CommandBuffer commandBuffer,
    int kernelHandle) {
        Camera camera = Camera.main;
```

```
commandBuffer.SetComputeMatrixParam(shader,
    "CameraToWorld", camera.cameraToWorldMatrix);
commandBuffer.SetComputeMatrixParam(shader,
    "CameraInverseProjection",
        camera.projectionMatrix.inverse);

commandBuffer.SetComputeVectorParam(shader,
    "SurfaceColor",
        new Vector3(surfaceColor.r, surfaceColor.g,
            surfaceColor.b));
    }
}
```

As you can see, my script contains a public variable for the surface color that can be set easily in the **Inspector**, and it then does a series of set operations on the `CommandBuffer` instance during the `Render` process to assign the required parameters. More specifically, we want to grab our current main camera and extract from it the two space conversion matrices, `CameraToWorld` and `CameraInverseProjection`, and then we want to pass in the r, g, and b components of the `surfaceColor` variable.

If we come back to the Unity editor, we now see two things:

- First of all, there is a large disc in the middle of our game view.

- Secondly, if we select our `ComputeRaymarchingSphere` ScriptableObject asset, its **Inspector** shows us an input for the color of the surface (see *Figure 8.10*). As we change this value, the color of the disc changes accordingly: our compute shader context is properly populated by the `Render` logic of our C# class!

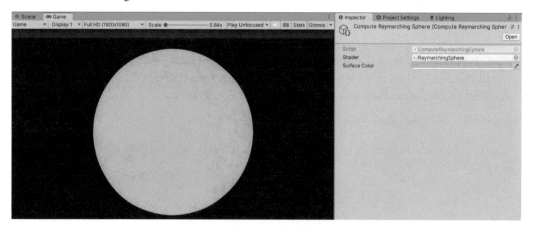

Figure 8.10 – Render of a single unlit yellow sphere using ray marching

But this is obviously incomplete because for the moment, our ray marching algorithm doesn't compute any shading – although we said in the *Understanding the fundamentals of ray marching* section that this was invaluable to creating interesting renders.

Time to add this logic to our compute shader and our C# wrapper, so that this procedural scene takes into account a virtual directional light and determines the shadows it creates on our sphere surface.

Adding shading

To integrate shading in our ray marching render process, we need to first add the approximation of our surface normal. To do this, we have to compute the gradient of our SDF by calculating our SDF at slightly offsetted points and getting the difference between those values.

So, let's create a new function in our compute shader, `estimateNormal`, as well as a new constant called `EPSILON`, for the small offset to apply:

```
static const float EPSILON = 0.001f;

float3 estimateNormal(float3 p) {
    float gradX = mapSceneSdf(float3(p.x + EPSILON, p.y,
        p.z)) - mapSceneSdf(float3(p.x - EPSILON, p.y,
            p.z));
    float gradY = mapSceneSdf(float3(p.x, p.y + EPSILON,
        p.z)) - mapSceneSdf(float3(p.x, p.y - EPSILON,
            p.z));
    float gradZ = mapSceneSdf(float3(p.x, p.y, p.z +
        EPSILON)) - mapSceneSdf(float3(p.x, p.y, p.z -
            EPSILON));
    return normalize(float3(gradX, gradY, gradZ));
}
```

Now, if we call this function in our `raymarch` process, we will be able to evaluate the normal of the surface at this specific sampling point. But, to compute what the shadows should look like (considering a simple Lambert lighting scheme), we will also need to have a light in our procedural scene.

To implement this, let's add a new parameter to our shader, `DirectionalLight`, which is a `float4` variable that packs together all the required data about our light source – its direction as the first three components, and its intensity as the last component:

```
float4 DirectionalLight;
```

We should, of course, pass this information to our shader from the C# side, by declaring some other variables in our `ComputeRaymarchingSphere` class and updating its `Render` function:

```
public class ComputeRaymarchingSphere : URPComputeAsset {
    // ...
    public Vector3 lightRotation = new Vector3(30, 25, 0);
    [Range(0, 4)] public float lightIntensity = 1;

    public override void Render(CommandBuffer commandBuffer,
    int kernelHandle) {
        // ...
        Vector3 lightDirection = Quaternion.Euler(
            lightRotation) * Vector3.forward;
        commandBuffer.SetComputeVectorParam(shader,
            "DirectionalLight", new Vector4(lightDirection.x,
                lightDirection.y, lightDirection.z,
                    lightIntensity));
    }
}
```

Now, in our `raymarch` function, we can calculate the dot product between our surface normal estimate and the direction to the light source, just like we did in *Chapter 1*. Remember, however, that the light direction has to go from the surface to the light, therefore we will need to negate our `DirectionalLight` direction components. Finally, we'll just have to multiply our diffuse intensity by the surface color and the light color, and this will give us our final lit pixel color:

```
float3 raymarch(float3 rayOrigin, float3 rayDirection) {
    float totalDistanceTraveled = 0;
    while (totalDistanceTraveled < MAXIMUM_TRACE_DISTANCE)
    {
        // ...
        if (dist <= MINIMUM_HIT_DISTANCE) {
            float3 normal = estimateNormal(
                currentPosition);
            float diffuseIntensity = saturate(dot(normal, -
                DirectionalLight.xyz)) * DirectionalLight.w;
            return SurfaceColor * diffuseIntensity;
        }
        // ...
    }
    return float3(0, 0, 0);
}
```

If we come back to the Unity editor, it will instantly recompile our shader and show us the final result of our ray marching render, with the right lighting – here is a screenshot of the output in the game view for the same yellow sphere as in *Figure 8.10*:

Figure 8.11 – Render of a single yellow sphere with Lambert-like shading using ray marching

And here we are: we have successfully implemented a basic ray marching logic that allows us to render a sphere... just using pure math! This scene is generated entirely procedurally, from an SDF, and yet we get a nicely lit scene with our shape in the middle and some easy-to-tweak parameters.

But this scene is obviously quite simple – it would have been way easier to just model it by hand and put our camera in front of the sphere mesh. So, now, let's see how procedural generation can really shine by upgrading this simple ray marching process to one that can draw multiple random shapes of various colors.

Upgrading our procedural generation logic to handle a multi-shape render

OK – to go one step further, we will create a second compute shader to render several shapes at the same time: `RaymarchingShapes.compute`. In this, more advanced, version, we will extend our ray marching render process to handle four types of shapes – spheres, cubes, toruses, and prisms – and combine multiple objects to create the final scene SDF.

`RaymarchingShapes.compute` will initially contain the same code as `RaymarchingSphere.compute`; we will then improve it little by little to integrate the multi-shape rendering.

The first thing we need to do is define some new SDFs in our shader to accommodate our new shapes. We can draw inspiration from Inigo Quilez's great list of common SDFs (available at https:// iquilezles.org/articles/distfunctions/) and create three new functions for the cube, torus, and prism shapes, like this:

```
float sdfCube(float3 p, float3 center, float3 size) {
    float3 o = abs(p - center) - size;
    float ud = length(max(o,0));
    float n = max(max(min(o.x, 0), min(o.y, 0)), min(o.z,
        0));
    return ud + n;
}

float sdfTorus(float3 p, float3 center, float r1, float r2) {
    float2 q = float2(length((p - center).xz) - r1, p.y -
        center.y);
    return length(q) - r2;
}

float sdfPrism(float3 p, float3 center, float2 h) {
    float3 q = abs(p - center);
    return max(q.z - h.y, max(q.x * 0.866025 + p.y * 0.5, -
        p.y) - h.x * 0.5);
}
```

Now, to know what shape we are supposed to render at which position, we are going to create a new data structure to represent a shape instance in our scene, naturally called Shape. This structure will contain four fields to store the type of shape (as an integer), the position of the object in the scene, the color of its surface, and its scale.

Of course, we also have to declare a StructuredBuffer variable containing elements of this Shape type, and we can keep track of the total number of shapes in the scene to automate the render step later on (this information will be passed from the C# logic):

```
struct Shape {
    int shapeType;
    float4 color;
    float3 position;
    float3 size;
};
StructuredBuffer<Shape> Shapes;
int NShapes;
```

By using the `shapeType` field of our `Shape` structure, we can easily choose which SDF to call for a given shape – I'll wrap this switch logic in a `sdfShape` function:

```
float sdfShape(Shape shape, float3 p) {
    if (shape.shapeType == 0) {
        return sdfSphere(p, shape.position, shape.size.x);
    }
    else if (shape.shapeType == 1) {
        return sdfCube(p, shape.position, shape.size);
    }
    else if (shape.shapeType == 2) {
        return sdfTorus(p, shape.position, shape.size.x,
            shape.size.y);
    }
    else if (shape.shapeType == 3) {
        return sdfPrism(p, shape.position, shape.size);
    }
    return MAXIMUM_TRACE_DISTANCE;
}
```

Now, we just need to update our `mapSceneSdf` process to have it take into account all the shapes in our procedural scene and combine the results properly. Basically, instead of just sampling the SDF for one sphere with a pre-determined position and radius, we are going to do the following:

1. First, we will loop through all of our shapes and use the `sdfShape` method we just defined to get the proper SDF (based on the shape's type):

    ```
    float4 mapSceneSdf(float3 p) {
        for (int i = 0; i < NShapes; i ++) {
            Shape shape = Shapes[i];
            float shapeDist = sdfShape(shape, p);
        }
        return float4(0, 0, 0, MAXIMUM_TRACE_DISTANCE);
    }
    ```

    You see that we pass in the whole `Shape` structure instance so that our SDF can position and size it properly.

    This snippet also highlights something important: in this new shader, our `mapSceneSdf` function now returns `float4` instead of a simple `float`. That's because since each shape can have a different color, we have to store this extra data when we sample the SDF at a given point, to deduce what the scene color should be for our pixel from the surface we hit. Therefore, our output will be `float4` with the color of the surface as the first three components, and the distance to the surface as the last component.

But for now, our `mapSceneSdf` always returns a black color and a maximum distance, because we are not really considering our SDF sampling results.

2. To actually use our shape's SDF sampling, we are going to store the smallest distance and associated surface color computed up until now in variables initialized outside the loop, and then whenever we get our results for a new shape, we will check whether the distance is smaller and, in that case, replace our variables.

    This will effectively give us a basic blend mode where the closest shapes are drawn on top of the other ones, which will properly simulate the depth system we would have in a classical render (here, we consider the simple case where everything is opaque, and ignore transparency).

    Our final `mapSceneSdf` logic will therefore look like this:

    ```
    float4 mapSceneSdf(float3 p) {
        float globalDist = MAXIMUM_TRACE_DISTANCE;
        float3 globalColor = float3(0, 0, 0);
        for (int i = 0; i < NShapes; i ++) {
            Shape shape = Shapes[i];
            float shapeDist = sdfShape(shape, p);
            float3 shapeColor = shape.color.xyz;



            if (shapeDist < globalDist) {
                globalDist = shapeDist;
                globalColor = shapeColor;
            }
        }
        return float4(globalColor, globalDist);
    }
    ```

3. Last but not least, we will need to update our `raymarch` function to have it re-extract the distance to the scene and the color of the surface for this pixel after its call to `mapSceneSdf`. The x, y, and z components will give us the surface color, and the w component will be the equivalent of the `dist` variable we had in the *Rendering a sphere with ray marching* section:

    ```
    float3 raymarch(float3 rayOrigin, float3 rayDirection) {
        float totalDistanceTraveled = 0;
        while (totalDistanceTraveled <
        MAXIMUM_TRACE_DISTANCE) {
            float3 currentPosition = rayOrigin +
                totalDistanceTraveled * rayDirection;
            float4 sceneSdf = mapSceneSdf(
                currentPosition);
            float dist = sceneSdf.w;
            if (dist <= MINIMUM_HIT_DISTANCE) {
    ```

```
        float3 normal = estimateNormal(
            currentPosition);
        float diffuseIntensity = saturate(dot(
            normal, -DirectionalLight.xyz)) *
                DirectionalLight.w;
        float3 surfaceColor = sceneSdf.xyz;
        return surfaceColor * diffuseIntensity;
    }
    totalDistanceTraveled += dist;
}
return float3(0, 0, 0);
}
```

4. In order to fill in all the variables of our compute shader at the moment of the dispatch, we will also require a C# wrapper `URPComputeAsset`-derived class, `ComputeRaymarchingShapes. cs`. This script will be similar to `ComputeRaymarchingSphere.cs`, except that it will use the `Setup` and `Cleanup` hooks to initialize and release the shapes buffer.

I won't go into too much detail about this `ComputeRaymarchingShapes.cs` file here, as it is mostly common C# logic for creating random instances of our `Shape` data structure; you can find the entire file in the GitHub repository of this book (`https://github.com/ PacktPublishing/Become-a-Unity-Shaders-Guru`).

The only relevant part to our discussion is the `Render` function, where we use a compute buffer to transfer our list of shapes to the shader, as explained in *Chapter 7*. We first compute the size of one instance of our `Shape` structure, then create a buffer of the right size for our entire list of shapes, and finally set its data to send it over to the GPU:

```
public override void Render(CommandBuffer commandBuffer, int
kernelHandle) {
    Cleanup();
    if (_shapes.Count == 0) return;

    Camera camera = Camera.main;

    int sizeofShape = sizeof(int) + sizeof(float) * (4 +
        3 + 3);
    _shapesBuffer = new ComputeBuffer(_shapes.Count,
        sizeofShape);
    _shapesBuffer.SetData(_shapes);
    commandBuffer.SetComputeBufferParam(shader, 0,
        "Shapes", _shapesBuffer);
    commandBuffer.SetComputeIntParam(shader, "NShapes",
        _shapes.Count);
```

```
commandBuffer.SetComputeMatrixParam(shader,
  "CameraToWorld", camera.cameraToWorldMatrix);
commandBuffer.SetComputeMatrixParam(shader,
  "CameraInverseProjection",
    camera.projectionMatrix.inverse);

Vector3 lightDirection = Quaternion.Euler(
  lightRotation) * Vector3.forward;
commandBuffer.SetComputeVectorParam(shader,
  "DirectionalLight", new Vector4(
    lightDirection.x, lightDirection.y,
      lightDirection.z, lightIntensity));
}
```

With all this in place, we can now switch our previous ComputeRaymarchingSphere ScriptableObject to a new ComputeRaymarchingShapes one (based on our ComputeRaymarchingShapes class) in the URP settings of our project, and we will get a new render with several shapes at the same time in the scene (I've also added a ground plane using my cube SDF to help better visualize the setup):

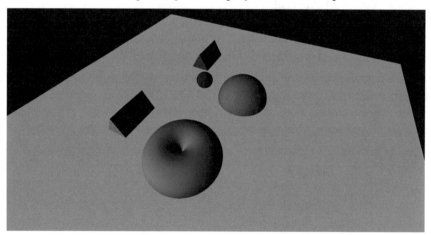

Figure 8.12 – Render of several random shapes with Lambert-like shading using ray marching

This is where we start to see the power of ray marching and procedural scene generation: simply by changing one random seed, we can instantly create a brand-new visual in the blink of an eye that follows our set of rules. So, we can make an infinite number of scenes, with no asset modeling or material preparation required!

Still, you might think that this is a bit of a dull experiment that just produces a few random geometric shapes. Sure, the processing speed is impressive, thanks to our off-loading of the computations to the GPU; but how could one use that for an actual game?

Well, it is time to take yet another step into the world of ray marching and discover a real-life application of this technique to a common video game problem: the rendering of clouds.

Studying a common use case – the rendering of volumetric clouds

So far, we have seen how ray marching allows us to create arbitrarily complex shapes based on SDFs and 3D surfaces. This makes it easy to create procedural scenes with solid shapes, like the ones shown in *Figure 8.12*.

But ray marching can also be taken one step further, to actually render 3D volumes. For example, thanks to this technique, we can create fairly realistic clouds like these ones:

Figure 8.13 – Volumetric clouds rendered on the scene skybox using ray marching

So, our goal here will be to create a material shader for the skybox of the scene, to have it display volumetric clouds similar to the ones shown in *Figure 8.13*.

In the following sections, we are going to implement our shader step by step and discuss how we can adapt our ray marching principles to the case of volume rendering. Then, we will see how we can use mathematical noise to create interesting shapes for our clouds, and finally how to apply these ideas to an actual Unity skybox shader written in HLSL code.

Using ray marching for volumetric clouds

Up until now, in this chapter, we have discussed how, by creating multiple rays, walking through them, and sampling a given SDF, we can approximate the shape of a solid object by rendering its exterior surface with some basic shading.

However, this application of ray marching is quite limited: unless you are willing to dive into crazy SDFs and crank up your shading technique a notch (we can again refer to Inigo Quilez's incredible experiments, for example, the ones listed over here: `https://www.iquilezles.org/www/articles/terrainmarching/terrainmarching.htm`), you will soon get bored with these spheres and cubes.

In video games, ray marching is often applied to another interesting problem: the rendering of smoke or clouds, or in other words, objects that are in a volume but aren't a filled shape.

Typically, if you think about clouds, it is quite clear that the big difference between a child's drawing and reality is that, in real life, clouds aren't bounded precisely by a stroke line and all filled inside! They are an ensemble of micro-droplets that come together to look like a large mass with more or less dense areas:

Figure 8.14 – Photograph of clouds in the sky, for reference

These shifts in opacity, color, light transmittance, light absorption, or light scattering you see in *Figure 8.14* are what we instantly picture when we hear the word "cloud," and they are definitely what players would expect from a realistic game.

So, how can ray marching help us create this type of visual?

In short, our goal here will be to take samples inside the cloud and evaluate their distance from the top and bottom surface of the cloud from within, rather than taking samples in the empty space of the scene until we hit a surface from outside (see *Figure 8.15*).

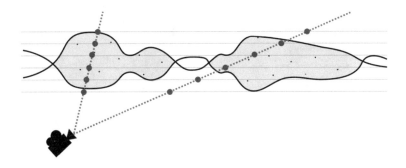

Figure 8.15 – Basic ray marching process for volumetric rendering

For each sample point inside the cloud, we will therefore be able to evaluate how opaque it is and by summing all those local opacities, we will get the final opacity for our skybox pixel.

So far, so good – but the next question we need to ask ourselves is: how are we going to determine these top and bottom surfaces? That is, how are we going to define the location and the density of our clouds? The answer is by picking a **mathematical noise** for our clouds.

Here, we are not talking about acoustics, but about functions that are used in computer graphics to generate procedural textures from a seed, some user-defined parameters, and a simple algorithm. These are the key to simulating controlled randomness. Typically, mathematical noise functions can create grayscale 2D images that look like this:

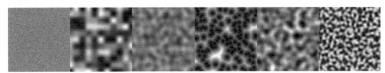

Figure 8.16 – Examples of 2D grayscale textures generated from various mathematical noise functions

In *Figure 8.16*, we see six common noise functions that are used in video game creation to generate textures procedurally: white noise, value noise, gradient noise, Worley noise, Perlin noise, and Simplex noise (from left to right).

Each noise has its own specific usage, and you should always consider which one (if any) is the best fit for your current situation. But, more generally speaking, the concept of mathematical noise can be used for many types of procedural content, from terrain heightmaps to object repartition, color blending, organic-like imperfections, or even stylized fluid visualization (such as a lava lamp or ink spots in water).

Oftentimes, it is also interesting to overlay multiple noise functions with slightly different parameters (and, in particular, different scales), to create more details and resolution in the final texture. For example, *Figure 8.17* shows the difference between a Perlin noise with a reference scale of 1, another Perlin noise with double the scale, and a third Perlin noise that mixes the two (from left to right):

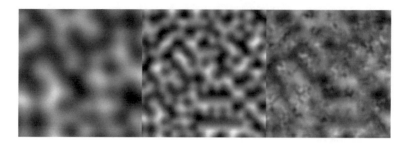

Figure 8.17 – Perlin noise functions with various scales (left and middle),
and a mix of multiple Perlin noise functions (right)

Alright, with this in mind, let's now see how we can use this knowledge to implement clouds in a Unity URP project, with the help of ray marching.

Creating clouds in Unity

Our goal here will be to create a common material shader for the skybox of the scene, to have it display volumetric clouds based on a mathematical noise like the ones shown in *Figure 8.13*.

The location and density of our clouds will be defined using a pre-computed Perlin noise – we will sample this 2D texture as is to get a heightmap of sorts for the top surface of the clouds, and then re-sample it in reverse to get the bottom surface of the clouds (as suggested in Matt Stark's experiment on the topic, available at https://matt.stark.scot/2019/02/27/volumetric-clouds.html).

We will create this shader in HLSL code, in a new shader file called RaymarchedSkybox.shader. For now, we will start simple and just make sure that we properly distinguish between the ground, the horizon, and the sky. To do this, we only have to get the view vector to our current pixel and check whether its y component is greater than, equal to, or less than 0. This will allow us to know easily whether this pixel is above, on, or below our line of sight. So, we will initialize our shader file with the following bits of code:

1. First, we'll have some properties for the color of the skybox and the amount of fog we want at the various altitudes:

```
Shader "Custom/RaymarchedSkybox" {
  Properties {
      _SkyColor("Sky Color", Color) = (0, 0, 0, 1)
      _GroundColor("Ground Color", Color) = (0, 0, 0, 1)
      _FogColor("Fog Color", Color) = (0, 0, 0, 1)
      _FogClouds("Fog Amount Clouds", Float) = 0.001
      _FogSky("Fog Amount Sky", Float) = 0.1
      _FogGround("Fog Amount Ground", Float) = 0.1
  }
}
```

2. Then, we will set up the `SubShader` tags, plus the culling and z-writing options, so it is rendered as a background and doesn't use culling or z-writing:

```
Shader "Custom/RaymarchedSkybox" {
  ...
  SubShader {
    Tags {
        "Queue" = "Background"
        "RenderType" = "Background"
        "PreviewType" = "Skybox" }
      Cull Off ZWrite Off
  }
}
```

3. The next step is, in the `HLSLINCLUDE` block, to include the URP `Core.hlsl` package, set up our parameters, and define the `appdata` and `v2f` data structures:

```
Shader "Custom/RaymarchedSkybox" {
  ...
  SubShader {
    ...
    HLSLINCLUDE
    #include "Packages/com.unity.render-pipelines
    .universal/ShaderLibrary/Core.hlsl"
    float4 _SkyColor;
    float4 _GroundColor;
    float4 _FogColor;
    float _FogClouds;
    float _FogSky;
    float _FogGround;

    struct appdata {
      float4 vertex : POSITION;
    };
    struct v2f {
      float4 vertex : SV_POSITION;
      float3 viewVector : TEXCOORD1;
    };
    ENDHLSL
  }
}
```

4. Finally, in the `HLSLPROGRAM` block, we will code up our `vertex` and `fragment` shader functions:

```
Shader "Custom/RaymarchedSkybox" {
  ...
  SubShader {
    ...
    Pass {
      HLSLPROGRAM
      #pragma vertex vert
      #pragma fragment frag
      v2f vert (appdata v) {}
      float4 frag (v2f i) : SV_Target {}
      ENDHLSL
    }
  }
}
```

The `vertex` function just needs to pass through the position of the vertex and the associated view vector, which is simply the position of the vertex in object space:

```
v2f vert (appdata v) {
  v2f o;
  o.vertex = TransformObjectToHClip(v.vertex);
  o.viewVector = v.vertex.xyz;
  return o;
}
```

The `fragment` function will use this view vector to determine whether the pixel is in the sky, at the horizon, or on the ground, and compute the right color:

```
float4 frag (v2f i) : SV_Target {
  float3 viewVector = i.viewVector;
  if (viewVector.y > 0) { // SKY
    viewVector = viewVector / viewVector.y;

    float cloudFog = 1 - (1 / (_FogClouds *
        length(viewVector) + 1));
    float4 col = float4(_FogColor.rgb * cloudFog,
        cloudFog);

    float skyFog = 1 - (1 / (_FogSky * length(
        viewVector) + 1));
    float4 totalSkyColor = lerp(_SkyColor, _FogColor,
        skyFog);
    col += (1 - col.a) * totalSkyColor;
```

```
    return col;
  }
  else if (viewVector.y < 0) { // GROUND
    viewVector = viewVector / viewVector.y;
    float groundFog = 1 - (1 / (_FogGround *
        length(viewVector) + 1));
    return lerp(_GroundColor, _FogColor, groundFog);
  }
  else { // HORIZON
      return _FogColor;
  }
}
```

The computation of the ground and horizon color is good as is, so we won't need to refine it any further; but, of course, we need to work on the sky part much more!

You'll notice, in these snippets, that to better blend the clouds with the actual sky background, and to properly handle the horizon delimitation, we also set up a basic fog system that allows us to lerp between our various colors depending on how dense the fog should be at the various altitudes.

If we create a new material asset from this shader and apply it to the skybox of our scene in the **Environment** tab within the **Lighting** panel, as shown in *Figure 8.18*, we will then be able to easily set up some colors for the ground, the horizon, and the sky of our scene.

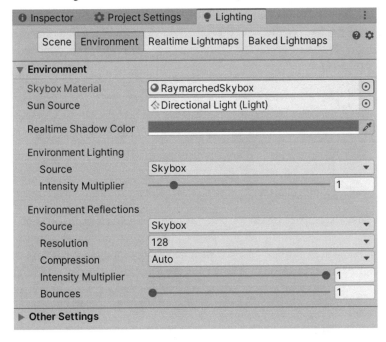

Figure 8.18 – Configuration of the scene's skybox material in the Lighting panel

For example, this screenshot shows what it looks like with a blue sky, gray ground, and light blue fog:

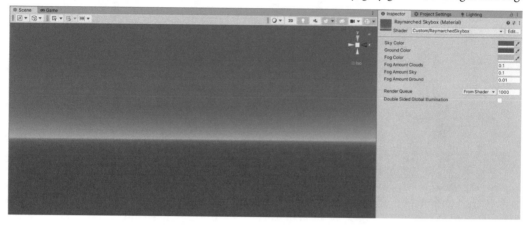

Figure 8.19 – Basic skybox shader with the separation of the ground, horizon, and sky altitudes

Let's now see how to actually add clouds to this blue sky. I won't detail all the properties' definitions and setup, but remember you can check out the entire code in the GitHub repository of the book (https://github.com/PacktPublishing/Become-a-Unity-Shaders-Guru). To create the clouds, we will proceed step by step, as follows:

1. First of all, we need to use our `viewVector` direction and the position of the camera to compute the position of the skybox pixel in world space. We will define the altitude of the clouds in the sky via a new float parameter called `_CloudHeight`, so here is our updated sky color calculation logic:

```
if (viewVector.y > 0) { // SKY
   viewVector = viewVector / viewVector.y;
   float3 viewerPosition = _WorldSpaceCameraPos;
   float3 position = viewerPosition + viewVector *
     (_CloudHeight - viewerPosition.y);
   ...
}
```

2. Then, we have to prepare two new values: `stepSize` and `stepOpacity`. These floats will correspond, respectively, to the length of a ray marching step and the opacity we will accumulate along our ray with each step. Those will depend on a constant integer, `SAMPLES`, and two new float parameters for our clouds, `_CloudThickness` and `_CloudOpacity`, as shown here:

```
if (viewVector.y > 0) { // SKY
   viewVector = viewVector / viewVector.y;
   float3 viewerPosition = _WorldSpaceCameraPos;
   float3 position = viewerPosition + viewVector *
```

```
    (_CloudHeight - viewerPosition.y);
  float3 stepSize = viewVector * _CloudThickness /
    SAMPLES;
  float stepOpacity = 1 - (1 / (_CloudOpacity *
    length(stepSize) + 1));
  ...
}
```

3. The next step is to do the actual ray marching. We will rely on a `for` loop with up to SAMPLES iterations, and we will accumulate small steps along our marching ray to walk through the cloud (remember *Figure 8.15*):

```
if (viewVector.y > 0) { // SKY
  viewVector = viewVector / viewVector.y;
  float3 viewerPosition = _WorldSpaceCameraPos;
  float3 position = viewerPosition + viewVector *
    (_CloudHeight - viewerPosition.y);
  float3 stepSize = viewVector * _CloudThickness /
    SAMPLES;
  float stepOpacity = 1 - (1 / (_CloudOpacity *
    length(stepSize) + 1));
  float cloudFog = 1 - (1 / (_FogClouds *
    length(viewVector) + 1));
  float4 col = float4(_FogColor.rgb * cloudFog,
    cloudFog);
  for (int i = 0; i < SAMPLES; i++) {
    position += stepSize;
  }
  ...
}
```

Note that this loop is inserted before the computation of the sky fog so that the clouds are included in the rendering before this final pass.

In each iteration, we will sample our cloud noise texture to get the top and bottom surface height for the cloud at this specific world position. For this, we will need a new `_CloudTex` property for the texture itself, as well as a `_CloudScale` vector for the overall scale of the cloud, to stretch the texture on the skybox. We will also declare some additional `_TopSurfaceScale` and `_BottomSurfaceScale` float parameters to better control the influence of the noise texture on the top and bottom surfaces of the cloud. So, here is our updated `for` loop with this new logic:

```
for (int i = 0; i < SAMPLES; i++) {
  position += stepSize;
```

```
    float2 uv = position.xz / _CloudScale.xy;
    float h = SAMPLE_TEXTURE2D(_CloudTex,
      sampler_CloudTex, uv).r;
    float cloudTopHeight = 1 - (h * _TopSurfaceScale);
    float cloudBottomHeight = h * _BottomSurfaceScale;
}
```

4. Then, we will check whether our sampling point is between these two bounds and, in that case, compute our distance to the nearest surface:

```
for (int i = 0; i < SAMPLES; i++) {
  ...
  float f = (position.y - _CloudHeight) /
    _CloudThickness;
  if (f > cloudBottomHeight && f < cloudTopHeight) {
    float dist = min(cloudTopHeight - f,
      f - cloudBottomHeight);
  }
}
```

With that new piece of information, we can easily deduce the local opacity of the cloud at this precise sampling point, and then the matching color increment for this ray (assuming for the moment that our clouds are just pure white):

```
for (int i = 0; i < SAMPLES; i++) {
  ...
  if (f > cloudBottomHeight && f < cloudTopHeight) {
    ...
    float localOpacity = saturate(
        dist / _CloudSoftness);
    float4 cloudColor = float4(1, 1, 1, 1);
    col += (1 - col.a) * stepOpacity * localOpacity *
      cloudColor;
  }
}
```

5. Finally, if we have our opacity value is close to 1, we will do an early exit of our ray marching process for this point and just set the color:

```
for (int i = 0; i < SAMPLES; i++) {
  ...
  if (f > cloudBottomHeight && f < cloudTopHeight) {
    ...
    if (col.a > 0.99) { // almost opaque:
                        stop marching
      col.rgb *= 1 / col.a;
```

```
        col.a = 1;
        break;
      }
    }
  }
```

If we come back to the Unity editor and recompile the shader, we will see that there are now clouds in our sky (check out *Figure 8.20*)!

Figure 8.20 – Skybox shader with basic volumetric clouds, rendered using ray marching

> **Important note**
>
> When you import the cloud noise texture, don't forget to set its **Wrap Mode** import setting to **Repeat** instead of the default **Clamp**; otherwise, the skybox won't display properly!

6. A quick way to improve the rendering of our clouds and simulate light absorption is to artificially darken the bottom half using a gradient texture. In short, the idea here will be to replace our constant `cloudColor` variable with a varying one that goes from white at the top of the cloud to a light gray at the bottom.

    We will store this blending color ramp in a texture like this one:

Figure 8.21 – Color ramp texture for the cloud darkness lerping

7. And then, simply by adding a new _GradientTex parameter to reference this image and sampling the texture in our loop iteration logic based on our current altitude in the cloud, we will be able to get a more realistic effect:

```
for (int i = 0; i < SAMPLES; i++) {
    ...
    if (f > cloudBottomHeight && f < cloudTopHeight) {
        ...
        float4 cloudColor = SAMPLE_TEXTURE2D(
            _GradientTex, sampler_GradientTex,
                float2(1 - saturate(cloudTopHeight - f),
                    0));
        col += (1 - col.a) * stepOpacity * localOpacity *
            cloudColor;
        if (col.a > 0.99) { ... }
    }
}
```

This simple update gives us our final skybox shader, shown in *Figure 8.13*.

So, here we go: we now have a nice sky with some clouds here and there! Thanks to ray marching, we created some cool volume effects with various shifts in opacity and light transmittance, which make for quite a realistic render.

We could, of course, improve our skybox shader further by implementing some extra turbulence variations, or an animation feature for our clouds (to have them move slowly as time goes by). What's also interesting with this method is that we can very quickly switch out the pre-computed density texture for one using another type of noise, and instantly see how this affects the rendering of our clouds. The GitHub repository of the book contains a full version with these additional functionalities and some other cloud noise textures if you want to check it out.

> **Using seamless textures**
>
> It is important to note, however, that the textures you use for the cloud noise should be seamless. This means that when you paste several copies of your texture side by side, you should not see the border of each instance (there shouldn't be any visible seam). Otherwise, the skybox will contain some strange discontinuities wherever the texture is repeated to fill the space.

We now know a new advanced shading trick that allows us to use fairly quick-to-produce assets, and then automatically transform them into a real sky for our scene!

Summary

In this chapter, we explored the technique of ray marching and discovered how to apply it to the rendering of simple shapes or more advanced effects, such as clouds.

We first talked about the theory behind ray marching and focused on the importance of SDFs for defining arbitrarily complex surfaces.

Then, we saw how to implement a basic ray marching algorithm in Unity to render either a sphere or several random shapes. We also took this opportunity to reuse the compute shaders we introduced in *Chapter 7*, and we discussed how this technique allows us to create an infinity of procedural scenes quickly and easily.

Finally, we dived into a famous application of ray marching: the rendering of volumetrics such as clouds. We made our own skybox shader that creates a blue sky filled with clouds and used ray marching to give the clouds more volume. We then simulated light absorption and transmittance using color gradients and clever visual tricks.

This concludes our overview of advanced shading techniques for video games. In the upcoming chapters, we will take a step back and discuss another crucial topic for experienced technical artists: the optimization of your visuals.

In that chapter, we will discuss the important inner workings of Unity's shader compilation process. We will see how we can introduce conditional behaviors in our shaders using branching and variants and focus on a few interesting built-in macros that can help us with creating cross-platform projects.

Going further

If you're curious about ray marching and volumetric cloud rendering, here are a few interesting resources to check out or continue your journey with:

- *Coding Adventure: Compute Shaders*, S. Lague (2019): `https://www.youtube.com/watch?v=9RHGLZLUuwc`

- *Coding Adventure: Clouds*, S. Lague (2019): `https://www.youtube.com/watch?v=4QOcCGI6xOU`

- *Coding Adventure: Ray Marching*, S. Lague (2019): `https://www.youtube.com/watch?v=Cp5WWtMoeKg`

- *Writing a ray marcher in Unity*, The Art of Code (2019): `https://www.youtube.com/watch?v=S8AWd66hoCo`

- *Unity URP Tutorial - Volumetric Raymarching Cloud Shader*, dmeville (2022): `https://www.youtube.com/watch?v=0G8CVQZhMXw`

- *Volumetric Clouds in Unity + Time of Day lighting*, PuckLovesGames (2018): `https://www.youtube.com/watch?v=LLUUIAKFgWg`

Part 4:
Optimizing Your
Unity Shaders

So far in this book, we've learned the basics of making URP shaders, before leveling up to more advanced shader techniques to simulate geometry efficiently or even create an entire scene, using just mathematics and shader code. In this fourth part, we're going to talk about another crucial topic for technical artists, which is ensuring the best possible performance for your game.

In this part, we will cover the following chapters:

- *Chapter 9, Shader Compilation, Branching, and Variants*
- *Chapter 10, Optimizing Your Code, or Making Your Own Pipeline?*

Shader Compilation, Branching, and Variants

9

In the first half of this book, we discussed various shading techniques that can help you create interesting visual effects in your game projects. We saw how to use Unity's new URP pipeline and, in particular, its node-based shader editor – the Shader Graph.

Coding or branching up a shader to render a specific visual on screen is, of course, an essential skill for any technical artist, but there is something else that you should take into consideration if you want to master shaders: the art of optimization!

Indeed, knowing the inner workings of the tools you use is crucial to getting the most out of them, and this is especially the case with shaders, because of how compute-intensive they are. Moreover, nowadays, with the growing trend of mobile games, ensuring the best performance for your visuals is becoming paramount to your product actually being cross-platform.

So, in this chapter, we will highlight some of the key settings and tools Unity provides us with for optimizing our URP shaders by covering the following topics:

- Learning some Unity shader compilation tricks
- Taking advantage of shader branching and shader variants
- Exploring shader macros and platform-dependent compilation

Technical requirements

To familiarize yourself with the settings panels and tools presented here, you will need to have Unity installed, with a version from 2022 or later. For good measure, you should create either of the following:

- A project with the common 3D template, which you will then upgrade to use the URP or HDRP render pipelines (see the *Stepping up with the URP render pipeline* section of *Chapter 2*)

- A project with the new 3D URP or 3D HDRP template (see the *Stepping up with the URP render pipeline* section of *Chapter 2* for guidance on how to download and pick this template)

This chapter does not rely on any specific scripts or assets.

Learning some Unity shader compilation tricks

As a seasoned shader artist, you probably know that when it comes down to it, rendering is no piece of cake. If you've ever tried to make your own rendering system from scratch instead of relying on a game engine such as Unity and its pre-made rendering pipelines, then you know that writing shader code is just one step among many to actually display something on the screen. Out in the wild, you also have to worry about graphics backends, platform-specific compilation, cross-platform API compatibility, and much more!

And with the ever-growing variety of possible target devices, and in particular, the growing usage of mobiles and tablets for gamers, saying that you are going to produce a fully **cross-platform game** means you'll need to think about dozens of graphics APIs and backends that can be very different from each other.

Now, of course, this is where 3D and game engines shine: by abstracting away this low-level rendering process, they allow us to focus on the fun and creative part because they handle the grunt work for us. Still, it is worth discussing some of Unity's under-the-hood compilation tricks so that you really understand when and how your shader logic gets fed to the hardware.

So, in the upcoming sections, we will discuss Unity's caching system for shaders, how the engine defaults to asynchronous compilation and why this option should sometimes be disabled, and finally, point out a few notable caveats you should keep in mind when organizing your game projects with AssetBundles.

Understanding Unity's shader caching system

Have you already had to build a large Unity project with hundreds of assets, materials, and shaders – a project that targets multiple platforms, and contains complex rendering processes?

If yes, then you've probably already seen this type of terrible popup, telling you about shader setup… and that you should get up and get yourself a coffee because it's going to be a long wait:

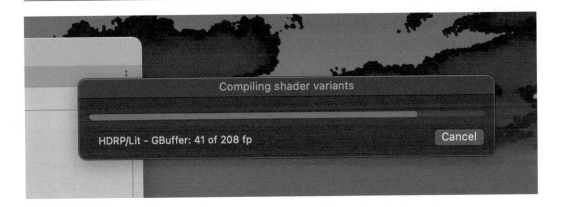

Figure 9.1 – Example of a Unity build popup at the stage of shader compilation

The reason Unity takes a while to build a project with a large number of shaders is that, as we've just said, shader code is just an abstraction of the real low-level deal, and this code, therefore, has to be compiled down for the hardware... for each possible hardware target!

So if you plan to distribute your game on Windows, Linux, macOS, Android, iOS, and some consoles, Unity will basically have to compile each of your shaders for each of these platforms. Of course, not every build requires every shader, and you don't build for all platforms all at once; but all in all, if your project contains many shaders, brace yourself because build times will be significant.

Now, if you pause for a second, you might have a question pop up in your head: since we can actually see the results of our shaders in real time in the editor, doesn't that mean Unity has already compiled the shaders and fed them to the computer's graphics card?

Well, yes – indeed, Unity *does* compile the shaders you see on screen. But it only compiles those ones to avoid interrupting your creative flow with such a long wait.

In a nutshell, the idea is that Unity relies on a cache system for the shaders so that it can keep track of which shaders it has already compiled, and which ones are brand new. Whenever you import (or create) a new shader asset in your project, the following happens:

1. The editor does some quick preprocessing on the shader.
2. Then, the editor checks its cache folder for a previously compiled identical shader code.
3. If it finds one, then the editor uses this compiled version to render the object in the viewport.
4. Else, it takes some time to compile the shader and store the compiled version in the cache folder for next time and finally, renders the object in the viewport.

> **Locating (and freeing) the shader cache folder**
>
> When it caches the compiled shader code, Unity stores it in the `Library/ShaderCache` folder of your project. This folder can thus grow quite a lot if you have many shaders that you modify often. If you need to free some space, you can delete this cache folder without any issues – it will simply require Unity to take a bit of time to recompile shaders the next time you use them (either in the editor or when you build the project).

This caching system allows Unity to stay reactive and re-update the viewport render quickly to not hinder your work pipeline. It is also useful at build time because the editor will be able to identify the shaders that have already been compiled and include them directly without losing time recomputing.

Unity's shader compilation process (called `UnityShaderCompiler`) can also be spawned multiple times to handle multiple shaders at the same time, in parallel; this is particularly useful at build time, to reduce the overall shader compilation time.

And to make this whole process even smoother, Unity has yet another trick up its sleeve: asynchronous shader compilation.

The magic of asynchronicity

Have you ever noticed that when you update a shader asset in your project, there's a little progress bar at the bottom of the screen that tells you it is being processed? And have you ever seen your scene objects suddenly turn cyan because you'd just saved a shader asset they used (like in *Figure 9.2*)?

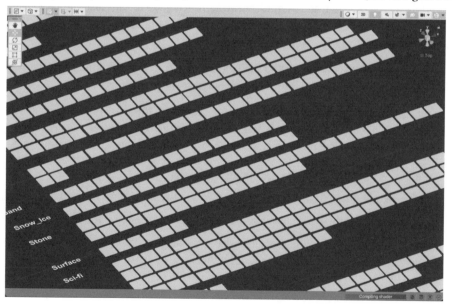

Figure 9.2 – Temporary render of a still-in-compilation shader using Unity's dummy cyan shader

The progress bar and the cyan color are two visual indicators that warn you that Unity's asynchronous shader compiler has kicked in and added your new shader code to the compile queue and that it is currently doing some heavy lifting behind the scenes to recompile the code and make the shader ready for render.

The great thing is that, because the compilation process is asynchronous, it doesn't block you in any way: you can still move around in the editor, select objects, and go about your work as you would normally. So, even if for some reason your shader takes a while to compile, there shouldn't be too much friction for your workflow.

However, this asynchronous behavior also means that until the shader has been compiled, the editor cannot display your updated visuals. This is why Unity automatically gives a temporary dummy shader to the objects that use this still-in-compilation shader – this temporary shader shows them as unlit cyan shapes, as shown in *Figure 9.2*.

This asynchronous compilation is enabled by default in Unity projects, and most of the time, it is best to keep this tool on – this will make it easier to change and refresh multiple shaders during the development phase.

There are, however, some cases where this asynchronous compilation can cause issues. Indeed, for some advanced rendering techniques, you'll want to generate your custom data only once at the beginning, and then reuse it for all the other frames; if asynchronous compilation happens during this initial generation step, then your data might be incomplete or corrupted.

So, of course, Unity allows you to opt out of using asynchronous shader compilation in order to avoid this problem. You can do so in different places, depending on the level of granularity you want:

- To completely disable asynchronous shader compilation in the whole project, you need to change your project's settings:

    I.   Go to the **Edit | Project Settings** panel.

    II.   Switch to the **Editor** settings in the left column.

    III. Scroll to the bottom and find the **Shader Compilation** section, then uncheck the **Asynchronous Shader Compilation** option (see *Figure 9.3*):

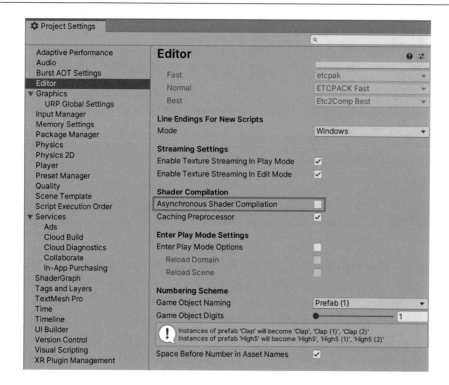

Figure 9.3 – Asynchronous Shader Compilation option in the project's Editor settings panel

- To disable asynchronous compilation temporarily for specific rendering calls, you can use the `ShaderUtil` C# API to turn this option on or off at runtime.

Typically, if you are submitting some custom rendering process using `CommandBuffer` (as we saw in *Chapter 7*), you can insert calls to the `ShaderUtil.SetAsyncCompilation` and `ShaderUtil.RestoreAsyncCompilation` functions to enable or disable this feature, like this:

```
// Create the CommandBuffer
CommandBuffer cmd = new CommandBuffer();
// Disable async compilation for subsequent commands
ShaderUtil.SetAsyncCompilation(cmd, false);
// Rendering commands that DON'T use the placeholder shader
cmd.DrawMesh(...);
// Restore the old state
ShaderUtil.RestoreAsyncCompilation(cmd);
```

Note that you can use this technique to enable asynchronous shader compilation in your own custom C# editor tools – because, by default, this built-in tool is only active for the **Scene** and **Game** views, not your additional custom docks and panels.

- Finally, you can disable asynchronous compilation for a specific shader to force the editor to always compile it synchronously. This can be particularly useful if this shader generates some initial data that is reused later on.

  To do this, you just need to add the following #pragma statement inside your shader code:

  ```
  #pragma editor_sync_compilation
  ```

  We already had a quick look at shader #pragmas in *Chapter 4*, but don't worry – we are going to explore them in more detail in the rest of this chapter!

Monitoring asynchronous shader compilation

Suppose that you are using advanced rendering, as described earlier in this chapter, and that your logic relies on generating data at the start and then reusing it for later frames, as described before. Then, another solution is to keep asynchronous shader compilation enabled but check when it is done to potentially remove the invalid data and regenerate correct values. For this, you can once again use the ShaderUtil C# API and, more precisely, its IsPassCompiled function or its anythingCompiling flag.

To sum up, Unity's asynchronous shader compilation tool is great because it speeds up the workflow of most technical artists. But if you ever dive into more complex rendering, and if you start to pre-compute or pre-generate data for upcoming frames, you might need to keep an eye out for data pollution and be ready to tune the magic down a little.

To be honest, this is quite the edge case. Playing around with this asynchronous compilation option is not required in the vast majority of Unity projects, and it is mostly something you should have in the back of your mind if you ever encounter strange rendering data initialization issues.

Another important risky optimization point that is way more frequent, however, is the usage of AssetBundles… and the few caveats it comes with for materials and shaders!

Handling AssetBundles

We know now that Unity's shader compilation system is well-thought-out and pretty optimized. It allows us to try out numerous shader variants on-the-fly in real time in the editor, and yet not be bogged down by compilation time, thanks to caching and asynchronous processes. And even though large projects with many shaders will take a while to build, the engine is doing its best to speed this up by doing parallel processing. Moreover, if your project has some special requirements because of advanced rendering logic, Unity lets you tweak the asynchronous compilation settings quite a lot to avoid any data corruption issues.

This is all nice and sweet but, as a technical artist, there are still a few areas where you have to be careful and understand Unity's secrets to use it to its full potential. And one of the notable gotchas when optimizing your shader and materials is the organization of your resource files, especially when your project relies on asset bundling.

What exactly are AssetBundles?

When you work on prototypes and small projects, you usually don't care that much about how your assets are organized in the project's folder. The point is to try things out, study new technologies, or perhaps ship a basic product that won't come under too much scrutiny. So, you may put all these 3D models, textures, sprites, materials, sound effects, animations, or even custom data objects somewhere in your project's hierarchy without too much concern.

On the other hand, when you embark on bigger projects and start using Unity for professional endeavors, you gradually discover that sorting all these objects is crucial to planning ahead and building a good game.

Over the years, Unity has provided us with more and more features to handle our assets, and we are no longer at the age where using the special `Resources` folder is the only way to pack assets in your game build. The new Addressables system, for example, allows us to design new asset workflows that are easier on both the artists and the programmers, and help with cross-platform distribution by better scoping and optimizing the data of your game.

At the heart of this new system are the **AssetBundles** – these archive files are basically a group of non-code assets that are packed together as a data folder. This data is usually compressed to reduce the required amount of storage, it is platform-specific, and it is quick to load from memory.

AssetBundles are therefore a powerful tool and an efficient way to distribute your game's content on a variety of platforms – in particular, because they allow you to start your game off with just a minimal amount of content, and then download more assets in the background to avoid long initial loading times on mobiles (which can lead to players' disinterest). The whole point of AssetBundles is thus to cut down your game resources into logical units of content so that you can access only what is required when it is required.

Of course, this is easier said than done!

Deciding on what should be packaged together can be difficult. You might choose to group your assets based on the part of the project they belong to (which is perfect for downloadable content and extensions), or based on the type of file they are (typically if you have some settings that are shared between multiple platforms), or even based on when those files are loaded by your game. Ideally, you should probably mix all those types of bundling in your project to get the best fit for each scenario.

But when working with materials and shaders, there is something you need to be very cautious about – the duplication of your assets, and the breaking of your draw call batching.

Using AssetBundles properly for shaders

One of the big advantages of AssetBundles is that they handle resource linking quite well – you can easily reference another asset, even if it is in another bundle, and construct a system of dependencies for your project data.

For example, a material in one bundle can reference a texture in another bundle. This can be interesting if you split your assets based on the file type, or based on the moment they are loaded, and this texture has to be reused several times.

But these dependencies do have an important limitation regarding our current topic: if a material references a shader that is not inside an AssetBundle, then the material will need to copy the shader to its own bundle in order to compile and use it. And even worse – if materials in multiple AssetBundles reference this external shader resource, then the shader will be duplicated in each AssetBundle!

Figure 9.4 shows a schematic representation of the issue:

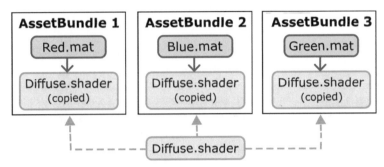

Figure 9.4 – Representation of the external shader duplication issue with AssetBundles

This obviously means that the shaders in your bundles will require more memory and storage space than expected, and if you are targeting mobile platforms (where storage is usually the limiting factor), it might hurt your distribution process quite a lot.

Also, because we are not referencing a single asset but rather creating redundant versions of it, the materials in each bundle effectively use a unique shader instance each time – although it contains the exact same code. Therefore, Unity cannot batch together the rendering of the meshes that use these materials because it has to consider every material as a different type of render. Your game thus cannot perform **draw call batching** and you will lose in performance.

To solve this issue, the easiest solution is actually to just put the external shader in its own AssetBundle. By wrapping it like this, you allow Unity to fall back on the dependency mechanism we talked about, and your materials will be able to directly access the shader without copying it locally to their own bundles.

This improved setup is illustrated in *Figure 9.5*:

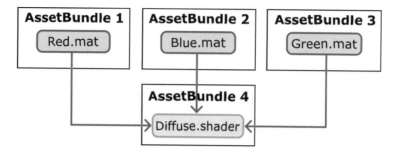

Figure 9.5 – Representation of an improved shader dependency with an additional AssetBundle

Typically, a common technique is to create an AssetBundle with all the shaders for your project to allow materials in the rest of the project to pick and choose what they need from this global data source. However, because AssetBundles cannot be partially unloaded, this will keep all of the shaders you ever required in memory, even if they are no longer in use. That's why, sometimes, it can be better to split your shaders into logical group units, such as a "nature" AssetBundle and a "city" AssetBundle.

Properly organizing your project files is therefore more than a good practice to please your team leads; grouping your assets the wrong way can actually impact the performance of your game, both in terms of storage and speed. AssetBundles are an extremely powerful tool that should definitely be considered for large Unity projects, but with great power comes great responsibility... and it is therefore your duty to build these bundles carefully, especially when manipulating shaders.

With that being said, compilation options and file organization aren't a silver bullet, obviously, and there are also essential tricks to keep in mind when actually writing your shaders to optimize them properly. We will see some shader programming tips in *Chapter 10*, but for now, let's discuss a fundamental tool for making cross-platform shaders – shader branching.

Taking advantage of shader branching and shader variants

When you first started your journey in the world of shaders and you took your first steps writing vertex and fragment functions, life was easy: you wrote a single piece of code that always executed the same (see the examples shown in the *Appendix: Some Quick Refreshers on Shaders in Unity*, or in *Chapter 1*).

But now that you are getting into more advanced rendering schemes, you might want to introduce some **conditional behavior** into your shader code so that it executes differently under different circumstances – for example, because of one of the following reasons:

- You want to distinguish between two target platforms and their respective graphics backends

- You don't want to execute expensive code such as vertex inputs or large loops

- You want your shader to sample a different texture depending on some instance-specific data

For all those cases, you might need to add some **branching** logic to your code.

In Unity, you can use several techniques to introduce these conditionals: static branching, dynamic branching, and shader variants. In the next sections, we are going to examine each and see their benefits and their downsides.

Using static branching – fast but restrictive

Static branching is a way to create different versions of your shader code based on some project-wide variables or platform-specific constants. These versions are computed at compile time, which means that when the compiler takes in your shader code and creates the compiled version, it will exclude all unused branches and only keep the contents of the chosen code paths.

The biggest advantage of shader static branching is that it doesn't have any negative impact on your game's performance. Since everything is resolved at compile time, the shader will be fully formed and determined at runtime, and Unity won't waste any time picking between code paths at this later stage.

The drawback, of course, is that when using static branching, your conditions cannot refer to variables that are computed at runtime because the code will have already been compiled with a specific branch before. Everything has to be known at the moment of compilation.

To do static branching in your shaders, you have two methods.

Method 1

You can use preprocessor directives such as #if, #elif, #else, and #endif to check for a specific condition. For example, suppose we have defined some Boolean flag called MAKE_GRAYSCALE in our shader or our project, and consider the following piece of shader code:

```
float4 frag(v2f i) : SV_Target {
#if MAKE_GRAYSCALE
   float v = SAMPLE_TEXTURE2D(_BaseMap, sampler_BaseMap,
     i.uv).r;
   float4 baseTex = float4(v, v, v, v);
#else
   float4 baseTex = SAMPLE_TEXTURE2D(_BaseMap,
     sampler_BaseMap, i.uv);
#endif
   return baseTex;
}
```

Here, we are using an `#if`-`#else`-`#endif` branching so that, if the `MAKE_GRAYSCALE` variable is true, our shader just considers the red channel of the sampled texture, and otherwise, it takes in all the colors. Because, with static branching, the code path to use is resolved at compile time, this code will therefore produce two different compiled versions, depending on the value of `MAKE_GRAYSCALE` at the time of compilation:

- If we decide to turn `MAKE_GRAYSCALE` on, our shader snippet will be compiled to the following:

```
float4 frag(v2f i) : SV_Target {
  float v = SAMPLE_TEXTURE2D(_BaseMap, sampler_BaseMap,
    i.uv).r;
  float4 baseTex = float4(v, v, v, v);
  return baseTex;
}
```

- If we switch `MAKE_GRAYSCALE` off, our shader snippet will be compiled to the following:

```
float4 frag(v2f i) : SV_Target {
  float4 baseTex = SAMPLE_TEXTURE2D(_BaseMap,
    sampler_BaseMap, i.uv);
  return baseTex;
}
```

In any case, the final compiled version doesn't contain any preprocessor directive anymore.

If you want to check whether a variable has been defined or not, you can use the `#ifdef` and `#ifndef` (for "if not defined") preprocessor directives. Again, don't forget that any opening `#ifdef` or `#ifndef` directive has to be matched with a closing `#endif`, like this:

```
float4 frag(v2f i) : SV_Target {
  float4 baseTex = SAMPLE_TEXTURE2D(_BaseMap,
    sampler_BaseMap, i.uv);
#ifdef MAKE_GRAYSCALE
  baseTex.g = baseTex.r;
  baseTex.b = baseTex.r;
  baseTex.a = baseTex.r;
#endif
  return baseTex;
}
```

While it is, of course, possible to define your own variables and parameters (such as `MAKE_GRAYSCALE` in these examples), Unity also provides us with some built-in macros that can be used for static branching, such as information on the target platform or texture coordinates orientation. We will see some of those in the last section of the chapter, *Exploring shader macros and platform-dependent compilation*.

Method 2

You can also use a simple `if` statement in your vertex or fragment shader functions where the condition only depends on compile-time constant variables and values.

Although `if` statements are used frequently for dynamic branching, Unity's compiler is able to detect whether the condition you use in your check is a constant value at compile time and automatically turn it into a static branch instead, to improve your shader's performance.

For example, we could rewrite our previous example without preprocessor directives, but with an `if` statement, and because `MAKE_GRAYSCALE` is constant at compile time, Unity will directly use static branching to produce the corresponding compiled code like before:

```
float4 frag(v2f i) : SV_Target {
  if (MAKE_GRAYSCALE) {
    float v = SAMPLE_TEXTURE2D(_BaseMap, sampler_BaseMap,
        i.uv).r;
    float4 baseTex = float4(v, v, v, v);
  }
  else {
    float4 baseTex = SAMPLE_TEXTURE2D(_BaseMap,
        sampler_BaseMap, i.uv);
  }
  return baseTex;
}
```

It is important to note that static branching is only available in shaders written in code. When you're working in the Shader Graph and you add a **Branch** node to a shader, it doesn't perform static branching. Instead, it does another kind of Unity shader branching – dynamic branching.

Turning to dynamic branching – adaptive but slow

We've seen that because it is resolved at compile time, static branching doesn't hinder your game's performance but has some restrictions. **Dynamic branching**, on the other hand, can be used to evaluate conditions at runtime. This technique, therefore, makes it easy to tweak the behavior of your code in scoped places without having to create a whole new version of the shader. It allows your shader to dynamically change its behavior based on runtime conditions.

Dynamic branching can be very useful if you want some of your materials to change dynamically based on some script event (such as the game entering winter has your visuals covered in snow) or global quality user-defined settings (such as letting players toggle fog on and off).

To use this tool, you simply need to include an `if` statement in your shader code with a condition that relies on the runtime state. For example, the following shader snippet shows a simple computation where we transform a value into its base-10 logarithm if it is not null (else we keep it as-is):

```
if (x != 0) {
    x = log10(x);
}
```

This condition could also be written as a ternary expression to condense the code, like this:

```
x = (x != 0 ? log10(x) : x);
```

Depending on the values inside your condition, dynamic branching thus comes in either of two flavors:

- Your condition checks for the value of a uniform variable
- Your condition checks for a value that is computed at runtime

Conditional behavior based on a shader uniform is slightly more efficient because the uniform value is constant for the entire draw call, and the GPU can therefore optimize the computation the next time it goes over the code.

The problem, however, is that, overall, dynamic branching decreases GPU performance. The impact can vary depending on the hardware you target and the code your shader contains, but as a general rule, the following applies:

- Whenever you introduce dynamic branching in your shader, you effectively ask your GPU to either perform different tasks at the same time (which breaks parallelism) or "flatten the branch" – in other words, maintain parallelism by computing the result for both branches and then throwing away the one that does not match the condition. And both those solutions have a negative impact on GPU performance!

Controlling an if statement compilation mode in HLSL

By default, the compiler will try and flatten the branches to allow for a parallel process. This can also be made explicit or enforced by adding the `[flatten]` attribute just before your `if` statement, and it is necessary if either one of your branches contains a gradient function, such as `tex2D` (or a Unity built-in macro that uses it). Conversely, if you want to force the compiler to use your `if` statement as a non-flattened branch, you can use the `[branch]` attribute – this is necessary if either one of your branches has side effects, such as a stream append statement.

If you use a **Branch** node inside a shader made in the Shader Graph, then this shader will always perform dynamic branching if you flatten the branches.

- You should avoid **asymmetric branches**, or in other words, branches where one code branch is longer or more complex than the other. These will require the GPU to allocate enough memory for the worst case of the two, and you will therefore waste a lot of space with the other one. This in turn means that the GPU won't be able to stack as many invocations of your shader in parallel as usual, and it will decrease the performance.

- Also, because dynamic branching takes place at runtime, both code paths have to be kept at the time of compilation. This means that a shader with this type of branching will usually be longer because all conditions have to be compiled in one shader program.

So, in short, you should use dynamic branching scarcely and only when it really fits your use case because, if you let it go out of hand, it will quickly hinder the performance and increase the amount of required storage of your game!

But guess what? If you absolutely need your shader code to adapt to some runtime condition but you cannot afford to suffer these GPU performance issues, there is one last card you can try and play: using shader variants.

Switching to shader variants... or not

Alright – let's quickly recap what we've seen so far about conditionals and branching in shaders. For now, we've said that Unity allows us to do either static branching, which doesn't impact your game's performance but can only check for compile-time values, or dynamic branching, which is very flexible but severely diminishes your GPU performance.

The situation looks quite dim, and it seems like there is no right answer. Right?

Luckily, Unity provides a third technique to introduce conditional behavior in our shaders, called **shader variants**. In short, this tool tries to mitigate the disadvantages of both static and dynamic branching by providing branching at runtime, but without any GPU performance downgrade.

How is that possible? By trading this computation cost for another resource: memory space.

Basically, the idea of shader variants is to prepare all the possible versions of your shader given by your various branches at compile time, and then pick the right version at runtime by checking the current state against the branch conditions. You therefore produce a gallery of small and specialized shaders beforehand, which you can then execute directly while the game runs without any impact on performance.

Using shader keywords via code

To utilize this feature, you need to include **shader keywords** using specific `#pragma` statements inside your code. You might remember how we briefly introduced this concept in *Chapter 4* – to create shader variants, we use the `#pragma multi_compile` and `#pragma shader_feature` directives and pass them the various keywords we want to define. For example, the following line defines three shader keywords:

```
#pragma shader_feature COLOR_RED COLOR_GREEN COLOR_BLUE
```

Because they were declared in the same `#pragma` statement, we say that these keywords form a **set**. You can define multiple sets of keywords in your shader by using multiple `#pragma` directives. The following snippet shows some examples of three custom shader keyword sets:

```
#pragma multi_compile COLOR_RED COLOR_GREEN COLOR_BLUE
#pragma multi_compile SHADOWS_ON SHADOWS_OFF
#pragma shader_feature USE_NORMALMAP
```

A single set of keywords cannot contain the same keyword multiple times, and a single shader cannot contain the same set of keywords multiple times.

To have Unity automatically add a variant of your shader when all of the keywords in a set are disabled, remember that you can add an underscore at the beginning of the list:

```
#pragma multi_compile _ SHADOWS_ON SHADOWS_OFF
```

By default, the keywords are declared with a global scope, which allows us to change their state at runtime with C# scripts. But sometimes, it can be useful to declare keywords with a local scope to protect them and to avoid reaching Unity's limitations in terms of shader keyword count. To declare keywords as local, you simply need to add the _local suffix after your #pragma directive:

```
#pragma shader_feature_local COLOR_RED COLOR_GREEN COLOR_BLUE
```

You can also help Unity pick the right variants for your shader by explicitly specifying which stage of the shader uses this keyword in a conditional in the #pragma declaration. This is done by adding a suffix, too, chosen from the following list:

- _vertex
- _fragment
- _hull
- _domain
- _geometry
- _raytracing

For example, the following statement declares shader keywords that are used in a conditional in the vertex shader function:

```
#pragma shader_feature_vertex OPTION_1 OPTION_2
```

> **Limitations of shader-stage-specific keywords**
>
> Note that this trick of telling Unity which shader stage this keyword will be used for does not work with all graphics APIs. In particular, OpenGL, OpenGL, ES, and Vulkan don't take this into account, and Metal will ignore the _geometry and _raytracing suffixes, and it will bundle together the _vertex, _hull, and _domain stages.

After being defined with `#pragma` statements, shader keywords need to be used inside your code in conditional preprocessor directives (such as `#if`, `#else`, `#ifdef`, and so on) to actually adapt the code behavior depending on the current context:

```
#if (COLOR_RED || COLOR_GREEN)
    // code for red or green enabled
#else
    // code for only blue enabled
#endif
```

Using shader variants in code is therefore quite straightforward – you just need to add your `#pragma` statements at the beginning to declare shader keywords, and then using them in the code, it looks a lot like static or dynamic branching.

Using shader keywords in the Shader Graph

You can also declare keywords in the Shader Graph editor, in the **Blackboard** panel (see *Figure 9.6*), which can be of three types: **Boolean**, **Enum**, or **Material Quality**.

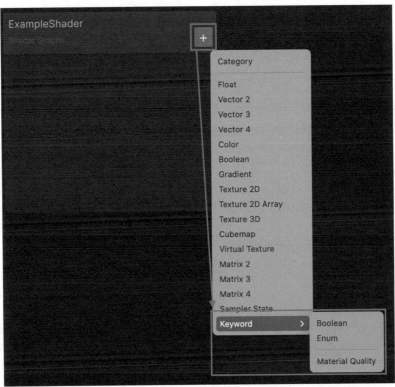

Figure 9.6 – Creation panel for keywords in the Shader Graph's Blackboard panel

Once you've added your keyword, you can set its properties just like you would for a variable by opening the **Graph Inspector** panel and selecting the keyword in the **Blackboard** panel:

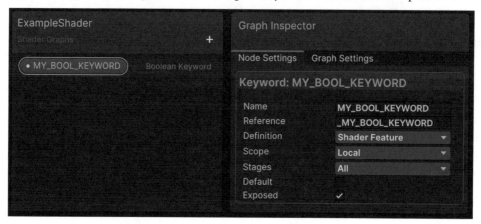

Figure 9.7 – Properties of a Boolean shader keyword in the Graph Inspector panel

These settings closely match what we discussed earlier in this section:

- The pretty display name of your shader is automatically associated with a matching reference string. This can be particularly important if you are not declaring a custom keyword of your own but want to use a built-in one from Unity – in that case, you'll want to make sure that the **Reference** field contains the right value to link to this built-in macro (casing and underscores count!).

- You can set the scope of your keyword by choosing **Local** or **Global** in the **Scope** dropdown. Note that here, keywords are *local* by default.

- The **Definition** dropdown allows you to choose between **Shader Feature** or **Multi Compiled**, just like we do with our #pragma statements in code. The dropdown offers a third option, **Predefined**, which will transfer the definition and configuration of your keyword up to the render pipeline.

- Finally, you get the **Stages** dropdown, which is equivalent to the shader stage suffixes we discussed in the *Using shader keywords via code* section, and helps Unity know where this keyword is used in your code.

Other than that, the Shader Graph keywords also have a default value, and they can be exposed in the inspector of the materials using this shader like normal variables. For keywords of the **Enum** type, the properties are also where you can define the possible values for the keyword, as a list of names and corresponding suffixes:

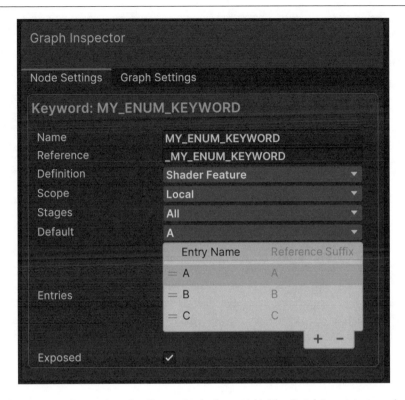

Figure 9.8 – Properties of an Enum shader keyword in the Graph Inspector panel

Typically, continuing on our previous examples, we could define an **Enum** keyword called COLOR, and then give it three possible values (Red, Green, or Blue) with the matching suffixes: RED, GREEN, and BLUE.

The **Material Quality** type is similar to an **Enum** type, except that the possible values are already fixed to **Low**, **Medium**, and **High**, and some other properties are locked.

Then, to use the keywords inside your shader logic, you'll need to create a node that references your keyword (you can do so by dragging the keyword to the area in the middle), and linking it to the rest of your nodes as usual. The input and output obviously depend on the type of keyword – *Figure 9.9* shows the different possibilities:

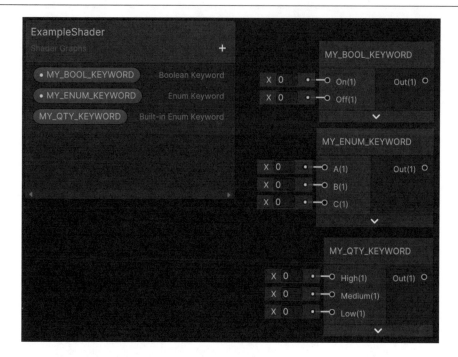

Figure 9.9 – Keyword nodes with type-dependent input and output

Using shader keywords is therefore extremely easy, both via code and via the Shader Graph. However, properly defining them, and in particular, choosing between a shader feature and a multi-compiled keyword, can be difficult. So, let's look at this in more detail!

Picking the right type of definition

To better understand the difference between the `#pragma multi_compile` and `#pragma shader_feature` directives, let's take a common example case for shader variants and shader keywords, which is changing the behavior of your shader code depending on the quality settings of our game. We will consider that we have three quality levels: QTY_LOW, QTY_MEDIUM, and QTY_HIGH.

We have three ways of declaring these as shader keywords and using them to make our code behavior conditional:

- If we know the value of our keywords at compile time, then we can use the `#pragma shader_feature` statement to define them:

    `#pragma shader_feature QTY_LOW QTY_MEDIUM QTY_HIGH`

    As we will see very soon in this section, using the `#pragma shader_feature` directive is interesting because it allows Unity to check for unused combinations and exclude them from the build, which makes for lower build times, reduces the runtime memory usage, and decreases the build file size.

The drawback is that any combination that is not used at compile time will therefore be inaccessible at runtime. More precisely, to know whether it should remove a shader variant associated with a keyword defined in a `#pragma shader_feature` statement, Unity looks through all the materials in your project and ensures that at least one of them uses the keyword. If there is none, then it means the variant is not actually needed by your game (at least for now, given the current build-time context), and can therefore be removed from the build.

- If we want to be able to change shader variants at runtime as our context evolves, then we need to ensure the engine compiles all possible combinations of keywords. To do this, we need to use the `#pragma multi_compile` statement instead:

```
#pragma multi_compile QTY_LOW QTY_MEDIUM QTY_HIGH
```

   With that setup, it is possible to enable or disable our shader keywords (here, `QTY_LOW`, `QTY_MEDIUM`, and `QTY_HIGH`) at runtime from a C# script without any risks – since Unity prepared all possible variants, it will be able to pick the one matching your context every time.

- Finally, we can declare our keywords but also decide to completely disable the creation of shader variants by forcing these keywords to be used with dynamic branching. To do so, we can use the aptly named `#pragma dynamic_branching` statement in a similar way as the two previous ones:

```
#pragma dynamic_branching QTY_LOW QTY_MEDIUM QTY_HIGH
```

   If you use this directive, then Unity will not create any variants for your shader. Instead, it will convert your shader keywords to Boolean variables and turn these variables on or off, depending on the keyword(s) you enable. The GPU then performs dynamic branching on the branches using these keywords as described in the previous section, *Turning to dynamic branching – adaptive but slow*, which therefore leads to the aforementioned performance issues.

You might actually be wondering why this third option exists: if dynamic branching is so bad, why would the Unity team allow us to re-integrate it inside this amazing tool that is shader variants?

Understanding the risks of shader variants

We need to be aware of the risks of using shader variants because a tool as powerful as shader variants is also hard to master – and diving too deep into shader variants can quickly turn your project into an unmanageable mess. As your number of shader variants starts to grow, you will experience longer build times, larger build files, higher runtime memory usage, and longer loading times. From a creator's perspective, it can also burden the daily workflow with additional complexity, typically if you want to preload your shaders.

Dynamic branching, on the other hand, does not imply compiling multiple versions of the same shader code – and even though the compiler will have to keep the contents of your various branches all in the same place, these slightly longer code files are usually far less consumptive of memory than shader variants.

Indeed, a key thing to keep in mind when using shader variants is that it is devilishly easy to inadvertently create too many versions: putting the wrong keyword in the wrong place can lead to dozens of variants suddenly popping up to slow down your game and your team. And Unity will need to consider each possible combination of your shader keywords – the number of shader variants, therefore, grows very quickly, being subject to what we call a combinatorial explosion.

Typically, consider two of the example sets of shader keywords that we showed in the previous section:

```
#pragma multi_compile COLOR_RED COLOR_GREEN COLOR_BLUE
#pragma multi_compile SHADOWS_ON SHADOWS_OFF
```

If a shader code contains both those `#pragma` statements, then Unity will need to compile six variants for this shader, for the following keyword combinations:

1. COLOR_RED and SHADOWS_ON

2. COLOR_RED and SHADOWS_OFF

3. COLOR_GREEN and SHADOWS_ON

4. COLOR_GREEN and SHADOWS_OFF

5. COLOR_BLUE and SHADOWS_ON

6. COLOR_BLUE and SHADOWS_OFF

And if we were to add just one another on/off shader keyword pair, the number of variants would instantly jump to 12! You can quickly see how this can cause memory issues for complex shaders.

The good news is that to avoid these problems, Unity has some available tools to help limit the impact of shader variants on your game's performance and memory usage, which are discussed next.

Deduplication of shader variants

Once it has compiled the different variants of your shader, the engine checks for code chunks that are identical between multiple shader variants within the same pass, and has them point to the same bytecode. This directly helps reduce the final file size.

However, deduplication only happens after the variants have been compiled, so you will still have longer build times; and it doesn't help with loading times at runtime. This is why, when possible, it is always best to try and strip unneeded shader variants.

Shader variant stripping

Because shader variants tend to multiply quickly, you should always try to limit the number of variants you ask Unity to compile as much as possible. A very interesting tool for this is **stripping**, which is a way to prevent variants from even being compiled.

Shader variant stripping happens when we use the #pragma shader_feature statement: as we highlighted in the *Learning some Unity shader compilation tricks* section, at compile time, Unity will then check whether these keywords are actually used and, if not, exclude the variants containing them from the build.

To better manage in-development projects and device limitations, you can turn stripping on or off depending on the platform you are building for. Typically, you may want to enable it for mobiles, but disable it on desktops. This is easy to do, thanks to preprocessor directives and Unity's built-in macros (which we will look at in more detail in the next section, *Exploring shader macros and platform-dependent compilation*). You just need to use a #pragma shader_feature statement to define your keywords in the first case, and a #pragma multi_compile statement in the second one, like this:

```
#ifdef SHADER_API_MOBILE
  #pragma shader_feature COLOR_RED COLOR_GREEN COLOR_BLUE
#else
  #pragma multi_compile COLOR_RED COLOR_GREEN COLOR_BLUE
#endif
```

By removing these unneeded variants from your projects, you'll significantly reduce the negative impact of shader variants on your project. The catch, however, is to keep in mind that since Unity excludes the variants that are not used by your project at compile time from the build, some variants may not be available at runtime. So, if you want your game to switch to a different variant at runtime because your context changed, then there is a risk this variant may not be available. This means that the software will be forced to fall back to another variant that is "close enough," which may result in unexpected or incorrect visuals.

It is therefore important to keep track of the shader variants in your project and to be aware of the different keyword combinations your materials will require at runtime.

Shader variants exploration

In order to help us identify the pain points of our project related to shader compilation, Unity offers some logging and profiling tools.

Indeed, as is always the case when trying to optimize software, it is crucial to first assess whether such optimization is needed and whether you should devote time to working on this issue. So, to better evaluate the weight of shader variants on your project, you can do the following:

- You can see a count of all the shader variants the Unity Editor currently uses in the **Scene** view and the **Game** view by going to the **Edit | Project Settings | Graphics** settings panel and looking at the **Shader Loading** section.

The number of variants is shown next to the **Currently tracked** label (see *Figure 9.10*):

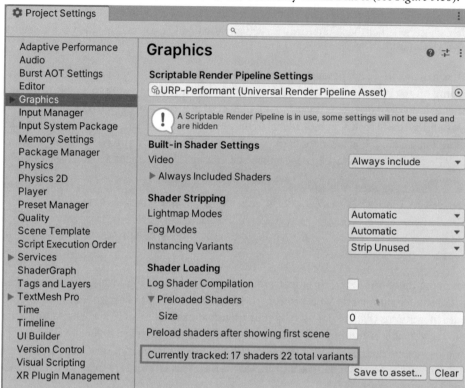

Figure 9.10 – Count of the shader variants currently in use by the Unity Editor in the Scene and Game views

- To know how many shader variants Unity creates at build time for your project, you can build your project and then open the `Editor.log` file to see how many variants the engine compiled and stripped. This log file contains some information about the shader compilation process that looks like this:

```
Compiling shader "Universal Render Pipeline/Lit" pass
"ForwardLit" (fp)
320 / 786432 variants left after stripping, processed in 6.77
seconds
starting compilation...
finished in 29.72 seconds. Local cache hits 202 (0.24s CPU
time), remote cache hits 0 (0.00s CPU time), compiled 118
variants (582.41s CPU time), skipped 0 variants
```

The `Editor.log` file is located in different places, depending on the OS of the computer you build the project on – you can check out the following link for the exact location of the file on your type of system: https://docs.unity3d.com/Manual/LogFiles.html.

- To see whether your project tries to use unavailable shader variants at runtime, you can configure it to highlight missing variants by showing a pink error shader instead of falling back to another variant.

  To enable this, go to the **Edit | Project Settings | Player** panel and open the **Other Settings** section. You'll then have a block called **Shader Settings**, with a **Strict shader variant matching** option you can toggle on or off:

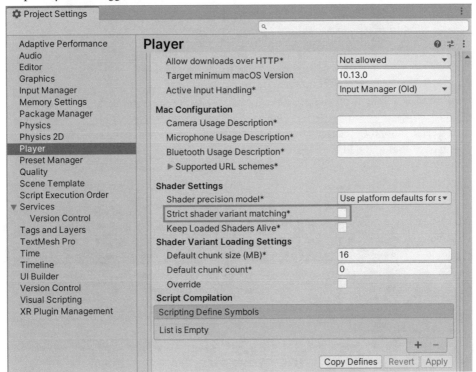

Figure 9.11 – Project Strict shader variant matching setting to highlight missing variants at runtime

---

Important note

This option is only available starting from the Unity Editor 2022.

- To check how much memory your shaders use, and point out the ones that consume too many resources and should be stripped of variants, you can use Unity's built-in **Memory Profiler** module or the more advanced **Memory Profiler** package.

  The **Memory Profiler** module is one of the tools available in the **Profiler** window of the editor. You can open this window by going to the **Window | Analysis | Profiler** menu, which will give you a new dockable panel that looks like this:

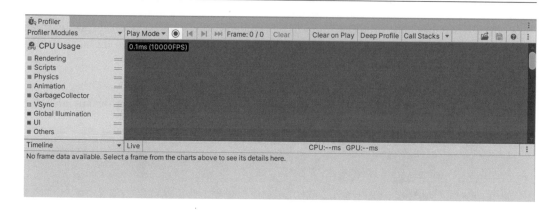

Figure 9.12 – Built-in Profiler window with no recorded data

You can choose the modules you want to show in the dropdown in the top-left corner, and after you have started the **Play Mode** for your game in the editor, you will see that **Profiler** starts to track the various data streams you asked it to monitor, as shown in *Figure 9.13*:

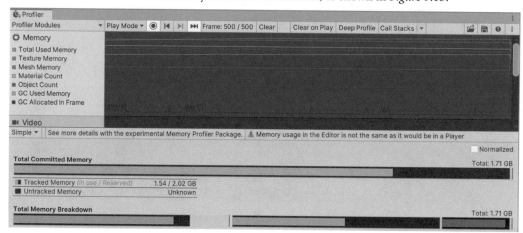

Figure 9.13 – Built-in Profiler window with a basic memory-related data analysis

The bottom part of the window gives you frame-by-frame detailed statistics on the data that **Profiler** collected (see *Figure 9.14*), which can help you narrow down the unexpectedly high resource-consumer assets and, therefore, focus your optimization work on specific parts of the project.

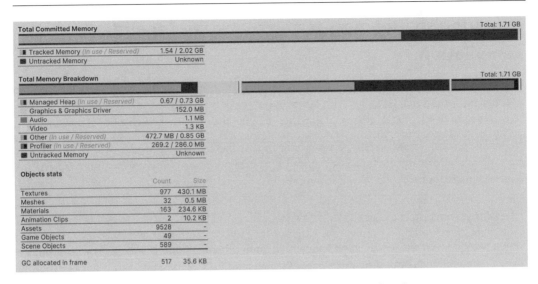

Figure 9.14 – Built-in Profiler detailed statistics section for a frame

> **Important note**
>
> When you profile your game in the Unity Editor, you will get higher data reports than if you were profiling the built project on a target device. That's because the editor itself uses some resources, and it relies on some extra objects that take up memory. To get an accurate evaluation of the bottlenecks of your application, it is thus essential to profile it with actual builds run on the target platforms and systems. In-editor profiling should mainly be used to quickly iterate on the issues you found in these build profilings. For more information, have a look here: `https://docs.unity3d.com/Manual/profiler-profiling-applications.html`.

This tool, and its more advanced version in the **Memory Profiler** package, are obviously complex, and I don't want to dive into too many details here. But hopefully, this gave you an introduction to what Unity has to offer in terms of logging and profiling, and you can now discover more about those tools in your own projects, and by browsing the internet!

To conclude, shader branching and variants are very interesting features of Unity for advanced technical artists, because they allow you to introduce conditional behavior in your code easily and with quite a high level of control on the compilation process – which is essential to optimizing large projects. But the preprocessor directives and `#pragma` statements we discussed so far are not the only ones you can use to improve your shaders' performance and plan for cross-platform distribution.

So, to wrap up this chapter, let's discuss some other valuable built-in macros you can use in your shaders to help Unity compile your code in the best possible way.

Exploring shader macros and platform-dependent compilation

Now that we have discussed various tricks to optimizing the organization of our project shader assets and adding conditional behavior with branching or variants, let's focus on another key aspect of cross-platform development for technical artists: handling the rendering specificities of each platform.

In this last section, we will explore various built-in macros that Unity provides us with for checking the type of platform we are building for, looking up the current Unity version, normalizing UV direction, and more.

Identifying the target platform

When working with shaders, it is fundamental to know what the target platform for your project is. Because although this obviously impacts many other areas of game development (such as UI/UX for controls, or responsive interfaces), the rendering tools you have at your disposal are inherently linked to the kind of device the game will run on.

Game engines such as Unity are obviously here to abstract away the low-level particularities of the various rendering backends – they allow you to develop the same code for multiple platforms, and handle several graphics APIs all in one go.

> **Important note**
>
> In this section, we will refer to common rendering backends and graphics APIs that are not specifically linked to Unity shader creation but are more of general culture for advanced technical artists. In this book, I will therefore not go into the details and will assume that you have prior knowledge.

Still, if you get into advanced renders, those APIs may have some differences that you'll need to handle yourself, by specifically distinguishing between the various cases. To do so, you can use the technique of static branching we discussed in the previous section, *Taking advantage of shader branching and shader variants*, and have your condition depend on one of Unity's built-in target platform macros, which can be the following (please note, *the support of OpenGL for macOS platforms is deprecated since June 2018 – most notably, you cannot submit applications using OpenGL/OpenGL ES to the App Store*):

Graphics API	Target platform(s)	Macro
Direct3D 11	Windows, Xbox	SHADER_API_D3D11
Direct3D 11 "feature level 9.x"	Universal Windows Platform	SHADER_API_D3D11_9X
Desktop OpenGL "core" (GL 3/4)	Windows, macOS, Linux	SHADER_API_GLCORE
OpenGL ES 2.0	Android, iOS, Windows, macOS*, Linux, WebGL	SHADER_API_GLES

Graphics API	Target platform(s)	Macro
OpenGL ES 3.0/3.1	Android, iOS, Windows, macOS, Linux, WebGL	`SHADER_API_GLES3`
Metal	iOS, macOS	`SHADER_API_METAL`
Vulkan	Android (some devices), Windows, Linux (+iOS, macOS using MoltenVK)	`SHADER_API_VULKAN`

Figure 9.15 – Available graphics APIs for Unity shaders and matching built-in macros

Additionally, Unity also defines the `SHADER_API_DESKTOP` and `SHADER_API_MOBILE` macros to represent the Windows, macOS, Linux, and WebGL platforms on the one hand, and the iOS and Android platforms on the other hand.

For example, we can use these target platform-related macros to enforce some quality settings and properly adapt the graphics level to the hardware limitations:

```
#ifdef SHADER_API_DESKTOP
    #pragma shader_feature QTY_LOW QTY_MID QTY_HIGH QTY_ULTRA
#else
    #pragma shader_feature QTY_LOW QTY_MID
#endif
```

But this is not all that the built-in macros can tell us! Let's see another interesting piece of data we can get thanks to them.

Checking the version of your tools

Another type of information you can gather easily with Unity's built-in shader macros is the version of your current Unity executable or the shader target model.

To know what Unity version you are compiling this shader code with, you can use the `UNITY_VERSION` variable and compare it to a specific version number, as follows:

```
#if UNITY_VERSION >= 502
    // executed if the Unity version is 5.0.2 or greater
#endif
```

As you can see in this snippet, the version number is the numeric value of the Unity version to check for – for example, `502` stands for Unity 5.0.2.

This kind of check can be useful if your script relies on built-in shader functionalities that have changed from one version to another, to perform a manual re-standardization.

Similarly, the shader target model can determine the capabilities of your shader, or whether you have to use some workarounds and approximations. To check for the current shader target model, you can use the SHADER_TARGET variable and, again, compare it to a given version in the numeric format:

```
#if SHADER_TARGET < 30
    // shader model is older than 3.0:
    // limited functionalities, do approximations
#else
    // more functionalities, use improved logic
#endif
```

Also, Unity's built-in shader macros can inform us about yet another thing: the orientation of our coordinates system.

Ensuring your coordinates are oriented properly

Indeed, one of the important points where graphics APIs differ is in how they orient the coordinates in texture and clip space. More precisely, there are two possible conventions that may affect the flipping of your UVs and clip space coordinates:

Graphics API	Texture space convention	Clip space convention
Direct 3D-like (Direct 3D, Metal, consoles)	The Y coordinate starts at 0 at the top and increases downward	The clip space depth goes from +1.0 at the near plane to 0.0 at the far plane
OpenGL-like (OpenGL, OpenGL ES)	The Y coordinate starts at 0 at the bottom and increases upward	The clip space depth goes from –1.0 at the near plane to +1.0 at the far plane

Figure 9.16 – Texture and clip space coordinate conventions for Direct 3D-like and OpenGL-like APIs

Unity obeys the OpenGL-like convention as much as possible – for example, by internally flipping the UVs to match this convention. Still, despite the engine trying to uniformize discrepancies, there are some cases where you need to take care of it on your own. Those situations are the following:

- **Image effects and grab passes**: When you use anti-aliasing, or when you process multiple Render Textures in a single image effect, Unity won't flip the UVs internally. This means that they might look upside-down on Direct 3D-like platforms.

  To solve this issue, you need to check the current context in your shader code using the UNITY_UV_STARTS_AT_TOP built-in macro. Then, you can verify how UVs are oriented for a given texture by looking at the sign of its texel size along the y axis, like this:

  ```
  #if UNITY_UV_STARTS_AT_TOP
  if (_MainTex_TexelSize.y < 0)
      uv.y = 1 - uv.y; // flip UVs vertically
  #endif
  ```

Similarly, grab passes may also be flipped on Direct 3D-like platforms, which is why you should use the `ComputeGrabScreenPos` function from the built-in renderer `UnityCG.cginc` include file. For more details on this, you can look at the files in the GitHub repository of this book from *Chapter 2* that implement the blurry refraction example.

- **Rendering in UV space**: In some cases, you might want your shader to render its output in the texture space, rather than the usual clip space. For example, this can be a good way to output the unwrapped version of a mesh to a texture for future reference.

However, outputting to a texture is different from outputting to a screen – this time, you should not flip the UVs vertically!

But since Unity cannot always guarantee the orientation of UVs, you need to find a way to standardize your texture renders by checking whether the UVs have been flipped internally by the engine. To help you with that, Unity has a nice built-in macro, `ProjectionParams` – and more precisely, its x component, which equals +1 if the UVs have not yet been flipped to obey the OpenGL-like convention, and -1 otherwise.

So, for example, the following snippet of code shows you how to check whether UVs have been flipped along the *y* axis and, if so, flip them back:

```
float2 standardizedUVs = uv;
if (_ProjectionParams.x < 0)
    standardizedUVs.y = 1 - standardizedUVs.y;
```

This may not be useful in all your shaders, but it is definitely worth keeping in the back of your mind for the day when you're faced with this sort of issue.

Additional resources

Now, these few built-in macros are interesting, but they are obviously just a small sample of what Unity has to offer! To really explore all of the available variables that the engine provides for optimization and cross-platform shader compilation, you should definitely take a look at the official documentation.

Among the pages related to the topic, we can highlight the following:

- Declaring and using shader keywords in HLSL: `https://docs.unity3d.com/Manual/SL-MultipleProgramVariants.html`
- Built-in macros: `https://docs.unity3d.com/Manual/SL-BuiltinMacros.html`
- Writing shaders for different graphics APIs: `https://docs.unity3d.com/Manual/SL-PlatformDifferences.html`

And, as usual, when exploring optimization techniques, the best way to learn is to practice and test it out on your projects. Discover the profiling tools and learn to log as much data as you can on your own assets so that you understand how all these factors can combine into a loss in performance, and don't hesitate to look up Unity's documentation and forums to explore all the possible solutions.

Summary

In this chapter, we discussed some inner workings of Unity's shader compilation system, and how advanced technical artists can leverage a few settings and clever tricks to further improve the performance of their shaders.

We began by presenting some important points about shader management in Unity, such as caching, asynchronous compilation, and AssetBundles organization.

We then explored the various forms of branching we can use in our Unity shaders, and what should be used in which case, between static branching, dynamic branching, and shader variants.

At the end, we listed some commonly used `#pragma` directives, and we saw how built-in macros and preprocessor directives can help us with platform-dependent compilation and cross-platform distribution.

In the next chapter, we will continue this talk on shader optimization and dive more into practical tips for improving the performance of your shaders through coding decisions. We will also quickly introduce some tools Unity offers us to go beyond the SRPs and see how you can create your own render pipeline!

Going further

If you're curious about URP shader optimization (in particular, using shader compilation tricks, shader branching, and shader variants), here are a few interesting resources to check out or continue your journey from:

- Official documentation on shader compilation, Unity: `https://docs.unity3d.com/Manual/shader-compilation.html`

- Official documentation on shader branching, Unity: `https://docs.unity3d.com/Manual/shader-branching.html`

- Official documentation on shader variants, Unity: `https://docs.unity3d.com/Manual/shader-variants.html`

- Optimizing shader runtime performance (official documentation), Unity: `https://docs.unity3d.com/Manual/SL-ShaderPerformance.html`

- *7 Ways to Optimize your Unity Project with URP*, Unity (2020): `https://www.youtube.com/watch?v=NFBr21V0zvU`

10

Optimizing Your Code, or Making Your Own Pipeline?

In the previous chapter, we explored some of the tools Unity provides us with for creating efficient cross-platform shaders. We talked about built-in shader compilation tricks, shader branching, and useful macros.

But, of course, compiling shaders properly is not the only way you can optimize your rendering. If you want to get the most out of your shaders, you also need to make the right choices when actually coding them up.

Or, even better, if you know your renders require very specific processing, you might opt out of Unity's default generalist pipelines and make your own!

So, in this chapter, we are going to explore a few tips and techniques for optimizing your shader code and gaining some precious extra milliseconds. To do so, we'll talk about the following topics:

- Picking the right shading model
- Optimizing your runtime performance
- Creating your own SRP

Technical requirements

To familiarize yourself with the settings panels and tools presented here, you will need to have Unity installed, with a version from 2021 or later.

For the first two sections, *Picking the right shading model* and *Optimizing your runtime performance*, you should set up a project using the URP pipeline. For the third section, *Creating your own SRP*, you should start a simple 3D Unity project with the legacy pipeline.

You can also find all the code files for this chapter on GitHub, at `https://github.com/ PacktPublishing/Become-a-Unity-Shaders-Guru/tree/main/Assets/ Chapter%2010`.

Picking the right shading model

To begin our exploration of scoped shader optimization techniques, let's first discuss an important property of any shader: its shading model.

Put simply, the shading model determines how the color of your object's surface will vary depending on its orientation, the position of the camera, or the lights in the scene. In other words, it is the set of mathematical computations that the engine will have to do in order to render your material for the current context.

Over the years, technical artists have developed a whole gallery of shading models to represent various types of surfaces and recreate various visual styles. While some models are dedicated to reproducing reality as accurately as possible (most notably, physically-based shading), others are simpler processes that either approximate realism or take a completely different route and apply their own look and feel to the render.

We've already touched upon this idea in *Chapter 5*, when we worked on our toon shader and we re-implemented our own lighting. What we did back then was define our very own shading model, by providing Unity with all the right formulas for aggregating together the current scene data (such as the lights' position and intensity, and the object's transform) into a final pixel color.

But, of course, toon shading is kind of a special case, and most of the time, you'll want to have the usual smooth shadows and nice lighting of a lit render. Luckily, Unity provides us with built-in shading models for this, so that we can quickly create shaders that process the scene data in the right way!

Exploring Unity's URP built-in shading models

In URP, there are four built-in shading models available:

- **Physically-based shading**: Aimed specifically at recreating photo-realistic surfaces, this model uses real-life physics principles to compute the amount of light reflected by objects.

  As we briefly mentioned in *Chapter 4*, this physically-based shading relies on two core concepts: energy conservation and microgeometry. Simply put, those principles ensure that you can never reflect more light than the incoming light and that your surface can be more or less rough at a microscopic level (which results in a more or less smooth effect). A key idea with physically-based shading is that the diffuse and the specular components of your light are correlated, since part of the incoming light is refracted, and part of it is reflected.

Of course, having such physical accuracy comes at a price – this model is fairly complex and thus quite compute-intensive. It is therefore not recommended to use it when you target less powerful platforms such as mobiles because it will severely hinder the performance of your app.

In that case, you should probably turn to the simple shading model instead.

- **Simple shading**: Contrary to the physically-based shading model, the simple shading model doesn't make truly realistic renders. It is based on the Blinn-Phong model, which we explored in *Chapter 1*, and in particular, it does not obey the energy conservation principle. You can thus reflect more light than the initial incoming light (effectively "creating energy").

Thanks to these approximations, this shader is less demanding than the physically-based shading model – which means you can use it on low-end hardware (mobiles, tablets, and so on) without too many performance issues.

Note that you can obviously also use it on a powerful PC or console, if your game's esthetics happen to have a more stylized look. The simple shading model can be a nice way of optimizing your shaders for all platforms, as long as it doesn't downgrade your render quality too much for your taste! We'll actually have a quick talk about this meta-question of whether your visual style can be influenced by your technical limitations at the end of the upcoming section, *Optimizing your runtime performance*.

Still, if you don't want to sacrifice your visuals for performance, you can try to go for the baked lit shading model.

- **Baked lit shading**: This model is different from the other ones because it does not support real-time lighting at all. When creating shaders with this model, you won't be able to preview the results directly as you would normally in the Unity Editor.

To compute lighting for the baked lit shading model, you need to use lightmaps or Light Probes in your scene and bake their light contribution beforehand – then, the engine will be able to read this data to light the object's surface using the baked lit shader.

The big advantage of this technique is that, since lighting is pre-computed, you can get away with quite advanced effects while still maintaining an okay runtime performance on low-end platforms such as mobiles. The drawback is that you have to do this in the first phase, and then re-update your baked data whenever you change the lighting in the scene... and most importantly, you cannot have dynamic lights that move around in your scene at runtime!

- **No lighting**: Finally, there can be some cases where you don't really need to compute any lights and shadows. Shaders using this lighting model are said to be unlit, and they compile extremely fast. Because there are no light computations or lightmap lookups of any sort, these shaders are the best possible choice for less powerful platforms in terms of performance.

A shader without any lighting cannot be used everywhere, but if your game has somewhat stylized esthetics, or if you are making a custom shader for 2D elements, then you might have a need for that simple model.

In short, if you already know that your object won't need any lighting, don't hesitate to switch over to this model to save build time and performance!

Thanks to these shading models, you can easily adapt your renders to the current target platform, so as to get the best possible visuals considering the hardware's limitations.

Now that we have an idea of what's available, let's see how to use these models in our shaders, be it directly with a built-in shader, or in a custom shader asset.

Using the URP shading models

If you don't need any particular options or optimizations in your shader and you just want to use one of the built-in shading models as is, then you can create a new material asset in your project and have it use one of the built-in URP shaders:

- **Complex Lit** or **Lit** (which is the default for a new mesh) for the physically-based shading model
- **Simple Lit** for the simple shading model
- **Baked Lit** for the baked lit shading model
- **Unlit** for the no-lighting shading model

On the other hand, if you want to actually edit and customize the shader code, then you'll need to create your own shader asset and implement the lighting logic inside.

So, once you have identified which URP shading model is the best for your shader, there are two different processes to actually set it up in your shader, depending on whether you are using direct HLSL code or the Shader Graph editor.

Using HLSL code

Defining your URP shading model in HLSL code requires you to include some files from the Unity URP library, and to configure a few options. Good references for this are Unity's built-in URP shaders, which you can access and open in your IDE by going to your project's file, in the **Packages** section, in **Universal RP | Shaders**:

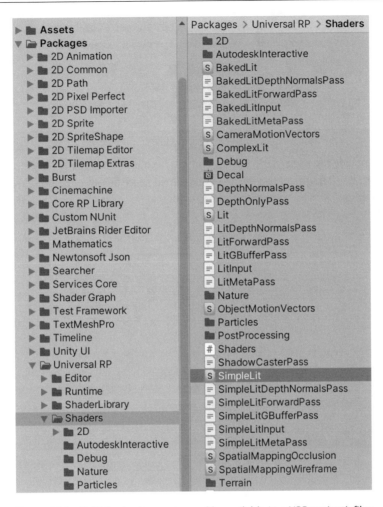

Figure 10.1 – Built-in shader assets, readily available in a URP project's files

If you examine one of these shaders (for example, the **SimpleLit.shader** asset), you see that the easiest way to have your shader use a specific shading model is by following these steps:

1. Add the `UniversalMaterialType` item to your `SubShader` tags with the type of lighting you want:

```
SubShader {
    Tags { ... "UniversalMaterialType" = "SimpleLit" }
    ...
}
```

The `UniversalMaterialType` tag can take two values: `Lit` (default) or `SimpleLit`.

2. In your `Pass` blocks that require lighting, set up the vertex and fragment shader functions reference using the `#pragma vertex` and `#pragma fragment` directives:

```
Pass {
    ...
    #pragma vertex LitPassVertexSimple
    #pragma fragment LitPassFragmentSimple
}
```

3. Finally, include the right files from the Unity URP library to actually import the definition of those vertex and fragment shader functions (or use these files as reference to recode and adapt the functions if you need specific customizations):

```
Pass {
    ...
    #include "Packages/com.unity.render-pipelines
        .universal/Shaders/SimpleLitInput.hlsl"
    #include "Packages/com.unity.render-pipelines
        .universal/Shaders/SimpleLitForwardPass.hlsl"
}
```

Note that you may use different vertex and fragment functions depending on the role of your `Pass` block; to know which functions you have at your disposal, you can directly look inside the HLSL files you included, which are located next to the shader assets in the project's **Packages** assets (in the **Universal RP | Shaders** folder).

Using the Shader Graph editor

To choose a shading model for a Shader Graph asset, you can either use one of the templates to automatically assign it on startup, or reconfigure it afterward in the Shader Graph editor panel.

The URP shader templates are available in the asset contextual menu (which you can open by right-clicking in the **Project** panel), in the **Create | Shader Graph | URP** menu, as shown in *Figure 10.2*:

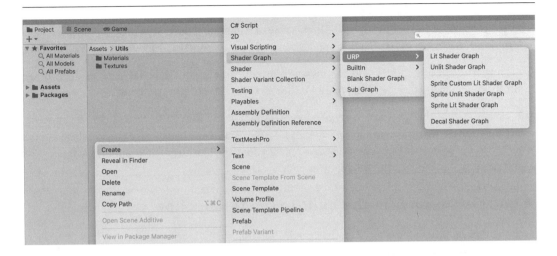

Figure 10.2 – Contextual menu for creating a new Shader Graph asset based on a URP template

If you want to have more control over the settings of your shader, or if you want to modify its shading model after initialization, you can use the **Graph Inspector** panel inside the Shader Graph editor, which has a **Graph Settings** tab focused entirely on the options of your shader asset:

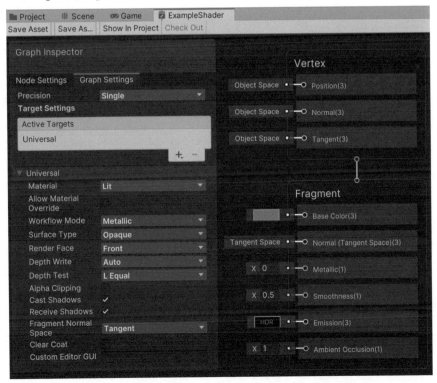

Figure 10.3 – Graph Settings panel for a basic Shader Graph asset

This panel provides you with various settings, some of which we looked at in previous chapters, that re-expose the shader keywords and other options you could set in your HLSL code via #pragma directives.

To change the lighting model, you can pick a different value in the **Material** settings drop-down control, among **Sprite Custom Lit**, **Sprite Lit**, **Sprite Unlit**, **Decal**, **Lit**, and **Unlit**.

Choosing the right shading model can go a long way in making your game faster because rendering is a taxing process that takes up a lot of resources. So when the time comes to optimize, always check whether your shaders use the right level of complexity for their lighting computation, or whether you could simplify it without losing too many of your visuals.

A quick side-note for the built-in render pipeline

Although we decided to focus more on the new SRPs in this book, there are still many situations where you'll have to deal with Unity's built-in rendering, in particular, when maintaining older projects. So, let's also have a quick look at a very common case when improving shaders for Unity's built-in render pipeline.

If you ever need to optimize rendering for this pipeline, chances are that a lot of the shaders you work on will be **Surface Shaders**. Those are the "easy" way to code up lit shaders in the built-in render pipeline with a higher level of abstraction than pure vertex/fragment shader functions, and they make it quicker to set up lighting or shadows for your material. In short, the idea is to define a "surface function" that takes in data and fills in a SurfaceOutput structure – this structure describes the properties of the surface (such as its color, its normals, its specularity, whether it's emissive, etc.). The Surface Shader compiler then transforms this code into actual vertex and fragment shader functions, so that the computer can ultimately handle the rendering of your shader.

> **Want to learn more about Surface Shaders?**
>
> The point here is not to re-introduce the notion of Surface Shaders in detail. If you are not too familiar with this tool or you want to re-discover the concept, feel free to have a look at the official Unity documentation here: https://docs.unity3d.com/Manual/SL-SurfaceShaders.html.

For Surface Shaders, there are some useful compile options that you can use to improve the performance of your scripts without too much loss in quality. To enable these extra settings, you just need to add them to your #pragma surface... directive (which designates the shader as a Surface Shader), located in a SubShader block, between the CGPROGRAM and ENDCG lines:

```
Shader "BuiltIn-Diffuse" {
    Properties {}
    SubShader {
        Tags { "RenderType" = "Opaque" }
        CGPROGRAM
```

```
        #pragma surface surf Lambert
        struct Input {};
        void surf (Input IN, inout SurfaceOutput o) {
            o.Albedo = float3(1, 1, 1);
        }
        ENDCG
    }
    Fallback "Diffuse"
}
```

This #pragma directive is of the following form:

```
#pragma surface <surface function> <light model> [options]
```

Of course, the <surface function> and <light model> parts have to be replaced with the name of the surface function in the shader (for example, in the previous code snippet, surf), and the name of the light model Unity should use to auto-compute the lighting in this shader. This light model can be either a built-in one (among the four available: Lambert, BlinnPhong, Standard, and StandardSpecular) or a custom one if you provide your own lighting function. For more information, you can have a look at this Unity tutorial: https://dev.rbcafe.com/unity/unity-5.3.3/en/Manual/SL-SurfaceShaderLighting.html.

And so, at the end, you can insert some options – typically, for optimization:

- noambient: Disables ambient lighting in the shader's computation, which can make performance slightly faster.

- noforwardadd: Disables additive passes for forward rendering so that the shader supports only one full directional light, and the other lights are computed per vertex. This makes the shader smaller and more efficient.

- approxview: Makes the view direction normalized per vertex instead of per pixel (which is approximate but often good enough). This improves the shader's performance because there are fewer vertices than there are pixels in a render – we'll discuss this a bit more in the next section, *Optimizing your runtime performance*.

- halfasview: Further speeds up the shader by replacing the view vector with the half-vector (meaning the vector halfway between the lighting direction and the view vector). This half-vector is computed and normalized per vertex and then passed on directly to the lighting function.

Depending on the visuals you are trying to achieve, you can simplify your Surface Shaders even more – at the cost of some render features – with other directives:

- noshadow: Disables shadows receiving support in the shader

- nolightmap: Disables lightmapping support in the shader

- nofog: Disables support for the built-in fog in the shader

These options are more "aggressive" since they completely turn off some features, which in turn means they will actually change the visual result. But it can be an interesting optimization for some stylized esthetics, or some low-resolution versions of your objects.

With this quick review of the Unity URP shading models out of the way, let's now dive into the nitty-gritty of writing optimized shader code, and discuss more low-level improvements.

Optimizing your runtime performance

There are various interesting low-level optimizations you can do to improve your shaders and keep your code fast.

In the following sections, we will see why the precision of your computations matters, which mathematical operations are considered "complex" and can slow down your shaders, and how some particular cases such as alpha testing may benefit from platform-specific implementations. Finally, we'll discuss how picking the right esthetics for your project can sometimes help with technical limitations.

Float, half, or fixed?

If you're a bit familiar with Unity shaders, then you've probably already seen that, depending on the tutorial you look at, fragment shader functions may return either `float4` or `half4`. This might be surprising at first: how come the same function can use different types like this, and why choose one over the other?

Well, a key idea to keep in mind when doing intensive calculations such as graphics rendering is that you always have to do a trade-off between precision and memory. Because computers can't just store infinite numbers, we have to decide where we stop decimals and truncate the ideal value into an actual hardware-compatible representation. The rule of thumb is that the more decimals you have, the more precise your computations are, but the heavier the toll on your machine.

Unity HLSL shaders largely rely on floating point calculations – but to represent these floating point numbers and control the precision of your computations, they don't just have the `float` variable type like in C#. Rather, to help optimize your calculations on mobile and low-tier platforms, the engine offers us three types of floating point data in our shaders: `float`, `half`, and `fixed` (along with the associated composite types, such as `float4x4` or `half3`).

Each data type has its own advantages and drawbacks, and consequently, its optimal use cases. Most notably, some types may not be available on your target platform, because they are not supported by all GPUs. So, depending on the hardware you are building your project for, your code might be "incompatible."

If you use floating point data types that are not available on the current architecture, then they will be converted automatically to the next best thing – usually, the first available data type that has as low precision as possible. But relying on these automatic conversions is not always error-proof, and even if it doesn't directly impact the results, it can still hinder your performance. That's why when you get into rendering optimization, it's important to understand which data type can be used in which case.

> **Beware of PC GPUs and performance testing!**
>
> Keep in mind that PC GPUs *always* use high-precision data, or in other words, `float`s, for their computations. Even if you use a `half` or `fixed` data type in your code, it will ultimately be converted to a `float` type. So remember that because the `half` and `fixed` types are only available for mobile GPUs, you should test your shaders on these target platforms to check whether you are experiencing precision and/or efficiency issues – otherwise, you run the risk of having an inaccurate assessment of the situation.

Figure 10.4 shows a summary of the usual size of each type, the associated precision level, the family of GPUs it is available on, and what use cases it is usually appropriate for (as presented in the official Unity documentation at `https://docs.unity3d.com/Manual/SL-DataTypesAndPrecision.html`):

Data type	Size	Precision	GPU families	Common use cases
`float`	32 bits	High	All	World space positions, texture coordinates, complex scalar calculations (for example, with power/exponentiation)
`half`	16 bits	Medium	PowerVR SGX 5xx, PowerVR Series 6/7, Qualcomm Adreno 4xx/3xx, ARM Mali T6xx/7xx, NVIDIA X1, NVIDIA Tegra 3/4	Small vectors, directions, object space positions, high dynamic range colors
`fixed`	11 bits	Low	PowerVR SGX 5xx	Regular colors, small computations

Figure 10.4 – Summary table of the three possible floating point data types (float, half, and fixed)

> **Important note**
>
> In *Figure 10.4*, the **Size** column shows the most common size on most platforms, but it may differ on some architectures.

At this point, you see that using `float` variables may seem like the better solution – at least in terms of cross-platform compatibility and computation precision. But never forget that they consume the most memory-wise and that this can be an issue on lower-tier devices and mobiles. 32 bits might not look like much, but because of the technical limitations on these devices, a graphically demanding project will absolutely require the technical artists to dive into the shader code and optimize the data types!

Moreover, thanks to "fast path" execution units and improved GPU register allocation, using lower precision is often faster and less taxing on the battery life of mobiles.

Another interesting gotcha to remember is that floating point number suffixes in HLSL shaders are actually ignored by Unity's shader compiler. For example, consider the following piece of code:

```
half3 normal = half3(1.0, 0.0, 0.0);
half3 recenteredNormal = normal * 2.0h - 1.0h;
```

In this snippet, we use the common h HLSL suffix to give Unity a hint that we want all the computations to be done using `half` types. However, because the suffix is ignored, this actually underperforms, as it will first calculate intermediate values of 2 and 1 as `float` variables, then do the computation in high precision and only convert the result back to a `half` value at the end.

To optimize this computation, we should explicitly use `half` values for our constants, like this:

```
half3 normal = half3(1.0, 0.0, 0.0);
half3 recenteredNormal = normal * half(2.0) - half(1.0);
```

Picking the right data type is obviously important, but it's not the only way to improve your shaders' performance. Sometimes, you also need to think about what operations you are doing with those numbers, and whether some should be rewritten to get faster calculations.

Avoiding complex mathematical operations

Nowadays, GPUs implement more and more mathematical operations in their hardware, which helps optimize low-level computations. However, there are still functions that are quite resource-intensive and should be avoided in your shaders when possible.

Most notably, transcendental mathematical functions (meaning functions that cannot be expressed as polynomials) are fairly demanding for the hardware – common examples of such transcendental functions are as follows:

- The power function, `pow`
- The exponential function, `exp`
- The natural logarithm, `log`
- The cosinus, `cos`

- The sinus, `sin`

- The tangent, `tan`

Of course, this is not to say that you should never use them in your shader code. There are many rendering schemes that rely on trigonometric functions or exponents.

But if you target a platform with severe technical limitations, you might want to try and replace these operations to improve the performance of your shader. To solve this issue, a usual technique is to use lookup textures: basically, you store the results of your computations in some image file, and then re-read the pixels of this image to instantly retrieve the values. The texture can either be prepared beforehand, if the result of the calculation can be guessed in advance, or generated at runtime but then saved in a cache to avoid recomputing the results.

> **Computation versus memory trade-off**
>
> This trick of using lookup textures is a handy way of reducing the compute time of your HLSL shaders and optimizing your calculations on low-tier platforms. However, it also means that you have to store those textures somewhere, which can sometimes be complicated on mobile platforms that have limited storage. This is once again an example of the common "computation versus memory" trade-off we need to make when improving the performance of resource-intensive code.

With that said, if you do need to use compute-intensive functions in your code, it is generally good practice to rely on Unity's built-in tools, because they have been expertly crafted to generate the best possible code for the various platforms. Typically, you shouldn't try and re-implement vector normalization or dot products; just use the built-in `normalize` and `dot` tools – they will make for more efficient shader code!

To sum up, mathematical computations are at the heart of shader code, so it is crucial to do your best to optimize them for each of your target platforms. But it's not the only type of scoped low-level improvement we can do!

Handling transparency in shaders

To continue on this idea, let's have a quick look at something we do quite often in shader code, and yet that can sometimes cause some performance issues – alpha testing, which is used to get transparent visuals.

As we've already peeked at in *Chapter 5*, for example, when describing the Shader Graph tool, one of the important characteristics of a Unity shader is whether it is opaque or transparent. Indeed, this impacts how objects with this shader will interact with the rest of the scene since it determines whether they block the view and hide what's behind them or not.

You probably also know that even opaque shaders can still support a very basic transparency system with just "on" or "off" pixels; in other words, you don't get nice, blended edges with decreasing alpha values, but rather you just have some parts of your mesh that are completely opaque and others that are completely transparent.

This is possible thanks to alpha testing, which allows you to directly discard some pixels from rendering, and therefore abort useless computations early. This process, also known as clipping, can be done in Unity HLSL shaders in two ways:

- Either you define the `Alpha Test` keyword in a `Pass` block of your shader, to define the direction and the value of the clip threshold – for example, to only render pixels with an alpha value of 0.5 or greater, you could use the following shader code:

```
Shader "Simple Alpha Test" {
    Properties {
        _MainTex ("Texture (RGBA)", 2D) = "" {}
    }
    SubShader {
        Pass {
            AlphaTest Greater 0.5
            // ...
        }
    }
}
```

- Or you use the built-in `clip` function to remove any pixel for which the value inside the `clip` function call is negative – the following snippet would once again keep only pixels with an alpha value above 0.5:

```
Shader "Simple Alpha Test" {
    Properties {
        _BaseTex ("Texture (RGBA)", 2D) = "" {}
    }
    SubShader {
        Pass {
            // ...
            float4 frag (v2f i) : SV_Target {
                float alpha = SAMPLE_TEXTURE_2D(
                    _BaseTex, sampler_BaseTex,
                        i.uv).a;
                clip(alpha - 0.5);
            }
        }
    }
}
```

This process of crudely discarding pixels to get fully opaque and fully transparent parts is the most efficient most of the time – that's why, when possible, you should try and replace your transparent shaders with opaque shaders that use alpha testing. This can, of course, lead to some visual artifacts and unappealing aliasing on foreground elements, but for objects in the distance, it can usually be used without too many consequences in terms of quality.

> **Improving the quality of clipped visuals**
>
> To mitigate these quality issues, a nice trick can be to design a shader with two `Pass` blocks, one that uses alpha testing and one that uses alpha blending. The alpha testing `Pass` block stores pixel depth and therefore improves the efficiency of the shader in the scene (by quickly blocking computations for any pixel behind an opaque one), and the alpha blending `Pass` block doesn't store pixel depth but helps improve the visuals. For more information, you can check out this example in the Unity documentation: `https://docs.unity3d.com/Manual/SL-AlphaTest.html`.

There is, however, one case where alpha testing is detrimental to the performance of your shader: on iOS and some Android mobiles (those using PowerVR GPUs), alpha testing is actually quite resource-intensive, and thus discarding pixels with the `Alpha Test` keyword or the `clip` function doesn't help with optimization.

Of course, this is somewhat of a special case, but is worth considering if you have a lot of transparent shaders in your project as it can significantly improve your runtime performance, but won't apply to all situations. Another valuable trick with a broader set of use cases is ensuring that your shaders are compatible with the SRP Batcher.

Creating SRP Batcher-compatible shaders

A while ago, in *Chapter 2*, we briefly discussed how, with the new SRPs, Unity also introduced some direct optimizations under the hood – in particular, for managing the CPU-to-GPU data transfers. We saw that thanks to some rewrites of low-level engine parts and with the introduction of the **SRP Batcher**, Unity is now able to better handle data persistence in the GPU memory and thus make quicker renders.

However, we also said that, when working on custom shaders, you needed to ensure they were compatible with this SRP Batcher in order for the engine to perform these optimizations. So, what does it mean for a shader to be compatible with the SRP Batcher? How can we make sure our shaders can be used by this tool?

Luckily, ensuring shader compatibility with the SRP Batcher is not too difficult. There are simply two things to keep in mind:

- All your material properties (meaning the exposed options in the **Inspector** for materials using your shader) have to be declared in a single constant buffer named `UnityPerMaterial`.

To ensure all the passes in your shader use the same buffer, we usually declare our properties along with their buffer at the `SubShader` level, inside the `HLSLINCLUDE` block. The buffer is declared thanks to the `CBUFFER_START` and `CBUFFER_END` built-in macros, which the engine will eventually replace with the appropriate code for declaring a constant buffer if the current platform supports it (basically, most platforms apart from OpenGL ES 2.0).

Typically, for a simple shader with a texture and a color, we could write something like this:

```
Shader "URPExample" {
    Properties {
        _BaseTex ("Texture (RGBA)", 2D) = "" {}
        _Color ("Color", Color) = (1, 1, 1, 1)
    }
    SubShader {
        HLSLINCLUDE
        #include "Packages/com.unity.render-pipelines
            .universal/ShaderLibrary/Core.hlsl"
        CBUFFER_START(UnityPerMaterial)
        float4 _BaseTex_ST;
        float4 _Color;
        CBUFFER_END
        ENDHLSL
        Pass { ... }
    }
}
```

The `CBUFFER_START` and `CBUFFER_END` macros are directly included from the `Core.hlsl` file from the Unity URP library, which is why we need to add the `#include` directive before using it in the `HLSLINCLUDE` block.

- All your built-in engine properties (for example, `unity_ObjectToWorld`) have to be declared in a single constant buffer named `UnityPerDraw`.

  This buffer is once again declared with the `CBUFFER_START` and `CBUFFER_END` macros; for example, for common Unity space transformation matrices, we could have the following code:

```
CBUFFER_START(UnityPerDraw)
float4x4 unity_ObjectToWorld;
float4x4 unity_WorldToObject;
float4 unity_LODFade;
real4 unity_WorldTransformParams;
CBUFFER_END
```

Be careful because even if you don't use all of the built-in properties from this group of values, you still need to declare all of them in the constant buffer in order for the SRP Batcher to consider your shader compatible (so, your `CBUFFER_START`/`CBUFFER_END` block needs to contain the declaration of `unity_ObjectToWorld`, `unity_WorldToObject`, `unity_LODFade`, and `unity_WorldTransformParams` as soon as your code uses at least one).

If your shader obeys those two rules, then it should be compatible with the SRP Batcher and Unity will be able to batch draw calls for the objects in the scene that use it.

By the way, remember that you can always check whether a specific shader file is SRP Batcher-compatible by looking at its **Inspector**, and checking the **SRP Batcher** property, as shown in *Figure 10.5*:

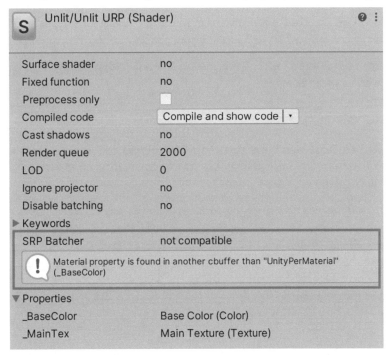

Figure 10.5 – Shader Inspector of a non-SRP-Batcher-compatible shader

Disabling the SRP Batcher – why and how

Despite all its merits, the SRP Batcher is not a silver bullet – and there are some situations where it can conflict with other features. Typically, the SRP Batcher cannot be used along with GPU instancing (which is a common optimization technique that bundles together all draw calls for meshes with the same material in a single draw call). If you render many meshes with the same material, GPU instancing can be more efficient than the SRP Batcher, and you may therefore want to disable the SRP Batcher.

To do this, you can either make your shader incompatible with the SRP Batcher (by breaking one of the two rules mentioned earlier in this section) or add a `MaterialPropertyBlock` variable to your renderer, which will automatically toggle off the SRP Batcher.

Okay, we now have an idea of some specific tricks we can use to improve the performance of our shaders – from picking the right floating point data type to reducing our usage of complex mathematical functions, alpha testing, or ensuring compatibility with the SRP Batcher. But of course, there is another obvious optimization technique worth mentioning: the removal of all the unnecessary fluff from your code!

Checking that you only compute what's needed

I know – this may look like a basic idea. You are, of course, aware that it's not great to compute useless results, and you probably always try and simplify your shader code as much as possible.

And yet, many of us Unity technical artists have a few habits that sometimes get in the way of performance without us realizing.

Having too much flexibility

A common slowdown for shaders is the "just in case" features we tend to add during the development phase to balance out efficiency and adaptability, which remain in advanced versions of the project although they aren't useful anymore.

Think of the basic diffuse shaders you often create at the beginning of a project to quickly populate your white-box scenes and help the level designers convey the core elements of the story. These prototype materials and shaders are, of course, meant to be as flexible as possible – you'll want the game designers to be able to easily change their colors, shininess, and even textures so that they can represent all the necessary information quickly. So you'll create a simple script that exposes a wide variety of properties, maybe even some dynamic branching (as we discussed in *Chapter 9* as a means of introducing conditional behavior in shaders), and then you'll handle all the different cases to create a powerful and adaptive asset.

But when the time comes to actually build and ship your game, and when you'll be down to optimizing the rendering performances, these materials might actually come back to haunt you.

Why? Because all of this flexibility is now fairly useless.

To put it simply, when the prototyping is done and the artists on your team have produced the right assets, the need for adaptability in shaders will become secondary – your mesh parts will have a given color, shininess, and texture. No need to let designers pick and choose anymore.

This means that, in your shader code, you don't have to define exposed properties for all those characteristics anymore, and you may not even need your branching directives. For example, if you know that a material will always be just pure white, it is far more efficient to hardcode this color in your script once and for all. This will avoid lookups and computations for each vertex or each pixel of your object, and will therefore improve the performance of the shader.

Ideally, a clean production workflow should enforce that all the prototype materials are eventually replaced with "production-ready" equivalents, which would be tuned specifically for the final assets and would thus sidestep this issue. But on smaller productions, or on all those projects that started off as a game jam but ended up growing into actual games, you don't always have that tidy a process, and you can easily run into this kind of problem.

So, remember that flexibility is a nice touch during development, but you may need to leave it behind when you optimize your project.

Off-loading to the vertex shader function

Sometimes, another possible improvement trick for shaders is to transfer some of your logic from the fragment to the vertex shader function.

Indeed, most of the time, there are many more pixels than there are vertices in a 3D scene render process, and so computing a value for each vertex is quicker than computing it for each pixel. Thus, if some part of your data or your logic is continuous on your mesh, you should take advantage of your computer's rasterizer and let it interpolate the value you output from the vertex shader function.

This cannot apply to all shaders, obviously, but it is a nice idea to keep in mind if you're struggling to optimize your rendering, and if moving computations to the vertex shader code doesn't impact the visuals too much.

Turning to "lighter" graphics altogether

As a final note in this section, we can mention a more meta idea, which is about the overall esthetics of your game. This is not an optimization per se, but I thought it interesting to briefly outline another level of reflection when considering the technical limitations of your game.

We are in an age of incredible technological achievements, and the video game industry has understood this. Our powerful GPUs have barely had the time to be amazed that we've already given them quite the workload – for the past decade, games have slowly closed the gap with movies, and it now seems like players' thirst for hyperrealism and lifelike graphics can never be quenched. This, in turn, means that you as a technical artist have to double down on the tricks to actually render all of these visuals (and even more so when you consider another huge evolution of gaming, which is the development of mobile platforms).

Still, while AAA game studios are battling for who'll produce the most realistic water, facial animation, or beast fur, many smaller companies have decided to go the other way around, and instead turn to low-poly esthetics. Among other things, these independent productions have brought back a retro vibe and some artistic trends such as pixel or voxel art, which totally assume their "low-quality" visuals but also take advantage of the reduced computational cost.

Typically, similar to the previous idea of off-loading calculations from the pixel to the vertex shader function, a common trick with voxel engines is to perform vertex lighting – in short, you don't compute shadows and lights per pixel but per vertex, and then you let the rasterizer handle the interpolation for you. And of course, since those worlds are all made out of cubes, you can use instancing and refer to a single geometry (namely, the cube) that you repeat again and again, which significantly reduces the memory requirements of your app.

Now, the point is not to have everyone do voxel art – part of the charm of the video game community is in the endless diversity, and in all the unique approaches people find to renewing style and gameplay. There are obviously many situations where realistic visuals are more suited to narrating the story and sharing your world with the players.

Just don't forget that sometimes, the best solution to finding your own style and escaping the pain of heavy graphics is simply not to use them!

And if you're really going for a unique style, then perhaps you can consider going further and cutting yourself from Unity's ready-made pipelines – so to wrap up this chapter, let's discuss why and how you can create your very own custom SRP in Unity.

Creating your own SRP

Developing performant code is never easy, and rendering is no exception. The famous programming mantra of "make it work, make it right, make it fast" typically applies very well to coding shaders. Usually, you'll need to iterate multiple times over your scripts to really get the effects right, and then when the optimization phase comes, you'll have to once again rework the whole thing to squeeze the performance out of your code.

We've seen, in the two first sections of this chapter, that this optimization step can be about choosing the right option for your shader lighting mode, or even doing some low-level data type conversions. But there might come a day when these fall short for you – if your project is really too special, and if it leverages really unique visual features, then perhaps Unity's built-in options won't be enough.

Because, despite our best efforts, we haven't yet reached a point where a single rendering pipeline can work perfectly for all types of games. This is why Unity offers us multiple options with the SRPs and even the built-in renderer, and why some independent productions or arty creations dare to take the bull by the horns and re-implement their own rendering scheme from scratch.

So, in this final section, we are going to discuss why you may want to turn to a custom rendering pipeline and what tools Unity offers us to do so, by doing a quick demo of a custom SRP that only renders unlit meshes.

Why use a custom render pipeline?

Choosing to go with your own pipeline is a strong technical choice. Unity's ready-made pipelines (be it the legacy one or the new SRPs) have been tried and tested for many years, thus guaranteeing a certain degree of robustness. Conversely, relying on your own render pipeline can be more risky and lead to some low-level issues that you'll need to deal with.

But using a custom render pipeline is also an incredible opportunity to tune the rendering process to your liking and really optimize the visuals for your specific case. Never forget that an engine as generalist as Unity has to do some trade-offs here and there, and can't provide top-notch efficiency for each and every situation – so creating a specialized system can be the key to boosting your game's performance and going the extra mile if your renders are very different from the norm.

With that said, Unity isn't just throwing us to the wolves on that one, and with their SRPs, they have actually introduced a way to develop custom pipelines in a fairly safeguarded environment.

Here, we will focus specifically on creating custom Unity SRPs – this is not quite as low-level as re-implementing an entire rendering engine from scratch, but it ensures a minimum level of safety and ease of use. This is sort of an in-between: we don't go down to the hardware and graphics backends, but we still specialize the rendering process to optimize our own kind of visuals.

Typically, a nice perk of using Unity's custom SRPs is that we can easily benefit from core systems such as culling, and just implement our tailor-made tweaks on top of them. And remember that the Universal Render Pipeline and High Definition Render Pipeline are both made based on this feature, so it's clearly quite powerful!

Alright, then – how does it work exactly?

Setting up a basic custom SRP

Okay, it is now time to put all of this into practice and discover how to create our own SRP! To end this chapter, we will do a quick demo of how to set up a simple unlit render pipeline in Unity.

> **Important note**
>
> As with the previous examples in this book, the custom render pipeline we will code up here is not optimized for the best runtime performance. Rather, it is designed to be as clear and readable as possible.

First of all, to test our custom pipeline as we develop it, let's create a basic scene with a few cubes and spheres. Since we want to make our own SRP from scratch, for now, we will start with the legacy pipeline.

Remember you can make your project use the built-in render pipeline by either creating it from a basic 3D template or removing the reference to the SRP render pipeline asset from your **Project Settings | Graphics** panel:

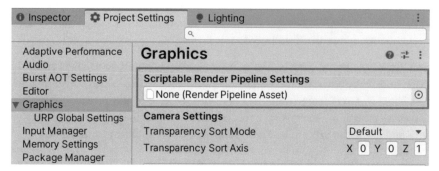

Figure 10.6 – Project settings with no SRP asset enabled, to use the legacy render pipeline

So, we'll give our objects various common built-in materials from the legacy pipeline such as the **Standard** and **Unlit** shaders, in either **Opaque** or **Transparent** mode. Don't hesitate to check out the Chapter 10 folder in the GitHub repo of this book (available at https://github.com/ PacktPublishing/Become-a-Unity-Shaders-Guru) if you want to see my exact scene setup.

Figure 10.7 shows what the scene looks like at the moment:

Figure 10.7 – Basic scene with test objects, rendered using Unity's built-in legacy pipeline

You can see in *Figure 10.7* that, because we are using the normal legacy pipeline, we see all of our objects, both the ones with and without lighting, as usual. Our goal in this section will be to create a custom pipeline that only renders the objects with an unlit shader (in other words, the three yellow spheres and the white transparent unlit sphere on the left).

To do so, we will process in three steps:

1. First, we will create our own render pipeline asset, instantiate it, and assign it in our **Project Settings** panel, in the **Graphics** section.

2. Then, we will prepare a custom render pipeline class – this class will be instantiated by our render pipeline asset at the time of the render and it will take care of filling all the right render data for Unity in each frame.

3. Finally, we'll discuss the basic operations of a simple render loop and implement them in our custom render pipeline logic.

Let's go through this step by step!

Creating our render pipeline asset

To begin with, we need to make our own pipeline asset by defining and instantiating a new C# script. We will call this script CustomRenderPipelineAsset.cs, and our goal will be to pass an instance of it to Unity in the **Project Settings | Graphics** panel, just like we do for the URP or HDRP pipeline assets. This script will tell Unity "how to render," by providing it with a RenderPipeline instance (and it would also allow us to define our pipeline's settings, if we had any).

Here, I'm going to reproduce Unity's folder structure for the URP pipeline, and nest my script inside a **CustomRP | Runtime** hierarchy, as shown in *Figure 10.8*:

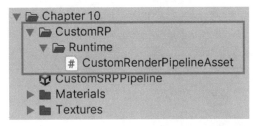

Figure 10.8 – Folder structure for the custom render pipeline scripts and assets

This script needs to inherit from the RenderPipelineAsset C# class, which we can find in the UnityEngine.Rendering package – so we can initialize our CustomRenderPipelineAsset class as follows:

```
using UnityEngine;
using UnityEngine.Rendering;

public class CustomRenderPipelineAsset : RenderPipelineAsset {}
```

Now, we can override the `CreatePipeline` method in our script, which will return the `RenderPipeline` instance Unity needs to perform the render:

```
public class CustomRenderPipelineAsset : RenderPipelineAsset {
    protected override RenderPipeline CreatePipeline() {
        return null;
    }
}
```

To actually make our script instantiable as an asset in the project, we need to give it the `[CreateAssetMenu]` attribute. As we saw in *Chapter 7*, we can define where the menu item will be located by passing the attribute a `menuName` parameter, like this:

```
[CreateAssetMenu(menuName = "Custom RP/Custom Render Pipeline")]
public class CustomRenderPipelineAsset : RenderPipelineAsset {
    protected override RenderPipeline CreatePipeline() {
        return null;
    }
}
```

At this point, we can create an instance of our `CustomRenderPipelineAsset` script in the project, thanks to our new menu item:

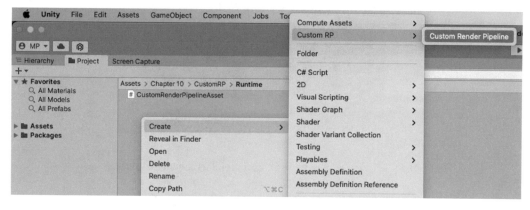

Figure 10.9 – Create menu item for our custom render pipeline asset

And then, we simply need to assign this `CustomRenderPipelineAsset` instance in our **Project Settings | Graphics** section, as with any SRP asset:

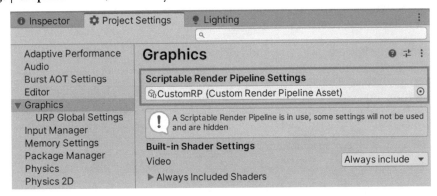

Figure 10.10 – Project settings with our custom render pipeline asset instance assigned

Of course, at the moment, our `CreatePipeline` method returns a null `RenderPipeline` instance, so the engine can't render anything anymore: our scene is completely black! The **Scene** and **Game** view aren't functional, and even material previews are now invalid.

So the next step is to create a valid `RenderPipeline` for our custom rendering process.

Making a custom render pipeline

Once again, we can start with a basic version of a custom `RenderPipeline` class, and then iterate to improve it. We are going to create another C# script, `CustomRenderPipeline.cs`, and place it in the same folder as `CustomRenderPipelineAsset.cs`: **CustomRP | Runtime**.

This class has to inherit from the `RenderPipeline` C# class, which is in the `UnityEngine.Rendering` package too:

```
using UnityEngine;
using UnityEngine.Rendering;

public class CustomRenderPipeline : RenderPipeline { }
```

The `RenderPipeline` base class also defines an abstract method that we need to override in our own derived class, called `Render`. This is the function that Unity will invoke every frame, which will actually fill the render buffers and write the proper data for each camera rendering the scene:

```
public class CustomRenderPipeline : RenderPipeline {
    protected override void Render(
        ScriptableRenderContext context,
            Camera[] camera) { }
}
```

You see in this code snippet that the `Render` method takes both the array of cameras enabled for the render and a render context. We will see very soon how to use these parameters but, for now, let's keep things simple and leave our function empty like this – this will already allow our `CustomRenderPipeline` script to compile.

This way, we can use it in our `CustomRenderPipelineAsset` class, in the `CreatePipeline` method, where we want to return a new instance of `CustomRenderPipeline`:

```
[CreateAssetMenu(menuName = "Custom RP/Custom Render Pipeline")]
public class CustomRenderPipelineAsset : RenderPipelineAsset {
    protected override RenderPipeline CreatePipeline() {
        return new CustomRenderPipeline();
    }
}
```

Now, to have our pipeline render something, we will need to add some logic in our `Render` function to compute the render of the scene for the active cameras we've been given. This means that we want to loop through all of our active cameras and run the render logic on each:

```
public class CustomRenderPipeline : RenderPipeline {
    protected override void Render(
        ScriptableRenderContext context,
        Camera[] cameras) {
            foreach (Camera camera in cameras) {
                // per-frame & per-camera render logic
            }
    }
}
```

Alternative code base organization

Note that for a more complex custom render pipeline, it could be a good idea to extract this per-camera render process to its own class. This would make it easier to browse the code base and understand the different steps each camera needs to take in order to create a valid render.

If you're curious, here is a great example of a step-by-step tutorial for an advanced custom SRP from the great *Catlike Coding* blog: `https://catlikecoding.com/unity/tutorials/custom-srp/custom-render-pipeline/`.

So, now, let's see how to implement the right logic in our `CameraRenderer` script to actually draw our different objects and render this scene.

Drawing our scene

To show something on the screen, we need to draw various things in the right order and implement what is called a **render loop**. This loop usually consists of these three steps:

1. **Clearing the render target**: Because we draw our scene contents at each frame, we need to make sure that we don't have leftovers from the previous frame before drawing the new data. So the first step is to clear our screen by removing all the previously rendered geometry from the last frame.

2. **Culling**: The culling process filters out the geometry that is not visible to a camera and avoids losing computing power on objects that are not in the field of view.

3. **Drawing**: Finally, we have to tell our GPU what to draw to render our geometry.

For these operations, we will reuse the concept of `CommandBuffer` that we already explored briefly in *Chapter 2*. In short, the point is to stack commands in a buffer in the right order, and then give this buffer to Unity to have the engine render the frame accordingly. We won't need to explicitly manipulate `CommandBuffer` instances at each step, because the `context` variable actually has a `CommandBuffer` instance that we can interact with thanks to shorthands and nice methods; but behind the scenes, all of this is about listing the right render commands for Unity.

Okay – time to re-implement these three operations in our `Render` method to recreate some nice custom visuals. We can work on each step one after the other.

Clearing the render target

For this first operation, we will create an explicit `CommandBuffer` instance, store a "clear command" in it, and then execute and clear the buffer to finalize the step.

For the sake of simplicity, we can consider that this operation is global to the entire frame, thus we will do it before our loop on the cameras; the code in itself is quite self-explanatory:

```
protected override void Render(ScriptableRenderContext context,
Camera[] cameras) {
    // 1. Clear the target render
    CommandBuffer cmd = new CommandBuffer();
    cmd.ClearRenderTarget(true, true, Color.black);
    context.ExecuteCommandBuffer(cmd);
    cmd.Release();

    foreach (Camera camera in cameras) {}
}
```

We could also clear the render target per camera, typically if we had multiple cameras with different background colors.

Culling

We'll then want each of our cameras to apply culling – meaning they should check which objects are in their field of view, and which ones can be ignored. Handling this for a multi-camera setup could be a pain but, luckily, Unity has some built-in tools to help us: the camera.TryGetCullingParameters and context.Cull methods.

All we have to do is, in our foreach loop, get the culling parameters for the current camera, and apply these settings to our render context (which will basically set this culling for all the upcoming drawing commands):

```
protected override void Render(ScriptableRenderContext context,
Camera[] cameras) {
    // 1. Clear the render target...

    foreach (Camera camera in cameras) {
        // 2. Cull
        camera.TryGetCullingParameters(
            out var cullingParameters);
        var cullingResults = context.Cull(
            ref cullingParameters);
    }
}
```

Note that you could manually update some parameters of the cullingParameters variable if you want, but it should always be retrieved with the camera.TryGetCullingParameters method so that its initial value is valid.

Drawing

And now, for the grand finale! We are finally about to store draw instructions in the render context to tell our GPU how to render our scene.

This drawing step is where we will look through our scene and gather all the geometry our pipeline can render, and then draw the corresponding 2D onscreen shapes based on our current camera settings.

So, first, we need to know what objects we will draw. To do this, the trick is to list the renderable meshes based on the LightMode pass tag inside their shader. This unique shader tag ID allows us to quickly get all the meshes compatible with our pipeline. In our case, since we only want to render unlit meshes, we can use the built-in SRPDefaultUnlit tag. And because it will stay the same throughout all the frames, we'll define it as a static variable in our CustomRenderPipeline class, as follows:

```
public class CustomRenderPipeline : RenderPipeline {
    static ShaderTagId shaderTagId =
        new ShaderTagId("SRPDefaultUnlit");
```

```
    protected override void Render(
        ScriptableRenderContext context,
            Camera[] cameras) { ... }
}
```

Now, we can use this shaderTagId variable and our current camera instance in the foreach loop to get our render settings, apply our culling, and render our meshes using the context.DrawRenderers method:

```
protected override void Render(ScriptableRenderContext context,
Camera[] cameras) {
    // 1. Clear the render target...

    foreach (Camera camera in cameras) {
        // 2. Cull...
        // 3. Drawing
        // update built-in shader variables
        context.SetupCameraProperties(camera);
        var sortingSettings = new SortingSettings(camera);
        DrawingSettings drawingSettings =
            new DrawingSettings(shaderTagId,
                sortingSettings);
        FilteringSettings filteringSettings =
            new FilteringSettings(RenderQueueRange.all);
        context.DrawRenderers(cullingResults,
            ref drawingSettings, ref filteringSettings);
    }
}
```

While we're at it, we can also restore the drawing of our skybox easily, thanks to the context.DrawSkybox method:

```
protected override void Render(ScriptableRenderContext context,
Camera[] cameras) {
    // 1. Clear the render target...

    foreach (Camera camera in cameras) {
        // 2. Cull...
        // 3. Drawing
        // update built-in shader variables
        context.SetupCameraProperties(camera);
        var sortingSettings = new SortingSettings(camera);
        DrawingSettings drawingSettings =
            new DrawingSettings(shaderTagId,
                sortingSettings);
```

```
        FilteringSettings filteringSettings =
            new FilteringSettings(RenderQueueRange.all);
        context.DrawRenderers(cullingResults,
            ref drawingSettings, ref filteringSettings);
        context.DrawSkybox(camera);
    }
}
```

And finally, we need to remember to actually send our current render context to Unity at the end of our loop iteration, by calling the context.Submit method – this will ensure that the commands we gradually stored in our context variable are indeed sent to the GPU (otherwise, they will just be discarded when the loop ends!):

```
protected override void Render(ScriptableRenderContext context,
Camera[] cameras) {
    // 1. Clear the render target...

    foreach (Camera camera in cameras) {
        // 2. Cull...
        // 3. Drawing
        // update built-in shader variables
        context.SetupCameraProperties(camera);
        var sortingSettings = new SortingSettings(camera);
        DrawingSettings drawingSettings =
            new DrawingSettings(shaderTagId,
                sortingSettings);
        FilteringSettings filteringSettings =
            new FilteringSettings(RenderQueueRange.all);
        context.DrawRenderers(cullingResults,
            ref drawingSettings, ref filteringSettings);
        context.DrawSkybox(camera);
        context.Submit();
    }
}
```

If you save the file and wait for Unity to recompile everything, you'll see that we have now restored a visual and that we have successfully managed to remove the render of lit meshes:

Figure 10.11 – (Incomplete) basic scene with test objects, rendered using our custom SRP

There's just one issue: we only see our solid unlit objects – the ones with a transparent shader aren't drawn anymore! Does that mean we've lost some geometry on the way, or that the transparent unlit shader cannot be retrieved using the SRPDefaultUnlit shader tag ID?

Well, in truth, our fourth unlit sphere is rendered, it's just that we can't see it. To check that, we can take advantage of Unity's **Frame Debugger** tool, available in the **Window | Analysis** menu. Once you open it, you'll see that the **Frame Debugger** window has an **Enable** button you can click to instantly get a detailed listing of all the draw calls that went into making the frame you are currently seeing:

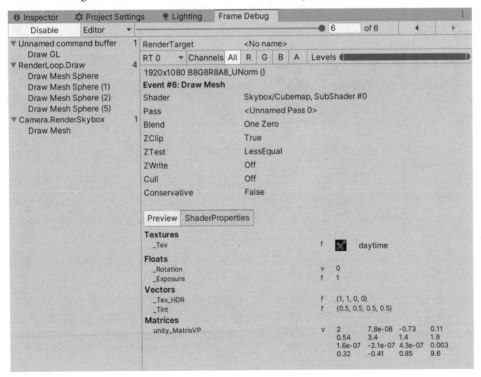

Figure 10.12 – Frame Debugger panel with the list of draw calls for the current frame

You can see in *Figure 10.12* that we indeed draw four spheres – but the final render of the skybox hides away the transparent one. To understand how exactly the various drawing steps combine, you can use the slider at the very top to see the intermediate renders one draw call at a time. For example, if we go back to step **5** out of **6** (or in other words, *before* the skybox is drawn) as shown in *Figure 10.13*, we see that our transparent sphere is indeed rendered:

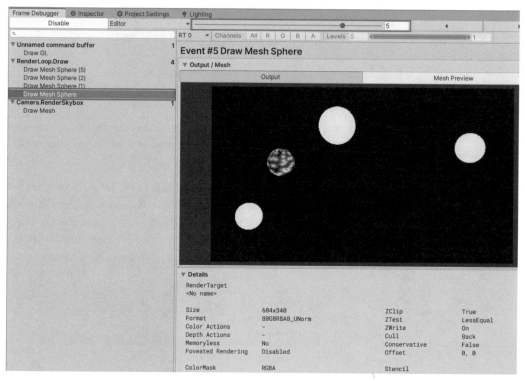

Figure 10.13 – Intermediate drawing state for our scene before the render of the skybox

What this means is that our mesh is found and drawn, but we have an issue with the ordering of the commands in the buffer. The good news is that it is actually very easy to fix – here, I intentionally made a little mistake in our `CustomRenderPipeline` script in order to introduce the **Frame Debugger** tool.

In fact, we should draw the skybox before we draw the meshes by inverting the lines at the end of our `foreach` loop like this:

```
protected override void Render(ScriptableRenderContext context,
Camera[] cameras) {
    // 1. Clear the render target...

    foreach (Camera camera in cameras) {
```

```
// 2. Cull...
// 3. Drawing
// update built-in shader variables
context.SetupCameraProperties(camera);
var sortingSettings = new SortingSettings(camera);
DrawingSettings drawingSettings =
    new DrawingSettings(shaderTagId,
        sortingSettings);
FilteringSettings filteringSettings =
    new FilteringSettings(RenderQueueRange.all);
context.DrawSkybox(camera);
context.DrawRenderers(cullingResults,
    ref drawingSettings, ref filteringSettings);
context.Submit();
    }
}
```

If we recompile, we see that our unlit meshes now render fine in the scene, all thanks to our custom SRP:

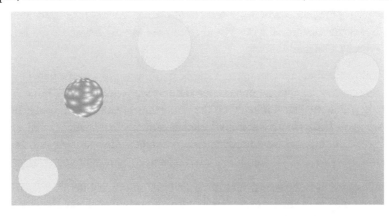

Figure 10.14 – Basic scene with test objects, rendered using our custom SRP

Here we are – we now have a simple example of how to create our own SRP step by step. With just a few assets and a dozen lines of code, we have managed to filter, sort, cull, and draw the meshes in our scene without even having to change their materials.

> **Quick note**
>
> If you set up your project to use a ready-made SRP, such as URP or HDRP, you will see all objects except the lit ones will render pink because these pipelines don't support the legacy **Standard** shader.

This is obviously just a toy example with no real applications, but hopefully, the process is now clearer for you, and you will feel ready to tackle this kind of highly-specialized task the day you need your own render process in Unity.

This concludes our brief overview of custom Unity SRPs and shader optimization tricks.

Summary

In this chapter, we explored various techniques and tools for improving the efficiency of our shader code.

We first talked about lighting models and discussed how Unity provides us with several built-in ones. We saw that they always do a trade-off between realism and power usage and that your target platform has a big impact on the kind of lighting you can use in your games.

Then, we dove into low-level optimization and studied different scoped improvements for shader code, from per-platform computation precision to mathematical operation complexity, alpha testing caveats, and even SRP Batcher compatibility.

Finally, we had a peek at another approach and introduced the basics of writing a custom SRP shader in Unity to completely tune the rendering process to our liking. We saw how the engine gives us easy-to-use and safe tools for customizing our visuals, and how we can debug the render steps in detail thanks to the **Frame Debugger** window.

As a final note, always remember that optimizations are only as good as the benchmarks you do to assess the bottlenecks of your application and that the science of performance boosting requires you to test in the right conditions (most notably, on the actual target platforms) to really narrow down the areas of improvement. There is no point in fixing a fake slowdown or spending hours on a negligible computation hiccup. Rather, you need to learn to analyze and profile your projects in order to focus your optimization work.

In the next chapter, we will move away from these advanced topics and enter the final part of the book, where we explore a gallery of shader examples to deepen our knowledge of the Unity URP shaders with hands-on examples. We'll start with 2D shaders and see how to apply various effects on sprites, such as negate, color-swap, pixelate, outline, dissolve, and many more!

Going further

If you're curious about URP shader code and making your own SRP, the following are a few interesting resources to check out or continue your journey from.

Shader code optimization

- Official documentation on the URP shading models, Unity: `https://docs.unity3d.com/Packages/com.unity.render-pipelines.universal@10.2/manual/shading-model.html`

- *Optimizing shader runtime performance* (official documentation), Unity: `https://docs.unity3d.com/Manual/SL-ShaderPerformance.html`

- *7 Ways to Optimize your Unity Project with URP*, Unity (2020): `https://www.youtube.com/watch?v=NFBr21V0zvU`

Custom SRPs

- Official documentation on custom SRPs, Unity: `https://docs.unity3d.com/Manual/srp-custom.html`

- *Custom Pipeline – Taking Control of Rendering*, Catlike Coding (2019): `https://catlikecoding.com/unity/tutorials/scriptable-render-pipeline/custom-pipeline/`

- *Custom SRP and graphics workflows | Battle Planet - Judgement Day - Unite Copenhagen 2019*, Unity (2019): `https://www.youtube.com/watch?v=91zUwJwkXNQ`

- *CREATE YOUR OWN RENDERER WITHOUT CODE in Unity!*, Brackeys (2019): `https://www.youtube.com/watch?v=szsWx9IQVDI`

Part 5:
The Toolbox

Throughout the first four parts of this book, we deepened our understanding of Unity shaders, especially when using the new URP pipeline, and we discovered how to use both HLSL code and the Shader Graph tool to create various effects and illusions. We also saw a few tricks to optimize our shaders and make the most of our devices.

To finish our exploration of shaders, we will go through the most common types of shaders and, for each category, discuss a few examples to expand our horizons, preparing a little toolbox of commonly used tools that you'll be able to refine and adapt in your own future projects.

In this part, we will cover the following chapters:

- *Chapter 11, A Little Suite of 2D Shaders*
- *Chapter 12, Vertex Displacement Shaders*
- *Chapter 13, Wireframes and Geometry Shaders*
- *Chapter 14, Screen Effect Shaders*

A Little Suite of 2D Shaders

In the previous chapters, we talked about shader performance, and we took quite a meta look at how technical artists can optimize rendering in a Unity project. These are obviously crucial skills to have as an advanced shader creator, but they're often not the most enjoyable part of the job.

Rather, a shader artist wants to create shaders, right?

Well, good news! In this chapter and the upcoming ones, we will go through little galleries of shaders and learn various techniques with a hands-on approach by studying a variety of common use cases. Ideally, these examples will serve both as references for your future projects and primers for more experimentation on your part.

And to begin with, let's discuss 2D shaders! To do so, we'll talk about the following topics:

- Implementing color-swap, hue-shift, saturate, negate, and pixelate effects
- Making 2D outlines
- Having fun with overlay textures, dissolves, and holograms

Technical requirements

To try out the shader examples shown in this chapter, you should install Unity with a version from 2021 or later and make a project using the **Universal Render Pipeline** (**URP**) pipeline.

In all the demos of this chapter, I will use the following three images:

- A dwarf image
- A pixel-perfect sphere image
- A pixel-perfect character sprite sheet by GrafxKid (available at: https://opengameart.org/content/classic-hero)

All these images are PNG images with a transparent background. They are used as sprites in a **Sprite Renderer** component placed on a simple empty Unity game object in the scene, like this:

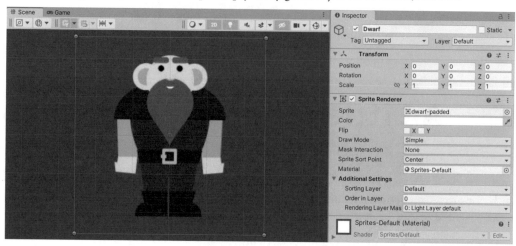

Figure 11.1 – Object setup with a 2D Sprite Renderer component and the sample dwarf image

You can check out how the scene is organized and find all the Shader Graph Assets for this chapter, as well as the demo images and textures in the GitHub of the book at `https://github.com/PacktPublishing/Become-a-Unity-Shaders-Guru/tree/main/Assets/Chapter%2011`.

Implementing color-swap, hue-shift, saturate, negate, and pixelate effects

To begin with, let's talk about some common operations we can do on sprites, such as inverting the colors, shifting the hue to re-colorize the image, or saturating the tint to exaggerate our colors. Then, we will discuss the technique of color-swapping for pixel-perfect sprites. And finally, we will see how to make a simple dynamic pixelation of our sprites to transform them into approximate pixel art equivalents.

Performing basic operations such as hue-shift, saturate, and negate

Because hue-shifting, saturation, and negation are such basic transformations, Unity actually has built-in Shader Graph Nodes for most of this – we will see which one corresponds to each operation.

First, we will work on our `Negate` shader. The point here is to invert the colors, meaning that black will become white and vice versa, but also that red will become blue, for example. Just to give you an idea, *Figure 11.2* shows the comparison of our original sample dwarf image on the left and its negated version with our shader applied on the right:

Figure 11.2 – Example of a sprite with our Negate shader applied

To create this shader, we will start from the **Sprite Unlit Shader Graph** template Unity provides us with for creating a new Shader Graph Asset. Remember you can access it in the asset **Create** contextual menu, by right-clicking in the **Project** dock and navigating to the **Create | Shader Graph | URP** menu:

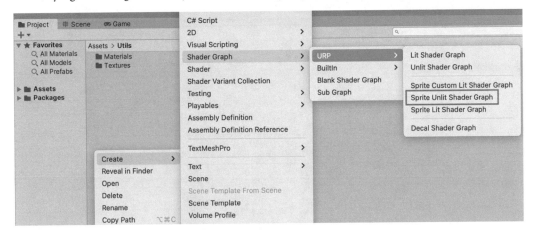

Figure 11.3 – Contextual menu for creating a new Shader Graph Asset based on a URP template

Once you've created this new asset and named it something like `Negate`, double-click on it to open it in the Shader Graph editor, and you will see that you have an empty graph with the **Vertex** and **Fragment** output contexts:

Figure 11.4 – Startup Negate shader configuration created from the Sprite Unlit Shader Graph template

In the **Fragment** context, you have a default solid gray **Base Color**, and in the **Alpha** output slot, there is a value of 1. Therefore, if you create a material based on this **Negate** shader and assign it to our 2D dwarf sprite, you will get just a square filled with gray:

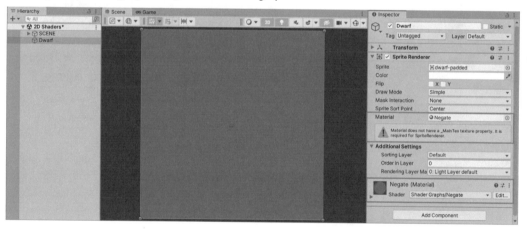

Figure 11.5 – Result of the startup Negate shader on our Sprite Renderer

We could, of course, change this color directly in the graph by hand and see how it affects the output or play with the alpha value… but in truth, what we want is to restore the actual texture and transparent background of our image. To do so, we need to do a couple of things:

- First, we have to add a `_MainTex` property to our shader (as indicated in the warning shown in *Figure 11.5*, this is necessary for sprite shaders), and sample this texture using the **Sample Texture 2D** node

- Then, we need to connect the **RGBA** output slot of the **Sample Texture 2D** node to the **Base Color** slot of the **Fragment** context and the **A** output slot to the **Alpha** slot

Here is the resulting graph and visual:

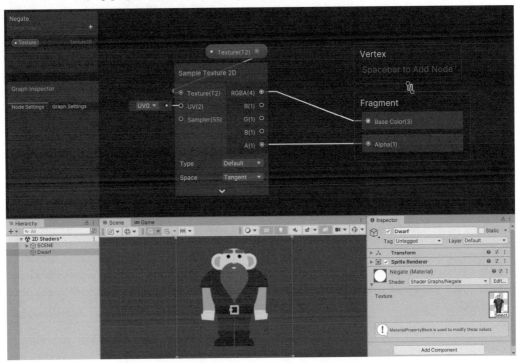

Figure 11.6 – Graph and the result of our Negate shader with just the initial texture sampling

You see that we now display our sprite normally again. To create a negate effect, we simply need to add one last node in our shader logic before outputting the texture color: **Invert Colors**. We will only invert the red, green, and blue channels and keep the alpha as-is:

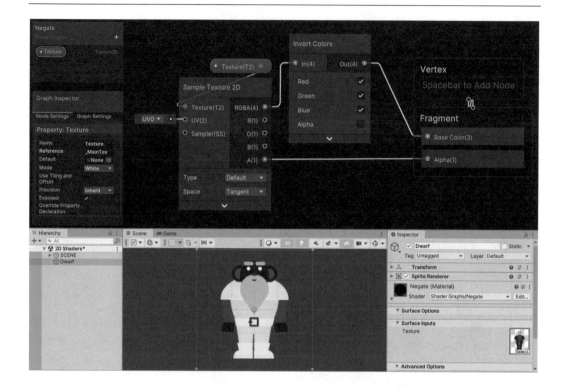

Figure 11.7 – Graph and the result of our Negate shader with the negate effect

And here we are! You can see that our image is now properly negated: we retain the transparent background, but the colors are inverted as expected.

For the hue-shift operation, the Shader Graph Asset will be quite similar. We will just add a `Shift` property so that users can easily control the color shift amount and use the **Hue** node instead of the **Invert Colors** one:

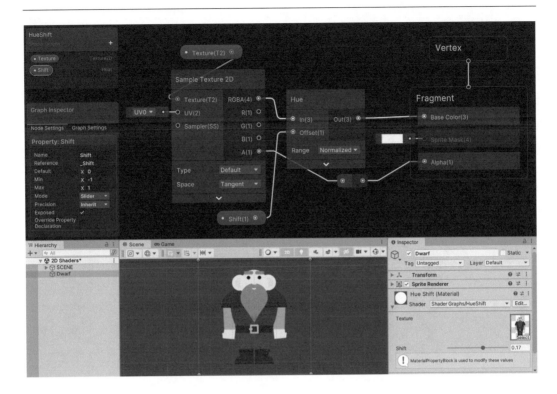

Figure 11.8 – Graph and the result of our HueShift shader

You can see in *Figure 11.8* how this shader colors our dwarf image with more greens when using a `Shift` value of `0.17`.

Finally, the saturate effect can be done once again with the same sort of setup, simply by replacing our `Shift` property with a `Saturation` property and replacing the **Hue** node with a **Saturation** one. We will keep the usual conventions and consider that a `Saturation` value of `0` means we turn the image to grayscale, a `Saturation` of `1` means we keep the original colors, and values above `1` "over-saturate" the tints:

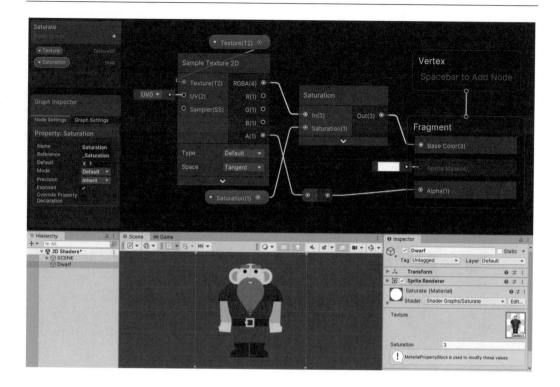

Figure 11.9 – Graph and the result of our Saturate shader

Figure 11.9 shows an example of the dwarf image "extra-saturated" with a `Saturation` value of 3.

OK – we now have some simple shaders that perform basic operations on our sprite to transform its colors in various ways. However, we have only seen how to apply the effect globally and affect the entire sprite all at once. Sometimes, you might want to be a bit more precise and only touch certain areas of the image – typically for color-swapping.

Creating a color-swap system

If you ever work with 2D sprites and need to easily re-colorize parts of your images, you are bound to stumble upon the color-swapping technique.

In a nutshell, the idea behind color-swapping is to write a shader that automatically replaces a given input color with another one for each pixel in your sprite. You can do it for either a single pair of input and output colors or for multiple pairs.

A very common use case for color-swapping is for player unit colors. Suppose you have a multiplayer game where each player is assigned a unique color and where players can produce three types of units: the guard, the archer, and the mage. Each type of character has its own sprite, and you would like for the unit's chest armor or robes to be colored according to the player's color to better identify each team. In that situation, you clearly want to avoid duplicating the character sprites for each possible player color – this will quickly grow into an insane amount of image files as soon as you add a new color or a new character type. Here, a better solution is to use this color replacement technique to transform your initial sprite with a default player color into its equivalent for other player colors on the fly and only store the default character spritesheets. For example, *Figure 11.10* shows the result of doing a color swap of the blue shirt on the hero spritesheet by GrafxKid:

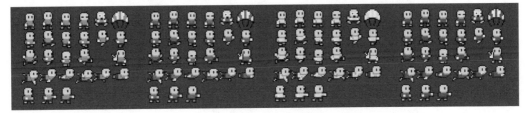

Figure 11.10 – Color-swapping on the hero spritesheet, replacing the blue shirt with red, yellow, or purple

Of course, because you're replacing an exact color value, the color-swapping technique should be used on **pixel-perfect sprites** with no **anti-aliasing** – otherwise, your swap logic will have trouble with the smoothed color gradients.

So, whenever you plan on using this process, make sure that in the import settings of your sprite, you turn the **Filter Mode** property to **Point** to disable anti-aliasing; to do so, follow these steps:

1. Select your image asset and scroll to the bottom of its inspector.

2. Use the **Filter Mode** drop-down selector and pick **Point (no filter)**:

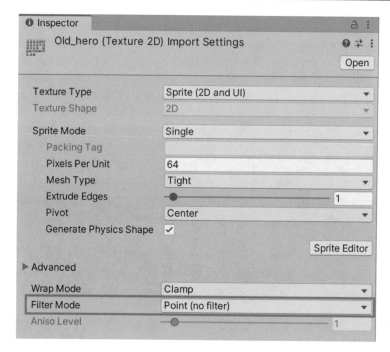

Figure 11.11 – Import settings for a pixel-perfect sprite with no anti-aliasing

By the way, this is also why for this section, I'll use the pixel-perfect character spritesheet by GrafxKid instead of the dwarf sprite.

Now, there are two possibilities to consider: either you are doing a single color swap, or a multiple color swap to replace several colors at once in your original sprite. Let's study each case in more detail.

Single color swap

If you just want to change a single color in your sprite, then you can take advantage of Unity's built-in **Replace Color** node in the Shader Graph. You simply need to give it the original texture in its **Input** entry, the color to replace in its **From** input, and the color to switch to in its **To** input. This means that we can create a basic single color-swapping shader that looks like this:

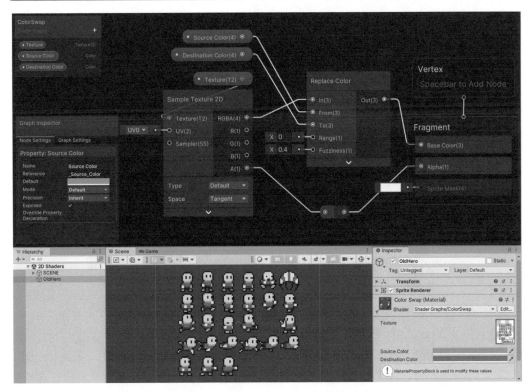

Figure 11.12 – Graph and the result of our single ColorSwap shader

Figure 11.12 shows how this shader replaces the blue color of the character's shirt with a red tint and leaves the rest of the image intact. This is great because it allows us to easily tweak the color to change and the replacement color to use... but it's a bit limited because it only handles one swap operation!

So let's have a look at how to implement a multiple color-swap shader.

Multiple color-swap

Our single-color swap shader is nice, and it would probably be enough for a basic color replacement scheme, typically for per-player unit colors. But what if we need something more advanced, where different colors get replaced by new ones?

We could, of course, add more **Replace Color** nodes in our graph to handle more color swaps – but this technique wouldn't be very scalable, and the graph would soon become quite unreadable. Moreover, having a chain of **Replace Color** nodes actually means our shader logic would contain multiple conditional statements, which is always an expensive operation.

This is why, usually, for multi-color swap, a better technique is to rely on a swap texture, to specify all the replacement values in a single data source. The trick is then to use one of the channels of our original image, for example, the red one, to serve as a "picker" inside this swap texture. So, typically, we could say that "any pixel for which the color has a red value of X will be replaced by color C" – and this way, if two pixels in our original image have different red components, we'll be able to easily map them to new colors in our swap texture. And since classical **Red, Green, and Blue (RGB)** images can have red values between 0 and 255, this technique will allow us to remap up to 256 different values at the same time.

Of course, we have to be careful because two colors that are different in our source image can have the same red value – *Figure 11.13* shows a few colors along with their red value, and you see that a pure black and a pure blue both have a value of 0 in the red channel:

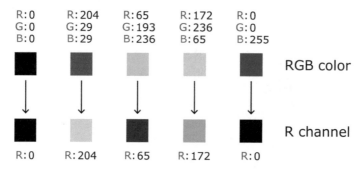

Figure 11.13 – Various RGB colors with their red component isolated

But if we ensure that all the colors in our sprite have different red components, then we can make a swap texture of 256x1 pixels, where each non-transparent pixel corresponds to a replacement color, and the position of the pixel along the horizontal axis corresponds to the red value to replace.

In *Figure 11.14*, you can see a simplified example of such a swap texture where we use 16-pixel wide replacement color blocks (instead of 1-pixel wide) so it is more readable:

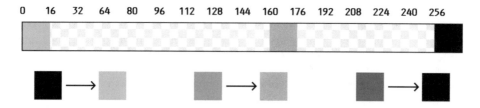

Figure 11.14 – Simplified swap texture with 16-pixel wide replacement color blocks

Here, a value of 0 to 16 in red (the block completely on the left) is remapped to a light blue, a value of 160 to 176 (the block further on the right) is remapped to an orange, and a value of 256 is remapped to black.

If you look at the files of the GitHub repository for the book, you will find a color-swap texture that works exactly the same but has 256 pixels along the horizontal axis to support the normal 256 red values of an RGB image.

OK, we know that we want to sample this swap texture based on the red component of our initial texture color at each pixel. This is actually easier to do as a short **High-Level Shader Language (HLSL)** shader code than a big Shader Graph Asset with multiple sampling chunks, so let's create a new shader file in our project and fill it with the base skeleton of a URP HLSL shader, like this:

```
Shader "Unlit/MultiColorSwap" {
    Properties {}
    SubShader {
        Tags { "RenderType"="Opaque" "RenderPipeline" =
            "UniversalPipeline" }
        Blend SrcAlpha OneMinusSrcAlpha
        ZWrite On

        HLSLINCLUDE
        #include "Packages/com.unity.render-pipelines
            .universal/ShaderLibrary/Core.hlsl"
        struct appdata {};
        struct v2f {};
        ENDHLSL

        Pass {
            HLSLPROGRAM
            #pragma vertex vert
            #pragma fragment frag

            v2f vert(appdata v) {
                v2f o;
                return o;
            }

            float4 frag(v2f i) : SV_Target {
                return float4(1, 1, 1, 1);
            }
            ENDHLSL
        }
    }
}
```

This code snippet simply contains a common HLSL shader structure, like in the examples we studied throughout the previous chapters of this book.

Now, we will build this shader step by step to implement our texture sampling logic and get the multi-color swap process we want. We can do this as follows:

1. First, we'll need two properties of the Texture type for the initial sprite, and the swap texture:

```
Properties {
    [MainTexture] [NoScaleOffset] _MainTex ("
        Main Texture", 2D) = "white" {}
    [NoScaleOffset] _SwapTex ("Swap Texture", 2D) =
        "white" {}
}
```

2. Then, we need to remember to create the associated low-level variables in our HLSLINCLUDE block with the texture samplers:

```
HLSLINCLUDE
#include "Packages/com.unity.render-pipelines
.universal/..."

TEXTURE2D(_MainTex); SAMPLER(sampler_MainTex);
TEXTURE2D(_SwapTex); SAMPLER(sampler_SwapTex);

struct appdata {};
struct v2f {};
ENDHLSL
```

3. Our appdata structure needs to contain the vertex's position and UV coordinates, and we'll then pass on this data in the v2f structure as well:

```
struct appdata {
    float4 vertex : POSITION;
    float2 uv : TEXCOORD0;
};
struct v2f {
    float4 vertex : SV_POSITION;
    float2 uv : TEXCOORD0;
};
```

4. Our vert function will implement the usual local-to-clip space conversion on the vertex's position and leave the UV coordinates unchanged:

```
v2f vert(appdata v) {
    v2f o;
    o.vertex = TransformObjectToHClip(v.vertex.xyz);
    o.uv = v.uv;
```

```
            return o;
    }
```

5. And finally, our `frag` function will first sample the initial sprite texture and then extract the red component of the resulting pixel's color and sample the other texture (the swap texture) at the *X* coordinate corresponding to this red value. Then we will simply get back the alpha value from the original sprite to properly set the opaque and transparent zones on our sprite and return the final color:

```
float4 frag(v2f i) : SV_Target {
    float4 col = SAMPLE_TEXTURE2D(_MainTex,
        sampler_MainTex, i.uv);
    float4 swap = SAMPLE_TEXTURE2D(_SwapTex,
        sampler_SwapTex, float2(col.r, 0));
    float4 c = lerp(col, swap, swap.a);
    c.a = col.a;
    return c;
}
```

You see in this snippet that to only consider non-transparent pixels in our swap texture, we use the `lerp` function based on the alpha value of the swap color. This means that if this alpha value is 0 and the swap color is transparent, then we just keep the original color as-is.

And that's it! If we create a new material asset using this shader and apply it to our pixel-perfect hero sprite, we can then use the swap texture we want to replace one or more colors at the same time and re-colorize multiple parts of the image in one swift process.

Figure 11.15 shows an example of this multi-color swap shader used to replace three colors – the outline and the hero's light and dark shirt parts:

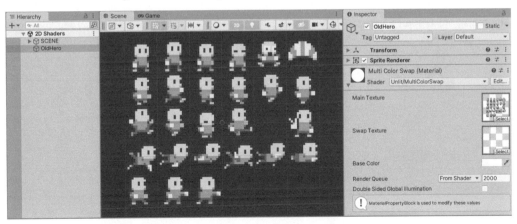

Figure 11.15 – Result of our MultiColorSwap HLSL shader with
three replacement colors in the swap texture

To sum up, color swapping is a powerful technique that can greatly reduce the number of sprite assets to make when used well because it allows you to dynamically re-adapt the colors of your images and therefore create variations. The example we saw here relied on the red channel as the differentiator, but depending on your use case, you can, of course, use any of the other two (or three) channels of an RGB (or **Red, Green, Blue, and Alpha (RGBA)**) image: green or blue (or alpha).

Now, all those color transformations are cool, but we could also just prepare our sprites with these other colors in advance. So what about making shaders that actually impact our image at runtime to apply some filter or effect? Let's start with a really cool one – the auto-pixelation of a sprite into a pixel-art approximation.

Pixelating a sprite dynamically

To wrap up this first series of basic sprite shaders, let's work on a nice effect: a dynamic pixelation system! Basically, this will allow us to quickly make an approximate pixel-art version of a "smooth" sprite. To do this, we will have a `Pixelation` shader property normalized between 0 and 1.

Now, the process of transforming a smooth texture into a pixelated image is as follows:

1. First, we will scale up our texture UVs based on our pixelation factor – more precisely, we will use the **One Minus** node to get the complementary value of our `Pixelation` property and multiply this value by 100 to get it as a percentage.

2. Then, we will take our scaled-up UVs and floor them to get the "pixel grid" effect.

3. Finally, we will divide the UVs by the same factor as before to retrieve the UVs in the proper range.

4. These final UVs will be used in the **UV** input slot of a **Sample Texture 2D** node, and then we will simply connect the **RGBA** and **A** outputs to the **Fragment** context slots as in our previous shaders.

All of this is fairly straightforward and relies on self-explanatory nodes we already know – so here is the final graph of the `Pixelate` shader and the resulting visual on our dwarf image for a `Pixelation` value of roughly `0.5`:

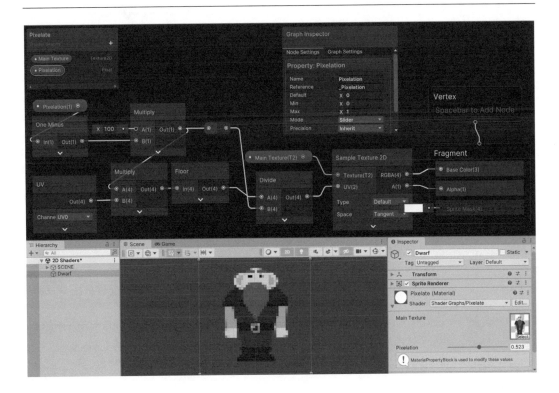

Figure 11.16 – Graph and the result of our Saturate shader

You see in *Figure 11.16* that we can play around with our `Pixelation` property to increase or decrease the effect and get more or fewer crude pixels on our sprite.

The various shaders we discussed in this section are quite simple and quick to make, and yet they implement a lot of the common operations we like to do on sprites. It is, therefore, interesting to know the basics of this toolbox because they can apply to many situations.

To continue our quick exploration of 2D shaders, let's now dive into another very common effect for 2D sprites – contouring and outlines.

Making 2D outlines

After this brief introduction to 2D sprite shaders, we will move on to another nice topic for 2D shaders: the auto-outlining of sprites, thanks to dynamic and tweakable stroke shaders. Our goal here is to build more and more advanced shaders to introduce new effects gradually and create more complex outlines around our sprites.

We will first begin with a simple outline using one solid color, then we will see how to use post-processing and HDR emissive colors to add glow, and finally, we will study how to make animated shaders that use the current time in their logic.

Implementing a simple outline

First of all, let's see how to implement a simple sprite outline for a pixel-perfect sprite. This is a simple technique for adding a stroke that relies only on copying and translating. It doesn't handle corners, so it doesn't work very well for smooth sprites, but here is how it will look on our sample pixel-perfect sphere:

Figure 11.17 – Pixel-perfect sphere sprite without (left) and with (right) our soon-to-be Outline shader

Of course, the nice thing is that because this is a shader, we can have some extra control parameters, such as the thickness or the color of the stroke (see *Figure 11.23*).

A pixel-perfect outline like this is fairly straightforward to make. The trick is to do the following:

1. Create four copies of our original sprite.

2. Translate each copy along the *x* or *y* axis slightly: we'll move one with a positive *x* offset, one with a negative *x* offset, one with a positive *y* offset, and one with a negative *y* offset. The offset will depend on the thickness we want for the outline, and these four copies will therefore correspond to an "extended" version of our image along these four strict directions.

3. Recombine all the copies into a single outline, and patch them along with the original sprite.

4. Make sure to use only the "shape" of the outline, but re-colorize it in a single color: the outline color.

We can start with the copy and translation part. To start off, we'll make a Sub Graph Asset to handle just one side of the outline: `OutlineSide`. This graph logic is quite simple, actually – we'll renormalize the outline thickness by our texture's base texel size (using the **Texel Size** and **Reciprocal** nodes) and then displace the texture by this offset value in the given direction. And since we only need to get the shape of this displaced texture and not its color, we'll only output the alpha value from our Sub Graph:

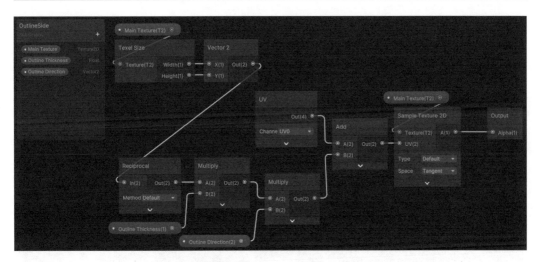

Figure 11.18 – A Sub Graph asset to compute one side of the outline

Now, we can make our actual `Outline` Shader Graph Asset, and inside use this `OutlineSide` Sub Graph four times to get the outline on the four sides of our sprite:

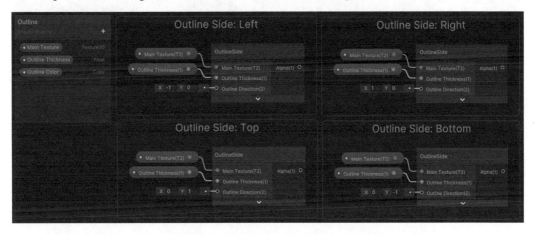

Figure 11.19 – Multiple instances of our OutlineSide Sub Graph inside the
main Outline shader with different displacement directions

You see in *Figure 11.19* that we always use the same `Main Texture` and `Outline Thickness` properties (directly passed from our main Shader Graph Asset properties to the Sub Graph), but we have a different value for the `Outline Direction` property in each Sub Graph instance.

We'll then combine the four outline pieces into one by adding them and saturating the result to avoid going outside the 0–1 range. Then, we'll re-compose the right color by using our previous result as the alpha value and the user-specified outline color as the **R**, **G**, and **B** values. The overall graph now looks like this:

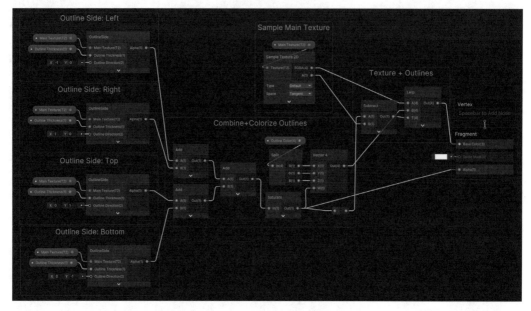

Figure 11.20 – The combination of the four Sub Graph instances into a single colorized outline (the text within this image is not important, and the image intends only to show the overall graph logic)

And for reference, here is a zoomed-in screenshot of the **Combine+Colorize Outlines** node group we've just added:

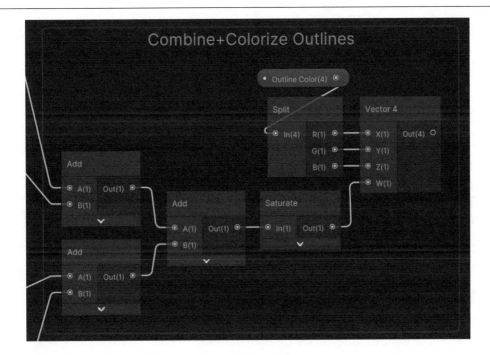

Figure 11.21 – A zoomed-in screenshot of the new Combine+Colorize Outlines node group

Finally, all that's left to do is sample the base texture and composite it with the outline. To properly mix the two, we want to get the actual stroke alpha – because remember that, for now, what we have computed is basically our sprite "spread out" by an offset in the four directions, but there is no hole in the middle. So first, we'll subtract the alpha of the initial sprite from the alpha of the outline to only get the actual stroke shape; and then, we'll use a **Lerp** node to switch between the original image's pixel color and the stroke pixel color, depending on the alpha value:

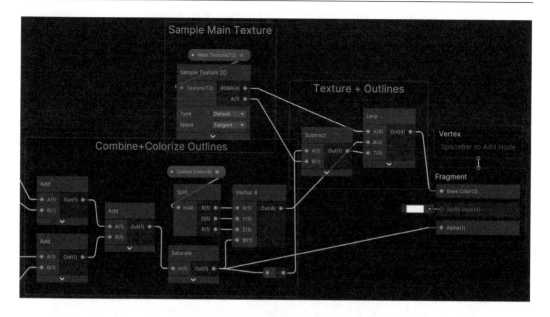

Figure 11.22 – Final mixing of the original sprite with the outline

Our `Outline` shader is now ready, and we can apply it, for example, to our pixel-perfect sphere image to instantly add a stroke around our initial sprite with a specific thickness and color:

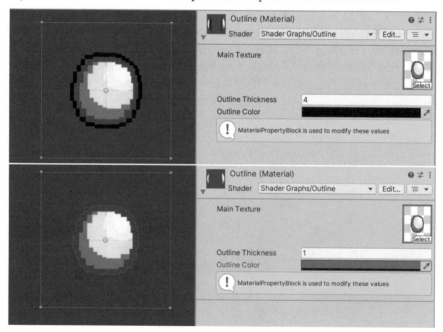

Figure 11.23 – Result of our Outline shader on the pixel-perfect sphere sprite with various values for the Outline Thickness and Outline Color properties

We can, of course, also use this basic outline shader on a smooth image such as our dwarf, but as expected, it doesn't handle the corners properly because we only have displacements in four strict directions:

Figure 11.24 – Result of our Outline shader on a smooth image with missing corners

To fix this, a simple solution would be to add the corners as well by instantiating our OutlineSide Sub Graph four more times with diagonal displacement directions. We can do this in a new Shader Graph Asset based on the Outline shader (that we call OutlineWithCorners, for example), which works exactly the same, except we also have these additional instances for the corners, like this:

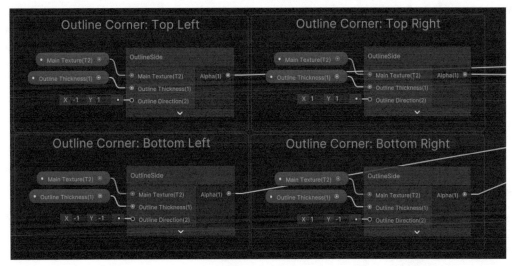

Figure 11.25 – A graph of our improved Outline shader with corners

Then by combining these results with the previous ones, we get a continuous stroke that also takes care of the corners and creates a smooth result:

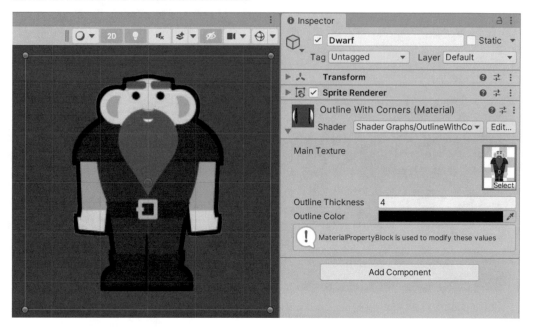

Figure 11.26 – The result of our improved Outline shader on a smooth image, with corners

So we now have a basic outline shader that can easily add some strokes around our sprites with a given thickness and color. There are still remaining artifacts that you might want to remove – in particular, the thickness is not exactly the same everywhere – but overall, this shader is easy to understand and quick to implement, and it makes for nice results in most cases (basically, unless you have a high value on your Outline Thickness property, the stroke thickness variations will probably not be too much of an issue).

But what if we wanted something a bit more arty? With even fancier effects, such as a glowy outline or an animation in the stroke? Let's level up and see how to make even more advanced outlines!

Making our stroke glow

At the moment, our Outline shader works with a simple color for the stroke. Our Outline Color property is applied to the whole outline shape – but it is a simple RGB value.

In order to add a glow effect to our stroke, a very cool thing we can do is modify this property so it is a **High Dynamic Range (HDR) color**. This way, it will also contain an intensity value that represents how emissive the color is.

So, let's create a new Shader Graph Asset based on the last one (`OutlineWithCorners`), called `OutlineWithGlow`, and edit our `Outline Color` property to change its mode to **HDR** in the drop-down menu:

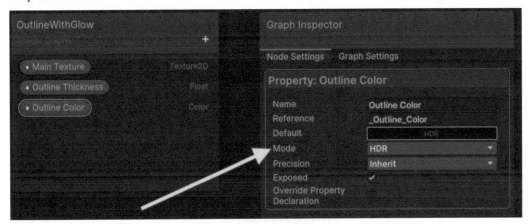

Figure 11.27 – The Outline Color property set in the HDR mode

Then we see that, in the **Graph Inspector** panel, the color input for this `Outline Color` property transforms into one marked **HDR**, and the color picker contains some additional buttons at the bottom to set the color's intensity:

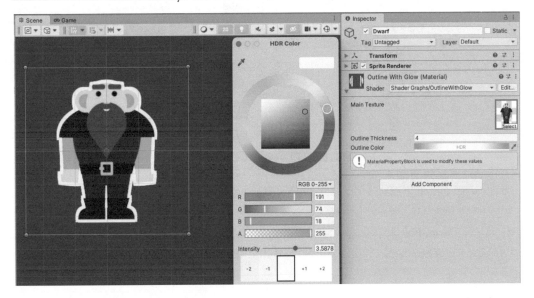

Figure 11.28 – New input color in HDR mode for the Outline Color property and result on our dwarf sprite

You'll notice in *Figure 11.28* that the outline around the dwarf does look more emissive... but it's not really *glowing*. That's because, in Unity, to achieve a real glow effect, you have to apply some **post-processing**.

It used to be that, in the built-in render pipeline, you'd need to download and install a specific package to do post-processing (**Post Processing Stack V2**). That package contains a lot of modules and premade effects, and it can be added to your project to boost your image in various ways.

But the great thing is that, with the new **Scriptable Render Pipeline** (**SRP**) pipelines, Unity decided to make things even simpler and directly integrate post-processing tooling in the render pipelines. So, in our URP project, we can actually do post-processing without having to install an additional package.

All we have to do is create a new object in our scene and give it a **Volume** component. Then, inside this component, we can create a new **Profile** asset by clicking the **New** button next to the slot and fill this post-processing profile with various effects by clicking the **Add Override** button. Typically, in our case, we want to add a **Bloom** effect for the glow:

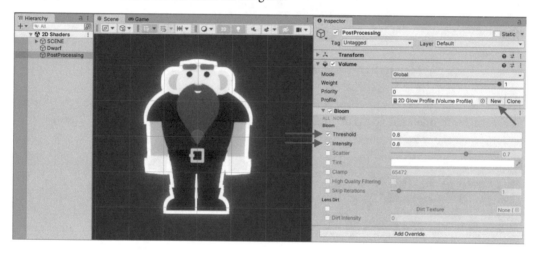

Figure 11.29 – Glowing outline with a Bloom post-processing effect applied

Here, I've set the **Threshold** property of my **Bloom** effect to 0.8 so that it mostly focuses on the parts of the scene with high-intensity color, and I've set the **Intensity** property of the **Bloom** effect to 0.8 as well to get something fairly visible. And, indeed, you see that my dwarf now has a nice glowing stroke that wraps him in a sort of halo.

Of course, the effect is pretty strong here, and chances are that, in a real game, you'd be a bit more subtle. But if you ever need to add some glow strokes to your levels, you now have a simple step-by-step process of how to do so!

Adding animation to our outline

As a last example, let's add another nice feature to our `Outline` shader: an animation that mixes two colors with a basic noise. This creates a cool "power-up" effect for your characters – for example, here is the result on our dwarf sprite with a slightly glowing yellow and red combo:

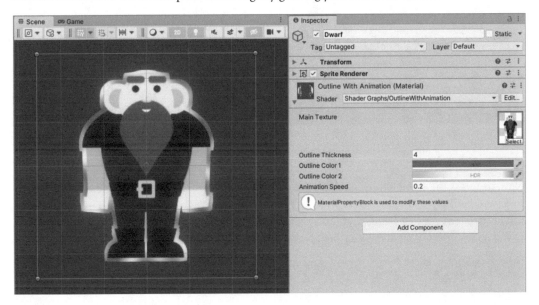

Figure 11.30 – Animated outline with multiple colors mixed together using a procedural noise

To create this effect, we can once again copy our last shader, `OutlineWithGlow`, and extend its logic to incorporate this animation. Basically, we will replace the outline colorization part (which until now was just about multiplying the alpha value by the `Outline Color` property) with something a bit more advanced so that the color changes over time.

This new shader, which I'll call `OutlineWithAnimation`, will have two color properties instead of one, `Outline Color 1` and `Outline Color 2`. It will also have a **Float** property, `Animation Speed`, to determine how quickly the noise moves around and the color mix changes:

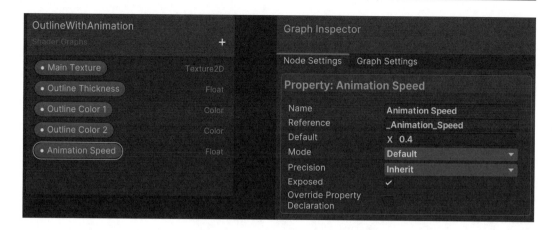

Figure 11.31 – Properties of our new OutlineWithAnimation shader

Now, to access the current time and have the property change as time goes by, we can use the **Time** node and multiply it by our speed. This will be the *Y* coordinate for our noise texture sampling, so we just need to feed it into a **Tiling And Offset** node – and then, we can use the output of this **Tiling And Offset** node as the **UV** input of a **Gradient Noise** node to get a nice random noise-based grayscale value:

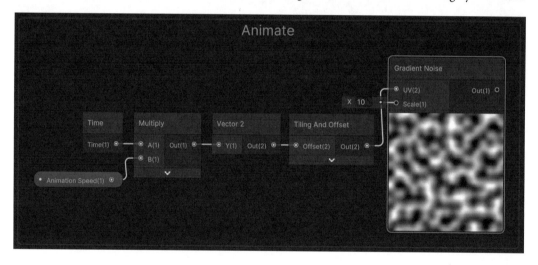

Figure 11.32 – Computation of an animated procedural noise grayscale mask

This black-and-white procedural texture can now be used to mix together our `Output Color 1` and `Output Color 2` properties. More precisely, we will use it directly as a mask for the first color and then invert it to get the complementary mask for the second color. Then all we have to do is add the two results, and we'll get our two colors moving together, side by side. This whole mixing process can be implemented easily with the following set of nodes, which we'll link after our previous group of nodes:

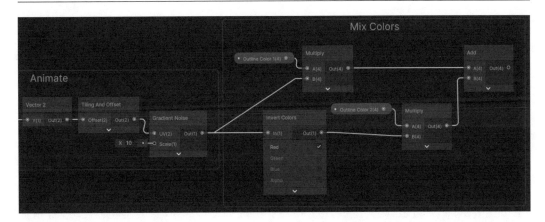

Figure 11.33 – Mixing logic for our two colors based on the procedural noise mask

Finally, we just have to use the output of this **Mix Colors** node group as the color multiplier for our outline and re-integrate it back into our previous logic:

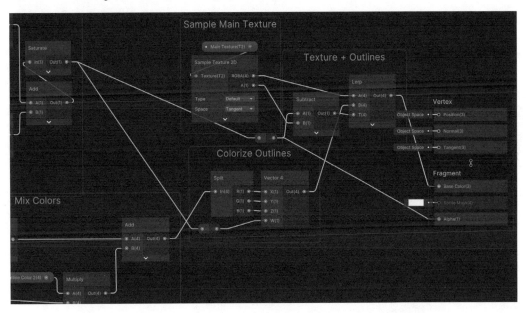

Figure 11.34 – Re-integration of the animated color mix in our previous logic

And there you go – you now have yet another version of this outline shader with a nice little animation to mix multiple colors and create a basic "power-up" effect!

These various shaders have shown us that it is actually quite simple to create a dynamic outline with adjustable properties, and we are now familiar with several sprite shader effects. However, we still haven't done much that couldn't be done beforehand in digital painting software, right? Apart from our last animated shader and the glow post-processing, the others were more "live hacks" for our sprites.

So, it is time to really dive into the power of shaders and make even more dynamic effects!

Having fun with overlay textures, dissolves, and holograms

For this final series of 2D shaders, we will examine useful yet easy-to-implement shader effects that can be directly applied in video games to show a specific state of a character or have it appear in an interesting way.

Namely, we will see how to overlay a texture on top of our sprite with various mixing operations, create a parametrized dissolve effect, and make our image look like a shiny hologram.

Showing an overlay texture

To start this series of advanced shaders, let's do an easy one: a basic texture overlay with controllable parameters. This is typically something that is very quick to do with shaders in a game engine and pretty much impossible without them.

In short, the idea is simply to use some mix factors to blend the colors of our original sprite with the colors of a user-defined overlay texture in a dynamic and easy-to-tweak way. You might remember that we already talked about that sort of mix in *Chapter 6* when we worked on parallax mapping and had to merge various layers.

In particular, back in this chapter, we prepared these two Sub Graphs:

- **BlenderMix** (see *Figure 11.35*):

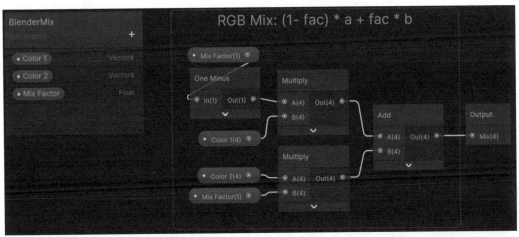

Figure 11.35 – The BlenderMix Sub Graph that re-implements Blender's alpha blend mixing logic

- **MixScreen** (see *Figure 11.36*):

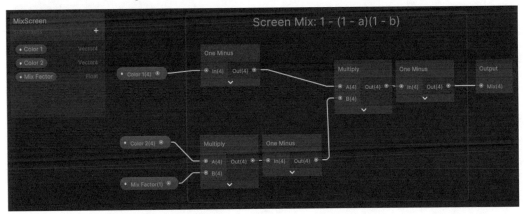

Figure 11.36 – MixScreen Sub Graph that re-implements Blender's screen compositing logic

These two Sub Graphs re-implement some mixing features from the well-known 3D software Blender into Unity to perform either an alpha blend or a screen compositing operation.

These two operations are quite common, and both can be interesting for a texture overlay, depending on the images you're trying to blend together. So we will make a `TextureOverlay` unlit sprite shader that has a **Boolean** property to switch between one operation or the other, and then we'll simply sample the original sprite and the overlay texture and pass their colors through the right mixing node to get our final result:

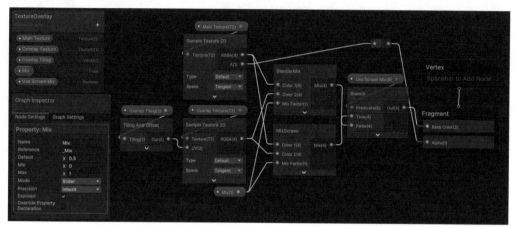

Figure 11.37 – The TextureOverlay unlit sprite Shader Graph

You can see in *Figure 11.37* that I've also added an `Overlay Tiling` property to better control the size of my overlay texture – this is totally optional, but it can be nice to give your shader users a bit more control over the final result.

We can now use this shader on our dwarf sprite to quickly create some fancy state modification effects, such as burning, frozen, or even poisoned (as you can see in *Figure 11.38*, here I'm using either the alpha blend operation, or the screen compositing operation by turning on the `Use Screen Mix` property):

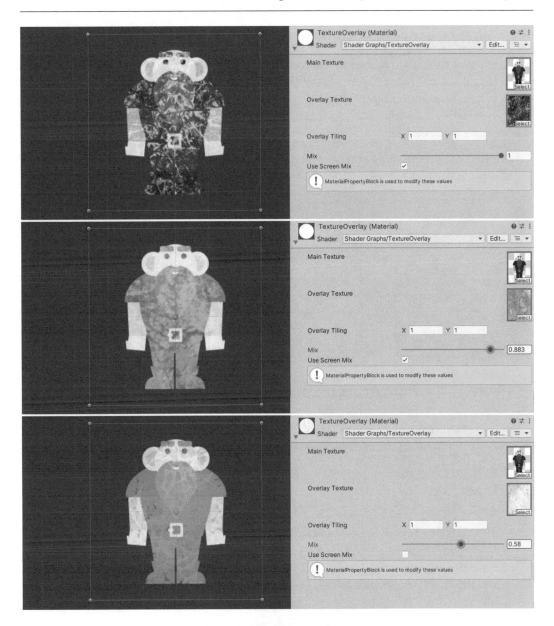

Figure 11.38 – Result of our TextureOverlay shader on the dwarf sprite with various overlays for various state modification effects (the text within this image is not important, and the image intends only to show the possible results with different textures or property values)

This TextureOverlay shader, therefore, makes it straightforward to mix the colors from two images, which is already neat. But now, let's go further and see a nice trick to make our sprite disappear and re-appear in a really cool way...

Making a tweakable dissolve effect

When you have an object in your scene that you want to show and hide, you may rely on various tricks to perform these transitions. You can just pop the element in and out instantly, which can be a bit harsh, or you can change its opacity to have it fade in and fade out; or if you're feeling adventurous, you can work out something even more catchy to the eye, such as a dissolve effect with emissive contouring, as we'll see here!

To give you an idea of what we are trying to achieve, here is our `Dissolve` shader applied to our dwarf sprite with a `Dissolve` amount of `0` (no dissolve) and `0.5` (half dissolved):

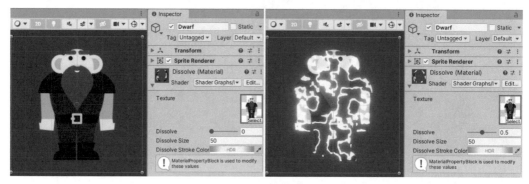

Figure 11.39 – The result of our Dissolve shader on the dwarf sprite with various Dissolve amounts

As you can see in *Figure 11.39*, our shader will integrate three main features:

- The `Dissolve` property (defined in the [0, 1] range) will determine how much of the original sprite is shown and how much is replaced by fully transparent pixels. We will thus need to compute a grayscale mask to combine the initial sprite's alpha value with the mask and hide more pixels as the `Dissolve` value increases.

- This masking will be done using a procedural noise map generated with one of Unity's built-in Shader Graph Nodes. We'll have a `Dissolve Size` property to control the size of this noise, and we'll need to make sure that our mask ultimately produces discrete values because, remember, we want to use it for the alpha channel as a sort of alpha cutoff.

- Our dissolved areas will be outlined with a glowy stroke that is colored using the `Dissolve Stroke Color` property (set in **HDR** mode, as we discussed in the *Making 2D outlines* section).

So, with that in mind, let's implement this logic gradually.

Computing a procedural noise-based grayscale mask

The first step is to get our mask for the opaque and transparent parts of the sprite. This mask should, of course, depend on the `Dissolve` value of our shader, and, as we said just before, it needs to be a discrete "on or off" black and white grayscale texture.

To get a procedural noise texture, we can use Unity's built-in **Simple Noise** node that creates a basic value noise. And then, to make it discrete, the trick is to use a **Step** node, which defines a threshold below which colors are white and above which colors are black. So we can create the first couple of nodes in our `Dissolve` shader that look like this:

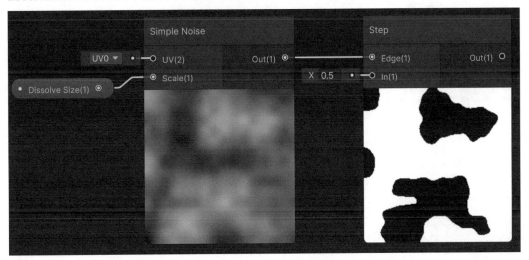

Figure 11.40 – Discretization of procedural value noise with a Step node

The threshold for black-and-white separation is defined by the **In** input value, and this is where we want our `Dissolve` property to intervene. Basically, if the `Dissolve` value is high, then we want to have a low **In** value so that there is more black, and the mask has more areas with an alpha of 0. Conversely, if the `Dissolve` value is low, we need to get a high **In** value.

Because our `Dissolve` value and the **In** value of a **Step** node both live in the [0, 1] range, we can easily get the right behavior by using a **One Minus** node, and using the result of this complementary value as the input for our **Step** node's **In** slot:

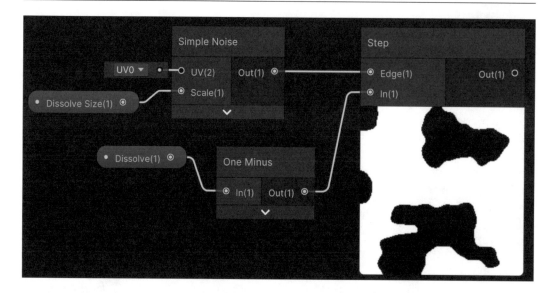

Figure 11.41 – Integration of our Dissolve property as the Step node's threshold

If we use this mask as-is and multiply it with the alpha of our original sprite texture, then we see our `Dissolve` property indeed creates more or fewer holes in the sprite:

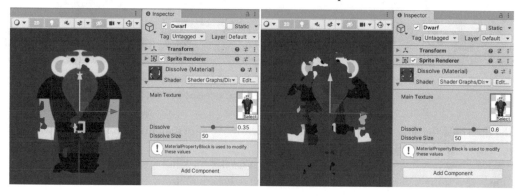

Figure 11.42 – The result of our procedural noise-based mask on
the dwarf sprite with various Dissolve values

So we've successfully managed to make a basic dissolve effect to "eat out" some chunks of our sprite based on a procedural noise. But now, we want to boost this shader and add a nice glowy outline, too!

Implementing the emissive stroke around the dissolved parts

In the previous step, we saw that changing the **In** input value of our **Step** node determines how big or small the white areas are. This means that if we were to take the complementary value of our current `Dissolve` value and remove a slight amount from it, we would get almost exactly the same mask but with slightly larger white areas. So, then, if we subtract this "expanded" mask from our first one, we'll get a stroke mask that precisely contours the dissolved parts of our sprite.

All of this can be implemented directly with some **Subtract** nodes, and in the end, we just have to multiply our result (meaning the stroke mask) with our `Dissolve Stroke Color` property value to get an emissive outline for our dissolved parts:

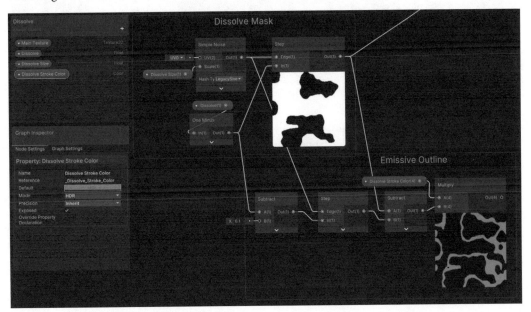

Figure 11.43 – A computation of the emissive outline around the dissolved parts

All that's left to do now is add this outline to our original sprite to get our final red, green, and blue components for the **Base Color** value and integrate this along with our previous mask-based alpha computation:

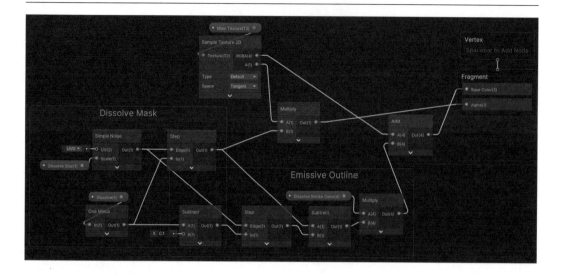

Figure 11.44 – The final Dissolve Shader Graph

And here we are: we now have a simple `Dissolve` shader with a cool emissive outline that can be used to make our character sprites disappear and re-appear in a very neat way!

Creating a hologram effect

For our final shader in this little gallery of 2D effects, let's do something that combines various features we've discussed throughout this chapter and shows some alternative methods for implementing them. Namely, we will make a hologram effect by mixing an animation, an approximate contour, and a re-colorization scheme.

Our effect will be composed of three logic chunks:

- Animated scanlines that move vertically on the sprite to simulate an old television screen damage
- A Fresnel-like outline effect to highlight the contours of our sprite
- The final mix that combines our original sprite with a specific color and adds everything up

To start, let's take care of the scanlines part. The point here will be to use some animated lines mask to both add white bands on the sprite of varying intensities and also impact the alpha of the image.

To generate these lines, we can either use a procedural technique or rely on a premade image texture. Procedural generation is nice because it is very controllable, but it also requires more work from our shader, and in our case, it will be quite hard to get all the little details that really make a good hologram. So, rather, I'm going to rely on a simple image that is available for free in a great GitHub repository by Brackeys: `https://github.com/Brackeys/Shader-Graph-Tutorials`, and that you can see in *Figure 11.45*:

Figure 11.45 – Scanlines texture by Brackeys

This texture is just a series of horizontal lines, with various tints from black to white and unequal thicknesses. We're going to import it in our Unity project and ensure that its **Wrap Mode** import setting is set to se**Repeat** mode so that we can move it indefinitely along the *y* axis without ever losing the texture:

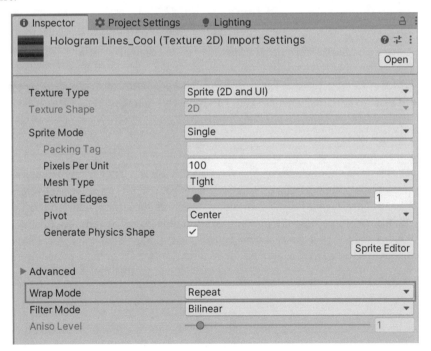

Figure 11.46 – The import settings for the texture with a Repeat value in Wrap Mode

And now, we can use it to create the scanlines effect in our new `Hologram` shader. To do this, we will simply sample our texture and extract its red and alpha components (since it's grayscale, we just need one color component).

But of course, we want the sampling position to depend on the current time so that these lines are animated. Thus we will once again use the **Time** node, multiply it by a `Scanlines Speed` parameter, and then use the result of this operation to create a UV offset thanks to the **Tiling And Offset** node, like this:

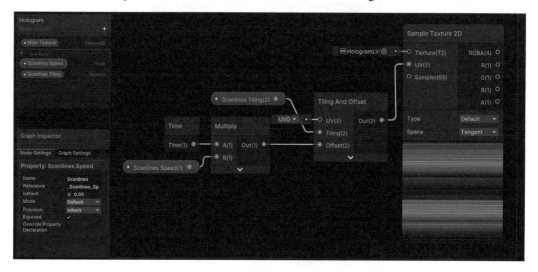

Figure 11.47 – The scanlines logic for our Hologram shader

As usual, you see in *Figure 11.47* that I've also added an optional `Scanlines Tiling` property to allow users to better control the size of the lines and their spreading on the sprite.

Before we mix these scanlines with our original image, though, let's prepare our second effect and take care of our Fresnel-like emissive 2D contour.

Now, the real Fresnel effect is actually a 3D concept that, basically, can be summed up as: "the more shallow the view angle of the surface, the stronger the reflection." It is, therefore, only available in 3D because it depends on the angle between the view vector and the surface, which doesn't make much sense for a 2D flat sprite like here. But the Fresnel effect also implies that, on round objects, we will get more intense specular reflections on the edges and have some highlighted glowy borders, which is exactly what we'll try to imitate here.

To put it simply, we are going to compute an inline for our sprite. This will be very similar to the outlines we made in the *Making 2D outlines* section, except this time, we will get an inner stroke, and also, we don't need as much precision. So we'll do it more quickly by sampling our original sprite two times, once at a smaller scale, and then subtracting the two:

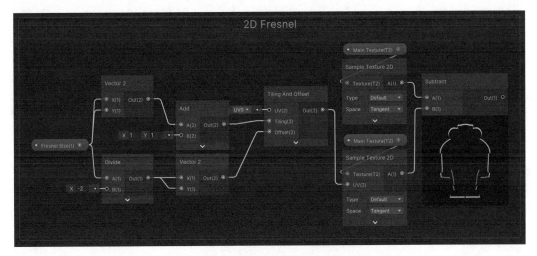

Figure 11.48 – Fresnel-like logic for our Hologram shader

And with all that ready, we can now mix the scanlines, the Fresnel-like contour, and our base image.

Now, because holograms are usually just one color, I am going to extract just a single component from my initial sprite (here, I've chosen the blue one, but this is arbitrary) and then add this value to a user-defined Base Color property. And then, I'll take the result of this operation and add it to the results of the two other node groups I've prepared, **Scanlines** and **2D Fresnel**:

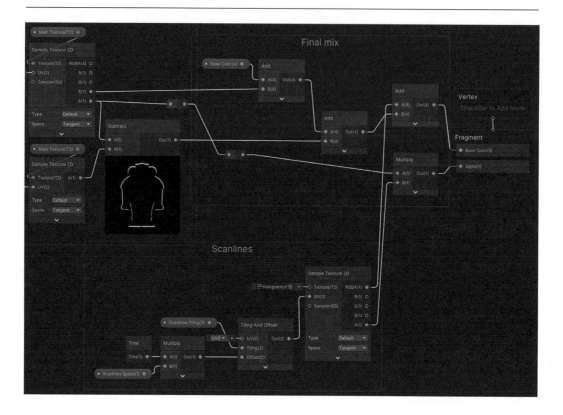

Figure 11.49 – The final mix of the scanlines, Fresnel-like effect, and base color
for our Hologram shader (the text within this image is not important, and
this image is only meant to show the overall logic of the graph)

Here, it is best to use an additive mix because holograms are famously all about light, so you'll want to make it look as if there is an exaggerated amount of energy coming from the sprite. We can further increase this feeling by re-using our **Bloom** post-processing effect from the *Making 2D outlines* section, which could give us a result like this one:

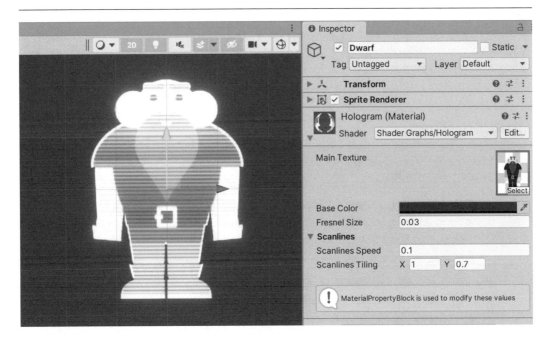

Figure 11.50 – The result of our Hologram shader on the dwarf image with a blue Base Color

This final shader concludes our quick peek at 2D shaders. Of course, this little gallery was just a short introduction to the topic, and there are many more effects we could discuss, such as glitches, retro-style filters, twists and vortices, or even shine and hit animations for game state highlights.

But hopefully, the shaders we've studied already give you some tools for experimenting – and don't forget that you can always try and combine this basic logic into more complex ones to achieve your own effects!

Summary

In this chapter, we explored a series of simple 2D shaders and effects.

We first discussed how to use Unity's built-in Shader Graph Nodes to easily tweak the colors of a sprite globally, for example by changing the hue or saturation. We then saw why color-swapping can be useful and how we can implement it via the Shader Graph editor or HLSL code before talking about dynamic pixelation for quick pixel-art approximation.

After that, we focused on 2D outlines and gradually built several shaders that implemented more and more complex effects, starting from a simple pixel-perfect stroke up to an animated emissive contour. We also took this opportunity to have a look at post-processing in URP and how we can use the built-in tools of the render pipeline to add a **Bloom** effect and make our HDR emissive colors glow in the scene.

Finally, we worked on a few shader utilities that could be used directly in a video game to show a specific character state with a texture overlay, a dissolve effect, and a hologram shader.

In the next chapter, we will shift our focus from 2D to 3D and discuss another important category of shaders: the vertex displacement-based shaders, which allow us to move the geometry of our objects efficiently, thanks to the power of GPUs. We'll see how this vertex displacement technique can be used to animate a butterfly, a fish, a water plane, and even a candle melting.

Going further

If you're curious about 2D URP shaders, here are a few extra interesting resources to check out or continue your journey with:

- *Unity 2021 Shaders and Effects Cookbook - Fourth Edition*, J. P. Doran (2021): `https://www.packtpub.com/product/unity-2021-shaders-and-effects-cookbook-fourth-edition/9781839218620`

- *How to Use a Shader to Dynamically Swap a Sprite's Colors*, D. Branicki (2015): `https://gamedevelopment.tutsplus.com/how-to-use-a-shader-to-dynamically-swap-a-sprites-colors--cms-25129t`

- *2D Outlines in Shader Graph and URP*, D. Ilett (2020): `https://danielilett.com/2020-04-27-tut5-6-urp-2d-outlines/`

- *Sprite Outline (Animated!) - 2D Shader Graph Tutorial*, Code Monkey (2019): `https://www.youtube.com/watch?v=FvQFhkS90nI`

- *Sprite Dissolve - 2D Shader Graph Tutorial*, Code Monkey (2019): `https://www.youtube.com/watch?v=auglNRLM944`

- *Get started with 2D Shader Graph in Unity - Dissolve Tutorial*, Brackeys (2020): `https://www.youtube.com/watch?v=5dzGj9k8Qy8`

- *Post Processing in the Universal RP*, Cyanilux (2020): `https://cyangamedev.wordpress.com/2020/06/22/urp-post-processing/`

- *How to make Unity GLOW! (Unity Tutorial)*, Code Monkey (2021): `https://www.youtube.com/watch?v=bkPe1hxOmbI`

12
Vertex Displacement Shaders

In the last chapter, we explored a gallery of 2D shaders, and we studied how to apply various effects on our sprites, from basic hue-shifting and saturation adjustments to advanced visuals such as holograms or dissolves.

To continue these experimentations, we're now going to focus on another common category of shaders – vertex displacement shaders. Those shaders, as the name implies, rely primarily on the vertex displacement technique, or in other words, the idea of using the vertex shader function in our code to slightly offset the position of the vertices of our model and simulate interesting deformations.

One of the big strengths of vertex displacement is that, because it is done in shaders, and thus on the GPU, it allows us to alter the model's geometry very efficiently. It is, of course, limited – in particular, it can only transform pre-existing vertices, and yet it can produce quite impressive results when used well. Most notably, when combined with time, it can create procedural animations for our 3D models that are adaptive and tweakable thanks to the shader's parameters.

To better understand the ins and outs of this technique, we're going to create a few example shaders using the Shader Graph and discuss the following topics:

- Animating fishes and butterflies
- Creating waves with vertex displacement
- Browsing some extra ideas

Technical requirements

To try out the shader examples shown in this chapter, you should install Unity with a version from 2021 or later, and make a project using the URP pipeline.

All the textures and models I use in the demos of this chapter, and all the shaders we'll create, are available in the GitHub repository for this chapter at `https://github.com/PacktPublishing/Become-a-Unity-Shaders-Guru/tree/main/Assets/Chapter%2012`.

Animating fishes and butterflies

To kick things off, let's discuss a very common application of vertex displacement – the creation of a simple movement animation for a fish or a butterfly.

To do this, we'll first learn the basics of creating vertex displacement in the Shader Graph; then, we'll focus on the fish animation and see how to introduce time in the mix. Finally, we'll reapply these concepts to our butterfly model and adapt the previous logic to create a wing-flapping movement.

Moving fishes thanks to a vertex displacement shader

Our goal will be to use a shader to automatically have our fishes wobble in the water, like this:

Figure 12.1 – A school of fishes deformed and animated thanks to vertex displacement shaders

First things first, we need to create our FishWobbling shader and learn how to do vertex displacement. Because we're working on 3D models, this time, we'll use the **Lit Shader Graph** URP shader template to create our asset (see *Figure 12.2*):

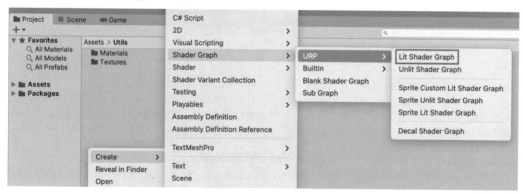

Figure 12.2 – The contextual menu to create a new Shader Graph asset based on a URP template

Then, we'll open it in the Shader Graph editor. At this point, it is just an empty shader, with the usual **Vertex** and **Fragment** contexts, that applies a gray color to our model:

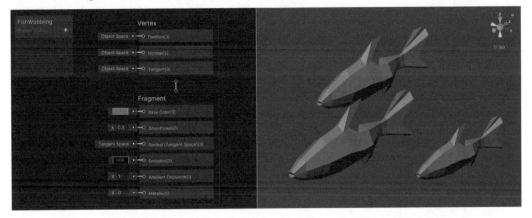

Figure 12.3 – A base empty Shader Graph for our FishWobbling shader

So far, in all the shaders we've made, we have hardly ever touched the outputs in the **Vertex** context – you might recall that we played around with it in *Chapter 6*, when we discussed the billboarding technique, but that's about it.

Here, we're going to rely extensively on the **Position** output slot in the **Vertex** context to create our vertex displacement effect. Indeed, the whole point of our shader will be to take the initial position of the current vertex using the **Position** built-in node (which can give us this position in any given space). The shader will then modify this value in various ways, before eventually inputting the transformed position of our vertex in object space in the **Position** output slot of the **Vertex** context. Don't worry if it's not perfectly clear yet – we'll go through this gradually in the upcoming paragraphs!

For this shader, the **Fragment** context will just be used to sample and map a texture on our fish to get something slightly more interesting than just a gray model. We can actually take care of this right now, since we're familiar with this process and it is very quick and easy to do:

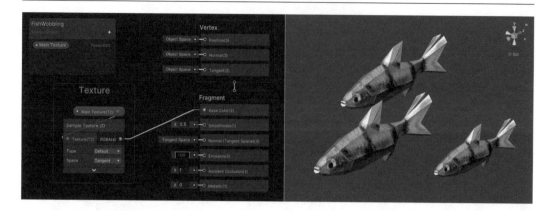

Figure 12.4 – Texture sampling in our FishWobbling shader

You can see in *Figure 12.4* that, at this point, we have a simple fish 3D model with an image texture mapped on it.

Now, to deform our model and really do vertex displacement, we need to start working on our vertex position transformation scheme. So, first, let's get the initial position of our vertex, thanks to the **Position** node; I'll directly set this node in **Object** mode to get the position in object space:

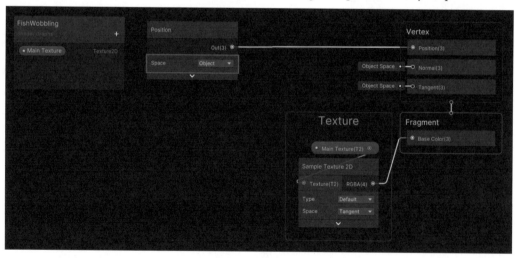

Figure 12.5 – The direct use of the Position node to get the (untransformed) vertex position

This graph doesn't do any displacement – it just reproduces the default behavior of the vertex shader function, which is to output the vertex positions in object space. However, if we then do some transformation on this position property, we can quickly create funny effects on our geometry.

Consider our fish model. In its own local space, meaning in object space, it has its body oriented along its upward vector (the green Y vector), as shown in *Figure 12.6*:

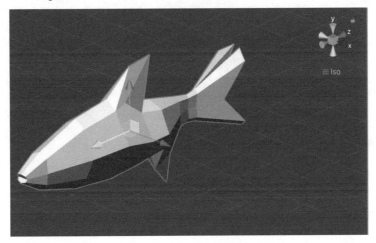

Figure 12.6 – A visualization of the local axis of our fish model, with the
body oriented in the direction of the upward Y green vector

So, let's suppose we isolate the Y component of our vertex position in object space and apply a sinus to it (multiplied by a certain amplitude). Then, we reintegrate this value as the X component of a new **Vector 3** node, and we add this to our initial position. Well, you see in *Figure 12.7* that this gives us an interesting deformation of our fish, as if its body was following a wavy curve:

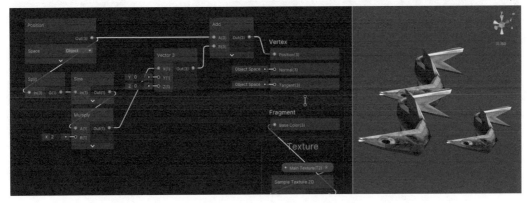

Figure 12.7 – The first example of vertex displacement in our FishWobbling shader,
with a strong sinusoidal deformation along the mesh's local Y axis

Of course, here, my amplitude of 2 is very high, and the effect is way too strong. But we can parametrize this factor, and we'll then be able to control the displacement to our liking:

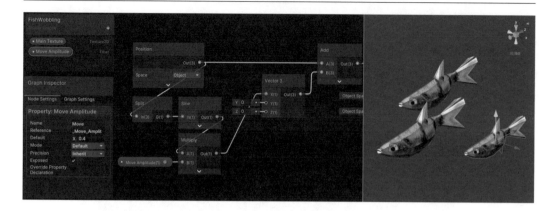

Figure 12.8 – Parametrized sinusoidal vertex displacement with a new Move Amplitude property

However, there is still a problem with this basic transformation – right now, it is applied the same on the whole body of our fish, which is not very realistic. In truth, we'd like for the head to be less affected by the displacement than the tail.

To solve this issue, we can use a **Lerp** node at the end of our graph logic to mix the displaced position with the initial position of the vertex differently, depending on where the vertex is along the model's main axis (meaning, in our case, how close or far it is from the fish's head). More precisely, we'll define two new parameters, `Min Mask` and `Max Mask`, to set the "influence zone" of the displacement, and then we'll use these values to vary the impact of the transformation on the vertex, like this:

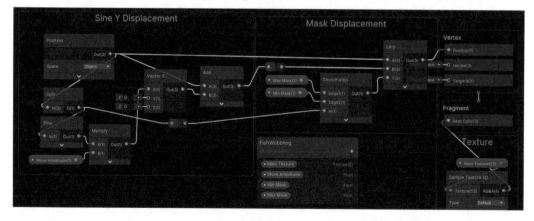

Figure 12.9 – Masked lerping logic to limit the influence zone of the vertex displacement

If we recompile the shader, we can see that, now, the geometry of our fishes is deformed around the tail, but their heads stay fixed at their original position, which looks more natural!

Figure 12.10 – The result of our non-animated FishWobbling shader on three fishes

We could, of course, improve this shader further – for example, by adding one extra parameter to have each fish instance wobble a bit differently (since, for now, they all have the exact same displacement). I won't detail this here, but if you're curious about how to do this kind of per-instance seeding using the model's world position, feel free to have a look at the Github repository for this book (https://github.com/PacktPublishing/Become-a-Unity-Shaders-Guru), which contains an advanced version of the FishWobbling shader with this extra bit of logic.

> **Beware your model's orientation**
>
> Once again, it is important to note that the shader assumes the main axis of the model is its up vector. Both the sinus computation and the masked lerping use the *Y* component of the initial vertex position because, for our model, the main axis is oriented along the green *Y* vector. If your model is oriented along another vector, you might need to adjust these transformations.

Anyway, our FishWobbling shader now implements all the core vertex displacement logic we want. Still, wouldn't it be cooler if it were moving, too? Time to level up our Shader Graph and see how to animate this geometry transformation to create a procedural movement.

Why not use basic Unity animation assets?

Usually, when you want to animate a 3D model in Unity with this level of precision, you need to rely on a **Skinned Mesh Renderer** component and a rigged skeleton to move around the different parts of the meshes, and then pass this **SkinnedMeshRenderer** some animation asset containing keyframes to tell the bones how to move and drag the geometry at each frame.

In addition to requiring quite the expertise to create the right animation, this pipeline also often requires artists to first prepare the animation in some external software, and then import and integrate the assets, which means that updating the animation necessitates a re-import, taking some time and effort.

Procedural animation is a new trend that is growing in the game development community because it mitigates the issues of this annoying pipeline and allows non-animators to give it a shot. It is by no means an "easy and all-in-one replacement," especially for humanoid models, because getting realistic animations with a procedural method can be extremely complex. However, in simpler cases, such as our fish here, computing the geometry movement via code can be a very interesting way of speeding up the pipeline and making a more controllable effect without too much loss in quality.

Among all the built-in nodes that Unity provides us with, there is one we already peeked at in *Chapter 11*, when we worked on our animated outlines and hologram shaders – the **Time** node. We saw that it allows us to get the current time value inside our shader and, in particular, feed this dynamic data to our computations to have the visuals change over time.

In other words, to create an animation for our basic wobbling shader, all we need to do is add a **Time** node in the right place. Specifically, we'd like for our sinusoidal displacement to "slide" along the body of the fish, which we can do by changing the input value of our **Sine** node a little. Thus, we simply have to add the current time to our vertex position Y component (with an optional custom speed parameter to better control the effect), and we're done:

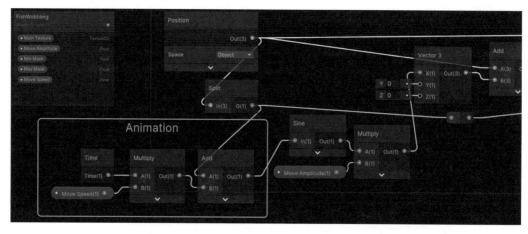

Figure 12.11 – The Animation node group for our final animated FishWobbling shader

Thanks to this new **Animation** node group, our fishes now move slowly over time, wobbling slightly as if they were swimming and swaying in the water.

And what's great is that this vertex displacement is not limited just to fishes – we can apply it to other types of movements, such as a flag fixed on a pole at one end but flying in the wind at the other, or a butterfly flapping its wings. So let's keep exploring the vertex displacement technique, and see how to use this nice trick to implement the butterfly example!

Displacing a butterfly

To continue our discussion on geometry transformation via shaders, we are going to apply the same vertex displacement trick to another use case – the butterfly.

In this section, we'll create a second shader, `ButterflyFlying`, that uses a similar logic to `FishWobbling` to deform a very basic shape, a simple quad with a split in the middle. Each face will be a wing, and we'll simply have them flap up and down to simulate the insect's movement. Finally, by slapping on a texture as we did before for the fishes, we'll get a credible and yet extra-light butterfly asset for our video game projects.

Figure 12.12 shows the 3D mesh (the split quad) without any texture on the left, and the same model with the texture applied on the right:

Figure 12.12 – A visualization of the wireframe of the split quad mesh
without any texture (left) and with the butterfly texture (right)

In a sense, the process we want to do here may remind you of the interior mapping trick we discussed a while ago in *Chapter 6*. You might remember that, back then, we explored how the combo of a quad, a simple texture, and a shader could simulate a whole 3D room quite well and very efficiently, which was perfect for distant or low-resolution building facades.

Our goal is kind of the same here – we want to use an ultra-simple geometry and an image to get an animated butterfly. The result will obviously not be extra detailed and high-resolution, but in the context of a video game, environment entities such as insect swarms, which are mostly meant to add to the global atmosphere, are rarely looked at from up close. Rather, they need to move about convincingly enough and not be too demanding in terms of resources so that more essential systems can use the computing power.

Thus, being able to render *and* animate a butterfly with just a quad and a shader is pretty interesting. Furthermore, it is actually quite straightforward to do!

In short, the idea is to reuse the logic we had for our `FishWobbling` shader, with the transformation of the current vertex position and the masking, and adapt it to instead move the wings of the butterfly up and down in a V-shape.

Since we're already familiar with the overall process, this time, we're not going to detail each step but rather focus on the result. So, here is a global overview of the final graph for this `ButterflyFlying` shader – *Figure 12.13* is just meant to give you a bird's-eye view of the connections between the node groups, but don't worry – we will zoom in and study each bit of this graph later on:

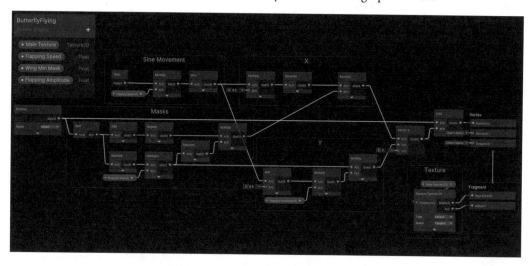

Figure 12.13 – The final graph of our ButterflyFlying shader (the text within this image is not important, and the image is intended to only show the overall graph logic)

If we apply this shader on our plane and let the animation play, we can take screenshots at regular intervals and decompose the movement as follows:

Figure 12.14 – The decomposition of the butterfly's movement, animated with our ButterflyFlying shader

Now, let's look at our shader more closely. Its graph, shown in *Figure 12.13*, is composed of four parts:

- In the top-left corner, the **Sine Movement** node group handles the animation:

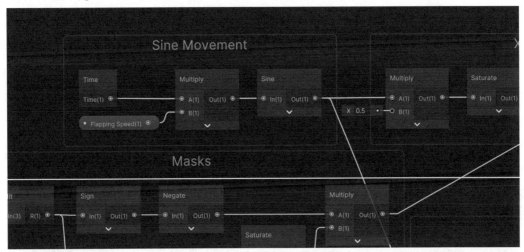

Figure 12.15 – The Sine Movement node group in our ButterflyFlying shader

Similar to the **Animation** node group in our `FishWobbling` shader, it uses a **Time** node to get the current time and multiplies it with a speed; then, it passes this value as input to a **Sine** node to get a sinusoidal movement.

- This movement is then applied along the *X* and *Y* local axes of the object to simulate the wings flapping:

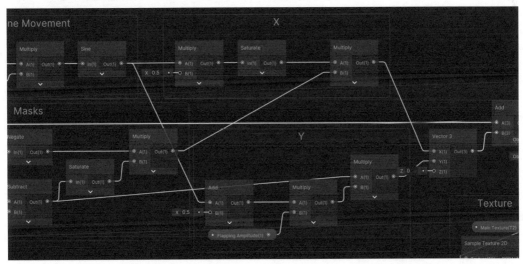

Figure 12.16 – The X and Y displacement node groups in our ButterflyFlying shader

At first glance, you might think that we only need to move our vertices along the vertical (Y) axis. However, if we do so, we will soon get a stretching of the wings that looks very unnatural. To compensate for this effect, it is important to also bring the wings inward when they are at their extreme Y positions, and outward when they are on the horizontal plane.

- The **Masks** node group on the left makes sure that the influence of the displacement is progressive along the wings:

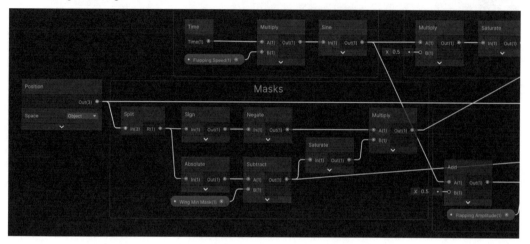

Figure 12.17 – The Masks node group in our ButterflyFlying shader

By using an **Absolute** node, we can completely cancel the deformation in the middle of the mesh and then have the displacement influence increase linearly as we get further away from this central axis in either direction. Once again, we can define a property to better control the reach of this mask, the `Wing Min Mask` **Float** parameter.

- Finally, the **Fragment** context contains very simple logic, like for the `FishWobbling` shader, that just samples the main texture we give our mesh – except we need to make sure to also retain the alpha value to get the right cutout around the wings on our plane:

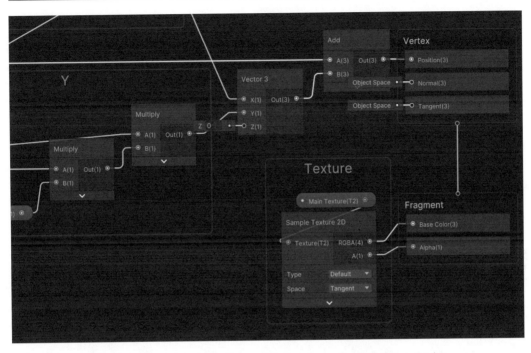

Figure 12.18 – Texture sampling node group in our ButterflyFlying shader

To properly apply the transparency on our shader and get the right effect on the butterfly's wings, we should also ensure that our graph's **Surface Type** property is set to **Transparent** in the **Graph Inspector** panel (under the **Graph Settings** tab):

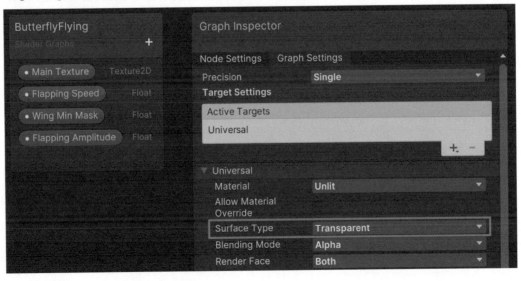

Figure 12.19 – Graph Settings for our ButterflyFlying shader with Surface Type set to Transparent

And there we go – our `ButterflyFlying` shader is now ready, and we can easily create swarms of insects just by copying and pasting a very simple quad geometry!

We've now got a good idea of how vertex displacement and masks can be used to animate 3D models of living creatures. But what about our game environments? Can they benefit from this technique too?

Well, yes – and to study that in more detail, we're going to explore how to apply vertex displacement to a water plane.

Creating waves with vertex displacement

In this second section, we'll continue our exploration of the vertex displacement technique with another common use case – the creation of waves on the surface of a water plane.

Here, we'll keep things simple and focus on sinusoidal waves. These are not the most realistic, but this way, the computation will remain fairly straightforward; still, this example will be a good opportunity to see how the resolution of a mesh can impact the result of a vertex displacement shader and how, sometimes, we can mathematically compute the exact value of displaced normals.

Understanding the importance of mesh resolution

Before diving into the shader itself, let's briefly talk about the geometry we need to get the proper effect.

In the previous section, *Animating fishes and butterflies*, we saw how vertex displacement shader can simulate interesting movements even on very simple geometries (for example, the split quad of our butterfly). However, it is important to also remember that we cannot create new vertices in a vertex shader function (or in the node logic used by the **Vertex** context of a Shader Graph asset). This shader stage is solely about modifying the existing mesh. This means that if we want a plane to be deformed into waves, we need to ensure that we have enough vertices on the surface to begin with. Otherwise, the effect won't work because we won't have enough details to tweak and adapt to create the intended shape.

In our case, to create waves on a water plane, we cannot use a quad anymore – instead, we should at least turn to Unity's plane primitive mesh that is subdivided into a grid of 10 by 10 quads:

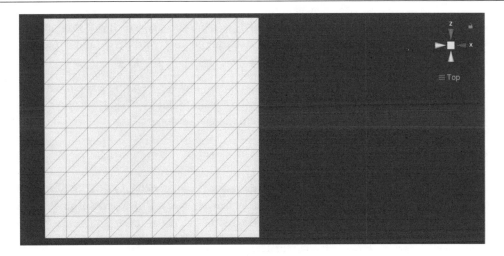

Figure 12.20 – A visualization of the wireframe of Unity's primitive plane mesh

This is the minimum level of detail, and the minimum **resolution** we need for our mesh to bend and curve properly when we displace it with our waves equation.

However, this primitive plane is still quite a low-resolution mesh of course – if we wanted to have more precise waves, with smoother curves and a nicer result overall, we would need to increase the number of subdivisions even more. For example, *Figure 12.21* compares the result of our soon-to-be Waves shader (which displaces the plane with a sinus to create waves on the surface), applied to Unity's primitive plane geometry (on the left) and a plane subdivided into 30 x 30 quads, made in Blender and re-imported into Unity (on the right):

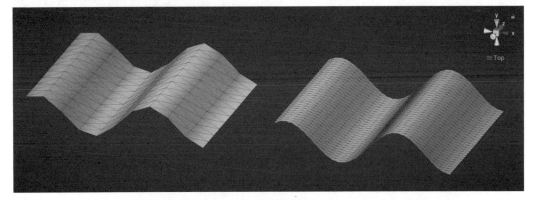

Figure 12.21 – A comparison of our Waves shader, applied on Unity's primitive plane geometry (left) and on a high-resolution subdivided plane made in Blender (right)

As you can see, the curve is way cleaner on the right of *Figure 12.21*, where the geometry has more subdivisions and, therefore, a higher resolution.

This highlights a key idea when creating vertex displacement shaders, which is that no matter how good your shader logic is, you also need to prepare your geometry properly (and, typically, with enough details) to actually get the expected result.

Anyway – with this in mind, we're now going to assume that we are using a mesh with enough subdivisions (I'll actually stick with the Unity primitive plane to not overload the demo screenshots with heavy wireframes), and we're going to dive into the shader *per se*.

Setting up waves displacement

First things first, let's create our new `Waves` shader asset. Again, it will be a lit URP Shader Graph (remember we saw in *Figure 12.2* how to create a shader like this from a URP template), but this time, we should make sure that we properly set its surface parameters and, in particular, its specular properties.

So, in our Shader Graph editor, we'll open the **Graph Inspector** panel and go to the **Graph Settings** tab; then, we'll switch the **Workflow Mode** setting of our shader from the default **Metallic** option to **Specular**, and in the **Fragment** context, we'll set its base color to a light blue and leave its smoothness at 0.5:

Figure 12.22 – Global settings, Base Color, and Smoothness for our Waves shader

This will ensure that our shader creates some reflections on the surface, as shown in *Figure 12.21*.

Now, we can recreate a basic vertex displacement logic, similar to what we did in the *Animating fishes and butterflies* section. We'll create the `Amplitude` and `Wavelength` parameters and extract the *X* component of our vertex position by reusing the **Position** node (in **Object** mode) and a **Split** node. Then, we'll mix our `Wavelength` parameters with this *X* coordinate to get an input value for a **Sine** node, multiply the result of this sinus by our `Amplitude` parameter, and apply this final value as a *Y* offset for our vertex:

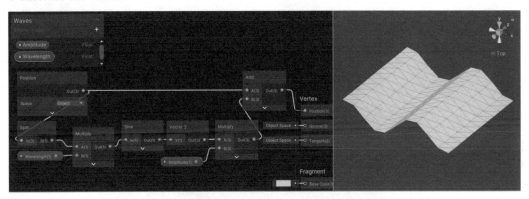

Figure 12.23 – Basic sinusoidal displacement in our Waves shader

At this point, you see in *Figure 12.23* that we already have some waves on the surface of our water plane.

The next step is simply to use a **Time** node as before to animate this sinus, using an arbitrary `Speed` parameter to offset our sinus input value by a given amount and get this continuous translation of our waves along the *X* axis:

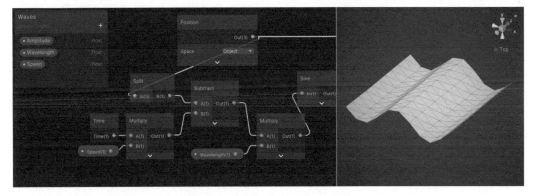

Figure 12.24 – Additional animation logic for our Waves shader

This is pretty nice, but there is one big issue – despite our shader being marked as **Lit** in **Graph Settings** (see *Figure 12.22*), it doesn't look like there are really any shadows on our waves! Instead, everything seems flat and uniform; this is because we aren't computing the right normals for our displaced mesh.

Computing our displaced normals

When we worked on our fish and butterfly examples in the first section, we only looked at modifying the vertex position value, and we ignored the two other slots in the **Vertex** output context – **Normal** and **Tangent** (see *Figure 12.25*). And yet, since we're moving vertices around and potentially changing the orientation of our mesh's faces, it would make sense to also take into account the vertices' normals or tangents, right?

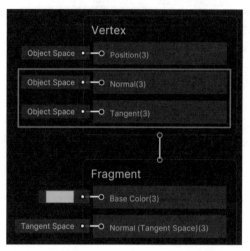

Figure 12.25 – A zoom-in on the Normal and Tangent output slots
in the Vertex context of a Shader Graph asset

The fact is, as-is, our `FishWobbling` and `ButterflyFlying` shaders aren't perfect because, among other things, they don't correct the model's shading to account for the displacement. For those use cases, it's not really an issue, since the point is not to have the players look at these objects from up close anyway.

But, for our waves, it causes a visible flaw that breaks the illusion and significantly hinders the impact of our displacement. Even though the vertices move about in pretty curves, our eyes can detect that something's wrong.

Basically, the idea is that because we've used a sinus to offset our points vertically depending on their horizontal coordinate, we get a smooth sinusoidal curvature. However, this curvature hasn't actually been *applied* to the model; it is just a fake done at the vertex function level, and in particular, the normals are still all pointing up. During the rasterization step, all these normals are interpolated into per-pixel normals that point upward too, and we end up with a completely flat shading on an apparently complex surface, which causes a visual discrepancy.

In some cases (including one that we will discuss in the upcoming *Browsing some extra ideas* section), it is impossible to get an exact value for the displaced normals, and we have to use approximation tricks to get a somewhat reasonable value that improves the shading a little bit. Yet, here, we are quite lucky because the movement of our vertices is simple enough that we can mathematically compute the exact equation for our normals.

We'll go through this computation in three steps:

1. First of all, we're going to group together the nodes we've created so far in our Waves shader that compute the input value for our **Sine** node – I'll name this group **Sine Input**:

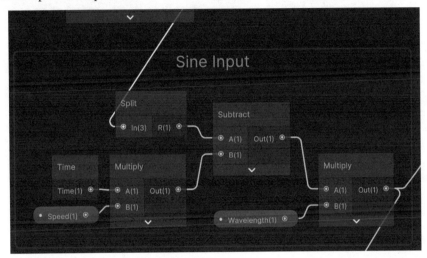

Figure 12.26 – The Sine Input node group in our Waves shader

2. Now, it is essential to note that the normal vector of a 3D point can be deduced from two of its tangent vectors in orthogonal directions – it is simply the cross-product of both those vectors. And in our case, those tangent vectors are easy to get.

    We don't have any movement along the Z direction, so in this direction, the tangent is the unit vector:

    $$T_z(x) = \left(T_z(x)_x, T_z(x)_y, T_z(x)_z \right) = (0,0,1)$$

    And we have a simple sinus wave along the X direction, so in this direction, the tangent is the derivative of the sinus function. If we have an amplitude A, a wavelength L, and a speed S for our waves, then this derivative is the following for the nodes in our **Sine Input** group:

    $$[A * sin(L*(x - S*t))]' = A*L*cos(x)$$

We thus end up with a 3D tangent vector for our vertex along the X axis that can be expressed as:

$$T_x(x) = \left(T_x(x)_x, T_x(x)_y, T_x(x)_z\right) = normalize((1, A * L * cos(x), 0))$$

Don't forget that a tangent vector should be normalized, which is why I've added the `normalize` operation around the end value.

This computation can now be reproduced easily in our Shader Graph:

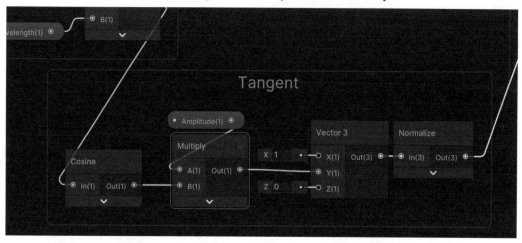

Figure 12.27 – Tangent node group in our Waves shader

3. Finally, we can use our two tangent vectors, $T_x(x)$ and $T_z(x)$, to compute the associated normal vector $N(x)$:

$$N(x) = T_x(x) \times T_z(x) = \left(-T_x(x)_y, T_x(x)_x, 0\right)$$

Again, this is easy to reproduce in the graph by taking the outputs of our previous node groups and applying a **Negate** node on the Y coordinate:

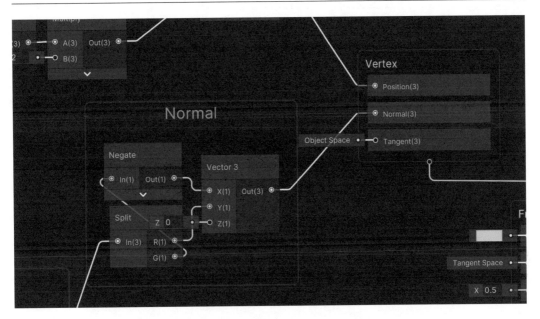

Figure 12.28 – The Normal node group in our Waves shader

And that's it! If we plug this normal vector in the **Normal** slot of the **Vertex** output context, as shown in *Figure 12.28*, and recompile our shader, we see that we now have lit waves with the proper shading:

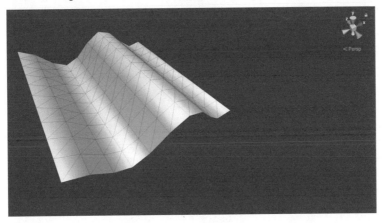

Figure 12.29 – The result of our Waves shader with the proper shading

> **Do you want to go further?**
>
> If you want to make a more realistic vertex displacement wave shader, I encourage you to check out this excellent tutorial by Catlike Coding: `https://catlikecoding.com/unity/tutorials/flow/waves/`. In this article, you'll learn about another equation model for waves called Gerstner waves, which better approximate reality, although they are slightly more involved than the basic sinusoidal movement we've described here. The post also explains how to overlap multiple waves together to create a more visually interesting effect, and how to tweak the mathematics in your shader to enforce your animation loops properly.

Our basic `Waves` shader is now complete, and we've even seen how, sometimes, it is possible to perfectly compute both the displaced position and the displaced normals of our vertices to recreate the right shading on a deformed mesh.

However, this is not always possible, and when you start to dive into more complex displacement shaders, you can be faced with situations where the only solution is to approximate some things. To better understand all of this, let's wrap up by discussing three great tutorials about vertex displacement that can expand our horizons on the topic.

Browsing some extra ideas

To end this chapter, I want to take a bit of time to mention amazing tutorials or resources that show vertex displacement shaders that I think are definitely worth studying to expand your knowledge of this domain. Never forget that learning about shaders (or any domain for that matter) is also about keeping an eye out for what other creators are doing, and what tools or techniques they're exploring – especially when you get to an advanced level and know all the basics.

So here, we'll discuss a simple Voronoi-based blob-like deformation shader, an interactive map shader, and a dynamic melting candle shader.

Unity's official vertex displacement tutorial

If you want to see a very common application of vertex displacement, you can have a look at Unity's official learning material on vertex displacement shaders, available at: `https://learn.unity.com/tutorial/shader-graph-vertex-displacement`.

In this quick guide, the team shares with us some mesh manipulation techniques using the Shader Graph to produce a blob-like deformation based on Voronoi noise. *Figure 12.30* (an image taken from Unity, from the tutorial page) shows the graph and the result of the shader on a sphere:

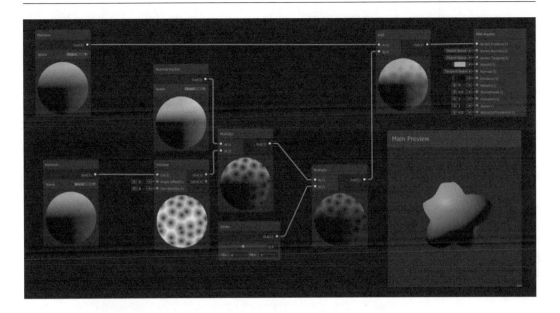

Figure 12.30 – The graph and result of a blob-like deformation shader from Unity's
tutorial on vertex displacement (the text within this image is not important,
and the image is intended to only show the overall graph logic)

In this tutorial, you'll revisit the basics of sampling a procedural noise texture via a built-in Shader Graph node, and you'll also see the difference between creating the effect in object space and world space.

So, even if this guide in itself probably won't teach you that many new tricks, it can be a nice basis for further experimentation, and it's also a quick summary of the steps to take to create, assign, and update a Shader Graph asset.

Alan Zucconi's interactive map

Have you ever wondered how these nice hologram maps were made in games and movies? You know, all those interactive tables with cool landscapes, as shown in *Figure 12.31* (this image was made by Baran Kahyaoglu for his Mapbox project and shared in the following Twitter thread: https://twitter.com/brnkhy/status/1118609807844442112):

Figure 12.31 – A screenshot of an interactive game map by Baran Kahyaoglu

In one of his tutorials, Alan Zucconi talks about how to achieve this effect in detail using just a base plane, a shader, and a few textures – you can check out the first part here: `https://www.alanzucconi.com/2019/07/03/interactive-map-01/`.

> **Important note**
>
> Alan Zucconi's tutorial uses the built-in Unity render pipeline and, most notably, its Surface Shaders. The code that he shares is, therefore, not compatible with a URP project as is.

Throughout the three parts of this tutorial, Alan Zucconi details a few important techniques and gotchas to have in mind when making such a shader, including the following:

- **Normal extrusion**: First, Alan Zucconi discusses how, by displacing each vertex in your surface along its normal by a given amount, you can give volume to your mesh and simulate the depths and peaks of a landscape. In order to control the extrude amount (and not just get a global offsetting of the base plane), the artist leverages heightmaps, just like we did in *Chapter 6* for parallax mapping.

- **Mipmapping and texture sampling**: The shader creator also highlights how, in a vertex shader function, if you ever sample a texture (typically, here, the heightmap), you need to be careful to use the `tex2Dlod` method instead of the usual `tex2D` (for the built-in pipeline), or `SAMPLE_TEXTURE2D_LOD` instead of `SAMPLE_TEXTURE2D` (for the URP pipeline).

In short, this is because, in the fragment shader function, the shader already knows what level of detail – that is, what **mipmap** of the texture – to use in order to get the best trade-off between quality and efficiency, based on the distance to the camera. Thus, we can call `tex2D` or `SAMPLE_TEXTURE_2D` and the program will automatically sample the right mipmap. In the vertex shader function, however, we cannot use these shorthands because the mipmap to use is not defined; therefore, we have to rely on `tex2Dlod` or `SAMPLE_TEXTURE2D_LOD`, which both accept an extra parameter to explicitly set the mipmap level we want.

- **Remapping vertex positions to UVs**: In order to create the scrolling effect, Alan Zucconi also introduces the idea of remapping the vertex positions to their UVs through computation (and not just by reading the vertex's data structure). This allows him to sample the heightmap for neighbor points too and, therefore, anticipate the displacement of these upcoming nearby points to get a smoother result.

  Although this is, in all generality, a complex problem to solve, in this case things are facilitated by the mesh being just a flat plane. Thus, the operation is mostly about re-normalizing the vertex's horizontal coordinates based on the overall dimensions of the mesh.

- **Tangent and normal computation**: Finally, in the last part of the tutorial, the artist talks about the most blatant issue when doing a simple heightmap-based normal extrusion – the incorrect normals and shading of the model.

  The problem is exactly the same as what we discussed in the *Creating waves with vertex displacement* section – we are offsetting the positions of our vertices using the heightmap and, thus, get a fairly complex surface, but the normals don't match and rather all point upward, which creates a flat shading.

  To solve this issue, Alan Zucconi shows a technique that reminds us of the approximate raymarching normal computation we studied in *Chapter 8*, involving the use of the nearby points on the plane and the heightmap to compute the tangent of the current vertex, and then the use of a cross product to deduce the normal from it.

To me, this shader tutorial is interesting because the creator goes through each step in detail, and he gradually brings up new questions and problems to refine the effect. He explores a variety of common shading techniques, offering many notes and remarks on subtle caveats to keep in mind when working on this kind of effect.

Cyanilux's melting candle

During my research for this book, I stumbled upon a great shader made by Cyanilux. The artist shared it in a Twitter thread here: `https://twitter.com/Cyanilux/status/1180084826961043456/`. In these screenshots, Cyanilux shares a vertex displacement-based logic that makes it possible to simulate a melting candle dynamically.

Figure 12.32 – The result of Cyanilux's melting candle shader on two candles of different sizes

By tweaking some parameters, this shader lets us change the height of the candle and the spread of the wax puddle at its base. There's even some random noise on the top surface of the mesh to create a more natural-looking destruction effect.

This shader is interesting because it relies on a combination of fairly straightforward techniques that, when put together, make this impressive result. If you take a look at the shader, you'll see that this entire effect relies on just a couple of parameters and very basic mathematical operations.

Figure 12.33 shows a slightly modified version of the shader, which I've adapted from Cyanilux's work for this book.

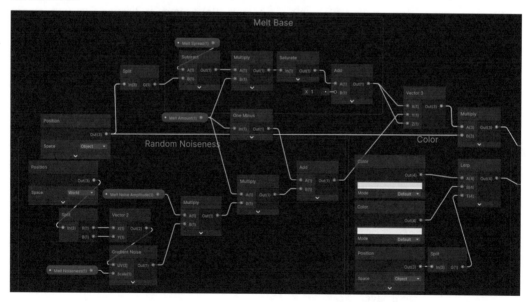

Figure 12.33 – An (adapted) graph of Cyanilux's melting candle shader

To me, this example is proof that you don't always need to overlap multiple levels of complicated logic to achieve a cool effect – it can just be about cleverly mixing together a few nodes in your graph, and properly abstracting the visual you're aiming for.

In addition to the main melting candle vertex displacement shader, Cyanilux also shares a second shader in this thread to create a teardrop-shaped flame above the wax, flickering in the wind.

> **Do you want to test this shader?**
>
> If you're curious and want to try out these two shaders for yourself, I've re-implemented them with some extra parameters in the GitHub repository for this book (`https://github.com/PacktPublishing/Become-a-Unity-Shaders-Guru`), so feel free to have a look!

On a final note, if you want to dive deeper into URP shaders and quick-wins for video game shaders, I highly recommend you follow Cyanilux's productions, either on Twitter or his blog (`https://www.cyanilux.com/`), because this artist always comes up with new ideas and offers neat breakdowns of the various effects he creates.

Summary

In this chapter, we studied the technique of vertex displacement.

We first explored how it can help us to create basic 3D animations in a procedural and tweakable way, such as giving some basic wobble-like movements to a fish or transforming a simple quad into a butterfly flapping its wings.

Then, we discussed how it can be applied to game environments and, in particular, to make sinusoidal waves on a water plane. We saw the importance of having the right resolution in our base geometry, and we studied how, sometimes, the displaced normals of a mesh can be computed exactly thanks to mathematics.

Finally, we mentioned several external resources and tutorials of creators that use vertex displacement to create interesting shaders, with valuable techniques to deepen our understanding of this type of shaders.

Throughout these few examples, we saw how vertex displacement can be useful to bring life to our 3D models efficiently, thanks to the power of shaders and GPUs. However, as we said in the introduction, using the vertex shader function in our code still has some limitations – most notably, the fact that you can't add any new vertices; you can only modify the existing geometry.

That's why, in the next chapter, we will have a look at another type of shader, geometry shaders, and how those allow us to dynamically create new geometry in our models. We'll see why they're interesting, how we can use them to create a wireframe shader for our objects, and also their limitations – in particular, the risks of using them when building games for Mac users.

Going further

If you're curious about vertex displacement shaders, here are a few interesting extra resources to check out to continue your journey:

- *Vertex Displacement*, Cyanilux (2019): `https://www.cyanilux.com/tutorials/vertex-displacement/`

- *Seaweed or Fish Animation Using Vertex Wave Shader Graph – Unity Tutorial*, Binary Lunar (2021): `https://www.youtube.com/watch?v=f0fWMHcbe20`

- *Waves – Moving Vertices*, Catlike Coding (2018): `https://catlikecoding.com/unity/tutorials/flow/waves/`

13

Wireframes and Geometry Shaders

In the two previous chapters, we studied various examples of shaders and focused on two specific types – 2D sprite effects and vertex displacement-based effects. When we worked on the vertex displacement technique, we saw that it was a neat way of creating procedural animations and environment decor efficiently, just by deforming the pre-existing geometry.

However, we also saw that there was a limitation to using vertex displacement, since it can only modify the vertices already present in the mesh – it cannot introduce new points or subdivisions, and it doesn't have access to the mesh's topology.

To go further and allow technical artists to manipulate geometry even more, there is another category of shaders worth diving into, called geometry shaders. So, in this chapter, we'll learn more about this other tool, as well as its limitations, and we'll discuss one of its most common applications. To do so, we'll discuss the following topics:

- Understanding the principles and limitations of geometry shaders
- Creating a URP wireframe shader

Technical requirements

To try out the shader examples shown in this chapter, you should install Unity with a version from 2021 or later, and make a project using the URP pipeline.

You can also find all the code files for this chapter on GitHub, at `https://github.com/PacktPublishing/Become-a-Unity-Shaders-Guru/tree/main/Assets/Chapter%2013`.

As detailed in the *Understanding the principles and limitations of geometry shaders* section, the geometry shaders we will make here are not compatible with recent macOS X architectures, so as a Mac user, you probably won't be able to try them out.

Understanding the principles and limitations of geometry shaders

First things first, we're going to start this chapter by having a quick look at the foundational principles of geometry shaders and their most important limitations. In particular, we'll focus on the specific cases of the macOS X and iOS platforms, which don't deal well with this type of code and have to be taken into consideration for cross-platform compatibility.

What are geometry shaders?

Geometry shaders are a special type of shaders that, in addition to the usual vertex and fragment stages, also contain an additional step in the render process – the **geometry stage**.

Contrary to vertex and fragment shader functions, the geometry shader function is totally optional. As we saw throughout this book, there are indeed many effects and renders that can be achieved without using this stage in the shader code. However, if you want to change the geometry of your meshes in depth and you need to add or remove vertices and faces, you'll have to go for it and start coding some geometry shaders.

The geometry program of a shader is executed at the very end of the 3D pipeline, just before the rasterization step:

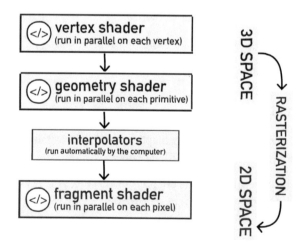

Figure 13.1 – A diagram of the render stages for a geometry shader

In *Figure 13.1*, you see that the geometry shader function runs between the vertex program and the interpolators, and takes 3D data as input. However, it doesn't work on vertices (such as the vertex shader function) but on 3D **primitives** – either triangles or lines – and it allows us to manipulate the geometry of our mesh by adding, removing, or modifying those primitives to create unique effects.

This distinction is important because it means that geometry shaders can gather and inject extra interesting **topology** data in the render pipeline for upcoming stages, or update the vertex properties with per-triangle or per-line information. Typically, geometry shaders can change the shading of a model from smooth to flat, or create normal-based mesh extrusions that actually dissociate and "explode" the model's faces, like this:

Figure 13.2 – Two normal-based extrusion shaders applied to the same sphere primitive, doing the extrusion respectively in the vertex stage (left) or the geometry stage (right)

That's because, whereas the vertex program acts on the base vertices without doubles (and, therefore, keeps all the faces linked together), the geometry program works with per-primitive data and has **doubled vertices**. Basically, since the vertices of a mesh naturally belong to multiple triangles in reality, the same point in space will appear multiple times as we browse our triangles, and we'll be able to assign the same coordinate in space to multiple vertex instances in our geometry shader function to create specific per-face data instances.

More generally speaking, geometry shaders have various applications, among which are the following:

- **Highlighting the geometry**: Because geometry shaders have access to the exact vertices of the mesh, they can be used to actually show these vertices at runtime. We'll discuss this in more detail in the upcoming *Creating a URP wireframe shader* section.

- **Adding custom details to the mesh**: Suppose you have a sphere and you want to add spikes on it. Thanks to geometry shaders, it is possible to add a new vertex in the middle of each face of your sphere, pushing these new points outward along the normals to easily create deformations on the mesh.

- **Instantiating primitives**: Geometry shaders also make it possible to transform an initial mesh into simple support for instantiated elements, such as grass blades in a field. As shown by Daniel Ilett in his great tutorial *Stylised Grass with Shaders in URP* (posted in August 2021 and available on his website here: `https://danielilett.com/2021-08-24-tut5-17-stylised-grass/`), you can easily create stylized grass in URP with this technique, by adding upward-pointing triangles on each vertex of a basic subdivided plane (see *Figure 13.3*, which shows an image from Daniel Ilett's article).

Figure 13.3 – A screenshot of several grass fields created thanks to a URP geometry shader

> **Going further with tessellation shaders**
>
> Besides geometry shaders and their specific shader stage, there is another type of shader that can create new primitives and modify a mesh – tessellation shaders. These allow you to subdivide and, thus, add details to geometry by inserting new vertices inside the pre-existing faces. The tessellation, which is defined in two shader functions named `hull` and `domain`, takes place between the vertex and the geometry shader functions.
>
> A tessellation shader can be particularly interesting if you want to create different **level of details** (**LODs**) on the fly for your mesh, or if you have some instantiation process in your geometry shader and you'd like to get more instantiation points. If you're curious about this last use case, Daniel Ilett talks about it in the aforementioned article on how to use geometry shaders to create stylized grass.

Geometry shaders are, thus, a powerful tool with many subtle use cases, and they nicely complement the vertex displacement technique we discussed in *Chapter 12* by providing us with topology data at the primitive level, and even the possibility to extend or simplify our geometry. However, as always with shader creation, this tool is not a silver bullet, and there are a few gotchas to keep in mind when working with geometry shaders, especially in Unity.

Some notable limitations of geometry shaders

First off, it is worth pointing out that, as geometry shaders are usually considered an advanced topic for people already very used to designing and writing shader code, there is not a lot of documentation on the topic out there. And the resources get even scarcer if you start to look for geometry shaders inside Unity! Most of the tutorials available will show you how to implement these concepts in Unity's built-in render pipeline, and there is virtually no information on how to do it for modern SRP pipelines.

Moreover, at the time of writing, it is not yet possible to create geometry shaders using the node-based Shader Graph tool. Some creators have tried to find some workarounds, such as the following:

- A cool GitHub project by Arturo Nereu (`https://github.com/ArturoNereu/WireframeShaderGraph`), where he shares a hack to make a wireframe effect like the one we'll create in the *Creating a URP wireframe shader* section using the Shader Graph

- A tutorial by Bill from GameDevBill (`https://gamedevbill.com/geometry-shaders-in-urp/`), where he explains how to create a custom HLSL node to add a geometry stage to our Shader Graph logic

Still, apart from these clever workarounds from the community, the Shader Graph tool doesn't have built-in support for geometry shaders, which is why in this chapter, the example we'll study will be written entirely in HLSL script.

Also, it is important to keep in mind that geometry shaders only work for a shader model with a target 4.0 or higher. So, although Unity automatically increases the target to this level if it was defined lower, you'll have to ensure that your target architecture can support this too.

But, in truth, the real thorn in our side as geometry shader artists today is, sadly, the macOS X and iOS platforms.

Watching out for incompatibility with Apple devices

Something essential to understand is that geometry shaders are a very unique sorts of shaders that are fairly specific to the DirectX 11 backend, and they are not really a Unity thing *per se*. In fact, some technical artists and graphics specialists even consider them to be a suboptimal and bad technique (especially since they don't match hardware architectures very well) and would like to see them disappear.

This is particularly true of Apple, since the company has decided to intentionally remove support for geometry shaders in their latest Metal graphics API, for both macOS X computers and iOS mobiles. This means that if your game contains shaders with a geometry stage, those will not compile and execute on most Apple devices – and your players will end up with some ugly missing shaders.

Actually, this trend of discontinuing geometry shaders doesn't seem to be slowing down, since newer graphics APIs such as Vulkan or DirectX 12 are just as reluctant to add support for them, preferring to integrate other stages in their shader pipelines (read, for example, this article by Sarah Jobalia from the DirectX development team: `https://devblogs.microsoft.com/directx/coming-to-directx-12-mesh-shaders-and-amplification-shaders-reinventing-the-geometry-pipeline/`).

If you're in doubt about whether your shader can work on your current computer architecture, you can check the compatibility directly in the Unity Editor, simply by inspecting your shader asset. For example, if you open a project with geometry shaders on a (somewhat) recent Mac computer and select a shader with a geometry stage logic, you will see a message in the asset's inspector telling you that these shaders cannot be compiled and used with this GPU (see *Figure 13.4*), and the meshes using this shader will be shown with the pink invalid shader display.

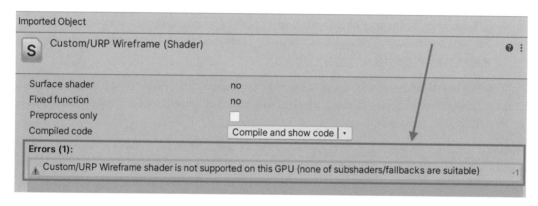

Figure 13.4 – The inspector of a geometry shader incompatible with the current GPU architecture

In other words, as a shader creator, if you know that your game will be cross-platform and that some of the target platforms use the Metal graphics API, you have to find some alternative to your geometry shaders.

There are a few common solutions, such as the following:

- Refining your vertex program to integrate the required computations at this stage of the render process (which is also more optimized, as explained in this cool article by Catlike Coding: `https://catlikecoding.com/unity/tutorials/advanced-rendering/flat-and-wireframe-shading/`)

- Using compute shaders (which we explored in *Chapter 7*) to efficiently prepare all the necessary extra data and/or extra geometry

> **A quick note on tessellation shaders**
>
> Note that the Metal API does support tessellation shaders via the use of specific options in your vertex, fragment, and/or compute programs. Those are viable even on recent macOS X and iOS platforms, and it is thus possible to "amplify" your geometry with subdivisions using this technique in a Unity tessellation shader, and then build your game for an Apple device.

To sum up, geometry shaders are nice from a developer's point of view because they allow us to easily integrate topology data in our pipeline, or to do some dynamic instantiating, but they are also quite weird from a computer's point of view, and fewer and fewer platforms support them. So, if you plan on building robust and cross-platform shaders, beware of geometry shaders and look instead at vertex transformations, or compute shaders!

With that being said, it is still interesting to peek at how to write geometry shaders and play around with them on a compatible Windows PC – that's why we're going to discover how to apply these principles in practice to create our very own URP wireframe shader.

Creating a URP wireframe shader

To better understand the ins and outs of these geometry shaders, let's take a very common use case – the creation of a runtime wireframe shader. Our goal in this section will be to make the geometry of our mesh apparent live, outside of edit mode. This type of effect can be very useful for debugging, sci-fi games, or even retro-futuristic visuals à la *Tron*:

Figure 13.5 – An example of a wireframe shader partially applied to a spaceship model

The shader will be unlit, and we will make the size of the strokes tweakable so that users can easily pick the thickness they want and modify the render to their liking. Therefore, let's go through this shader step by step by first setting up our URP shader, then adding the geometry stage, and finally, fine-tuning a few details to get smoother visuals.

Preparing our URP wireframe shader

To begin, we're going to create our shader as a new script `URPWireframe` asset in the project. For now, we'll simply prepare this script with a basic URP shader skeleton as follows:

```
Shader "Custom/URP Wireframe" {
    Properties {}
    SubShader {
        Tags { "RenderType" = "Opaque" "RenderPipeline"=
            "UniversalPipeline" "Queue"="Geometry" }

        HLSLINCLUDE
        #include "Packages/com.unity.render-pipelines
        .universal/ShaderLibrary/Core.hlsl"
        struct appdata {};
        struct v2f {};
        ENDHLSL
        Pass {
            HLSLPROGRAM
            #pragma vertex vert
            #pragma fragment frag

            v2f vert (appdata v) {}
            float4 frag(v2f i) : SV_Target {}
            ENDHLSL
        }
    }
}
```

In this snippet, we've just set up the base structure of our shader, so we're now ready to actually fill the script with our shader logic.

First, let's make a basic unlit URP shader. It will be even simpler than the one we created in *Chapter 3* because it will only use a solid color property. Therefore, we'll update our code in four places:

- First, we'll declare our `_Color` property in the `Properties` block:

```
Properties {
    _Color ("Color", Color) = (1, 1, 1, 1)
}
```

And we'll create the matching low-level `float4` variable in the following HLSLINCLUDE block:

```
HLSLINCLUDE
    #include "Packages/com.unity.render-pipelines
    .universal/ShaderLibrary/Core.hlsl"

    CBUFFER_START(UnityPerMaterial)
    float4 _Color;
    CBUFFER_END

    struct appdata {};
    struct v2f {};
ENDHLSL
```

Note that in this snippet, I've used the CBUFFER_START/CBUFFER_END macros to make this shader compatible with the SRP Batcher (as we discussed in *Chapter 10*), but this is, of course, optional, and you could remove these two lines.

- Then, we'll modify the appdata and v2f data structures to pass through the vertex positions, thanks to the POSITION and SV_POSITION semantics:

```
struct appdata {
    float4 vertex : POSITION;
};
struct v2f {
    float4 vertex : SV_POSITION;
};
```

- We'll also fill the vertex shader function, vert, to have it transform the position from object to clip space:

```
v2f vert (appdata v) {
    v2f o;
    o.vertex = TransformObjectToHClip(v.vertex.xyz);
    return o;
}
```

- And finally, in the fragment shader function, frag, we'll return our _Color parameter directly to get the expected unlit shading on our meshes:

```
float4 frag(g2f i) : SV_Target {
    return float4(_Color, 1);
}
```

At this point, our shader makes a flat shading for our objects in a single solid color:

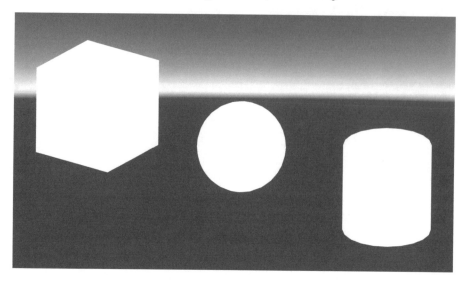

Figure 13.6 – A visualization of our (incomplete) wireframe
shader, with just flat shading on a few primitives

While we're at it, let's also add two properties to our shader for the wireframe color (_WireframeColor) and the wireframe stroke thickness (_WireframeThickness):

```
Properties {
    _WireframeColor ("Wireframe Color", Color) = (0, 0, 0,
        1)
    _WireframeThickness ("Wireframe Thickness", Range(0,
        800)) = 10
}
...
CBUFFER_START(UnityPerMaterial)
float4 _Color;
float4 _WireframeColor;
float _WireframeThickness;
CBUFFER_END
```

These properties will determine the color and the width respectively of the wireframe stroke on our model.

Of course, we don't want to do just an unlit shader here – we want to show some wireframes! Therefore, it's time to upgrade our code and inject the geometry shader function in the middle to process all of this per-vertex data, creating our own geometry-related effects.

Implementing the geometry stage in our shader

To create this wireframe shader, the core idea is to change the return value of our fragment shader based on the distance of the pixel to the nearest edge of the model. If we are beneath a certain threshold, then our pixel will be part of the wireframe, and we will give it the `_WireframeColor`; otherwise, it will not be part of the wireframe, and we will give it the base `_Color` value.

This means that to create this effect, we'll need to have our fragment shader function access some topology-related data, namely this distance to the closest edge. And to get this data, we're going to use the geometry stage of our shader.

Specifically, we'll leverage a neat notion called **barycentric coordinates**. Simply put, this is a sort of normalization operation but one that determines the position of a point in a triangle, relative to the three vertices of said triangle. As shown in *Figure 13.7*, the goal is to assign each vertex a unit coordinate along one axis (**(1, 0, 0)**, **(0, 1, 0)** and **(0, 0, 1)** respectively) and then interpolate between these extrema to give the inner positions relative coordinates with respect to those three vertex-defined axes:

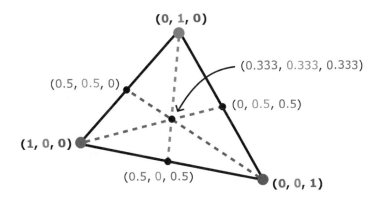

Figure 13.7 – Barycentric coordinates inside a triangle

In *Figure 13.7*, we can see the relative positions of the middle points of each edge of the triangle, and of the center of mass of the triangle. In our render pipeline, these barycentric coordinates will be computed automatically during the rasterization phase, as long as we assign each of the three vertices of the triangle their own extreme barycentric coordinates.

With this new piece of information, it is then pretty straightforward to know whether a point is close to an edge or not inside our fragment shader function; we simply have to check whether the smaller component of the point's barycentric coordinate is below our `_WireframeThickness` property, and voilà! Indeed, if any component of this barycentric coordinate is lower than our thickness threshold, then it means the point is really close to one of its triangle's edges, and it belongs to the wireframe.

A little note on wireframe edge thickness

It is worth mentioning that, with this technique, the inner edges of the model will appear with twice the thickness in the wireframe because the thresholds from the two triangles on each side of the edge will add up, while the outer edges of the model will appear with the single thickness. However, this is usually not really noticeable, as there are a lot more inner edges than there are outer edges.

Now that we have a rough idea of how our wireframe shader geometry stage will work, let's implement it gradually.

First of all, because we're adding a new stage in our shader script, we need to change our data structures a little to accommodate this intermediary step. Rather than having just a v2f structure to pass the data from the vertex to the fragment stage, we'll have to use both a v2g structure to pass the data from the vertex to the geometry stage, and a g2f structure to pass this new data from the geometry to the fragment stage:

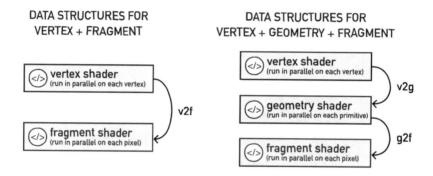

Figure 13.8 – Usual data structures for shader scripts with more or fewer stages

In *Figure 13.8*, you see the difference between a shader using only the vertex and fragment stages (on the left), and one using the vertex, geometry, and fragment stages (on the right) from a data standpoint.

We'll make these changes in our HLSLINCLUDE block by removing the v2f structure we had previously and adding the v2g and g2f ones instead:

```
struct appdata { ... };
struct v2g {
    float4 vertex : SV_POSITION;
};
struct g2f {
    float4 vertex : SV_POSITION;
    float3 barycentric : TEXCOORD0;
};
```

In this snippet, we can see that the information that we input into our geometry shader function is simply the vertex positions, but with the SV_POSITION semantic. Then, when going from the geometry to the fragment stage, we transfer both the position of the vertex and the matching barycentric coordinates for the wireframe display.

Now, we can define the geometry shader function in our code by adding a pragma directive in our HLSLPROGRAM block, preparing the prototype of the new geom function, and updating the input and output types of the vert and frag functions as follows:

```
HLSLPROGRAM
#pragma vertex vert
#pragma geometry geom
#pragma fragment frag

v2g vert (appdata v) { ... }

[maxvertexcount(3)]
void geom(triangle v2g i[3], inout TriangleStream<g2f> stream) {}

float4 frag(g2f i) : SV_Target { ... }
ENDHLSL
```

As you can see, when writing down the prototype of a geometry shader function, you have to specify several important elements:

- Before the actual function prototype, you need to use the maxvertexcount attribute to tell the function how many vertices it will output. In our case, we'll work with triangles, so we'll always output three vertices.

- Then, the first input parameter of our geom function is the incoming data from the previous stage, the vertex stage, passed as a v2g data instance. We have to explicitly set the type of primitive our geometry shader will work on, which in our case is triangle, and because triangles have three vertices, we'll get an array of data instances with three items inside.

- Finally, we need our function to actually output something for the next stages of the render process, but you'll notice that it has a void return type! That's because, since technically the number of output vertices of a geometry shader function can vary, it is not possible to use a hardcoded return type. Instead, a geometry shader writes to a stream of primitives that have been prepared beforehand and passed as input in read-write mode (thanks to the inout keyword). Here, we're manipulating triangles, so we'll use TriangleStream containing instances of our g2f data structure.

In order for our shader to compile properly, we're going to add some temporary logic inside our geometry shader function to simply transfer the data as is, unmodified, to the rest of the render pipeline. We want to put vertex data in our read-write primitive stream, which we can do with the Append function of the TriangleStream object:

```
void geom(triangle v2g i[3], inout TriangleStream<g2f> stream) {
    stream.Append(i[0]);
    stream.Append(i[1]);
    stream.Append(i[2]);
}
```

With these updates, our shader now compiles. And although it still looks exactly the same, it actually includes an extra geometry stage in the middle that we'll be able to customize by providing the right instructions to our geom function. More precisely, remember that we want it to set up barycentric coordinates on our triangle's vertices so that those are then interpolated by the rasterizer, and fed to the fragment stage.

The geometry function logic is quite easy to write – we just have to prepare new g2f data instances for each vertex in our triangle, assign their vertex field to the initial value from the incoming v2g data, and then give them the three extreme barycentric coordinates, like this:

```
void geom(triangle v2g i[3], inout TriangleStream<g2f> stream) {
    g2f o;
    o.vertex = i[0].vertex;
    o.barycentric = float3(1, 0, 0);
    stream.Append(o);
    o.vertex = i[1].vertex;
    o.barycentric = float3(0, 1, 0);
    stream.Append(o);
    o.vertex = i[2].vertex;
    o.barycentric = float3(0, 0, 1);
    stream.Append(o);
}
```

Here, we don't simply transfer our vertices unmodified anymore – we also give them barycentric coordinates, as expected in the g2f data structure, that can be blended for each inner point of the triangle during rasterization.

So now, in our frag function, we can take the incoming g2f interpolated data and extract from it the smallest of the barycentric coordinate components, meaning the closest distance to an edge for this fragment. And then, all we have to do is lerp between our _Color and _WireframeColor values, depending on whether or not this distance is below the _WireframeThickness threshold:

```
float4 frag(g2f i) : SV_Target {
    float3 wire = step(_WireframeThickness, i.barycentric);
    float dist = min(wire.x, min(wire.y, wire.z));
```

```
        return float4(lerp(_WireframeColor, _Color, dist).xyz, 1);
}
```

If we recompile the shader and apply it on a few test primitive meshes, we can see that it shows us the geometry of our mesh live, auto-computed thanks to the additional geometry stage:

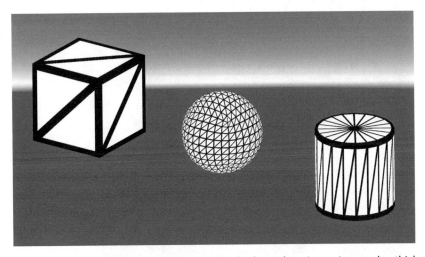

Figure 13.9 – A visualization of our wireframe URP shader with an inconsistent edge thickness

However, in *Figure 13.9*, you'll quickly notice that our shader currently creates inconsistent strokes with varying thicknesses, which doesn't look very nice. That's because, despite using a constant threshold, we define our edges based on proportions – thus, a larger triangle will show up with a thicker wireframe contour. To get a more aesthetically pleasing and controlled visual, we have to renormalize our distances with regard to the triangle size.

Making fixed-width antialiased wireframe edges

In order to renormalize our computations and get a fixed-width wireframe effect, we have to know the rate of change between two barycentric positions in our triangle. Luckily, HLSL has a built-in function that gives us this exact result in one go, called `fwidth`.

This means that if we apply this `fwidth` function to the barycentric coordinate of our input fragment in the `frag` function, we'll essentially get the unit width for the given triangle. And then, simply by multiplying our `_WireframeThickness` constant with this unit width, we'll get a renormalized threshold for our edge:

```
float4 frag(g2f i) : SV_Target {
    float3 unitWidth = fwidth(i.barycentric);
    float3 wire = step(unitWidth * _WireframeThickness,
        i.barycentric);
```

```
        float dist = min(wire.x, min(wire.y, wire.z));
        return float4(lerp(_WireframeColor, _Color, dist).xyz,
            1);
}
```

If we come back to the editor after updating our script, we can see that the wireframe thickness is now consistent across all triangles and all models:

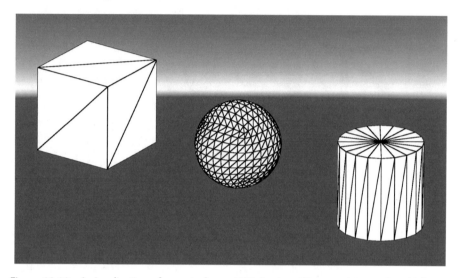

Figure 13.10 – A visualization of our wireframe URP shader with a consistent edge thickness

To improve the effect a little more and remove the bad aliasing, we can also replace our `step` operation with a `smoothstep` one, like this:

```
float4 frag(g2f i) : SV_Target {
    float3 unitWidth = fwidth(i.barycentric);
    float3 wire = smoothstep(float3(0, 0, 0), unitWidth *
        _WireframeThickness, i.barycentric);
    float dist = min(wire.x, min(wire.y, wire.z));
    return float4(lerp(_WireframeColor, _Color, dist).xyz,
        1);
}
```

This will instantly blur the borders of the edge and make an antialiased wireframe:

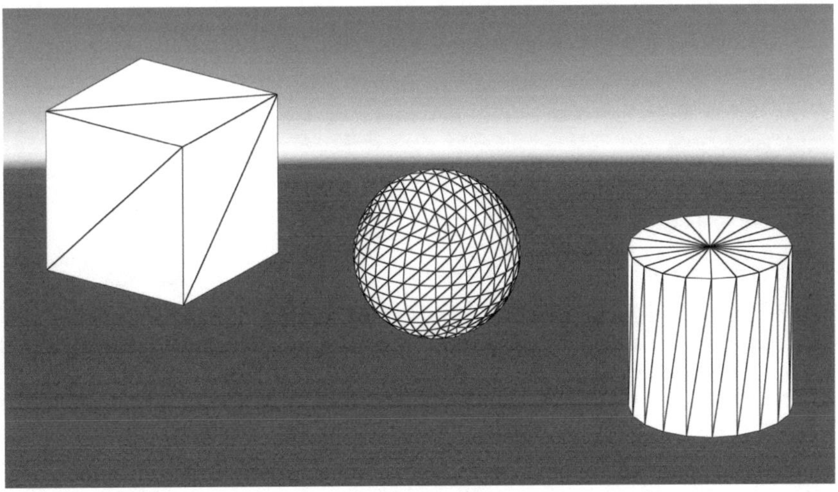

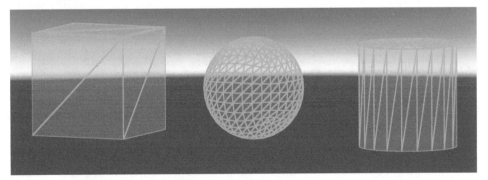

Figure 13.11 – A visualization of our wireframe URP shader with antialiased edges

And that's it – we've successfully implemented a basic wireframe unlit shader in HLSL code for the URP pipeline. We can now play around with the different properties to get a whole gallery of wireframe renders.

And we could even use this technique to not only toggle between two colors but also make the mesh semitransparent outside of the wireframe, by using the threshold to determine the alpha value of the final pixel color. This could create the neat hologram effect we showed in *Figure 13.5*, and demonstrated again here in *Figure 13.12*.

Figure 13.12 – A visualization of a semitransparent wireframe URP shader

If you're curious to see how to write such a shader, feel free to have a look at the GitHub repository for this book (https://github.com/PacktPublishing/Become-a-Unity-Shaders-Guru).

This concludes our quick overview of geometry shaders. There are, of course, plenty more applications for these – displaying a wireframe is a very common one, but it doesn't show the full strength of the tool. Therefore, as usual, don't hesitate to experiment and tinker with these base shaders to create your own effects!

Summary

In this chapter, we've discussed geometry shaders.

First, we talked about the base principles behind geometry shaders – we saw what they are, how they work, and also why they can be limited or risky to use. In particular, we focused on the case of Apple devices, which are now discontinuing the support for this kind of shader, thus requiring us to think twice before using them if we need full cross-platform compatibility.

We then studied a classical geometry shader application, which is rendering a wireframe version of our meshes. In just a few dozen lines, we were able to code a URP unlit shader script that highlights the geometry of our 3D models by drawing the edges of each triangle, which even works in-game, at runtime.

We are now nearing the end of this book, and we have seen a lot of examples that have taught us various tricks about modern Unity shaders and the new URP pipeline. To wrap all of this up, our next and final chapter will examine one last important category of shaders – screen-effect shaders.

Going further

If you're curious about geometry shaders and their limitations, here are a few interesting resources to check out to continue your journey:

- *Geometry Shader*, J. de Vries (2014–present): `https://learnopengl.com/Advanced-OpenGL/Geometry-Shader`

- *Geometry Shaders Made Easy In Unity URP! For Those New to Shaders! 2020.3 | Game Dev Tutorial*, Ned Makes Games (2020): `https://www.youtube.com/watch?v=7C-mA08mp8o`

- *Intro to Compute Shaders in Unity URP! Replace Geometry Shaders 2020.3 | Game Dev Tutorial*, Ned Makes Games (2020): `https://www.youtube.com/watch?v=EB5HiqDl7VE`

- *Unity Vertex Shader and Geometry Shader Tutorial*, GameDevBill (2020): `https://gamedevbill.com/unity-vertex-shader-and-geometry-shader-tutorial/`

- *Stylised Grass with Shaders in URP*, D. Ilett (2021): `https://danielilett.com/2021-08-24-tut5-17-stylised-grass/`

- *[Unity3D] Intro to Geometry Shader*, J. Liu (2018): `https://jayjingyuliu.wordpress.com/2018/01/24/unity3d-intro-to-geometry-shader/`

14

Screen Effect Shaders

Our journey through the world of modern Unity shaders is almost over, and we've looked at quite a number of examples. In the past few chapters, we explored a gallery of 2D and 3D shaders, and we learned several handy tricks for boosting our visuals and creating easy-to-tweak effects on our sprites and meshes.

In this final chapter, we'll discuss one last common type of shader – the fullscreen effect shader. These are global filters applied to the entire render image that make it possible to make our own custom postprocessing effects and improve the overall atmosphere of the scene.

Still, if you've ever lurked around the Unity forums and the shader-related threads, you've probably seen how the arrival of URP has sadly complicated things a little for screen effects… so we'll definitely have to take a moment to talk about the required setup for using fullscreen shaders in URP.

In this last chapter, we'll discuss the following topics:

- Using fullscreen shaders in URP
- Creating a security camera effect
- Making a fullscreen box blur

Technical requirements

To try out the shader examples shown in this chapter, you will need to install Unity with a version from 2022.2 or later and make a project using the URP pipeline.

All the shaders and assets for this chapter are also available in the GitHub repository of this book at `https://github.com/PacktPublishing/Become-a-Unity-Shaders-Guru/tree/main/Assets/Chapter%2014`

Using fullscreen shaders in URP

Before we get to actually creating fullscreen shaders, let's take a second to see how this kind of shader works in URP, and in particular how this render pipeline evolved to gradually make this feature easier and easier to use.

In this first section, we're going to have a quick look at the old way of doing things with the built-in render pipeline, and then we'll see how the URP pipeline changed over the years to eventually incorporate fullscreen shaders as a readily available tool.

The case of the built-in render pipeline

In the past, any shader creator who worked with the built-in render pipeline was fairly pleased to create a fullscreen effect shader, because it was simple. You would just need to do three things:

1. Prepare your screen shader.

2. Create a new material asset using this shader.

3. Add a `MonoBehaviour` script to your scene camera object containing the `OnRenderImage` function, to essentially apply this material on the scene render, thanks to `Graphics.Blit` being built in, with a structure such as the following:

    ```
    using UnityEngine;

    [ExecuteInEditMode]
    public class CameraPostProcessing : MonoBehaviour {
      public Material postProcessingMaterial;

      public void OnRenderImage(RenderTexture src,
      RenderTexture dest) {
        Graphics.Blit(src, dest, postProcessingMaterial);
      }
    }
    ```

    Note that here, the `[ExecuteInEditMode]` attribute allows us to preview the result of the shader on the scene render live in the editor, without having to start Play mode first.

This meant that in just a few minutes, you could prepare and set up your scene with a nice fullscreen effect totally customizable via your shader code, and you would only manipulate basic shaders, materials, and scripts – or in other words, classic graphics-related objects that you were used to.

But then, the new SRP pipelines arrived, and people started switching over to the URP as time went by... and got a bit stuck when it came to creating screen effect shaders. You could still find some workarounds with custom renderer features (which we studied in *Chapter 5* and *Chapter 8*, for example), yet there wasn't a straightforward built-in tool to handle this use case anymore.

That is, until version 14 of URP came out.

Switching our fullscreen effects over to URP

In the most recent versions of Unity, starting with Unity 2022.2, the **Universal RP** package (which, as you might remember from *Chapter 2*, defines all the core objects necessary for using the URP pipeline in your project) now contains very cool features that make it easy to create custom postprocessing effects using shaders.

In short, ever since version 14 of the **Universal RP** package, we've had two new objects at our disposal in our technical artist's URP toolbox – the **Full Screen Pass Renderer Feature** object and the associated **Fullscreen Shader Graph** template.

First, ensure that you are using the **Universal RP** 14+ version in your **Package Manager** window, as shown in *Figure 14.1*:

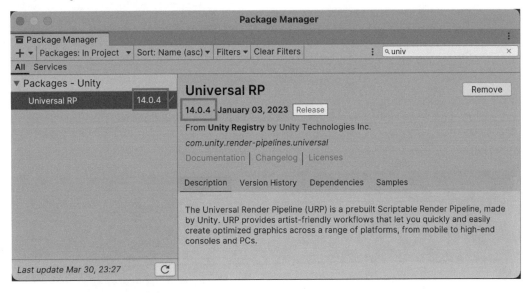

Figure 14.1 – Universal RP package in the Package Manager in version 14.0.4

Then, you will have access to a new URP shader template, called **Fullscreen Shader Graph**, in the contextual **Create | Shader Graph | URP** menu:

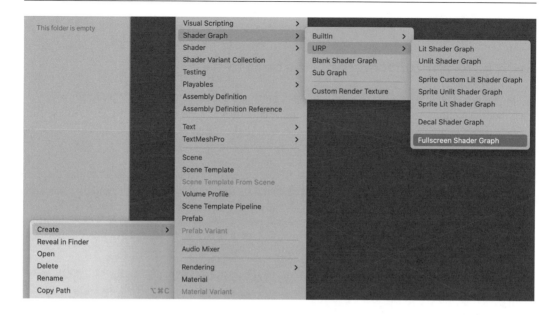

Figure 14.2 – New contextual menu item for the Fullscreen Shader Graph URP template

If you click on this menu item to instantiate a new Shader Graph in your project using this template, and you open it in the Shader Graph editor, you'll see in the **Graph Settings** window that the type of this shader is set to **Fullscreen**, and we just have two outputs in the **Fragment** context – **Base Color** and **Alpha**.

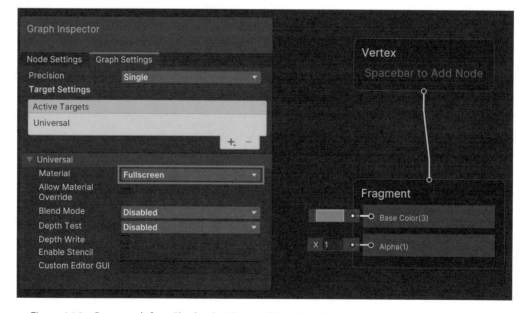

Figure 14.3 – Base graph for a Shader Graph asset based on the Fullscreen Shader Graph template

To put it in another way, in just one click, we created a new URP shader that can be edited via the beginner-friendly node graph system and works perfectly as a fullscreen effect shader.

Except that, to really apply this shader to our scene render, we're going to need the second feature in our toolbox – the **Full Screen Pass Renderer Feature** object.

For this example, and the rest of the chapter, we'll assume that we have a simple 3D scene containing three primitives and a default skybox, like this one:

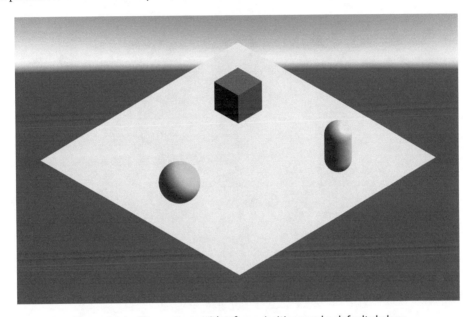

Figure 14.4 – Demo scene with a few primitives and a default skybox

Moreover, something neat is that the **Universal RP** 14+ package actually comes bundled with a `FullscreenInvertColors` material (based on a basic color invert fullscreen effect URP shader), which we can use directly to test the feature and check everything works properly.

So, just like any other custom URP renderer feature, we just have to add the **Full Screen Pass Renderer Feature** object to the settings asset of the project's URP pipeline. This is done by selecting the asset and examining its **Inspector** – here is the updated asset with the new renderer feature added and the `FullscreenInvertColors` material loaded in as the custom postprocessing fullscreen effect:

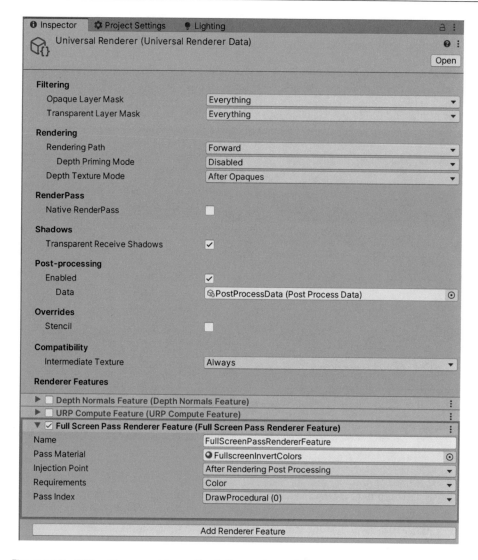

Figure 14.5 – URP settings asset to use the FullscreenInvertColors material as a fullscreen effect

Figure 14.5 shows that the **Full Screen Pass Renderer Feature** object relies on a material asset – which is equivalent to the `postProcessingMaterial` variable used in the previous snippet, in the case of the built-in render pipeline – and offers a few interesting options (for more information, see the official documentation at `https://docs.unity3d.com/Packages/com.unity. render-pipelines.universal@14.0/manual/renderer-features/renderer-feature-full-screen-pass.html`):

- **Injection Point**: This determines when the effect will be rendered in the render process

- **Requirements**: This selects some additional passes necessary to the shader logic used by this renderer feature
- **Pass Index**: This selects a specific pass inside the material used by this renderer feature

And that's it! If you look back at your **Scene** or **Game** view (both get updated instantly when you enable the renderer feature, and both get the screen effect applied), you'll notice that the colors are now inverted, thanks to the `FullscreenInvertColors`-based custom postprocessing:

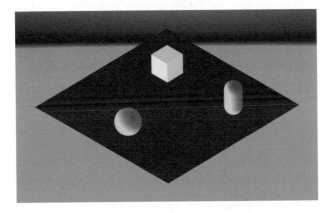

Figure 14.6 – Demo scene with the fullscreen color inversion effect applied

This is great because it allows us to keep our usual shader creation workflow. Simply picking the right shader type in our **Graph Settings** panel inside the Shader Graph editor makes assets that can be used in this renderer feature instantly work as fullscreen effects.

Of course, the next step is to see how to truly create our own effects, instead of just using a ready-made color inversion filter. That's why we're going to study a similar effect in more detail and discuss how to use these tools to desaturate the scene render.

A little example – turning our render grayscale

Alright – now that we're a bit more familiar with the process of making a URP fullscreen shader, let's apply this in practice. The first effect will be extremely simple: we'll just reduce the saturation of the output frame to 0 in order to make the image black and white.

This will allow us to explore how to set up a fullscreen shader in URP step by step and configure the pipeline to use it; plus, we'll have a look at the base Shader Graph node for fullscreen effects.

To start off, let's create our `Grayscale` shader asset. It will be a Shader Graph asset like all the others except, this time, it uses the new **Fullscreen Shader Graph** URP template (see *Figure 14.2*). If we open it in the Shader Graph editor, we get back the default fullscreen shader graph shown in *Figure 14.3*.

The first step is to get back the initial render frame – this is the original image produced by Unity based on the current scene camera properties that is displayed by default if we don't apply any screen effect shader.

To get this image, we can use the built-in **URP Sample Buffer** node with the **Source Buffer** dropdown set to the **BlitSource** value:

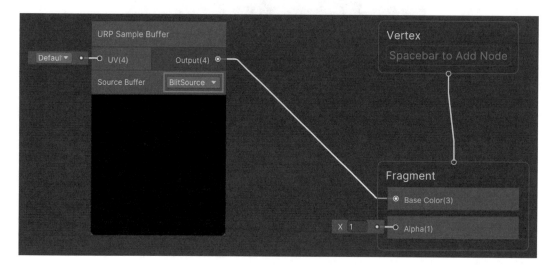

Figure 14.7 – Basic URP fullscreen shader using a URP Sample Buffer node

If we connect the output of this node to the **Base Color** output of our shader (in the **Fragment** context), then we're basically transferring the original render as is.

So, let's say that we create a material from our `Grayscale` shader and use it in our **Full Screen Pass Renderer Feature**, inside our URP settings asset:

▼ ☑ Full Screen Pass Renderer Feature (Full Screen Pass Renderer Feature)		⋮
Name	FullScreenPassRendererFeature	
Pass Material	◉ Grayscale	◉
Injection Point	After Rendering Post Processing	▼
Requirements	Color	▼
Pass Index	DrawProcedural (0)	▼

Figure 14.8 – URP settings asset to use the Grayscale material as a fullscreen effect

As you can see in *Figure 14.8*, I have kept the other properties, such as **Injection Point** and **Requirements**, at their default values, **After Rendering Post Processing** and **Color**, respectively.

For now, the **Scene** and **Game** views remain exactly the same, but we've actually included our effect in the render process.

So now, we can integrate a **Saturation** node in our `Grayscale` shader graph, change the **Saturation** input to `0`, and save the asset, like this:

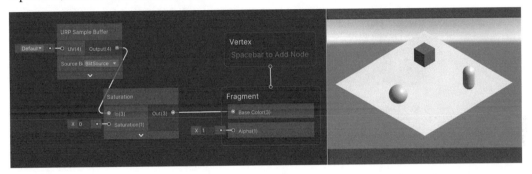

Figure 14.9 – Result and graph of the Grayscale shader

Then, as shown in *Figure 14.9*, our final image in the **Scene** and **Game** views indeed gets transformed into a black-and-white version.

We've thus successfully included our very own screen effect shader in Unity's render process and discovered the **URP Sample Buffer** node, which makes it easy to retrieve the current original render image.

With this in mind, it is time to level up and set up a more interesting fullscreen URP shader – a security camera effect.

Creating a security camera effect

To continue our study of fullscreen shaders, let's work on a classic security camera-like render, with a single-colored image, some glitchy scanlines, a bit of lens distortion, and a grainy filter (see *Figure 14.10*).

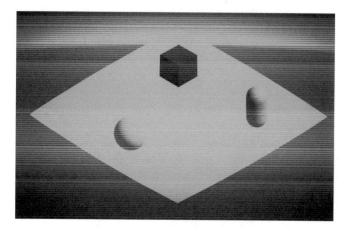

Figure 14.10 – Demo of our soon-to-be fullscreen Security Camera shader

To do this, we'll rely on both a fullscreen shader and a couple of built-in postprocessing effects. We'll start by implementing all the base features of our security camera effect, before adding in the postprocessing filters to boost the result even further.

Implementing the color tinting and scanlines

Our security camera effect will be handled by a `SecurityCamera` Shader Graph asset that is, once again, based on the **Fullscreen Shader Graph** URP template.

We will start by using the **URP Sample Buffer** node to get our initial render image, and multiply it by a single green color to tint it globally, as follows:

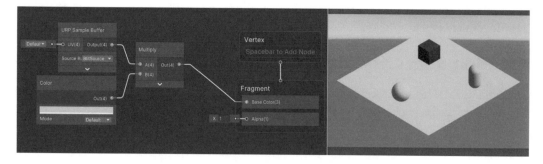

Figure 14.11 – Graph of the Security Camera shader with the base color tinting

Of course, you can change this color to anything you like, and even turn it into a shader property if you want users to be able to tweak this parameter.

Then, we'll reuse the scanlines texture from *Chapter 11* (the one we used for our hologram effect, shared by Brackeys in their open source GitHub project at `https://github.com/Brackeys/Shader-Graph-Tutorials`):

Figure 14.12 – Scanlines texture, by Brackeys

The shader logic will be almost identical to the one from the `Hologram` shader in *Chapter 11* – we'll just add a **Multiply** node at the end to slightly reduce the opacity of the lines, and then add it on top of or previously tinted image:

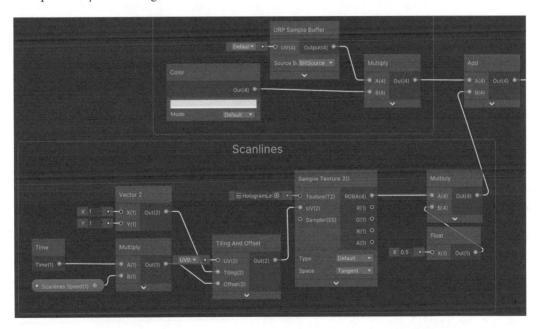

Figure 14.13 – Graph of the scanlines logic for the Security Camera shader

Now, all we have to do is create a material using this shader, and replace the reference in our URP settings asset so that this material is used by the **Full Screen Pass Renderer Feature** object. This time, we will set **Injection Point** to be **Before Rendering Post Processing** because we want our postprocessing effects to run *after* the shader:

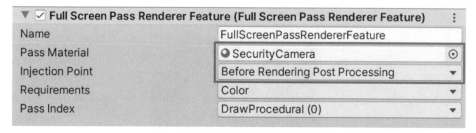

Figure 14.14 – URP settings asset for using the Security Camera material as a fullscreen effect

At this point, the render in the **Scene** and **Game** views has turned green, and we have little scanlines moving vertically over time:

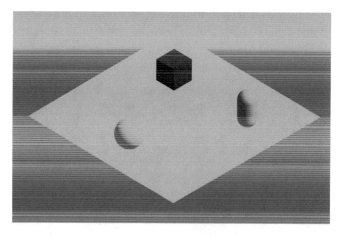

Figure 14.15 – Result of the fullscreen Security Camera shader (without postprocessing effects)

That's pretty nice, but we can go even further with some additional postprocessing effects!

Improving the effect with postprocessing

Usually, video game security cameras are even more distorted and old-looking than our current setup. So, we're going to improve the effect by using some of Unity's built-in postprocessing effects, as we saw in *Chapter 11*.

In our case, we can use three effects:

- **Vignette**: This darkens the corners of the screen and thus highlights the central area in the eyes of the viewer. Usually, the middle zone is defined by a circle or an ellipse.

- **Lens Distortion**: This simulates a real-world camera by distorting (or undistorting) the scene render.

- **Film Grain**: This adds animated spots on the image to re-create the feeling of a coarse camera film (Unity uses a coherent gradient noise function behind the scenes).

To set up this postprocessing in the scene, we just need to create a new Game Object and add a **Volume** component to it. Then, we'll make a new post processing profile asset in our project and add our three effects, like this:

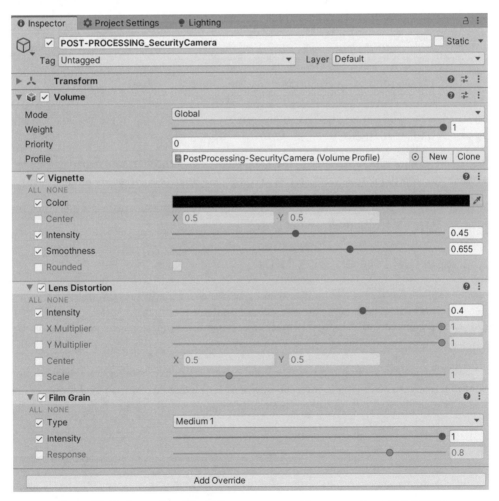

Figure 14.16 – Inspector of the Volume component for our scene postprocessing

Of course, feel free to play around with the values of the different parameters in those filters to adjust the effect to your liking. Also, don't forget to actually enable the **Post Processing** option on your scene camera:

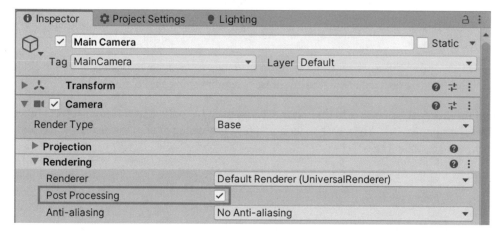

Figure 14.17 – Inspector of the scene camera with Post Processing enabled

You'll see that the render now includes our postprocessing filters on top of the screen effect shader, and that we get the result shown in *Figure 14.10*.

So, there you go – we've now finished a nice URP security camera effect and explored how to mix fullscreen shaders with postprocessing filters to completely transform our scene render.

To wrap up this chapter, let's see another way of getting screen data and creating a fullscreen shader without the use of the **URP Sample Buffer** node.

Making a fullscreen box blur

Up until now, we've seen how to implement some screen effect shaders thanks to the **URP Sample Buffer** node, and we've played around with the original render image in various ways. In this last section, we're going to discuss another method for creating fullscreen shaders with the Shader Graph tool and apply it to a box blur filter effect.

We will start by getting a quick reminder of how the box blur effect works; then, we'll see how to implement it thanks to a Sub Graph asset; and finally, we'll re-integrate this Sub Graph into a fullscreen URP shader to apply our box blur filter to the whole render.

What is a box blur?

The box blur is a very simple low-pass filter that lets us easily blur an image thanks to a few mathematical operations. It relies on a basic idea, which is to replace the initial value of each pixel in the image with the average of their neighbor pixel values.

This technique is far from perfect, but it is a good way to efficiently approximate more precise blurs, such as Gaussian blur.

Here, we will make a basic box blur-like effect by taking the original pixels of our scene render image, shifting them slightly in four directions (+X, -X, +Y, and -Y), and finally, adding those offsetted values to the original ones.

Because we will only do one shifted copy in each direction, we say that our box blur is single-step. We could improve the quality of the result by adding more steps (or in other words, doing multiple copies in each direction with various offsets, to get more details). But this is a trade-off against performance, and the more precise the effect, the more resource intensive the computation – so we will stick to a single-step example here.

What is interesting is that we will use the same "copy-and-shift" operation in each direction; therefore, by abstracting away this process in a Sub Graph asset, we can easily set up a 2D box blur filter for the entire render. So, let's now see how to do all of this in Unity step by step.

Creating a box blur Sub Graph

OK – to make it easier to create the final 2D box blur effect, we'll start by preparing a Sub Graph asset in our project that takes care of creating the displacement in one direction, with a given offset amount. Basically, this Sub Graph will take the current screen render and, for each pixel inside it, sample a neighboring pixel instead – essentially shifting the render to the side in some direction.

To do this, the trick is to rely on the **Screen Position** and **Scene Color** nodes. The **Screen Position** node gives us the position of the pixel, and **Scene Color** allows us to sample the scene render at a specific 2D UV coordinate; so, by taking in the initial UVs from the **Screen Position** node and applying an offset on them, we can get updated UV coordinates to re-sample our image at and get our shifted render.

More precisely, here is the graph for our `BoxBlur` Sub Graph asset:

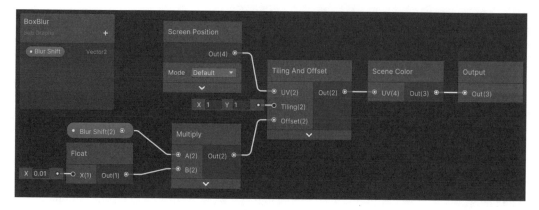

Figure 14.18 – Graph of the BoxBlur Sub Graph asset

You see, in *Figure 14.18*, the following:

- We use the initial UV output from the **Screen Position** node as the **UV** input for a **Tiling And Offset** node.

- We pass in a **Vector2** `Blur Shift` shader property as the **Offset** value, except we artificially divide by 100 to get something more controlled. This remapping will let us pass easy-to-manage values in the 0-1 range without having a huge shift in our render.

- Finally, we use our updated UV output from the **Tiling And Offset** node as the **UV** input of the **Scene Color** node, and we use the resulting color as the RGB color for our Sub Graph asset.

We can then create a fullscreen `Blur` shader as a new Shader Graph asset (again based on the **Fullscreen Shader Graph** URP template), and instantiate our Sub Graph in it twice – once with a null shift to get our original render, and another time with a shift of 1 along the X axis. Then, we'll add the two images on top of each other, and divide by 2 to renormalize the result and avoid having surexposed visuals, like this:

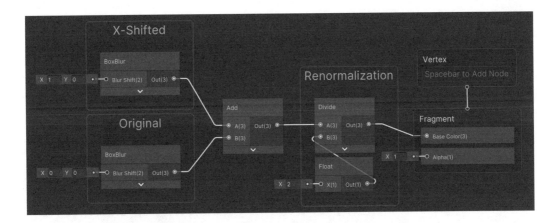

Figure 14.19 – Example of a base Blur fullscreen shader graph with a single shifted copy of the render

If we make a material based on this shader and apply it in our URP settings asset as the current material for the **Full Screen Pass Renderer Feature** object, we see that our render now shows two copies of the scene, one being slightly offsetted to the right side:

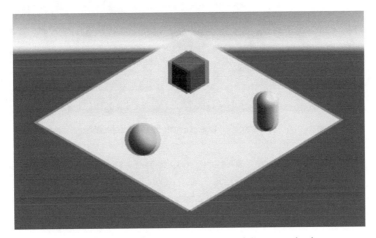

Figure 14.20 – Result of our basic Blur fullscreen shader

Here, the effect is, of course, a bit extreme, and it only takes one direction into account among the four we need. But this means that our BoxBlur Sub Graph works as expected and that we can now rely on this little brick to make our full 2D box blur effect.

Setting up the 2D box blur screen effect

For our real box blur screen effect, the goal will be to repeat this blend-and-renormalize chunk several times, in order to overlay five copies of our image: the original render, the render shifted to the right, the render shifted to the left, the render shifted to the top, and the render shifted to the bottom. This will create a basic single-step box blur.

In the end, our `Blur` shader will therefore look as follows – *Figure 14.21* is just an overview of the logic; we will zoom on each of the parts afterward:

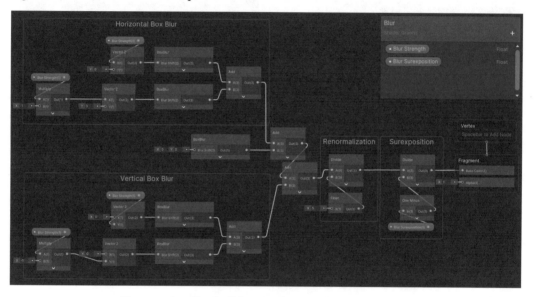

Figure 14.21 – Graph of the complete Blur fullscreen shader

This shader uses a `Blur Strength` property to determine the amount of offset to apply in each direction, as well as another `Blur Surexposition` property to artificially increase the exposition of the final result and force the brightness. This is by no means mandatory, and it is not directly linked to the blur effect, but I feel it adds to the example and gives a little extra boost to the shader.

The graph is composed of four parts:

- The **Horizontal Box Blur** node group in the top-left corner handles the left- and right-shifted renders (see *Figure 14.22*). It contains two instances of our `BoxBlur` Sub Graph asset. Those subgraphs take in a `Blur Shift` value composed of the `Blur Strength` property for the X component, and a null Y component, and the vector is reversed for the left-shifted version.

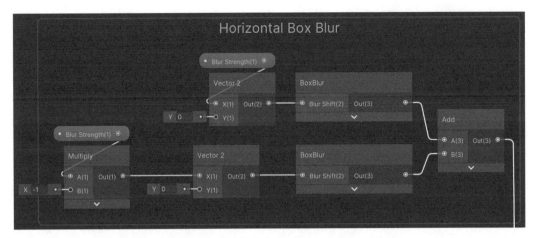

Figure 14.22 – Graph of the Horizontal Box Blur node group

- Similarly, the **Vertical Box Blur** node group handles the top- and bottom-shifted renders, again with two instances of the BoxBlur Sub Graph asset – except this time we fill in the Y component and leave the X component null:

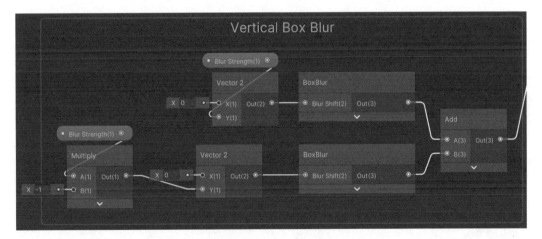

Figure 14.23 – Graph of the Vertical Box Blur node group

- The middle part recombines the five renders together with a series of **Add** nodes, and then renormalizes the result by dividing by 5:

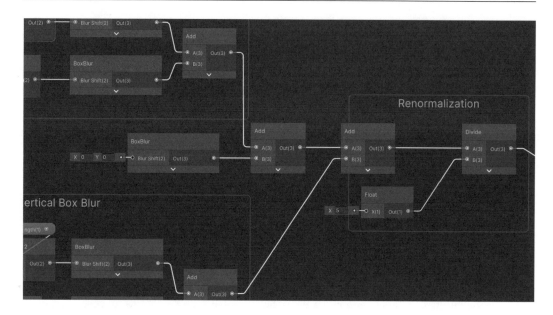

Figure 14.24 – Graph of the blend and renormalization logic in the Blur shader

- The final node group on the right, called **Surexposition**, is the extra option I talked about earlier in this section that allows us to increase the brightness of the final render to our liking and boost our effect even more:

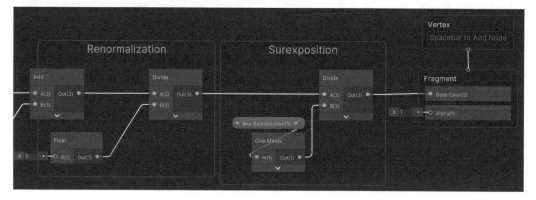

Figure 14.25 – Graph of the Surexposition node group

If we save our Blur asset, then the render of our scene will update to show us a blurred version. We can control how much blur we want by changing the value of the Blur Strength property, and we can increase the Blur Surexposition value to get the artificial brightness boost. *Figure 14.26* compares the blur effect without (at the top) and with (at the bottom) surexposition:

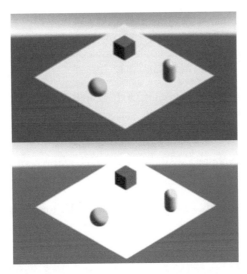

Figure 14.26 – Result of the complete Blur fullscreen shader
without (top) and with (bottom) extra brightness

This concludes our brief exploration of URP fullscreen shaders.

Thanks to this tool, you'll be able to create quite a variety of filters and transformations on your scene renders, from a simple color conversion to screen-wide pixelation (similar to what we did in *Chapter 11* for a single sprite), water ripples and heat deformations, global outlines, and even retro looks such as a Game Boy or an old CRT monitor.

Summary

In this final chapter, we've studied fullscreen effect shaders.

We first examined how the built-in and URP pipelines compare in terms of tooling for fullscreen effects, and we set up our first URP screen effect to turn the scene render black and white. Then, we worked on a common screen effect – a security camera-like filter that turns the image green, adds scanlines, and uses a few built-in postprocessing effects to set up lens distortion or vignetting. Finally, we talked about another method for accessing the screen data and discussed how to implement a basic 2D box blur filter effect with Shader Graph in Unity.

This marks the end of our adventure!

Throughout this book, we've studied the art of shaders and discussed a lot of techniques for using the new URP render pipeline in Unity. We've explored optimization tricks and plenty of examples, dived into writing modern Unity shaders using HLSL code, and learned how to use the node-based Shader Graph tool via various hands-on use cases.

Now, it's up to you to continue this exploration further and take advantage of all those ideas in your own projects – because remember that testing and tweaking is the best way to learn. So, I hope you've discovered a few interesting things in this book, and that the little gallery of shaders we've developed in the last few chapters will help nurture your creativity.

And on that note – have fun creating amazing Unity visuals!

Going further

If you're curious about screen effect shaders, here are a few interesting resources to check out or continue your journey with:

- *Custom post-processing*, official Unity URP documentation: `https://docs.unity3d.com/Packages/com.unity.render-pipelines.universal@16.0/manual/post-processing/custom-post-processing.html`

- *How to create a custom post-processing effect*, official Unity URP documentation: `https://docs.unity3d.com/Packages/com.unity.render-pipelines.universal@16.0/manual/post-processing/post-processing-custom-effect-low-code.html`

- *Full Screen Shaders in HDRP, URP, and Built In Renderer*, Game Dev Bill (2020): `https://gamedevbill.com/full-screen-shaders-in-unity/`

- *Custom Post Processing in Unity URP*, Febucci (2022): `https://www.febucci.com/2022/05/custom-post-processing-in-urp/`

- *Full Screen Shaders in URP?*, Unity forum thread: `https://forum.unity.com/threads/full-screen-shaders-in-urp.1228512/`

Appendix:
Some Quick Refreshers on Shaders in Unity

No matter how many tutorials you watch, and how many books you read, chances are that you won't be able to get to the real stuff if you don't have the basics. So, if you want to have a quick run through the fundamentals of shaders and how to create them in Unity with the built-in legacy system before diving deeper into Unity's newest render pipelines and shader tools, go ahead and take a peek at these core notions on shaders.

In this appendix, we will cover the following topics:

- Diving into what shaders are exactly
- Rendering 3D scenes on a 2D screen
- Exploring SubShader and Pass tags
- Recalling the basics of z-buffering and blending modes
- Reviewing textures and UV mapping

If you feel you are a bit shaky on some aforementioned points or you would like to remember all the neat words technical artists use to talk about their masterpieces, stick with me for this rapid review of the shader essentials.

Diving into what shaders are exactly

As the famous shader wizard Freya Holmér says, shaders can be thought of as **low-level frontends**. In short, shaders are computer programs that are able to take some 2D or 3D input and perform computations to eventually produce colors for every pixel on your screen. Thus, shaders are considered *low-level* because you are working with hard-to-grasp, computer-level info, and *frontend* because you are creating an image for your audience to look at and admire.

Now, you might be thinking that the definition of shaders we just discussed is fuzzy, and you would be right. Truth be told, it looks like the definition of a shader varies from one source to the other. If you are a gamer, a shader is actually just a visual effect that you can download into your Minecraft data folder to drastically improve the lighting or the textures of the cubic world. But in more tech-oriented communities, some people talk about shaders to describe code that runs on 3D vertices, while others refer to instructions applied on pixels or even to larger programs that are actually composed of both 3D-related and pixel-related code.

Yep – it looks like a mess. So, time to try and remerge all of this into a coherent whole!

Suppose you have an image, and you want to show it on a screen. Overall, it is quite straightforward: the computer just needs to read the contents of the file and "paste" (we usually say, *blit*) the color of each pixel inside this image on your screen at a given position, one next to the other, to gradually reconstruct the image and print it. This is similar to sticking a postcard on a board. You'll then have successfully displayed your 2D image on the screen.

Figure A.1 shows a simplified representation of this blit process:

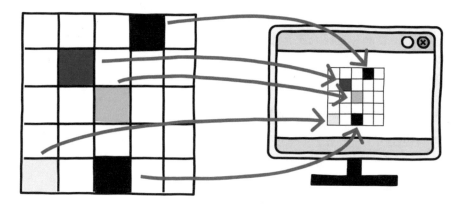

Figure A.1 – Simplified representation of the basic pixel-to-pixel
blit process that displays a 2D image on a screen

But now, imagine another scenario: you have a 3D scene in your Unity project with a cube on a plane, and Unity is kind enough to display a live visual of this scene on the screen for you.

If all we had was this *pixel-to-pixel blit* method, this visual of the 3D Unity scene simply couldn't exist, as this time, you don't have pixels to blit back on the screen! All the computer knows about is a set of virtual 3D positions used by your scene – nevertheless, it manages to show you a live visual of these 3D shapes on your screen, just like our 2D image before.

How is it possible? The answer is, of course, thanks to shaders!

In a nutshell, shaders are complex snippets of code that, in their fullest form, allow a computer to render a 3D space into a 2D image. This process implies several steps, which we will go through in the *Rendering 3D scenes on a 2D screen* section, some of which are optional: this is why we sometimes refer to a subset of the code as a shader in itself. For now, we can keep it simple and say that shaders are able to properly associate 3D positions and render data, such as material color or roughness, to the right color for the matching 2D pixel in the final image. This is similar to the example of our Unity scene in this section, where we saw some 3D shapes being magically blitted on our screen.

As an aside, because shaders use intermediary data structures and, at one point, work on pixel-to-pixel transformations, they can also be used for image transformation or screen visual effects. For example, if we wanted to apply some filter on our initial image and tint it red for our new horror-game menu screen, a simple blit process would again be too limiting. Even if we don't use 3D, shaders still allow us to customize and transform pixels to make interesting visuals. We don't talk too much about this pure 2D application of shaders in this book, though, apart from *Chapter 14*, because we are focusing on games in Unity and, today, most games rely on 3D.

Rendering 3D scenes on a 2D screen

We've seen that a 3D shape cannot be blitted on a screen as-is. This is because the computer just doesn't have the required information to fill the entire set of pixels from the virtual positions of the shape's vertices. So, in practice, how do shaders achieve this? In the following sections, we will discuss the working of shaders, both in general and in Unity.

A typical 3D rendering pipeline

Shaders are able to bridge the gap between the scarce 3D data and the denser 2D pixel information, thanks to the following three-step process:

1. **Vertex shader**: First of all, the shader has to gather all the data about the shape that is necessary for its render. This is done in the vertex shader: this piece of code is run in parallel on all vertices of the 3D mesh and transforms the initial raw per-vertex data into processed per-vertex data. Usually, this process implies converting the vertex's position from object space to clip space using the Model-View-Projection matrix; but it can also play around with this vertex position to perform some compute-efficient mesh deformation (we see more about that in *Chapter 12*).

2. **Rasterization**: The next step is to go from this scarce 3D representation of the shape as a set of vertices and triangles to a much thinner grid of cells: the pixels of our screen. This transformation is done by feeding the processed per-vertex data to the **interpolators** – this phase, called rasterization, is performed automatically by the machine (it is not a script that we have to write). The interpolators simply take all the inputs they have and blend (or *interpolate*) them linearly for all intermediary slots, hence the name. By the end of the rasterization phase, we therefore have a set of tiny 2D cells spreading over the entire screen, each filled with a set of blended 3D properties: the pixels, or **fragments**.

3. **Fragment (or pixel) shader**: Finally, we can use this per-fragment data to compute the actual color to show on screen in the second part of our shader code, the fragment shader. This is where we can sample a reference texture based on the input UVs, apply some tint on a color, or even use the input data and some global variables to compute lighting.

Here is a diagram of this entire process on a simple 3D cube with different colors on each vertex:

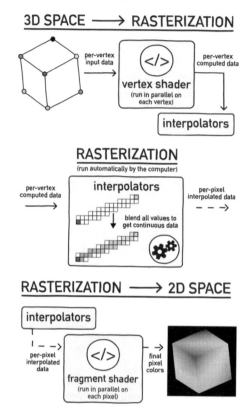

Figure A.2 – Full process to render a 3D cube to a 2D image by applying the three rendering steps: vertex shader, rasterization, and fragment shader

Since the two parts we can influence are the vertex shader and the fragment shader, a shader code is usually a combination of two functions that correspond to *step 1* and *step 3* of the process we just discussed. By convention, they are often named `vert` and `frag`, although some shader editors simply put the contents of each function into a separate function and don't bother with naming. The fragment shader returns a direct 4-component number (typically, `fixed4` or `float4`) to represent our final RGBA color for the given pixel.

In Unity, however, the basic structure of a shader code is a bit longer...let's have a look!

Using shaders in Unity

Shaders are a type of asset that cannot be used on its own. When you develop a game in Unity, to apply your shader to an object in your scene, you actually need to create an intermediary Material asset that relies on this shader, and then set the mesh of your object to use this material.

But of course, the Shader assets are also linked to their actual content, which can be edited in various ways depending on your current Unity version and render pipeline. We'll discuss it in further detail in the *Using shaders in Unity – code or graph?* subsection. If you create these Shader assets via code, then you can open them in your favorite IDE, and you'll have a file that contains the vert and frag functions we mentioned in the *A typical 3D rendering pipeline* subsection:

```
Shader "Custom/TransparentUnlit" {
    Properties {
        _Color ("Color", Color) = (1, 1, 1, 1)
    }
    SubShader {
        LOD 100
        Tags { "Queue" = "Transparent" }
        Pass {
            Blend SrcAlpha OneMinusSrcAlpha
            ZTest LEqual

            CGPROGRAM
            #pragma vertex vert
            #pragma fragment frag

            #include "UnityCG.cginc"

            float4 _Color;

            struct appdata { float4 vertex : POSITION; };
            struct v2f { float4 vertex : SV_POSITION; };

            v2f vert (appdata v) {
                v2f o;
                o.vertex = UnityObjectToClipPos(v.vertex);
                return o;
            }

            float4 frag (v2f i) : SV_Target  {
                return _Color;
            }
            ENDCG
```

```
            }
        }
    }
```

In the preceding code block, you'll notice the following:

- The basic vertex/fragment shader functions (`vert` and `frag`) are wrapped into some additional objects marked by the `SubShader` and `Pass` keywords.

- We have explicit data structures for the incoming per-vertex data and the processed per-vertex data, `appdata` and `v2f` (as in "vertex to fragment"). Here, they contain various fields for the vertex position: the incoming position (in `appdata`) is in object space, whereas the processed position (in `v2f`) is in clip space.

> **Changing the data structure names in Unity shaders**
>
> The names `appdata` and `v2f` for our data structures are once again conventions by the Unity team. You can rename them as you wish – just make sure you use the right type of structure in your vertex and fragment shader function prototypes.

If we just need the two basic vertex and fragment shader functions, and the `appdata` and `v2f` structures, then why are there all these other extra lines? Because Unity has its own shader language, ShaderLab, which allows the engine to mix all of the shaders used in your scene together and keep the various versions of your shader in one place. This can be useful if you want your game to work on multiple types of platforms with more or less computing power, or if you need to support a very specific (manually written) shader logic on several architectures. Don't worry, though: in truth, this *language* is more of an extension of the common Nvidia CG or HLSL shader programming language you might be used to. In fact, that's the reason why, inside `Pass`, you have the CGPROGRAM and ENDCG lines: they indicate the start and end of the low-level hardware shader code, to separate it from the outside Unity fluff.

Inside this code section, the `vert` and `frag` functions are explicitly designated as the source code for the vertex shader phase and the fragment shader phase by the two **pragmas**:

```
CGPROGRAM
#pragma vertex vert
#pragma fragment frag

#include "UnityCG.cginc"

float4 _Color;
...
ENDCG
```

Also, it is important to notice that the data structures and the fragment shader definitions use **semantic signifiers**, such as POSITION or SV_Target, to tell the GPU what each variable means.

At the very top of the script, just under the unique name and category of your shader, you also have the list of **shader properties** exposed in the **Inspector**. Those are the floats, colors, textures, toggles, and other variables you can tweak when you select a material that uses your shader, or a mesh that uses such a material. Each property has a unique reference (this is the variable's name, which you can use in your shader code to access its value), a display name for the **Inspector**, a type, and a default value. Here are a few examples of common property definitions:

```
Properties {
    _Color ("Color", Color) = (1, 1, 1, 1)
    _MainTex ("Main Texture", 2D) = "white" {}
    _Gloss ("Gloss", Range(0, 1)) = 0.5
}
```

Note that you can even add some optional attributes at the beginning of the line to customize the display of the property in the **Inspector** – we learn about this in *Chapter 1*, with the help of a practical example.

To use the variables in your code, you have to re-declare them inside your Pass object so that Unity can properly inject the value of the property as specified in the **Inspector** into the code when it is actually run. That is why we had this repetition of the _Color variable in the first code snippet:

```
CGPROGRAM
#pragma vertex vert
#pragma fragment frag

#include "UnityCG.cginc"

float4 _Color;
...
ENDCG
```

Unity also offers numerous ready-made shader libraries that we can include to easily compute some common values and useful variables to access the position of relevant objects, such as the camera, the main light, the Model-View-Projection matrix, and more. These imported libraries, often called the **includes**, depend on the render pipeline we are using. In *Chapter 3* and *Chapter 4*, we see the common ones used for the URP pipeline. But if you created a shader in a Unity project that uses the built-in render pipeline, you'll most probably have an include statement of the UnityCG.cginc library. This package provides us, among other things, with the variables I mentioned earlier in this section about the objects' positions, the camera, the main light, and more. It is imported with a #include instruction, like this:

```
CGPROGRAM
#pragma vertex vert
```

```
#pragma fragment frag

#include "UnityCG.cginc"

float4 _Color;
...
ENDCG
```

At that point, we've gone through most of the contents of a typical Unity ShaderLab structure, except for the few lines at the beginning of the `SubShader` and `Pass` objects in the first code block of this section:

```
SubShader {
    LOD 100
    Tags { "Queue" = "Transparent" }
    Pass {
        Blend SrcAlpha OneMinusSrcAlpha
        ZTest LEqual
        ...
    }
}
```

These lines are here to tell Unity when and how to use this `SubShader` block.

All of these instructions are optional, and some are easy to understand; for example, the LOD (level of detail) value just indicates how computationally expensive this shader is, which helps Unity prioritize shaders and pick the right `SubShader` depending on the context. Even if, contrary to a mesh LOD, a `SubShader` LOD value is set manually and does not derive from the distance to the camera, there isn't really more to say of this property.

But other properties such as the tags, the blend mode, or the z-buffering involve a bit more explanation, so let's take a look at them in detail.

Exploring SubShader and Pass tags

First of all, the **shader tags** are a list of one or more key-value pairs that allow you to custom-configure your `SubShader` or your `Pass` blocks. There are several built-in ones, and you can also define your own to then access them in your C# script using the `Material.GetTag` API. Most of the time, however, the predefined ones are enough.

At the time of writing this book, Unity documents list a total of eight `SubShader` tags. Some are very specific and rarely used, but there is one that is worth addressing: the `Queue` tag. It defines in which render queue a geometry with this shader will be. This is one of the key options that determines in which order this geometry will be rendered compared to the others.

To have precise control over the render order of your shaders, Unity lets you choose between two types of queue values:

- Either you use one of the built-in queues, among `Background`, `Geometry`, `Alpha Test`, `Transparent`, and `Overlay` (from first to last)

- Or you can use one of these reference queues as a base, and then offset it with an integer, for example, by defining a tag as follows:

```
Tags { "Queue" = "Geometry+1" }
```

This can be useful if you want the render to occur at a very specific moment, such as after the opaque objects, but before the transparent objects in your scene for water.

Picking the right queue can be an easy fix if your shader is not behaving as expected, in particular, if you are trying to use alpha for transparency. Forgetting to set the shader on the `Transparent` queue can result in an incorrect alpha output, as shown here:

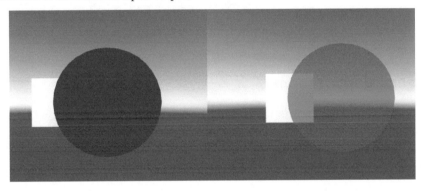

Figure A.3 – An example of the same shader without (on the left)
and with (on the right) the Transparent queue tag

As you can see in *Figure A.3*, when the tag is not passed, alpha-based transparency is not computed properly. But with the exact same shader code and just the right `Transparent` queue, it works perfectly!

Now that we have discussed the Unity shader tags, time to move on to the next interesting properties: z-buffering and blend modes!

Recalling the basics of z-buffering and blending modes

Another essential component of a shader is how it interacts with the rest of the environment, or in other words, what kind of behavior you expect from an object using your shader. Should it always be rendered in front of the rest? Should it be visible both from the front and the back? Should it be partially transparent and mix with the background color?

This scene interaction can be separated into two parts:

- On the one hand, it is crucial to decide whether your camera should render your shader *in the front* or *in the back* – to optimize the rendering process, a clever thing to do is to check whether some opaque objects are masking others, and thus we can decide whether we can ignore the ones further away or discard all the faces that are not visible from our point of view. To do this, we can rely on the technique of z-buffering.

- On the other hand, there are still cases where you will have one or more objects that overlap in the camera view. That's when you have to decide on a second important feature of your shader: how should it blend with the rest? In other words, do you want the nearest visible objects pasted atop the other ones, or do you want to have some transparency and mix their colors somehow? Or are we aiming for some flashy VFX, in which case, could we use an additive mode to boost its presence? All of these can be done via the definition of the proper blending mode for our shader.

So, first of all, let's dive into z-buffering and see how depth testing and culling can help optimize our rendering process. Then, we will see how blending modes can be the icing on the cake that gives a real uniqueness to your shader.

Culling and depth testing

A very usual question with shaders is: what is the maximal distance from the camera I want my object to be rendered, and should it be hidden by the others in front of it? To answer this, we usually use the **z-buffer**, a type of data buffer that stores the depth information for every pixel in our 3D image and allows us to know which shapes are closest to our camera eye in the scene.

So, here, the *depth* is the distance to the render camera; the shorter this distance, the more *in front* the object is compared to the others. Typically, when you work with fully opaque objects, if two shapes overlap in the camera view, then the one with the smallest depth will overwrite the output of the one further away and essentially block out its pixels on the screen in the final render.

A second depth-related concept is **culling**. This time, it is a property at the polygon level to ensure that, by default, the parts of our meshes that face away from the camera are ignored.

Depth testing, therefore, makes it easy to optimize the render efficiency by completely discarding all the data that would end up being overwritten – because it is run in-between the vertex shader and the rasterization steps, it avoids performing interpolation on unused vertices, and instead, helps the process focus on the visible object and faces in the scene.

But things obviously get harder when you want to create a visual effect that requires double-sided geometry, or when you have transparency in your shaders – for these special cases, Unity provides us with three interesting shader instructions, which are as follows:

- Cull: The Cull keyword lets us choose whether we want to ignore only polygons looking away from the camera (Cull Back, the default), ignore only polygons facing it (Cull Front), or don't ignore any polygon (Cull Off).

  The default Cull Back option is the logical choice in most situations: it simply discards the faces the camera cannot see. It makes sense to keep this setting when we want to render opaque objects since, by definition, we don't want the faces in the back to appear and we can, therefore, ignore them early in the process to save computing power.

  The Cull Front option can be useful for turning objects inside out. For example, if you want a simple box-shaped room in your game, just set this culling mode on a Unity primitive cube and it will automatically flip its faces for the camera.

  Cull Off is a good option whenever you have geometry with single faces but still regularly want to see them from both sides. Common usages are for clothing, leaves or grass blades, and VFX, where you often have just a single plane that renders the entire visual, but that should be visible from everywhere.

  Here are all three examples of culling:

  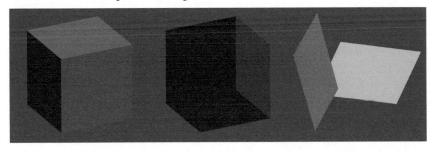

  Figure A.4 – Cull Back (on the left), Cull Front (in the middle), Cull Off (on the right)

  The Cull Off example on the right shows two planes with the same shader but different normal orientations.

- Zwrite: This is a Boolean option that you can toggle with the On or Off value. The default value is On. It is the usual z-buffer overwrite we discussed earlier in this section where objects are considered opaque – they each write their depth to the z-buffer and, if needed, replace the pixel depth of a previously stored object that is behind them.

  Turning it off is mostly relevant for semi-transparent shaders, or in other words, shaders where part of the mesh is visible and part of the mesh is transparent.

- ZTest: Finally, the `ZTest` instruction allows us to specify in detail how to perform depth testing for our shader. Basically, instead of relying on the usual front-to-back rendering where front objects overwrite the z-buffer of the ones behind them, we can decide to show only the parts of the mesh that are at a greater distance than the current buffer, or at the exact same distance, or even show everything at all times.

The `ZTest` keyword can be followed by one of seven values: `Less`, `Greater`, `LEqual` (the default), `GEqual`, `Equal`, `NotEqual`, and `Always`. Here are a few common examples:

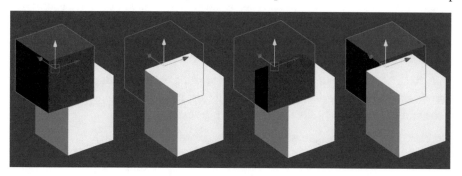

Figure A.5 – Several examples of z-test configurations – from left to right: Always, Equal, Greater, and LEqual (default value)

> **Extra notes about depth-related optimizations**
>
> If you are interested in these z-buffering mechanics and want to optimize your render process even more, another nice technique is occlusion culling. Although it can be taxing for large environments and should be used with caution, whenever you have an interior scene with large walls or items that completely block the view and constrain the camera's field of vision to a short distance, occlusion culling can help you go the extra mile.

After this short review of the z-buffer, let's now recall what blending modes are and how they work in Unity shaders.

Blending modes for the quick win

Sometimes, you'll have designed a shader that looks nice on its own but fails to properly integrate with the rest once used inside your game scene. Although there are several ways of fixing this issue, picking the right blending mode is often an easy yet powerful way to solve the problem.

We have studied most of the optional keywords a Unity shader `Pass` can contain; the only one that is left is `Blend`, which you can find at the top of a `Pass` block followed by two words, like this:

```
SubShader {
    Tags { "Queue" = "Transparent" }
```

```
    Pass {
        Blend One One
        ...
    }
}
```

The `Blend` keyword simply refers to mixing colors, as is usual in the world of shaders. But then, what are the two `One` keywords after it? Are they values, or enums?

In fact, Unity's **blending** mechanism is a common cheap trick for rendering to a single target, where at the end of the fragment shader, you run a little mathematical computation on both the color that is being outputted by this function (called the **source color**, `src`) and the one already in the background (called the **destination color**, `dst`). The formula always has the same form:

```
blended color = src • A + dst • B
```

And the tricky part is that to define your blending mode, the only values you can modify are the `A` and `B` factors.

Changing the blending operator

In general, shader blending may allow you to also change the operation in the middle to be either an addition or a subtraction, too. However, by default, Unity forces a plus sign here, and you therefore need to change the sign of the `B` factor if you want to subtract the `dst` color from the `src` color. If you really need a different operator, then you can use an extra `<Op>` keyword in your blend instruction. Read the docs for more details: `https://docs.unity3d.com/2018.4/Documentation/Manual/SL-Blend.html`.

Let's say that, for example, we want to use additive blending to make an object brighter in the background – which is always a nice technique for highlighting your visual effects. Then, we want the final formula to be as follows:

```
blended color = src + dst
```

This application of our formula means that, here, we would like to have `A = 1` and `B = 1`. Recognize anything? Yes, it's the `One` and `One` keywords from the code block we discussed at the beginning of this subsection! In Unity, the blending mode is defined by adding an instruction in your `Pass` block of the following type:

```
Blend <SrcFactor> <DstFactor>
```

By default, the mode is set to `Blend Off`, which is why objects are opaque. But, similar to the additive shader, we can get other well-known blending modes by using various keywords:

Blend options	Blending mode
`Blend SrcAlpha OneMinusSrcAlpha`	Traditional transparency
`Blend One OneMinusSrcAlpha`	Premultiplied transparency
`Blend OneMinusDstColor One`	Soft additive
`Blend DstColor Zero`	Multiplicative
`Blend DstColor SrcColor`	2x Multiplicative

Figure A.6 – Examples of the Blend options to use to get common blending modes

Even if the available keywords are limited, they allow us to recreate all the common mixes we need. If you feel like your shader doesn't fit into the world as expected, don't hesitate to have a look at blending modes to find one that would be more appropriate.

At this point, we've recalled the three main options you can add to a shader to better specify how it interacts with the rest of the scene: its tags, its culling, and depth testing configuration, and its blending mode. We will now take a look at one last essential notion for creating many shaders: handling textures and UV sets.

Reviewing textures and UV mapping

To finish this quick review of the shader fundamentals, let's have a short discussion on textures and UV mapping. Although we often think of the albedo (which means, the main color) when we hear the word *texture*, the truth is that shaders use a wide range of textures for diverse reasons, and they can be a valuable tool for optimizing your rendering. Of course, using 2D textures on 3D objects naturally implies converting between these two worlds, thus the need for the UV mapping process.

In the following sections, we are going to quickly refresh our knowledge of UVs and textures before discussing special types of textures and studying how to declare and use textures in a Unity shader code.

Wrapping a 2D image on a 3D shape

Textures are, as you know, 2D images. Therefore, the first step to using them in a 3D scene, and on 3D objects, is to find a technique to project this 2D plane onto the 3D shape. This is done via the process of **UV unwrapping**. The goal is to associate each vertex in the 3D object to a position in the unit 2D square so that the texture has *anchors* to bind itself to the shape when it wraps around it. Here is an example:

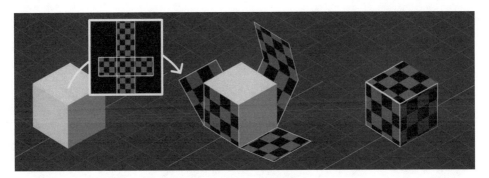

Figure A.7 – An illustration of the texture mapping process on an unwrapped cube

Therefore, in order to use any shader with a texture, an object will need to undergo this UV unwrapping process. The vertex-to-UV remapping data is then carried along with the 3D vertex-face information to completely define the object, and it can be accessed in your Unity shader in the `appdata` structure by giving the `TEXCOORD0` semantic to an input variable.

> **Using multiple UV sets**
>
> If you need to match your vertices to several UV positions (for example, to store baked light data or even custom 2D data into your object in addition to the base albedo-related UVs), you can use extra UV sets. In C#, you can access the different UVs in a mesh by getting or setting its `uv`, `uv2`, `uv3`… `uv8` properties. In a shader, those are provided via the `TEXCOORD0`, `TEXCOORD1`, `TEXCOORD2`… `TEXCOORD7` semantics, respectively.

Broadening our definition of a texture

At first glance, textures might look like they are simple plain images that you use to put some colors and details on a 3D object. Yet, textures can also be seen as 2D data containers since, in reality, nothing forces you to fill them with just one image spreading its colors over the four R, G, B, and A channels.

A very typical use of textures is for **masks**, or for defining specific material properties, such as roughness or transparency. For these examples, since you want a single value, you usually create a lightweight grayscale image with just this one black-and-white color channel.

Here are two examples of mask usage:

Figure A.8 – Mask usage for alpha clipping (top) or for custom-shaped roughness (bottom)

Another more complex type of texture is **normal maps**. This time, you do use multiple color channels, but the data you encode is not meant to be shown directly – it will be sampled and interpreted in your shader to efficiently fake surface details on your model, such as bumps or grooves.

Here is an example of a normal map:

Figure A.9 – Normal map used to simulate surface details efficiently

If you have a custom set of data you want to transfer to your shape for its rendering, you can have a similar process and create some custom texture, where the different color channels are used to store different quantities. This can be a nice alternative to using multiple UVs because, by packing everything in the same file, you reduce the required amount of read-write operations to the disk, which is always a bottleneck.

Using textures in a Unity shader

Whenever you import an image file in a Unity project, it is converted to a `Texture` asset that can be used as a texture, a sprite, a normal map, or more. Usually, for shaders, you will want to set it to the **Default** or **Normal Map** modes, and then create exposed properties on your shader so that you can drag this asset to your material's **Inspector** into the texture's slot.

If you auto-generate a Unity unlit shader, which is one of the simplest starters for the built-in render pipeline, you will see that ShaderLab often uses two variables for textures – `sampler2D`, which can access the actual image file data, and a `float4` variable with a very similar name.

Here is an excerpt of the code to highlight those texture-related instructions:

```
Shader "Custom/ExampleUnlit" {
    Properties {
        _MainTex ("Texture", 2D) = "white" {}
    }
    SubShader {
        Tags { "RenderType" = "Opaque" }
        Pass {
            CGPROGRAM
            #pragma vertex vert
            #pragma fragment frag
            #include "UnityCG.cginc"
            struct appdata {
                float4 vertex : POSITION;
                float2 uv : TEXCOORD0;
            };
            struct v2f {
                float2 uv : TEXCOORD0;
                float4 vertex : SV_POSITION;
            };
            sampler2D _MainTex;
            float4 _MainTex_ST;

            . . .
```

In this code block, we see our `MainTex sampler2D` variable declared at the top as an exposed property and then redefined in the shader program alongside the `float4 MainTex_ST` variable. This companion variable, which is always named based on your real texture variable with an _ST suffix, is what allows us to scale and offset our texture in the **Inspector**. Along with Unity's `TRANSFORM_TEX` built-in function, it helps the engine apply the values you passed in your material's **Inspector** to the shaded object.

This `MainTex_ST` variable is the one you set when you change the values of the **Tiling** and **Offset** fields inside the material's **Inspector**, as shown in *Figure A.10*:

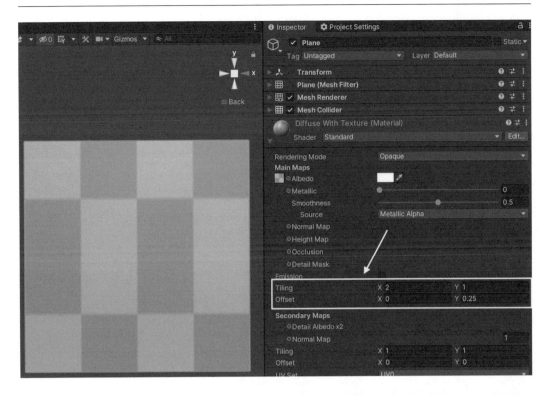

Figure A.10 – An object using a texture with scale and offset

Ignoring or preventing texture scale-offset

Using this additional _ST variable is completely optional. If you don't need to scale and offset the texture in your shader, you can use the [NoScaleOffset] attribute before your texture property definition to hide these inputs in the **Inspector** and remove the variable in your shader code.

Besides declaring the texture property, we also need to get the aforementioned UVs of our mesh. This is done in the following two steps:

1. In the vertex input data structure, we add a float2 field with the TEXCOORD0 semantic.

2. In the vertex output data structure, we transfer it to the fragment shader.

These "computed" UVs may or may not be different from the initial ones – if you don't have any scale or offset and just need the raw data transferred to the next phase, then your processed UVs will simply be a copy of the input.

Finally, in the fragment shader, we can read the data of the texture at a given UV position, thanks to the `tex2D` function, like this:

```
fixed4 frag (v2f i) : SV_Target {
    // sample the texture
    return tex2D(_MainTex, i.uv);
}
```

The `tex2D` function returns a number with one or more components depending on the number of channels in your texture image (usually one for grayscale, three for R, G, and B colors without alpha, or four for colors plus alpha) that you can then pass as the output of the fragment shader to get your final pixel color.

Summary

In this appendix, we recalled the fundamentals of shader theory and various useful tips for writing shaders in Unity.

We recalled the three steps of a common rendering pipeline (the vertex shader, the rasterization, and the fragment shader), before showing how they are implemented in a basic Unity ShaderLab shader code. We also discussed Unity shader configuration with tags, z-buffering options, and blend modes. We followed that up with some reminders on UV mapping and how to handle textures in the game engine.

With this review of all the essential notions of shaders done, you should now be clear on what shaders are, how they are implemented in Unity with the built-in render pipeline, and what a ShaderLab script usually looks like.

Index

Symbols

A

www.packtpub.com

Subscribe to our online digital library for full access to over 7,000 books and videos, as well as industry leading tools to help you plan your personal development and advance your career. For more information, please visit our website.

Why subscribe?

- Spend less time learning and more time coding with practical eBooks and Videos from over 4,000 industry professionals

- Improve your learning with Skill Plans built especially for you

- Get a free eBook or video every month

- Fully searchable for easy access to vital information

- Copy and paste, print, and bookmark content

Did you know that Packt offers eBook versions of every book published, with PDF and ePub files available? You can upgrade to the eBook version at packtpub.com and as a print book customer, you are entitled to a discount on the eBook copy. Get in touch with us at customercare@packtpub.com for more details.

At www.packtpub.com, you can also read a collection of free technical articles, sign up for a range of free newsletters, and receive exclusive discounts and offers on Packt books and eBooks.

Other Books You May Enjoy

If you enjoyed this book, you may be interested in these other books by Packt:

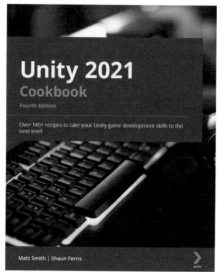

Unity 2021 Cookbook

Matthew Smith , Shaun Ferns

ISBN: 978-1-83921-761-6

- Discover how to add core game features to your projects with C# scripting
- Create powerful and stylish UI with Unity's UI system, including power bars, radars, and button-driven scene changes
- Work with essential audio features, including background music and sound effects
- Discover Cinemachine in Unity to intelligently control camera movements
- Add visual effects such as smoke and explosions by creating and customizing particle systems
- Understand how to build your own Shaders with the Shader Graph tool

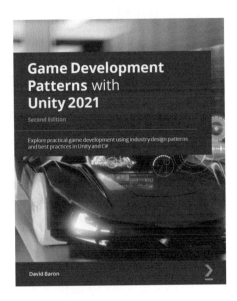

Game Development Patterns with Unity 2021

David Baron

ISBN: 978-1-80020-081-4

- Structure professional Unity code using industry-standard development patterns
- Identify the right patterns for implementing specific game mechanics or features
- Develop configurable core game mechanics and ingredients that can be modified without writing a single line of code
- Review practical object-oriented programming (OOP) techniques and learn how they're used in the context of a Unity project
- Build unique game development systems such as a level editor
- Explore ways to adapt traditional design patterns for use with the Unity API

Packt is searching for authors like you

If you're interested in becoming an author for Packt, please visit `authors.packtpub.com` and apply today. We have worked with thousands of developers and tech professionals, just like you, to help them share their insight with the global tech community. You can make a general application, apply for a specific hot topic that we are recruiting an author for, or submit your own idea.

Heya!

I'm Mina Pêcheux, the author of Become a Unity Shaders Guru. I really hope you enjoyed reading this book and found it useful for increasing your productivity and efficiency in Unity Shaders.

It would really help me (and other potential readers!) if you could leave a review on Amazon sharing your thoughts on Become a Unity Shaders Guru.

Go to the link below or scan the QR code to leave your review:

`https://packt.link/r/1837636745`

Your review will help me understand what's worked well in this book, and what could be improved upon for future editions, so it really is appreciated.

Best Wishes,

Mina Pêcheux

Download a free PDF copy of this book

Thanks for purchasing this book!

Do you like to read on the go but are unable to carry your print books everywhere?

Is your eBook purchase not compatible with the device of your choice?

Don't worry, now with every Packt book you get a DRM-free PDF version of that book at no cost.

Read anywhere, any place, on any device. Search, copy, and paste code from your favorite technical books directly into your application.

The perks don't stop there, you can get exclusive access to discounts, newsletters, and great free content in your inbox daily

Follow these simple steps to get the benefits:

1. Scan the QR code or visit the link below

https://packt.link/free-ebook/9781837636747

2. Submit your proof of purchase

3. That's it! We'll send your free PDF and other benefits to your email directly